PSYCHOLOGICAL CONTRACTS IN EMPLOYMENT

Natasha

all my best wishes,

Dawn Bowman

2000

PSYCHOLOGICAL CONTRACTS IN EMPLOYMENT

Cross-National Perspectives

Edited by

Denise M. Rousseau / René Schalk

Sage Publications, Inc.
International Educational and Professional Publisher
Thousand Oaks ▪ London ▪ New Delhi

For information:

Sage Publications, Inc.
2455 Teller Road
Thousand Oaks, California 91320
E-mail: order@sagepub.com

Sage Publications Ltd.
6 Bonhill Street
London EC2A 4PU
United Kingdom

Sage Publications India Pvt. Ltd.
M-32 Market
Greater Kailash I
New Delhi 110 048 India

Printed in the United States of America

Library of Congress Cataloging-in-Publication Data

Main entry under title:

Psychological contracts in employment: Cross-national perspectives /
edited by Denise M. Rousseau and René Schalk.
    p.   cm.
    Includes bibliographical references and index.
    ISBN 0-7619-1680-6 (cloth : alk. paper) — ISBN 0-7619-1681-4 (pbk.:
alk. paper)
    1. Organizational behavior—Cross-cultural studies. 2. Contracts—
Psychological aspects—Cross-cultural studies. 3. Commitment
(Psychology)—Cross-cultural studies. 4. Industrial relations—
Cross-cultural studies. I. Rousseau, Denise M. II. Schalk, René.
    HD58.7 .P757 2000
    158.7—dc21   00-008446

00 01 02 03 04 05 06 7 6 5 4 3 2 1

Acquiring Editor:	Harry Briggs/Marquita Flemming
Editorial Assistant:	MaryAnn Vail
Production Editor:	Astrid Virding
Editorial Assistant:	Cindy Bear
Typesetter:	Tina Hill
Indexer:	Kathy Paparchontis
Cover Designer:	Candice Harman

Contents

Acknowledgments

This book has been a team effort in the writing as well as in the production process. We wish to thank Carole McCoy for word processing and Cathy Senderling for copy editing; both having displayed great creativity and patience. Harry Briggs and Marquita Flemming of Sage Publications supported us from the outset of this project to its completion. Astrid Virding coordinated the final editorial work on the manuscript. It is a blessing to work with people who love books.

Support for this project was provided by the H. J. Heinz II Endowment and the Carnegie Bosch Institute. Particularly we thank Mark Kamlet and Michael Trick for making this support available to us and taking a developmental (i.e., long-term) view of this project.

1

Introduction

Denise M. Rousseau
René Schalk

Promises create debt.
Dutch Proverb

To break an oral agreement which is not legally binding is morally wrong.
The Talmud

The movement of progressive societies has hitherto been a movement from status to contract.
Henry James Sumner Maine

Employment, the exchange of work for compensation, is a social fact the world over. But what that exchange means to workers or employers is a subjective experience for each participant, affected by personal values and upbringing, the relationship's history, and the broader society. All of these factors merge to create a central feature of employment: the psychological contract.

Psychological contracts in employment are the belief systems of individual workers and employers regarding their mutual obligations (Figure 1.1). These obligations grow from the promises made as employment arrangements are started and sustained, from the hiring process through day-to-day interactions. The society in which employment takes place shapes how these promises are

AUTHORS' NOTE: We thank Jianmin Sun for his helpful comments on an earlier version of this chapter.

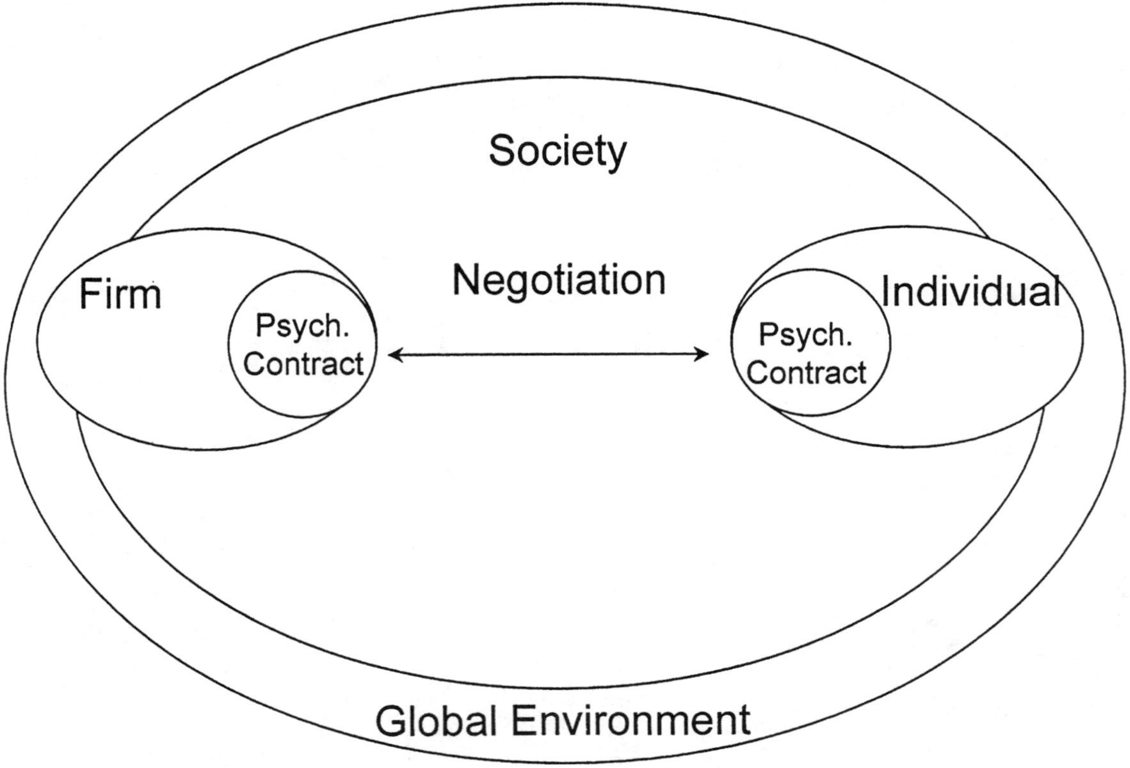

Figure 1.1. Key Contexts for Psychological Contracting

conveyed and interpreted. As the quotes opening this chapter indicate, promises can form the foundation of social relations and obligations, particularly as they are reinforced by a society's moral standards. This book examines the forces underlying the obligations between employee and employer and the role that societal factors play in shaping psychological contracts. In addressing the societal impact on psychological contracts at work, we can better explain such widely different experiences of employment as

- Psychological contracts based on conflict, rather than agreement, in French employment relations
- The sense of belonging at the heart of the Japanese experience of organizational membership and how economic changes affect it
- Workers' perceptions of whom their employment relationship is *really* with (whether the employer, as is typical in the United States; coworkers, as in Australia; or the state itself, as in France)
- The meaning of "high performance" for workers in societies where many workers are reluctant to be singled out as high performers, such as Australia and the Netherlands
- Societal forces that create highly similar psychological contracts across workers and firms, as in Belgium
- The highly idiosyncratic deals of many American workers and the institutional factors that promote such differences

The fundamental issue this book addresses is how participants in an increasingly globalized economy can better understand the impact of society on the psychological contracts experienced by the local workforce.

This book is the product of an international team including members from 13 countries. Understanding employment relations globally requires local knowledge and experience as well as a big-picture perspective that recognizes general patterns and shared meanings. Our team brings together social scientists with deep knowledge of the particular societies they describe, whose personal scholarship pertains to psychological contract phenomena locally as well as abroad.

This introductory chapter provides several themes to help frame the chapters that follow. First, we address the distinct status of the psychological contract in discussions of employment, proposing some ways in which psychological contracts might differ internationally. Next, we explain why a cross-national view of psychological contracts is important for today's managers, social scientists, and public policy makers. Finally, we address the conceptual approaches typically taken to cross-national research and propose a framework to help tease out the influences of societies, firms, individuals, and global factors on psychological contracts worldwide.

THE UNIQUE STATUS OF PSYCHOLOGICAL
CONTRACTS IN RELATION TO WORK

Historically, the emergence of psychological contracts for work coincides with the development of voluntary employment relationships. When one person chooses to work for another in exchange for compensation, their employment relationship is distinct from traditional roles (such as feudal duty) and coerced labor (slavery). How the worker and employer understand the terms of this voluntary agreement constitutes a psychological contract. Although the two parties can interpret their agreement differently, some degree of mutuality is essential for the psychological contract to achieve the interdependent goals each participant seeks. When people believe they owe each other something, the odds are better that both will get what they desire.

In addition, workers and employers who believe that a voluntary arrangement exists between them can reap tremendous benefits. This belief enhances commitment so that agreed-on actions are more likely to be performed. It also increases the predictability of behavior, giving each party a better idea of what to expect from the other. As a result, workers and employers can reduce the amount of time they spend monitoring or scrutinizing each other's behavior.[1]

Though we maintain that effective psychological contracting is critical to creating competitive opportunities for workers and firms in the global economy, not all societies support individually created agreements. Countries differ substantially in the conditions of employment that their infrastructures promote. In particular, international differences exist in the extent to which individuals are able to bargain for work conditions rather than accept preexisting conditions. In this volume, striking contrasts can be observed in the level of prespecified employment conditions between highly regulated labor markets such as Australia (Chapter 2) and Belgium (Chapter 3) and more loosely regulated markets such as New Zealand (Chapter 11) and the United States (Chapter 14).

Two Key Requirements

The primary requirement for the creation of a psychological contract is some degree of *personal freedom*. Psychological contracts are voluntary commitments that individuals make with others. Their creation, and the ability of a firm to benefit from the fulfillment of a psychological contract, depends on the existence of some degree of individual choice. People with no rights have nothing to freely give another—they can choose neither to work nor to quit. Similarly in some societies, rights or entitlements derive from particularistic relations, such as close ties to a superior or higher authority. The right to ask for something or to bargain for it does not reside in the individual but is derived from relations with another, higher authority (consistent with many employment relationships emerging in modern China; J. Sun, personal communication, July 1998). When the higher authority is inspired to know the individual's needs, those needs may be met quite effectively. However, the person may not have the right to ask or bargain in the first place. Legal entitlements and cultural traditions affect the extent to which employers and workers are able to shape the terms and conditions of employment. Nonetheless, freedom is always a matter of degree, with each society creating different solutions to basic problems regarding the forms and degrees of liberty and security that people can access (D'Iribarne, 1989).

Social stability, to some minimum degree, is the second critical requirement for psychological contract making. Before they can create agreements regarding the future, both the employer and the worker must have confidence in one another's intention and ability to keep commitments. The promise of future career opportunities in exchange for today's personal sacrifice is neither realistic nor credible in many firms operating within transitional economies, as in the case of eastern Europe, where a short-term focus dominates employee-employer relations. This time-limited orientation is in part a function of the difficulty of predicting the future during times of transition. Another contributor to the limited time frames associated with exchanges in transitional economies is the lack of sanctions for contract breaking. Transactions based on narrower time frames are easier to monitor, and relations are easier to sever in the event of one party's failure to perform. In a country with unstable social structures, threats of litigation or loss of reputation will not be credible enough to enforce promise keeping. The transitions in eastern Europe illustrate the importance of stable societies and governments, the rule of law, coherent social norms, and functioning markets when it comes to making and keeping voluntary agreements. Although developing countries with less stable societies can still have psychological contracts in employment and access the advantages of a motivated workforce, such arrangements may be for shorter periods of time or entail less extensive commitments.

A Caveat and a Question

On the basis of two requisite features for emergence of psychological contracts in employment, it is apparent that the concept is not applicable in some societies. To refer to psychological contracts in China as the "iron rice bowl" is more metaphoric than accurate because these agreements are not voluntarily entered into. In this book, we charge ourselves with the responsibility to tread carefully in inferring psychological states from behavior. Consider how misleading behavior can be: Although people may appear to be cooperating, there is no guarantee that they trust each other or have exercised any choice in their actions. Cooperation can be coerced, and the resultant trust may be very limited. Credible evidence for the existence and functioning of psychological contracts in employment is directly related to the quality of participation each party has in shaping the conditions of its exchange and in meeting its needs.

Participation is not always societally valued: Compliance might signal greater commitment to the relationship in a highly authoritarian society. Nor is participation in negotiating terms of employment always possible: Law, statute, pre-existing collective bargaining agreement, or custom can limit the latitude of individual workers to be party·to employment terms different from those of their peers. Nonetheless, psychological contracts in any society are bounded somewhat by what is legal or socially acceptable.

Thus, we must raise this fundamental question: To what extent is the construct of a psychological contract generalizable across societies? In developed societies, prevailing practices support the belief that employment relationships should be voluntary, and a perception of choice appears to be the key to creating the commitment to keep a psychological contract. In this book, authors address the extent to which voluntariness is prevalent. They also examine whether *other* bases exist in different societies for creating psychological contracts in employment (e.g., where employment arrangements are specified by law or collective bargaining agreement). In doing so, these authors contribute to our understanding of the dynamics and boundaries of the concept of psychological contracting.

WAYS THAT PSYCHOLOGICAL CONTRACTS CAN VARY INTERNATIONALLY

Psychological contracts are a subjective phenomenon not only individually but culturally. They are based on promises that can take many forms. Although we frequently think of promises as verbal (e.g., "I agree to work for 8 hours a day"), they can also be inferred (e.g., by observing how coworkers are rewarded). Workers and employers tend to believe that past practices, such as basing pay on performance or seniority, and employees' willingness to accept these practices indicate the actions they can expect from each other in the future. Reliance on words as opposed to observations of behavior in inferring promises can vary from country to country.[2]

A Promise Means Different Things

Societal norms play a major role in exactly what people believe a promise means: Is it a promise to *do* something or simply to *try?* For example, a Japanese student at an American university may battle icy roads and poor visibility during a heavy snowstorm to keep an appointment with a fellow student. She gets to their arranged meeting place on campus, only to find that the American student has stayed home, believing no one would expect him to keep an appointment in the middle of a blizzard. The Japanese student, upset that her friend let her down, says that "a promise is a promise." The different perceptions of these two students regarding the commitment they made suggests that what promises mean and the degree to which they are binding are subject to different sets of cultural assumptions.

Whether a promise means to do or to try is in part a function of the locus of control and the resulting degree of personal responsibility that individuals attribute to their actions. How tolerant people are of uncertainty can shape the way they view promise keeping. In the above example, part of the difference in perception can be attributed to the different tolerance for uncertainty that Japanese and Americans have. Similarly, in agricultural societies with high environmental uncertainty, it may be more reasonable to say "We'll see" or "I will try" than to say "I promise to do it."

Culturally, promissory behavior can take on broader meaning than any specific relationship, as reflected in Israeli psychologist Moshe Krausz's description in Chapter 7 of the link that Judaism makes between promises between people and promises between a person and God. The moral underpinnings of the act can create a greater sense of personal responsibility and binding obligation absent in a more secular view. Another factor affecting the degree of personal responsibility may be the scope of the individual's network of obligations. Other things being equal, the more people an individual is obligated to, the more difficult it may be to keep any specific commitment. One may need to break a promise to one person in order to keep a promise to another. Although employment relationships are frequently thought of as bilateral, there may be multiple parties to which workers or managers believe themselves obliged (e.g., team, union, occupation, customers, firm), and little is known regarding the dynamics of conflicting psychological contracts.

Differences in the Zone of Negotiability

The freedom to enter into exchange agreements is always a matter of degree. The vast majority of important legal contracts in which the average person participates have terms that are imposed (e.g., few people have the opportunity to negotiate the price they will pay when purchasing electricity for their house). Psychological contracts in employment follow a similar pattern: All societies impose some limits on the bargaining power of employees and firms. For example, a worker typically cannot sign away the legal protection that his or her nation's labor laws provide. In other words, societies guarantee workers and firms some a priori employment conditions because bargaining for every aspect of the employment relationship is not desirable from the standpoint of either efficiency or social welfare. An ongoing debate among our international team of scholars pertains to the meaning of freedom. Of course, none of us is against freedom *qua* freedom. Rather, the dispute pertains to whether the absence of legal protections for workers promotes greater worker choice or results in greater inequality between the haves and have-nots. These issues mirror those discussed in economic sociology (Swedberg, 1993). From the perspective of psychological contracts, however, this debate raises a funda-

mental question regarding the boundaries distinguishing psychological contracts and their consequences for firms and workers from other forms of binding obligations, such as those imposed by law or civic duty.

Societal or cultural beliefs also influence the kinds of exchanges that are negotiable in employment relationships and the terms that parties are willing to
accept. A manager in an American firm, for example, might avoid hiring workers who were close friends or family members of a board member, whereas a
Mexican manager might believe that hiring his superiors' *compadres* was in
the firm's interest and consistent with his role in it. Similarly, promising new
recruits that a job with the firm will help them be employable elsewhere might
be attractive in a highly mobile society but might signal an employer's unreli-
ability in a less mobile one.

In effect, there is a "zone of negotiability" associated with each society that
can be broad or narrow regarding specific contract terms, depending on law
and custom. Conditions of employment that are prespecified through legal
requirements, custom, and other societal institutions restrict the conditions
that must or can be bargained for by employee and employer. National holidays
mandating paid time off on certain days are not subject to bargaining, except
perhaps in the payment of overtime for those willing to work then. The same is
true of government-mandated pension benefits (e.g., social security) to which
firms and workers are required to contribute. A worker preferring to manage
his or her own pension fund is constrained from doing so, as are firms that
would prefer to base pension benefits on employee merit or firm performance.
Where conditions such as these are extensive, there is a narrow zone of
negotiability. Zones of negotiability vary with worker status, such as independent contractor, full-time employee, or part-time employee. The flexibility
to enter into agreements can also be constrained by cultural factors. Family
roles and responsibilities vary within and between societies, making acceptance of certain work conditions difficult or even intolerable. For example,
whether mothers can travel for work varies between Saudi Arabia and Canada.
Workers and owners who are party to numerous other obligations, as in many
nations where relationships play a key role in establishing business opportunities, may be constrained in entering new agreements because of the volume of
their existing commitments. In sum, broad-scale institutions shape the
employment conditions that a society readily supports and the degree of flexibility that workers and firms have in deciding on the terms that constitute
employment.

A broad zone of negotiability means both fewer constraints and fewer institutional protections or guaranteed resources for workers. A narrow zone indicates an array of constraints on the actions of one or both parties. In one sense,
legal protection for workers and other constraints on firm behavior limit freedom (or, one might argue, the excesses of freedom). But legal protection can
also offset imbalances in power between the parties, particularly because
employers tend to have greater financial resources than employees. To illus-

trate one difference between workers and firms, consider this: Can a production worker in Nice—or Tilburg or Chicago—exchange 15% of her human capital investment in her employer for an equity stake in an architect in Toulouse? The answer is likely to be no.

Despite the differences in power between workers and firms, societies still vary considerably in the value they place on employment flexibility versus worker protection. How societies regard these power differences may be an important factor in shaping the legal protections that constrain the negotiability of employment terms at the individual level. Typically, Britain and the United States have been less concerned with mitigating power differences between firms and workers than have France and Germany. The different infrastructures that result from societal concerns about power differences cause more variability in individual-level employment relations in the former countries than in the latter.

Group Identity

Group identity gives rise to highly generalizable behaviors pertinent to promise making. Social psychologists report that members within a group experiencing interpersonal conflicts are likely to make promises to each other in an attempt to settle the dispute. In contrast, intergroup or international disputes are more likely to result in threats than in promises (Betz & Fry, 1995). It is likely that the psychological contracts arising in employment relations involving "in-group" members (i.e., people with some common identity, such as ethnicity, firm membership, or nationality) differ from those involving people with different affiliations, or "out-group" members. This difference in the nature of exchange agreements among in- and out-group members may be a function of the broader potential zone of negotiability associated with high-trust relationships.

How people define "we" and "they" can be critical to both trust and promise making. In the United States, a classic example of we/they thinking is the historic dispute between European settlers and indigenous people over treaty violations. Two centuries of contention have led each group to believe that the other lies and breaks promises (while of course each believes that its own members are truthful and trustworthy) (Rotenberg & Cerda, 1994). Across groups and societies, trust is generally higher for in-group members than it is for out-group members, with corresponding effects on the kinds of promises exchanged.

Although the dynamics of in-group/out-group relations are generalizable, it is often difficult to determine who is "in" at a given point in time. The cultural diversity of Italy, England, Spain, France, and Germany before and after the formation of the European Economic Community (EEC) is at least as great as that characterizing the former Yugoslavia before it disintegrated. Identity can both form and vanish through the forces of politics and culture. The "in-group" (or "we") had meaning in Austro-Hungary as well as in the Ottoman Empire (where each had a long history of conflict with the other), though each has been gone for almost a century (Simon, 1992). "We" is particularistic and temporal, a dimension of sociology that influences psychology and is subject to revision and reformation. Despite this instability, in-group/out-group effects on beliefs and behavior endure over time, as witnessed in the recent conflicts following the breakup of the former Yugoslavia as well as Rhodesia (Zimbabwe).

These effects give us all the more reason to observe carefully the aftermath of acquisitions that cross national boundaries. In the case of Credit Suisse First Boston, American management practices were introduced to support a shift in competitive strategy in a traditionally managed Swiss bank. Yet the bank retained its Swiss identity and, as of this writing, its use of traditional Swiss languages (French and Swiss-German) in day-to-day business. In another case, an identity shift may occur, as exemplified by the creation of Daimler Chrysler, where one of the "Big Three" American car manufacturers became a German-owned company. Such a change has tremendous implications for labor and employment practices and psychological identification—and provides an opportunity to test the generalizability of psychological processes, such as in-group/out-group effects, as they pertain to psychological contract formation and change.

One danger facing cross-national managers is that once ineffective decisions have been made using incompatible assumptions from another society, it can be difficult to reverse those decisions and the negative consequences they have caused (this appears to be the current situation at Eurodisney).[3] On the other hand, we note that the global expansion of "lean" manufacturing has successfully introduced many of the same management practices worldwide. To inform the practice of working and managing in cross-national situations, this book identifies some important relationships between societal factors and the psychological contracts that arise between firms and workers that can affect both acceptance and implementation of change.

WHY WE NEED AN INTERNATIONAL VIEW
OF PSYCHOLOGICAL CONTRACTS

Several things motivate this cross-national analysis of psychological contracts.

Expansion of Multinational Firms and Labor Markets

Global firms and international labor markets give rise to concerns over the meaning of the employment relationship within and across nations. Psychological contracts are beliefs in a mutual agreement between worker and employer. These are mutually beneficial when the agreement supports the strategic interests of the firm as well as the personal needs of the worker. However, there does not have to be a harmonious consensus. As Loïc Cadin describes in his chapter on France (Chapter 4), mutuality can entail a bilateral agreement that reflects the inherently distinct interests of the parties involved. Societies vary regarding the nature of employment agreements, but the key issue is creation of a commitment to a course of action consistent with the belief that the other party agrees to be obligated in some way as well.

In the modern economy, there can be no productive employment or successful firms without functioning psychological contracts. But the term *functioning* may have society and context-specific meanings. One factor in support of more effective agreements, both in employment and in business generally, is a worldwide trend toward comparable laws and similar business practices. To reconcile local differences in laws affecting commercial and employment agreements, legal mechanisms such as contract laws and trade practices are becoming somewhat more compatible across countries. Perhaps the most developed infrastructure supporting globalization at present is the European Economic Union (EEU), which promotes common laws and practices in its member nations. Nonetheless, labor laws have been among the most resistant to homogenization. For instance, whereas the United Kingdom has seen expanded use of temporary workers, Belgium, France, and other continental countries have maintained institutional constraints on the types and numbers of jobs in which such a workforce may be employed.

Moreover, we must question whether even common laws would be sufficient to lead to common understandings of the employment relationship. The practices managers use to motivate workers may be more readily implemented if they are compatible with prevailing societal patterns. Conveying prestige or exercising power in the process of implementing a change may work well in societies where hierarchy and status differences are emphasized but may arouse organized opposition where group harmony or egalitarian values predominate (Schwartz, 1994, in press).

It can be difficult to understand the way people respond on the job when their psychological contracts are based on societal assumptions different from our own. An example of misapplied cross-cultural perspectives is found in attempts to use participative conflict resolution mechanisms in France. The French tend to avoid face-to-face conflict among people of equal status, preferring centralized authorities to settle disputes instead. Informal operations that require people to address their differences directly, as in many work-team systems, threaten the "equality" of members. A foreign (non-French) manager attempting to introduce a bonus system alongside an existing salary system set up a series of meetings with the workforce to explain the benefits of the new system and get agreement on how it should be implemented. The plan met with tremendous worker resistance both publicly and privately, which took the manager aback. No progress was made until the manager met privately with officials from several unions involved in the plant. After a day of private meetings featuring a good deal of chitchat and beer drinking but little negotiation about the issues at hand, the decision was made to implement the new program, with minor modifications. In this example, direct participation of workers was not effective, but publicly voiced concerns followed by the symbolic participation of authority figures legitimated the decision. This illustration reminds us that societal assumptions regarding worker and employer roles shape the nature of the relationships on which psychological contracts are based.

The introduction of one society's employment practices into another can run into trouble in two basic ways. In some cases, the practices may be societally incompatible, whereas in other instances the practices are acceptable but the chosen implementation process is incompatible. To understand the complex dynamics underlying the success and failure of employment practices worldwide, we need a rich understanding of the roles of society, firms, and individuals in shaping employment relations.

Advancing Scientific Knowledge Regarding Psychological Contracts and Their Generalizability Across Societies

As social scientists, we are interested in the extent to which the formation and maintenance of psychological contracts in employment is a generalizable process. More specifically, we are interested in what aspects of psychological contracting occur across societies. What role does choice play in creating beliefs in binding obligations? How important is participation to the creation of individualized employment terms? How does the zone of negotiability vary within as well as between societies? Key research issues for social scientists include the nature and meaning of promises across cultures and the role that societal differences related to promise making play in the formation of psychological contracts.

The role of promises is one central feature of psychological contract theory. Much is known about the conditions under which people are willing to make promises and trust others to keep their commitments. We know far less about how individuals interpret promises (e.g., to do vs. to try) and how different settings shape promise making and keeping (e.g., the influence of other parties on the capacity or perceived responsibility to keep promises).[4] Promise keeping can mean a fulfillment of a close-ended commitment in one setting or can result in even greater obligations in another.

A psychological contract is, in effect, a model of the future—what its parties believe can or should or will happen. The level of uncertainty regarding the fulfillment of a psychological contract varies with societal stability, which can shape an individual's locus of control and interpersonal trust. Presumably, we see more promises broken during the societal instability that occurs in conjunction with economic downturns and during personal crises. In both cases, individuals are likely to attribute any promise breaking on their part to events beyond their control. However, such circumstances can be chronic occurrences in transitional societies, as in the former Soviet Union. The vagaries of promise making are reflected in a quote from a Chinese government representative: "We don't break promises, we just make new ones."[5] More typically, we might expect people to be more inclined not only to break promises but also to avoid making new ones when uncertainty seems high.

How societies conceptualize the future, and time in general, is also important to the creation and interpretation of exchange agreements. A society's orientation toward time is evident in the extent to which people focus on the past, present, or future in their daily deliberations. Some societies are profoundly grounded in the present: The Ethiopian language, for example, has no past or future tense. Psychological contracts that entail commitments over the long term may be avoided in societies with low orientation toward the future. In contrast, long-term cycles of exchange promoting extensive relationships are characteristic of highly future-oriented societies, such as Japan.

This book pays special attention to the building blocks of psychological contracts—the meaning of promises, perceptions of uncertainty, and beliefs regarding the future and time—and their differences across societies. By doing so, we seek to better understand the generalizability and boundaries of our knowledge regarding promise making and keeping across societies.

Public Policy Implications of Psychological Contracts

A social system that supports the making of implicit and explicit agreements makes it possible for people to impose obligations on themselves through formal and informal contracts. Understanding how society shapes psychological contracts in employment helps identify the types of legal, educational, and other supports that permit firms and workers to make employment agreements that best serve their interests. By comparing societal factors shaping psychological contracts in a variety of nations, this book attempts to inform public policy discussion regarding the role of law and government in promoting effective agreements between workers and employers.

OUR APPROACH TO UNDERSTANDING CROSS-NATIONAL DIFFERENCES

Two schools of thought, anthropological and psychological, dominate research on cross-national differences affecting the employment relationship. The anthropological view maintains that national differences, especially cultural variations, are so fundamental and pervasive that cross-cultural, shared meanings—which are crucial for the mutuality seen in effective psychological contracts—are unlikely to ever exist. An example is the 1993 furor in France over the labor policies of McDonald's, Inc. The fast-food chain's commercial jingle proclaimed "Ça se passe comme ça chez McDonald's" ("That's what things are like at McDonald's"), an advertisement that became an ironic catch-phrase as the French press reported the labor strike, pickets, and ugly chants that arose nationwide against the company. At issue were its work hours, structured labor practices, and dress requirements. McDonald's, which operates in 79 countries, appeared to have touched a cultural nerve that constrained it from applying its otherwise global labor practices in France (Roquelle, 1993). An anthropological interpretation of the McDonald's debacle would focus on the idiosyncratic features of French culture, especially the society's attitudes toward authority and non-French influences, the value it places on individual expression, and its pro-labor sentiments.

The psychological view, in contrast, maintains that human cognitive processes are fundamentally shared, adapted to but not wholly formed by social settings, and therefore generalizable to some degree. A case in point can be made regarding the phenomenon of trust, which exists in all societies regardless of culture or political structure. Trust's meaning (whether it is based on faith or experience) and range (whether it involves insiders or outsiders) shift across settings. A general trust in authorities often seems like blind faith to the Dutch or to Anglo-Americans, an abdication of responsible judgment. Yet in an Islamic country, trust in authority can reflect both deep respect for the role that authorities play and a sense of duty. Despite cultural differences, trust exists in some form in societies as diverse as the Netherlands, England, Mexico, and Japan and can be explained with many of the same parameters across these societies. Returning to the McDonald's incident described above, a psychological analysis would emphasize issues of identification and in-group/out-group effects while downplaying the finer-grained aspects of French society.

Our position includes both approaches: In our discussion of psychological contracts, we examine both features *unique* to a particular society, by having experts analyze their own countries, and features that appear to be *generalizable* across many societies, using comparative analysis by our multinational team of researchers.[6] Our fundamental assumption is that psychological contracts have features that are both unique and generalizable across societies.

A society comprises political, religious, familial, and economic institutions that are closely intertwined with the phenomenon of "culture," each of which can powerfully shape employment practices and how individuals experience them (Carnoy, 1993; Carnoy, Castells, & Benner, 1997; Castells, 1996). But the role of societal factors, and particularly of culture, remains problematic. It may seem that understanding culture is like nailing gelatin to a wall: Its amorphous quality makes it difficult to represent adequately. Consider that lean manufacturing systems are used in global firms across many nations. However, their introduction into a specific firm in a particular country typically entails some distinctively local implementation practices: drinking beer with union leaders to gain their support, talking to the fathers of young female workers, sending a negotiating team to a workers' council meeting to discuss a strategic change, or flying the chief executive officer in from headquarters to address assembled employees before rolling out the change. (The reader can make his or her best guesses regarding where each of these is implemented.[7]) Cultural differences frequently act more as a disclaimer or caveat to claims regarding generalizability than as an explanation for international employment practices and organizational experiences.

The same employment practices can have very different functional roles across societies. Lifetime employment is viewed as a given by Westerners commenting on Japanese society, although there is evidence that this practice reflects a post-World War II arrangement between large Japanese firms and their workforce, which was created to avoid labor strife (Ozaki, 1991). Moreover, government workers in Italy also have "lifetime employment," even though the cultures of Italy and Japan differ tremendously. "Culture," when used to explain everything, may wind up explaining nothing—unless we more carefully address the societal institutions that compose and support it and their link to employment practices and individual experiences.

This book addresses societal factors and broadly examines the roles of government, law, education, and the civil society in representing social values, norms, and the role of family and community. Recent research in organizational psychology has highlighted some of the connections between national culture and individual-level differences in motivation and cognition (Erez & Early, 1993; Hofstede, 1980; Meaning of Work International Research Team, 1987). However, the role played by broader societal factors in shaping employment relations, such as credentialing practices, school-to-work connections, or family structure, has received less attention—a condition this book hopes to remedy.

Traditional cross-cultural research conducted by organizational researchers has downplayed the mechanisms whereby societal differences influence work behavior (Goodman, Olivera, & Ranganujam, 1998). To date, most organizational research that takes societal factors into account evokes a single institutional explanatory factor (e.g., culture) and employs a simplified representation of cultural values (e.g., individualism-collectivism).[8] That connection between organizational factors and cultural values is presumed to be a *direct* effect—for example, collectivism *causes* teamwork. However, values such as collectivism occur in conjunction with other societal factors. The actions of government or the educational system can have just as powerful an effect on the practices firms use (e.g., hierarchical decision making, use of teams). Culture can *mediate* the effects of such institutions on firm practices by giving rise to a shared meaning regarding the government's or educational system's actions. Alternatively, culture can *confound* our understanding by co-occurring with the actions of such systems but having no well-understood connections to them (as in the case of Russia, which had a hierarchical government similar to that of China without a comparably collectivistic culture).

Our authors explore the formation and dynamics of psychological contracts, recognizing that societal effects can take a variety of forms. By highlighting particular ways in which social institutions link to firms and workers, we hope to offer the reader a more comprehensive understanding of society's role in the employment relationship, both generally and specific to psychological contracts. We will address both the generalizable psychological processes underlying psychological contracts and the local social institutions that shape them.

FRAMING THE MULTILEVEL EFFECTS ON PSYCHOLOGICAL CONTRACTS

In this book, we recognize that effects at several levels—individual, firm, and society—shape psychological contracts in employment. To understand how these effects operate at different levels, we need to differentiate psychological contracts from other related concepts such as general meta-obligations or socially derived duty (Figure 1.2). Psychological contracts are based on promises made to a person or firm and are specific to that relationship. They differ from meta-obligations, such as honesty, acceptance of authority, and contribution to a social security fund, which might stem from the broader social experience of the individuals involved and which are based on societal norms and laws.

Differentiating meta-obligations from promise-based obligations is critical to understanding employment relationships across societies. The Meaning of Work (MOW) International Research Team (1987) suggested that whether people consider work to be something society has a duty to provide or a duty that people owe society can be a major distinguishing factor in work values across societies. The social and political history of a nation contributes to a broadly shared ethos regarding individual and societal work responsibilities. The MOW team reported that some societies are high in both, where people tend to believe work should be provided but accept substantial personal responsibility when it is (as in the case of Israel). On the other hand, the American sample indicated very little belief in society's obligations to provide them with work but a substantial belief in the duty of individuals to contribute to society by working. The "Protestant ethic" formulated by Weber (1963), in which work is an indicator of individual worthiness, reflects such a belief system. This work ethic arose in medieval Europe, concomitantly with capitalism and a market orientation. A different view of the world based on similar social dynamics has been proposed by several proponents of a "Catholic ethic," entailing a societal obligation to provide work that fosters human dignity (MOW International Research Team, 1987; Tropman, 1995; Weber, 1963). Both of these ethics are examples of meta-obligations. Work-related ethics that arise from the multifaceted influence of church and state (though distinct from a specific psychological contract between individual and firm) can substantially influence individuals' and employers' view of the particular employment arrangements they create. To understand the dynamics of psychological contracts, we must try to tease out the general effects of individual psychological

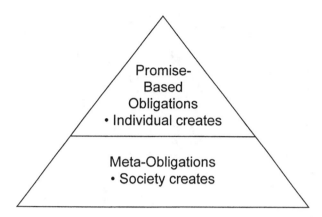

Figure 1.2. Two Levels of Obligation

processes as well as the local impact of social institutions on firms and people, while recognizing that these effects cannot be completely separated.

Our focus is on three levels of analysis: *societies,* or national-level institutions; *firms,* recognizing that different firms in the same society can have distinct approaches to employment based on strategy, technology, and other business-related factors; and *individuals* (workers and employers, as represented by owners and managers) within that society. Given the mix of unique and generalizable factors that shape psychological contracts, it is impossible to specify completely the interactions among these three levels. However, the framework shown in Figure 1.3 sketches out some potentially important factors affecting psychological contracts internationally.

Societal Effects

An essential question this book raises about the role of society in shaping the psychological contract is how much of the terms and conditions of work is negotiable and how much is prespecified by society's institutions. Within a given nation, local influences shape the human resource practices that firms adopt, including legal requirements (from holidays to termination practices), the degree of governmental support for free markets, and broader institutional forces such as the educational system and culture. Society affects the psychological contracts between firm and workers through two fundamental dimensions: first, the resources that societies make available to firms (e.g., skilled workers, capital for investment and development) and workers (e.g., access to employment opportunities) that can shape the terms of the agreements between them; and second, the regulations or legitimacy constraints that a soci-

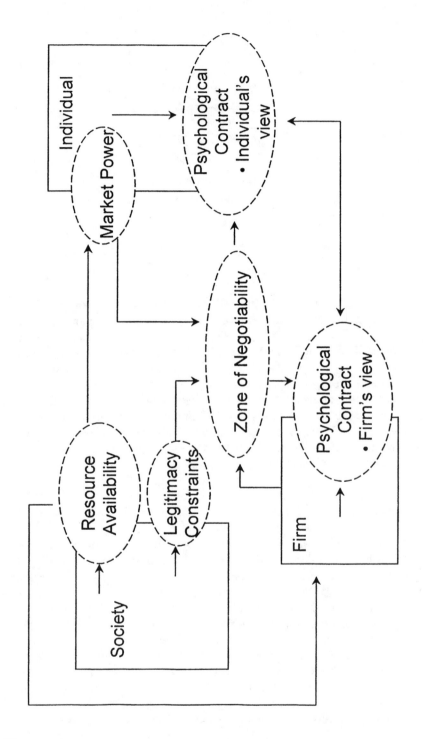

ety places, by either law or custom, on the range of activities and behavior available to workers and firms.

We consider here three basic aspects of society: law, government, and the civil society and its broader social institutions.

Law

Law plays a key role in legitimating the terms of psychological contracts. What people in society believe the law permits, forbids, or requires is a powerful determinant of both making and keeping psychological contracts. We must note that a psychological contract is a psychological fact, not necessarily a legal one. Legal scholars argue that all contracts are inherently "psychological" in that they are interpreted by the parties who made them, although psychological contracts are not always legally binding.[9] Nonetheless, psychological contracts reflect "bargaining in the shadow of the law," beliefs regarding exchanges between firm and worker affected by the participants' understandings of societal institutions (Macaulay, 1985).

What people in a society believe about its laws can be at odds with both academic law (the law as written) and reality (the law as enforced). In a classic study of this difference between perception and reality, residents of the U.S. state of Nebraska were asked their beliefs regarding the legal rights of employers to terminate employees at will. An overwhelming number of people surveyed said that firms had no right to terminate employees without cause. However, the reality is that Nebraska law supports termination at will, although the general public believed otherwise (Forbes & Jones, 1986). A similar discrepancy between the public's belief and the reality of law is illustrated by an experiment in which people given a written contract specifying conditions for renting an apartment believed those conditions to be legal and enforceable because they were presented on a preprinted form. (In fact, the terms printed on the form were *not* legal.) Not only do people often have inaccurate perceptions of the law, but they may not claim all the rights to which they are entitled under law. People often suppress potential disputes or make compromises to keep a relationship alive, indicating that what they are willing to tolerate or accept from those with whom they have contracts is often far broader than what the law requires (Macaulay, 1985, pp. 467-468).[10] Because laws have the power to enforce sanctions but not to maintain agreements, the human tendency toward extralegal relationship maintenance is probably functional. Nonetheless, the fact that psychological contracts are created and sustained in the shadow of the law means that what people *believe* to be law affects their behavior.

All societies impose limits on contractual arrangements related to employment, yet societies vary greatly in the degree of freedom they support. The problem of externalities is the main reason that people's choices regarding employment exchanges are never totally free (Atiyah, 1981, p. 23).[11] An externality is a side consequence of a free exchange that affects a third party. Even if an exchange benefits the two parties who make it, it will not be in the public interest if there are externalities that outweigh the private gain (e.g., employers that terminate workers during economic downturns can place burdens on the state and create social instability). Legal interventions to reduce externalities tend to focus on economic efficiency, as in the case of antitrust legislation to promote competitive markets, and on distributional goals, reflecting concern for weaker parties (e.g., the power of labor is generally less than that of owners and stockholders). Laws have tremendous impact on the rights of workers and employers to bargain, as well as on the scope of those negotiations.

Historically, freedom of contract has been a labor issue in most developed countries. Typical labor laws have addressed whether employment can be terminated at will, subject to the giving of reasonable notice. Recall that termination at will is legal in the United States, though the general public may believe otherwise. However, the legal doctrine of at-will employment has been discarded in Germany, where termination is socially unwarranted, and in France, where the termination of an employee is an "abuse of right" (Glendon, Gordon, & Osakwe, 1985, p. 1045). Moreover, legal systems can sometimes introduce obligations into the employment relationship that are not anticipated at the time of hire. For example, Muslim law does not articulate a set of guiding principles around which contracts operate, leaving judges the power to reconstruct or adjust existing obligations. As a result, extracontractual obligations may be imposed on parties through judicial intervention. In Islamic societies, the legitimacy of contractual obligations typically is determined by religious law. Legal intervention has broad societal impact on the zone of negotiability in employment agreements.

Government

Aside from the code of laws governing markets and contracts, government plays three other critical roles in shaping the psychological contracts of employment: It supports or constrains markets, empowers or impedes collective bargaining, and can be a major employer in its own right. First, the state's ability to support a market economy is a major factor in employment agreements. The relatively weak states that were formerly part of the Soviet Union have had difficulty creating market economies that include a stable monetary system and laws of contract. Thus, Ukrainian garment workers might be paid in T-shirts because Ukraine has only a limited cash economy. In addition, governments can impose constraints on both capital and labor markets. Germany is a case in point, where organized labor is prohibited from having equity stake in the employing firm. Governmental market policies affect the resources that are potentially available for exchange within employment agreements, from cash and stock options to goods and job security.

The state's role in determining conditions of employment is influenced by its power over other sectors such as collective bargaining. As Cadin describes in Chapter 4 of this book, the French central government is, relatively speaking, more powerful than organized labor in shaping employment, primarily because France's policies do not support the existence of large unions representing broad numbers of workers and because unions themselves are often composed of activists rather than a broad membership. (In contrast with institutionalized U.S. government support for a unified labor organization, the AFL-CIO, the French government traditionally has promoted competition among unions.) In contrast, the German government shares power with collective bargaining mechanisms, giving the state moderate influence over employment but less than that enjoyed by the French central government. Collective bargaining influences both the resources available for negotiation and the legitimacy of any processes used to arrive at a negotiated agreement.

The third critical role that government can play is as an employer itself. Government is one of the largest employers in many societies (if not the largest), from Nigeria and India to China and Italy. In Italy, one saying goes, "You celebrate two things: your marriage and the day you get a government job." Similarly, the Indian constitution sets aside certain jobs for members of particular castes as a means of income distribution. As Snehal Shah describes in Chapter 6, an Indian civil servant working for the state has a job with the same pay and benefits regardless of how hard he works or for which supervisor he works. In many societies throughout the world, the state itself can be a powerful psychological contract maker, establishing normative standards for local employers.

Civil Society and Social Institutions

Civil society is composed of the social institutions that create community life, including education, family, and broader cultural values and norms. The education system is particularly important because it directly affects the key resources available to a firm—the knowledge and skills of a society's workforce. Literacy, exposure to computers, and technical skills are resources clearly linked to societal levels of education. But although there are definitely skill differences among workers from different nations, a firm in Mexico and one in Canada might still be able to select workers with similar skill levels. Although firms might prefer to select only workers with particular skills, the ease with which this selection occurs may differ across societies. A society's education systems constrain or facilitate its firms' ability to obtain employees with the skills they need.

Education systems make their own promises regarding their students' future and, in doing so, shape the legitimacy of new employment arrangements. Established school-to-work pipelines, whereby generations of young people have accessed specific kinds of employment on the basis of their educational credentials, create powerful expectations regarding future career opportunities. The Japanese school system is an example: Children and families make sacrifices to obtain the highest academic rankings in elementary and secondary education, complete with long hours of homework each night and classes after school and on weekends. These sacrifices are based on the promise that academic success in childhood leads to admission to a prestigious college or university, such as Tokyo University. On graduation, the school-to-work pipeline historically holds the promise of employment with the Japanese government and the nation's largest firms. Credentialing systems, such as the apprenticeship training that exists in Holland and Germany, are also presumed to guarantee employment in a specific trade (Sorge, 1992). Such systems provide firms with resources in the form of workers whose "credentials" are clear signals of their experience and competency and also define the career paths that are legitimate and socially acceptable to those who have passed through the pipeline. In sum, the effects of 20 years of societal expectations, as in the case of a Japanese student, or 2 to 4 years of apprenticeship training in much of western Europe can sustain practices that firms might otherwise prefer to change.

Similarly, family structure can influence firms and the psychological contracts of their members, as evidenced by the overseas empires created by extended Chinese families, which are based on loyalties among family members (Granrose & Chua, 1996). The centrality of family in Mexican culture, as Hector Diaz-Saenz and Patricia Witherspoon describe in their chapter, influences both the nature of mobility (people may not be willing to move unless they are able to bring their extended family with them) and the motivations people have for working (to educate one's children rather than to advance oneself) (Abitia, 1986, 1991). Paying attention to family ties can also facilitate the implementation of change. An automobile manufacturer operating on the U.S.-Mexican border gained acceptance for proposed changes in the workplace by sending its supervisors to talk with the fathers of the young women who worked in the plants. Gaining the fathers' support for a change virtually guaranteed that the workers would also agree to it. Similar management efforts to promote organizational change would be considered intrusive in many other countries.

Societal values may also influence internal firm practices such as organizational structures and reward systems. The structure of firms appears to differ in systematic ways across societies, with empowerment differences being particularly evident. Latin societies tend to have more hierarchical firms (meaning unequal power and resources from top to bottom) than northern European ones (Lammers & Hickson, 1979). Similarly, although a study of firms in five countries found hierarchies in all of the organizations, the differences between top and bottom were greatest in Italy and Austria and least in Israel, the United States, and Yugoslavia (Tannenbaum, Kavcic, Rosner, Vianello, & Wieser, 1974). As always, we must add the caveat that variability in employment practices within a country can be as great as differences between nations: Flexible participation systems exist in Latin societies (Semler, 1989), and hierarchies characterize governmental bureaucracies in virtually all nations. We should note also that in most studies, a large portion of the variance among individual responses goes unexplained, with societal effects accounting for as much of 10% of the variation (no other competing explanations are tested).

In sum, societal factors affect members' desires and needs as well as the resources available to them (e.g., skills or credentials), which in turn affect their ability to participate in the labor market. Societal factors also influence individual bargaining power, with people who have greater bargaining power enjoying a broader zone of negotiability in employment agreements. Similarly, the resources that societies make available to firms, in the form of workforce skills, and government impact on free-market behavior affect the firms' ability to respond to competitive pressures and opportunities. Moreover, societal factors shape the legitimacy of the actions of both individuals and firms and thus the range of readily negotiable employment conditions.

Firm Effects

Firms do not respond passively to societal pressure; rather, they react to and sometimes shape societies in several ways. First, firms derive resources (particularly labor) from within societies but can exercise control over the kinds of resources they seek and use. Recruitment and selection practices permit a firm to target a specific segment of the labor force, whether it seeks to attract the highest-skilled or lowest-cost labor. Moreover, although skills and cultural values may have particular levels and distributions in a given society, firms can and do adapt, innovate, and otherwise alter these skills and values. Those firms whose human resource practices improve the quality of the workforce over the levels typically available in society should realize a comparative advantage in performance.

Multinational firms that seek to compete through innovative products and services typically invest heavily in developing their workforces at home and abroad, leading to the creation of worldwide training centers such as Motorola University and the International Banking School (Credit Suisse's in-house development program). Training and development activities not only create skills that might be unavailable otherwise in the broader society but can be the linchpin of a firm's efforts to socialize members into its distinctive practices, beliefs, and values. For example, high-involvement team work systems operate in a variety of nations, despite substantial cultural differences regarding collectivism and authority. High-involvement work systems generally are introduced along with a high degree of employee selection and training, producing a workforce with skills and values that differ significantly from those of typical workers in the broader society. Thus, although the educational system and other cultural factors shape the national workforce, these factors do not completely constrain the skills and motivations of workers *within* a particular firm. Through recruitment and selection, training and socialization, firms can improve the quality of their workforce beyond the abilities typically available in the larger society.

A firm strategically focused on innovation and change is likely to have a structure, technology, and culture different from those of a firm whose strategy is to defend a well-established market segment. But societal factors can act as constraints on or supports for a firm's actions. For example, the predominance of family-owned firms in Mexico, Korea, and China alters the businesses' dynamics and shapes the career prospects of nonfamily employees. Such businesses are unlikely to grow or restructure unless a family member is available to manage such a change (Fukuyama, 1995).

Global Effects

Firms operating in a broader multinational environment are also affected by global factors. Multinational firms can have distinct organizational cultures and human resource strategies that enhance their ability to operate in several countries (e.g., uniform pay structures worldwide vs. pay by country-specific standards). Moreover, such firms are highly visible to both government and the public. Thus, the human resource practices that multinationals use often reflect responses to political factors, including pressure for legitimacy, consistency with societal norms, and adherence to broader moral standards (as in the case of Nike, the athletic equipment manufacturer that was found to be using child labor in Asia, or in Chinese joint ventures providing pension and housing benefits to workers commensurate with those traditionally offered by state enterprises).

With the globalization of markets and the common competitive pressures that firms face, nations may be growing more similar in the way their firms are structured and managed. In a cross-national study, MacDuffie (1995) observed that variations in employment practices within countries are actually greater than differences between countries. High-involvement work systems exist on virtually every continent. Outsourced labor is a trend in the automobile industry from Japan to Canada; temporaries work at both Toyota and Ford. Thus, forces appear to be creating more widely shared ways of managing and motivating people, particularly in societies and firms that are actively engaged in the global economy. That global economy promotes the mobility of four resources key to economic success: technology, information, capital, and workers. Note that people are often less mobile than the other three. Pittsburghers and Parisians are often reluctant to leave home, and the social ties that bind people to places are part of what makes one society different from another.

Practices such as teamwork, total quality management, and just-in-time inventory systems may be used worldwide and yet have distinct meaning and implementation from one locality to another. Contracts have been called "a model of the future based on the past." The past (and present) experiences of people in a given society shape their relations with others, and in a world where practices have become more standardized, how those practices are understood and reacted to may not be always so easily homogenized.

Individual Effects

Finally, it is important to acknowledge the tremendous variation possible among individuals in a given society. Of particular concern in our analysis are differences in individuals' access to education, employment, and market power as a function of their experiences in a given society. Different employment opportunities based on gender, race, ethnicity, national origin, and citizenship exist in all societies, sometimes with legal complicity but virtually always with some degree of cultural legitimacy. Demographic factors such as gender and race affect an individual's personal zone of negotiability, broadening it for members of favored groups and constraining it for others. Moreover, individuals with different backgrounds, skills, and experiences have different levels of market power. People with highly sought-after skills bargain differently and create different employment agreements than those with less market power (Arthur & Rousseau, 1996). In developing countries, more modernized workers (who have experience with a market system) participate differently in employment relationships than their traditional counterparts. All societal analyses of employment must address how individual factors affect the individual's negotiating power and the resulting content of the employment agreement.

CONCLUSION

The psychological contracts of workers and employers are shaped by societal factors such as freedom of contract, employment protection, the existence of a market economy, the relative power of the state, and collective bargaining. However, these societal influences do not necessarily have a direct effect on psychological contracts. Organizational practices can mediate between society and individuals, and in many cases firms themselves can actively mitigate the effects of the larger society by introducing their own means for selecting and adapting the workforce to their needs. The effort firms exert to implement their business strategies can vary by country and according to the nature of the firm's relationship with a specific workforce. Last but not least, throughout the process of creating an exchange relationship between workers and employers, the individual worker has his or her own impact and subjective experience. This book is a first step toward unpacking the bundle of influences on psychological contracts in employment across societies.

NOTES

1. A detailed treatment of the theory of psychological contracts is found in Rousseau (1995).

2. Markus and Kitayama (1991) reported greater reliance on implicit interpersonal cues among individuals with highly interdependent models of self, in contrast to the more explicit communications of individuals with independent models of self.

3. Crocker, Fiske, and Taylor (1984) pointed out that incorrectly applied mental models can act as self-fulfilling prophecies. Thus, psychologists who have been told that people are mentally ill and then read case descriptions of normal individuals judge those individuals as mentally ill although they manifest no objective symptoms. People who have been misdiagnosed as mentally ill have difficulty reversing the perception. A manager who views certain behaviors (e.g., timeliness) as "typical" of workers from another culture may have a difficult time rating those individuals as effective workers on other performance indicators. The conflict between American management practices and French culture is evident in the uproar that Eurodisney's dress code created. In 1995, a former Disney Paris manager (himself French) was fined 3,000 francs for violating French labor law ("Ex-Executive Fined," 1995).

4. Other relationships that the parties to an employment agreement may have can also be factored into an individual's psychological contract and can affect beliefs regarding when the individual can or cannot keep that contract. Chinese workers might consider the influence of their boss's boss in making commitments to their supervisor, given that this person can have tremendous influence over the supervisor's ability to perform his or her part of the exchange.

5. This statement reflects relations between Chinese officials and non-Chinese businesspeople regarding the rental of government property. It also may reflect a style of exchange with out-group members.

6. Scholars have characterized the focus on society-specific versus generalizable processes using a variety of distinctions: emic (setting specific) versus etic (generalizable across settings) (Morey & Luthans, 1984); inductive (developing theory from experience) versus deductive (using experience to test existing theory); and local knowledge (richly detailed and fine-grained descriptions of specific settings) versus general knowledge (including attributes, characteristics, and phenomena presumed to be universal). For a more detailed discussion of these issues, see Brett, Tinsley, Janssens, Barsness, and Lytle (1996).

7. Drinking beer with union leaders to gain their support (France), talking to the fathers of young female workers (Mexico), sending a negotiating team to a workers' council meeting to discuss a strategic change (Germany), and flying the chief executive officer in from headquarters to address assembled employees before rolling out the change (Canada). Note that we do not claim that these practices are generalizable throughout the entire country—only that in each case a firm used a different tactic in one country than it did in another.

8. Walton (1987) and Lincoln and Kalleberg (1985) are exceptions.

9. According to MacNeil (1985), every legal contract is an agreement, but not every agreement is a legal contract. In a psychological sense, however, the perception of agreement is the defining feature. British common law stresses that a belief that the other intended to follow agreed-on terms is one condition of a legal contract. Similarly, the French make a point of stressing that agreement/matching of the wills must have existed between parties at some moment for a contract to exist (see Atiyah, 1989).

10. The social accounts that people accept are far broader than what the law recognizes. According to Macaulay (1985), "Potential disputes are suppressed, ignored, or compromised in the service of keeping the relationship alive" (p. 468).

11. Atiyah (1981) maintained that freedom of contract experiences a pendulum oscillation and is now on the upswing again, though some changes are irreversible.

REFERENCES

Abitia, E. A. (1986). *Los valores de los Mexicanos* (Vol. 1). Mexico City: Banamex.

Abitia, E. A. (1991). *Los valores de los Mexicanos* (Vol. 2). Mexico City: Banamex.

Arthur, M. B., & Rousseau, D. M. (1996). *The boundaryless career: A new employment principle for a new organizational era.* New York: Oxford University Press.

Atiyah, P. S. (1981). *An introduction to the law of contract* (4th ed.). Oxford, UK: Clarendon.

Atiyah, P. (1989). The binding nature of contractual obligations. In D. Harris & D. Tallon (Eds.), *Contract law today: Anglo-French comparisons* (pp. 21-80). Oxford, UK: Clarendon.

Betz, B., & Fry, W. R. (1995). The role of group schema in the selection of influence attempts. *Basic and Applied Social Psychology, 16,* 351-365.

Brett, J., Tinsley, C. H., Janssens, M., Barsness, Z. I., & Lytle, A. H. (1996). New approaches to the study of culture in I/O psychology. In P. C. Earley & M. Erez (Eds.), *New perspectives on international organizational psychology.* San Francisco: Jossey-Bass.

Carnoy, M. (1993). *The new global economy in the Information Age: Reflections on our changing world.* University Park: Pennsylvania State University Press.

Carnoy, M., Castells, M., & Benner, C. (1997). *What is happening in the U.S. labor market? Part 1: Review of the evidence.* Unpublished manuscript, Stanford University.

Castells, M. (1996). *The rise of the network society.* Malden, MA: Blackwells.

Crocker, J., Fiske, S. T., & Taylor, S. E. (1984). Schematic bases of belief change. In J. R. Eiser (Ed.), *Attitudinal judgment* (pp. 197-226). New York: Springer-Verlag.

D'Iribarne, P. (1989). *La logique de l'honneur: Gestion des entreprises et traditions nationales.* Paris: Editions du Semil.

Erez, M., & Early, P. C. (1993). *Culture, self-identity, and work.* New York: Oxford University Press.

Ex-executive fined over U.S. dress code at Disneyland Paris. (1995, January 24). *Wall Street Journal,* pp. B2, B5.

Forbes, F. S., & Jones, I. M. (1986). A comparative, attitudinal, and analytical study of dismissals of at-will employees without cause. *Labor Law Review, 37,* 157-166.

Fukuyama, F. (1995). *Trust: The social virtues and creation of prosperity.* New York: Free Press.

Glendon, M. A., Gordon, M. W., & Osakwe, C. (1985). *Comparative legal traditions: Text, materials and cases on the civil law, common law and socialist law traditions, with special reference to French, West German, English and Soviet law.* St. Paul, MN: West.

Goodman, P. S., Olivera, F., & Ranganujam, R. (1998). *Linkages between societal culture and organizational practices.* Unpublished paper, Carnegie Mellon University.

Granrose, C. S., & Chua, B. L. (1996). Global boundaryless careers: Lessons from Chinese family businesses. In M. B. Arthur & D. M. Rousseau (Eds.), *The boundaryless career: A new employment principle for a new organizational era* (pp. 201-217). New York: Oxford University Press.

Hofstede, G. (1980). *Culture's consequences: International differences in work-related values.* Beverly Hills, CA: Sage.

Lammers, C. J., & Hickson, O. J. (1979). *Organisations alike and unlike: International and interinstitutional studies in the sociology of organizations.* London: Routledge & Kegan Paul.

Lincoln, J., & Kalleberg, A. (1985). Work organization and workforce commitment. *American Sociological Review, 50,* 738-760.

Macaulay, S. (1985). An empirical view of contract. *Wisconsin Law Review,* pp. 465-482.

MacDuffie, J. P. (1995). Human resource bundles and manufacturing performance: Organizational logic and flexible production systems in the world auto industry. *Industrial and Labor Relations Review, 48,* 197-221.

MacNeil, I. R. (1985). Relational contract: What we do and do not know. *Wisconsin Law Review,* pp. 483-525.

Markus, H. R., & Kitayama, S. (1991). Culture and self: Implications for cognition, emotion, and motivation. *Psychological Review, 98,* 224-253.

Meaning of Work International Research Team. (1987). *The meaning of work.* New York: Academic Press.

Morey, N. C., & Luthans, F. (1984). An emic perspective and ethnoscience methods for organizational research. *Academy of Management Review, 9,* 27-36.

Ozaki, R. S. (1991). *Human capitalism: The Japanese system as a world model.* New York: Kodansha International.

Roquelle, S. (1993, December). McD's gets French fried. *Crain's Chicago Business,* sec. 1, p. 13.

Rotenberg, K. J., & Cerda, C. (1994). Racially based trust expectancies of Native American and Caucasian children. *Journal of Social Psychology, 134,* 621-631.

Rousseau, D. M. (1995). *Psychological contracts in organizations: Understanding written and unwritten agreements.* Thousand Oaks, CA: Sage.

Schwartz, S. H. (1994). Are there universal aspects in the structure and contents of human values? *Journal of Social Issues, 50,* 19-46.

Schwartz, S. H. (In press). Cultural value differences: Some implications for work. *Applied Psychology: An International Journal.*

Semler, R. (1989). Managing without managers. *Harvard Business Review, 67*(5), 76-84.

Simon, H. (1992). *Is international management different from management?* (Carnegie Bosch Institute Tech. Rep.). Pittsburgh, PA: Carnegie Mellon University.

Sorge, A. (1992). Human resource management in The Netherlands. *Employee Relations, 14*(4), 71-84.

Swedberg, R. (1993). *Explorations in economic sociology.* New York: Russell Sage.

Tannenbaum, A. S., Kavcic, B., Rosner, M., Vianello, M., & Wieser, G. (1974). *Hierarchy in organizations: An international comparison.* San Francisco: Jossey-Bass.

Tropman, J. (1995). *The Catholic ethic in American society.* San Francisco: Jossey-Bass.

Walton, R. E. (1987). *Innovating to compete: Lessons for diffusing and managing change in the workplace.* San Francisco: Jossey-Bass.

Weber, M. (1963). *The sociology of religion* (E. Fischoff, Trans.). New York: Beacon.

2

Psychological Contracts in Australia

A "Fair Go" or a "Not-So-Happy Transition"?

Boris Kabanoff
Nerina L. Jimmieson
Malcolm J. Lewis

> *The American has traditionally expected to find a gamut running from rags to riches, from tramps to millionaires. . . . Equality did not mean uniform position on a common level, but it did mean universal opportunity to move through a scale which traversed many levels.*
>
> David Morris Potter (1954, pp. 91-92)

> *The conception of equality which prevails in Australia is one which places great stress on the enforcement of a high minimum standard of material well-being for all. . . . Constitutional liberalism, which thinks in terms of uniform general laws, would create a set of bureaucratic rules to enforce equal treatment.*
>
> Solomon Encel (1970, p. 57)

The changing nature of the psychological contract has been a topic of emotional debate in contemporary Australian society (see Exhibits 2.1 and 2.2). The heart of this debate is captured by the above quotes. These authors

EXHIBIT 2.1 Getting to Work on the Workplace (*Australian Financial Review,* October 27, 1998, "Opinion," p. 19)

In the coming months it will be vital for job growth and job security and the nation's business effort that a new dialogue is established about how to build better and more productive workplaces.

Employers, unions, political parties of all persuasions—and the media as well—need to find a way to progress the important issues outside of the old class-warfare, "winners-and-losers" paradigm. It's now a tired paradigm that only succeeds in polarizing the community and throwing the legislative process into gridlock.

In the mainstream, there is an understanding emerging between employers and employees that the very serious challenges to productivity and business performance are real, and that they must be confronted. And if there is no effective response, the cost will be counted in falling job numbers, reduced investment, lower capacity to pay wages, less training, and less fulfilling jobs.

What cannot be denied is that Australia's workplaces need to continue to change and reinvent themselves in order to keep businesses competitive in their markets.

What it means is that employers need—more so now than ever before—some sensible changes if they are to employ more people, invest in training, and improve the employability and job security of their workforces. Some of the changes they need are:

- Skills must be able to be deployed flexibly across an enterprise. We need innovative broadbanding, re-classification and job design, functional team approaches and the elimination of demarcation, and to deploy labor efficiently, and selectively, as the job requires.

- Greater innovation is required from some management, which is currently constrained by the traditional industrial relations culture and its informal customs and practices.

- Unions' first aim must be to help create sustainable jobs, not simply increase membership (if they do the former, they will improve their chances of the latter).

- An end is needed to the "industrial mentality" and workplace antagonisms that inhibit the establishment of common values around the organization of the workplace or the business strategy.

- Management has to be able to manage (without negative interference) the efficient allocation and design of overtime, rostering, shift work, and the like that affect the use of capital and add significantly to costs.

- To boost training, limitations must be lifted on the way work is carried out. These restrictions currently mean there is inadequate return on additional training commitments, which leads to under-investment.

- The statutory mandate of the Australian Industrial Relations Commission must be placed on a contemporary footing.

. . . In the day-to-day reality of most Australian workplaces, there are few deep divides between employers and employees that cannot be bridged. The political and legislative process—and the media as well—should build on this reality, not defy it.

—David Buckingham, Executive Director, Business Council of Australia

---

describe two societies' different views regarding the nature of equality, justice, and fairness. The first describes how one society, the United States, values equality of opportunity but not equality of outcomes. Indeed, Americans expect equal opportunity to lead to unequal outcomes. Australian society, on

EXHIBIT 2.2 IR "Reforms" Fuel Insecurity (*Australian Financial Review,*
October 22, 1998, "Opinion" p. 20)

Recent cases of workers losing their wages and a lifetime's worth of leave entitlements through
corporate insolvencies are one demonstration of a pressing need for reform, defined by the
Macquarie Dictionary as "the improvement or amendment of what is wrong, corrupt, etc." But
that's not what the Government means—for the Coalition, reform is equated to deregulation of the
labor market.

Deregulation means removing restrictions on employer capacity to dismiss employees, or to
force unfair wages and conditions on employees. It also, inconsistently, means increasing the regulation of trade union activities, in particular through restrictions on their ability to negotiate collectively on behalf of employees. . . . Growing insecurity in the community is well justified when the
following is considered:

- The richest 10 per cent of families control almost half of Australia's wealth, and their
  share is growing.
- In the last three years, Australia has dropped from seventh to 15th out of 20 developed
  countries on the UN Human Development Index (based on a comparison of life
  expectancy, education, and income levels).
- The gap between rich and poor has widened, with the top 20 per cent of income earners
  paid 10 times more than the bottom 20 per cent. The gap has increased by four per cent
  over the past two years.
- One in four employees is a casual, while full-time job opportunities are declining.
- Australia has one of the highest proportions of part-time employment in the developed
  world.
- One in 15 workers has been retrenched in the three years from 1994 to 1997.
- The Melbourne Institute for Applied Economic and Social Research has found that job
  security in Australia is rapidly declining. Over a seven-year period (1989-90 to 1996-
  97), the number of workers who considered themselves in secure jobs fell by more than
  half from 73 per cent to 36 per cent. . . .

Deregulation of the Australian labor market has gone too far, with too little attention given to
the real factors inhibiting improved industry performance.

The kind of flexibility supported by the Australian Financial Review is essentially about wage
reductions and associated uncertainties; it does nothing to build a more committed and productive
workforce. Rather, it leads to the kind of anger and disillusionment that is to be found in many
workplaces and communities. . . .

—Tim Pallas, Assistant Secretary, Australian Council of Trade Unions

the other hand, seeks greater equality of outcome and is more inclined to idol-
ize "the battler" (i.e., one who overcomes adversity while still retaining his or
her modesty) than "the high achiever" or "the leader" (Renwick, 1991).

In this chapter, we seek to explain how and why the psychological contract
has emerged as a key political, social, and cultural issue in contemporary Australia. For the purposes of this chapter, the United States will be our major reference point rather than, say, the United Kingdom, as might seem more natural,
for several good reasons. First, as Renwick (1991) put it, "Australians and
Americans have usually had rather high regard for one another—as long as

they were some distance apart" (p. 1). Although we would expect the two countries to get along, they frequently do not. This creates an interesting paradox or tension that needs to be explained and understood. Second, there is no doubt that American organizations, managers, and workplace practices are currently seen by many Australians as the benchmark against which Australian managers, organizations, and workplace practices should be compared. Australian management has been under a critical spotlight of late, and most often it is an American model with which unflattering comparisons are made (Karpin, 1995). The CEOs of a significant number of Australia's largest companies are Americans, including Broken Hill Proprietary Company (Australia's largest diversified resources company), Telstra (Australia's largest telecommunications company), Coles Myer (Australia's largest retailer), Australian Mutual Provident (Australia's largest insurance and investment company), and Westpac (Australia's third-largest bank). It is clear that Australian organizations have felt a need to infuse a more American flavor into the psychological contracts that they offer their employees.

Although the psychological contract is a psychological phenomenon, as Chapter 1 observed, contracts are shaped by a great variety of nonpsychological factors, including the organizations in which the contracts are formed, executed, and (sometimes) broken. This chapter deals with the organization—specifically, the types of human resource management (HRM) practices that Australian organizations employ and what this tells us about the implied psychological contracts that they offer to their employees.

AN ORGANIZING FRAMEWORK

Figure 2.1 represents the framework around which this chapter is organized. Though it features a number of theoretical elements, it is not intended to be a theory of psychological contracts; rather, it is intended to provide an integrating perspective on a complex phenomenon.

Australia's historical background and cultural development are held to be key influences on the institutional context (i.e., the laws, the major institutions, and the forms of business organizations) as well as the individual and cultural values that help shape the nature of psychological contracts in Australia. Values, the institutional context, and the nature of psychological contracts all influence the shape of organizations' HRM practices (as do a number of other factors, such as strategy). This linkage is reciprocal—though not equally strong in both directions—because psychological contracts can also exert some influence on broadly cultural values and institutions. In this case, the main reciprocal effect is between HRM practices and psychological contracts rather than between HRM practices and broader contextual factors. That is, HRM practices and individual psychological contracts exert a stronger influence on one another than on cultural values and institutional contexts.

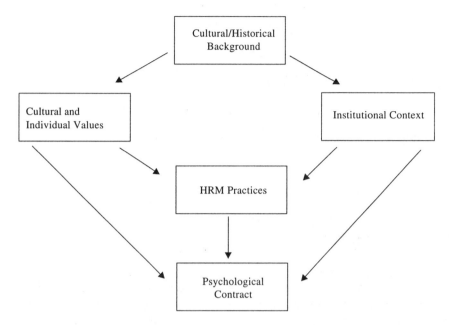

Figure 2.1. An Organizing Model for the Chapter

MAIN TYPES OF PSYCHOLOGICAL CONTRACTS

Rousseau and Wade-Benzoni (1994) suggested that HRM practices determine the nature of the psychological contract that exists between organizations and their employees. They argued that HRM practices are one of the major mechanisms through which employees come to understand the terms and conditions of their employment. Generally, HRM practices have at least two core dimensions: time orientation and specificity of performance requirements. These two dimensions help illustrate how different HRM practices shape employees' interpretations of their psychological contracts. In this respect, psychological contracts typically vary on a continuum of time that indicates the contractual aspects of employment, such as the duration of the employment contract (Guzzo & Noonan, 1994; MacNeil, 1985; Rousseau, 1989). *Performance requirements,* on the other hand, refers to the degree of specificity of performance standards provided as a condition of employment. Rousseau and Wade-Benzoni arranged these two features in a matrix to produce four major types of psychological contracts: relational, transactional, balanced, and transitional (see Figure 2.2).

Relational psychological contracts pertain to open-ended (i.e., nonspecific in terms of time) relationships that involve considerable investments by both employers (e.g., the provision of training) and employees (e.g., organizational

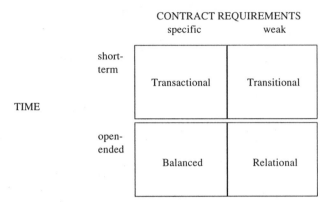

Figure 2.2. Typology of Psychological Contracts
SOURCE: Rousseau and Wade-Benzoni (1994).

commitment) and a high degree of mutual interdependence. Thus, organizations that create relational contracts with their employees are more likely to spend resources to develop employees, most notably in the training of staff to develop knowledge, skills, and abilities that are specific to the company. However, relational contracts tend to have poorly defined performance standards and requirements. In contrast, transactional psychological contracts are more likely to focus on monetary exchanges that are shorter in duration but entail well-specified performance standards. Organizations with transactional contracts typically enhance their ability to respond to changing market conditions by selecting individuals who already have specialized education and experience (rather than investing resources in general employee development). Balanced contracts tend to be more relationship oriented but have clearly defined performance terms (although these may change over time). Finally, transitional contracts are described as a breakdown in the psychological contract in which there are no guarantees concerning future employment and no explicit performance demands. Rousseau and Wade-Benzoni (1994) argued that organizations in transition are likely to be moving toward a transactional environment.

Implications for Employee Attitudes

How employees interpret HRM practices affects the way in which they assess the psychological contract. Subjective appraisals of one's psychological contract with an organization are likely to manifest themselves in a range of different employee attitudes. Favorable assessments relate to positive attitudes such as job satisfaction and organizational commitment, whereas less favorable assessments are likely to foster negative job attitudes (e.g., intentions to leave). These employee attitudes, in turn, may influence job-related behaviors such as performance, absenteeism, and turnover.

For example, employees working in organizations with relational psychological contracts are thought to have high levels of commitment to the company and, ultimately, lower rates of turnover (which helps to instill a strong institutional memory). In contrast, employees working in a transactional organization are likely to be less loyal to the organization and therefore less likely to stay with the organization for a long time. Balanced psychological contracts are believed to develop a sense of trust among employees, who also develop high levels of organizational commitment and expect to be involved in organizational decision making. Finally, transitional organizations are typically characterized by a lack of trust in management and low intentions to remain with the organization.

PSYCHOLOGICAL CONTRACTS IN AUSTRALIA

Historical Background

The European settlement of Australia began with the establishment of a British penal colony in 1788 at the present site of the city of Sydney. The penal colonies, which grew out of harsh economic and legal conditions in Britain, inhibited private investment and retarded free immigration. As time progressed and British needs changed, the Australian colonies came to favor private enterprise. Agriculture and mining were the foundational industries and remain vital to the Australian economy today. In 1985-86, these two industries accounted for 62% of export income, although the individuals who helped earn this income were less than 8% of those employed. However, it was not until the discovery of gold in 1851 that Australia was propelled into nationhood. Not only did the population increase and become more geographically dispersed after 1851, but alternative industries were established to provide infrastructure and support for thousands of hopeful gold diggers.

The changes wrought by the gold rushes were more than superficial—they altered the demographic character of the colonies. Wealth and economic power were no longer concentrated in the hands of a mainly land-based upper class, and the "radical" idea of a representative government took hold (Smith, 1993). This marked the beginning of a tradition of egalitarianism with the overriding principle of a "fair go" for everyone. This attitude was reflected not only in the 1854 Eureka Stockade (a gold prospectors' rebellion against unfair taxes) but in Australia's position as a world leader in adopting concepts such as male suffrage (and later, universal suffrage) and in the rapid growth of the Australian labor movement at the end of the 19th century.

The formation of the sheep shearers' union was a defining event in institutionalizing this ethic of equality and mutual solidarity. From 1888 to 1902, shearers' strikes raged across the states of New South Wales and Queensland,

and although the strikes ultimately failed, this defeat led to the birth of the Australian Labor Party. During the same period, an association of pastoralists was formed that ultimately became the National Party. These parties, along with the Liberal Party, are now the dominant political parties in Australia.

The concern with protecting the "underdog" and providing a "fair go" for all, as well as protecting the right to protest against perceived injustice, played a powerful role in shaping the national constitution that was adopted when the colonies federated in 1901. The period of strikes seemingly proved the need for the new Australian federal government to be granted powers in the labor relations arena, and the unions' actions had a potent influence on the industrial relations system that subsequently developed. As an editorial in the Australian Financial Review ("A Dangerous Obsession," 1992) described it:

> After crushing the unions in the industrial conflicts of the 1890s, employers displayed little interest in recognizing or dealing with organized labor. Compulsory arbitration was imposed on the initially unwilling employers, who eventually learned to live with external regulation of industrial relations, particularly when the notion of "protection all round" extended State assistance from the manufacturing sector to non-manufacturing enterprises. (p. 16)

The egalitarian principle discussed here may be uniquely Australian. In Australia, the emphasis on equality extends beyond the equality of opportunity that is evident in the American expression of egalitarianism. Rather, Australians demand a "fair and reasonable" standard of living for everyone and are less tolerant of unequal wealth. As noted by Feather (1975), this emphasis on equal outcomes tends to be accompanied by a distrust of excellence in many areas, the so-called "tall poppy" syndrome. The noted Australian sociologist Encel (1970) summed it up as follows:

> The conception of equality which prevails in Australia is one which places great stress on the enforcement of high minimum standards of material well-being, on the outward show of equality and the minimization of privileges due to formal rank, and almost by implication restricts the scope for the unusual, eccentric, or dissenting individual. (p. 57)

However, the pursuit of equality has also had some paradoxical outcomes, as Encel (1970) observed:

> Constitutional liberalism, which thinks in terms of uniform general laws, would create a set of bureaucratic rules to enforce equal treatment. Herein lies the paradox of egalitarianism in Australia: The search for equality of the redistributive kind breeds bureaucracy; bureaucracy breeds authority; and authority undermines the equality which bred it. (p. 57)

Institutional Context

In the end, the search for "redistributive equality" spawned a powerful and highly centralized industrial relations system. The system adopted soon after federation featured the underpinning principles of comparative wage justice, such as central wage fixing, regulated dispute resolution, and adversarial arbitration based on a judicial model. The arbitration system featured industry-wide employment conditions negotiated by employer and union representatives before a government commission in a formalized and legalistic setting. This had the benefit of providing economic security for employees with limited bargaining power, greater compression or less differentiation in wages, and a relatively low level of competition among employees.

In terms of the psychological contract, this system offered a sense of predictability and job security that guaranteed employees a fair wage, cost-of-living adjustments, nonwage benefits that were generous by world standards, and a reasonable chance of promotion as long as economic and organizational growth persisted. Larger organizations rewarded commitment and loyalty with career opportunities within the company. Further, a high degree of unionization and powerful unions in many industries ensured job continuity in normal circumstances, and the intervention of the union could reasonably be relied on if expectations were not met or employment conditions were threatened. In the next section, we consider how these historical and institutional characteristics relate to both individual and cultural values.

Individual and National Values

Hofstede's (1980) seminal study still offers a useful reference point for characterizing the broad cultural values shaping psychological contracts within Australia. Overall, Hofstede's findings place Australia squarely within what he called the "Anglo" group of countries, which includes Great Britain, the United States, Canada, New Zealand, Ireland, and Australia. Thus, Australian values are oriented toward greater equality; more tolerance of dissent; a reliance on individual judgment rather than on rules, laws, and hierarchies (i.e., lower uncertainty avoidance); greater individualism (i.e., preference for greater individual autonomy); and an emphasis on the pursuit of financial and personal success through competition and independence. Thus, concerns with equality, individual freedom, and the enjoyment of material well-being (i.e., hedonism) emerge as important characteristics of Australian cultural values.

One area where there appears to be some disagreement between the "historical" picture and a Hofstede-based classification is on the dimension of uncertainty avoidance. Australia's highly formalized, rule-based industrial relations system, which tends to provide greater certainty and less differentiation among people, seems much more congruent with high, rather than low, uncertainty avoidance. This apparent inconsistency between Australia's "Anglo" heritage and its possibly higher uncertainty avoidance may be, as Encel suggested, a paradoxical outcome of its search for "mandated equality." That is, the formalized and standardized industrial relations system may be a "collateral" outcome of the culture's pursuit of equality rather than a result of relatively higher uncertainty avoidance per se, though in fact Australia scores somewhat higher on this dimension than any other country in the "Anglo" group. Another major cross-cultural study of national values conducted by Schwartz (1992, 1994) found that the only three value dimensions on which Australia was located in the top 50% of the 38 countries ranked were affective autonomy (closely related to hedonism values), conservatism (closely related to security values), and egalitarian commitment.

We next discuss some research findings related to individual values, which shed further light on the issue of Australian values. Feather (1996), whose most recent work has drawn on the values framework developed by Schwartz, is the best known researcher of individual values in Australia. Schwartz (1992, 1994) developed a theory incorporating 56 separate values, describing universals in the content and structure of values. Importantly, he organized these values into 10 broad value types or systems and identified both the compatibilities and conflicts among these types. For example, hedonism and stimulation are compatible value systems because both entail a desire for affectively pleasant arousal. However, hedonism conflicts with conformity and tradition in that indulging one's desires contradicts the restraint of one's own impulses and the acceptance of externally imposed limits. The 10 types along with their constituent dimensions are as follows: *power* (e.g., authority and preservation of social image), *achievement* (e.g., success and ambition), *hedonism* (e.g., pleasure and enjoyment of life), *stimulation* (e.g., a varied and exciting life), *self-direction* (e.g., freedom and selection of one's own goals), *universalism* (e.g., equality and unity with nature), *benevolence* (e.g., responsibility, honesty, and loyalty), *tradition* (e.g., humility, devotion, and acceptance of one's position in life), *conformity* (e.g., obedience and respect for family members), and *security* (e.g., social order and reciprocation of favors).

Feather (1996) investigated the association between people's scores on the Schwartz value types and their level of identification with Australia, based on reports of how much pride people felt about being Australian and how much their nationality meant to them. He interpreted the correlations between values and national identification as indicating the values people perceived as central to the culture or capable of being satisfied within the culture. He hypothesized that identification with Australia would be associated with the importance attached to the values of hedonism, security, achievement, and equality (a dimension of universalism). This hypothesis was largely supported in that individuals who more strongly identified with Australia were more likely to endorse values of hedonism, security, and achievement. However, egalitarianism failed to emerge, possibly because it was just one aspect of the universalism type, which incorporated a number of values receiving low endorsement from Australians, including broadmindedness, wisdom, a world of beauty, and so on.

Implications and Paradoxes

Some implications of this analysis for understanding psychological contracts are relatively straightforward. Other implications are less so; indeed, they are paradoxical. The history of Australia and empirical research into its cultural and individual values lead us to suggest that the "typical" psychological contract in Australia has been shaped by concerns over predictability and security as opposed to autonomy and self-direction; hedonism as opposed to tradition and conformity; an emphasis on egalitarianism and "social justice" as opposed to authority and social power; and, to some extent, achievement of individual success as opposed to benevolence or more spiritual values. A concern with the pursuit of egalitarianism through a quasi-legal and redistributive system is a defining characteristic of Australia that distinguishes it from the United States but not necessarily from all European countries.

Thus, one major difference between the American and Australian cultures is quite evident: In the United States, meritocracy rules, whereas in Australia, citizens are less comfortable with distinctions based on achievement or purely on status. As Renwick (1991) described it:

> Australians tend to base their trust on the capacity for loyalty and commitment a person has and on *their own sense* [italics in original] and estimation of that person. Americans tend to base their trust on the person's capacity for performance and consistent behavior, and on *other people's* [italics in original] recognition, ranking, and accreditation of that person. (p. 25)

Australians tend to be more impressed by whether a person is "a good bloke" (guy) rather than the person's achievements and qualities as judged by an impersonal system.

Some further interesting evidence on the differing prevalence of meritocratic values in the two countries is provided by a study conducted by the first author in cooperation with an American colleague (we can work together, you see!). Kabanoff and Daly (in press) compared the values espoused in annual reports from a matched sample of Australian and American companies. One of the main differences they found was that more American than Australian organizations embraced a value set that could be characterized as meritocratic. The American organizations were more likely to espouse a mix of values that included relational as well as performance-oriented values; this value profile is very similar to what Rousseau and Wade-Benzoni (1994) described as a balanced contract.

However, there is also a rather paradoxical aspect to Australian culture and the nature of the psychological contract. We indicated this earlier in the quote from Encel (1970), who observed that in their search for a mandated equality, Australians may have built a reliance on authority and regulation that undermines the very egalitarianism they pursue. This is as much a paradox as the fact that Americans' equal and unhindered right to pursue individual achievement and success results in great inequalities in people's outcomes.

Australians' simultaneous distrust of and dependence on authority was commented on by the American expatriate managers mentioned earlier, whom Moodie (1998b) recently interviewed for a book about leadership in Australia. As Telstra CEO Frank Blount remarked,

> In general, I was shocked by the lack of "stepping up to the bar" and of people saying the "buck stops here." The trend is more to bring in a consultant to do the job and make a recommendation to the board. It may be caused by the notion of "mateship" in Australia. Nobody sticks their head up and everyone goes as a group, which means accountability is diffused and no one is in charge of anything. When I came here, I couldn't believe the number of papers coming across my desk for approval, which wasn't needed. So I kept sending them back with a note saying "You do it." (quoted in Moodie, 1998b, pp. 293-294)

Bob Joss, CEO of Westpac and a former executive of Wells Fargo Bank in California, suggested that this behavior is caused by Australia's more formal and structured business environment. He commented: "Australians like to think of the country as more egalitarian. But I found there were lots of graduations of power—a pecking order if you will—as well as [more] internal politics" (Moodie, 1998a, p. 3).

Once again, the study by Kabanoff and Daly (in press) provided some corroborating evidence in terms of organizations' espoused values. Although Australian organizations were less likely than American organizations to espouse a meritocratic set of values, they were more likely to have a value profile labeled by the researchers as "elite": that is, focused mainly on the role of senior managers. Perhaps this paradoxical combination of a simultaneous dislike for and dependence on authority is the basis for this famous English quip: "Australians are very well balanced people—they have a chip on both shoulders."

THE CONTEMPORARY PICTURE:
PRESSURES FOR CHANGE

The traditional Australian industrial relations system ensured that disputes were resolved, but its inherent inflexibilities meant that organizations, managers, and employees that were inefficient and nonproductive received the same rewards as those that were efficient and productive. Because occupational awards and union structures created wage movements that then spread to all of their domestic competitors and because a tariff barrier protected them from foreign competitors, neither managers nor employees had an incentive to become more efficient or innovative—instead, everyone had a comfortable if rather bureaucratically controlled existence. The attempt to protect the rights of all parties led to the institutionalization of industrial conflict in patterns of adversarial behaviors between employers and union bodies. These groups were given no incentive to address real issues, learn to bargain directly, or progress through collaboration and compromise.

This system lasted for more than 80 years, with no serious attention given to its deficiencies until negative economic circumstances arrived. In the 1970s, the Australian economy, its vulnerability long hidden by a trade surplus based on the export of raw minerals and wool, was shaken by the simultaneous occurrence of unemployment and inflation along with plummeting world commodity prices. These events provided a powerful stimulus to employers to reduce staff and introduce new work practices. At a national level, the need to become more economically competitive spurred increased attention to private sector performance and reform of the industrial relations system by the national government.

The Workplace Relations Act of 1996 facilitated direct workplace bargaining between employers and employees, with or without the involvement of trade unions, by introducing new mechanisms that allowed both parties to choose the most appropriate form of agreement for their circumstances. A central goal of this new legislation was to limit the matters that the Australian Industrial Relations Commission (AIRC) could deal with (by reducing its jurisdiction so that it could make awards to settle disputes in relation to only 20 allowable matters) and to reduce the need for trade union representation in the bargaining process. Thus, the Workplace Relations Act was designed to ensure that primary responsibility for issues affecting the employment relationship would rest with employers and employees in the workplace.

The act also modified the requirements for Certified Agreements (CAs) so that they would reflect a full range of working conditions for a specified period of time and would be negotiated directly with employees or with trade unions on behalf of all employees. The CAs are designed to override any preexisting awards and typically include procedures for settling industrial disputes. The AIRC must be satisfied that a valid majority of employees genuinely approve a CA, which often is ensured via a ballot process. Furthermore, the AIRC must be satisfied that the CA meets the "no disadvantage" stipulation by ensuring that it does not result in a reduction in the overall terms and conditions of those employees under relevant awards.

In addition, the Workplace Relations Act provides for Workplace Agreements (WAs). Under federal legislation, WAs are similar to CAs in that they reflect a full range of working conditions for a specified time period. However, WAs are individual agreements that must be negotiated with employees, either individually or collectively. The employee can appoint a bargaining agent, who may or may not be a union representative, to represent him or her during the negotiation. Further, WAs do not need to be registered with or approved by the AIRC. Rather, they are filed with the employment advocate, who provides advice to employers and employees and is responsible for ensuring that the WA meets a global "no disadvantage" test (the WA as a whole cannot be less favorable than the relevant award or any other relevant legislation). With WAs, unlike CAs, strict confidentiality requirements prohibit disclosure of specifications to outside parties. In light of such changes, the trade union movement has cautioned that this represents a deterioration of the AIRC's power and is likely to lead to the reduction and removal of important conditions and rights of employees (Kramar, McGraw, & Schuler, 1997).

This new legislation, though politically contentious, consolidated a decade of evolutionary changes during which employers, employees, and trade unions were increasingly required to undertake direct bargaining and productivity-based wage negotiations. Under the new legislation, wages and conditions can be linked (either collectively or on an individual basis) to workplace productivity measures, with little involvement of any central institution.

In Australia, trade union membership has steadily declined since the 1960s, to the point where the unions' financial restrictions and low representation in the workplace are constraining their ability to challenge management. It can be argued that the effect of this change, coupled with the Workplace Relations Act, has been a removal of the formerly systemic and union-based protection of individual employees. In the next section, we consider data that provide some insight into the consequences of these changes for the state of psychological contracts in Australia.

SOME RECENT DATA ON HRM PRACTICES
AND EMPLOYEE ATTITUDES

As explained earlier, Rousseau and Wade-Benzoni (1994) identified four major psychological contracts on the distinct continuums of time and specificity. They also described the relation of these four psychological contracts to employees' perceptions of the management-employee relationship and subsequent job attitudes, such as satisfaction and commitment. To provide some empirical evidence on the current state of HRM practices and the psychological contract in Australia, we drew on data collected by the Australian Workplace Industrial Relations Survey in 1995 (AWIRS 95; Morehead, Steele, Alexander, Stephen, & Duffin, 1997). This is a major national survey undertaken by a specially formed research team within the policy division of the Department of Workplace Relations and Small Business. The data collection process involved 2,001 workplaces (with 20 or more employees) in which senior managers, employee relations managers, and union representatives were surveyed about a wide range of employment practices, including HRM practices. In addition, a large sample of employees ($N = 19,155$) from these organizations were surveyed with regard to a range of different job attitudes.

Our conclusions, though based on some fairly complex analyses of these data, are straightforward. First, it was evident that a relatively large proportion of Australian organizations are using HRM practices that are oriented toward measuring both individual and organizational performance. The AWIRS 95 survey collected information about formalized processes for monitoring employee performance through traditional performance appraisal systems and the evaluation of more direct productivity measures, such as the use of key performance indicators, benchmarking against other workplaces, and the measurement of labor productivity. It was found that in 68% of workplaces, the work performance of at least some nonmanagerial employees was formally appraised at least once a year, compared to 61% in 1990. Sixty-eight percent of managers, representing both the public and private sectors, said that key performance indicators were in use at their workplace. However, such indicators were more likely to be used by larger organizations. Sixty-seven percent of organizations benchmark against other workplaces, a practice that is more likely to occur in the private sector and also in larger organizations. In 1995, 69% of workplaces indicated that they had procedures in place to measure labor productivity, a proportion that had remained relatively constant over the 5-year period (68% in 1990). In such organizations, 64% reported that the measurement of labor productivity was across the entire workplace, but some organizations used measures based on the performance of individuals (49%), groups (42%), or departments (50%) (Morehead et al., 1997). In short, Australian organizations appear to be shifting toward more specific or transactional HRM activities.

Employee responses to these transactional practices were equally clear: Workers in organizations employing all or most of the practices listed above typically had more negative attitudes toward their jobs. We note that these were average trends across a large and diverse sample and that the effects, though clear, were not large. Nevertheless, the employees surveyed in 1995 reported feeling less secure and having less trust in management when the organization used these types of HRM practices. Furthermore, employee tenure exacerbated this effect—the longer the tenure, the more negative employees' attitudes. Drawing on the arguments of Rousseau and Wade-Benzoni (1994) to interpret these trends, we suggest that in 1995 a significant proportion of Australian employees believed that they had transitional psychological contracts, an interpretation that stemmed from their organizations' adoption of HRM practices that were becoming more specific and less open-ended.

The trends are clear, but how are Australian organizations, employees, and society as a whole likely to develop in the future? Inevitably, the answer to this question involves some value judgments. One possible answer is put forth by the union movement in Exhibit 2.2: that is, to move toward reregulation and recentralization of employment relations management. Union proponents could certainly use the results of the AWIRS 95 study to support this argument. However, one could also argue that a sense of transition (and consequently insecurity) is inevitable, if not desirable, and is necessary for the future viability of Australian organizations. From this perspective, represented in Exhibit 2.1, the issue is not about the need or direction of change but rather about how that change is managed.

Is there another way to view the current situation in Australia that is not captured well by either side in Exhibit 2.1 or Exhibit 2.2? A third way that some have suggested sees market forces coexisting with a caring social order. Notably, virtually all of the practices identified as the "new wave" of HRM have an American origin. Management practices such as benchmarking and formal performance appraisal clearly have American roots and, as noted above, are congruent with the meritocratic values of the United States. We could view these results as a challenge to the innovative abilities of Australian organizations, managers, and HRM specialists. The challenge for Australia is to achieve the benefits of more flexible, meritocratic practices without seriously violating the country's traditional egalitarian values, if possible. This might involve modifying or adapting the practices that come from cultures such as the United States, implementing these practices in skillful ways, or—the most exciting but difficult option—developing "indigenous" Australian practices that achieve similar outcomes without the costs associated with dissatisfaction and distrust in the workplace.

The latter solution requires creativity on the part of Australian managers and human resource practitioners, as well as flexibility and tolerance of change by Australian employees. The prospects of this happening, though not entirely dim, are not necessarily encouraging. Australia has produced many successful inventors, scientists, and engineers, and individual Australians commonly have a high level of acceptance for new technologies, but the country's organizations have a poor reputation in terms of being innovative or entrepreneurial. Australians decry the fact that "good ideas" pioneered by Australians often end up being developed and commercialized by overseas companies that see their potential, while Australian companies avoid taking any risks on innovation. In the same way, it has been said that Australian organizations fail to innovate in their HRM practices.

There have, of course, been some success stories, including companies like ICI (now called Orica) and Australia Post. What distinguishes these organizations appears to be their greater focus on building trust and cooperation with their employees (sometimes involving unions) and sharing any gains from changed practices. Most practitioners or academics would not view these approaches as uniquely Australian; nevertheless, they suggest that managers might view their need to earn the respect and trust of employees as particularly important in the Australian context, with its distrust of authority and preference for "good blokes" rather than "great leaders." One social historian, Stretton (1985), has observed: "A national myth says Australians are good at everything except leading and being led" (p. 197). Perhaps Australians prefer their managers to encourage them to "have a go" rather than to exhort them to "join the crusade." To date, not enough work has been done to identify any truly distinctive Australian features that characterize successful efforts to redefine psychological contracts in Australian organizations.

If the tale of unhappy transitions indicated here is to end, Australians— managers and employees alike—must find a way to develop psychological contracts that are compatible with both the competitive demands of the next century and the core national values that were shaped largely in the last century. Ongoing conflict between the two is not sustainable, and the victory of one over the other could only be Pyrrhic.

REFERENCES

A dangerous obsession. (1992, August 7). *Australian Financial Review,* p. 16.

Encel, S. (1970). *Equality and authority: A study of class, status, and power in Australia.* Melbourne, Australia: Longman Cheshire.

Feather, N. (1975). *Values in education and society.* New York: Free Press.

Feather, N. (1996). Social comparisons across nations: Variables relating to the subjective evaluation of national achievement and to personal and collective self-esteem. *Australian Journal of Psychology, 48,* 53-63.

Guzzo, R. A., & Noonan, K. A. (1994). Human resource practices as communications and the psychological contract. *Human Resource Management, 33,* 447-462.

Hofstede, G. (1980). *Culture's consequences: International differences in work related values.* Beverly Hills, CA: Sage.

Kabanoff, B., & Daly, J. P. (in press). Values espoused by Australian and US organizations. *Applied Psychology: An International Review.*

Karpin, D. S. (1995). *Enterprising nation: Renewing Australia's managers to meet the challenges of the Asia-Pacific century. Report to the industry taskforce on leadership and management skills.* Canberra: Australian Government Publishing Service.

Kramar, R., McGraw, P., & Schuler, R. S. (1997). *Human resource management in Australia.* South Melbourne, Australia: Addison Wesley Longman.

MacNeil, I. R. (1985). Relational contract: What we do and do not know. *Wisconsin Law Review,* pp. 483-525.

Moodie, A. (1998a, November 13). First things first: Leaders found key contrasts in corporate culture. *Australian Financial Review,* p. 3.

Moodie, A. (1998b). *Local heroes: A celebration of success and leadership in Australia.* Sydney, Australia: Prentice Hall.

Morehead, A., Steele, M., Alexander, M., Stephen, K., & Duffin, L. (1997). *Changes at work: The 1995 Australian Workplace Industrial Relations Survey.* South Melbourne, Australia: Addison Wesley Longman.

Potter, D. M. (1954). *People of plenty: Economic abundance and the American character.* Chicago: University of Chicago Press.

Renwick, G. W. (1991). *A fair go for all: Australian/American interactions.* Yarmouth, ME: Intercultural Press.

Rousseau, D. M. (1989). Psychological and implied contracts in organizations. *Employee Rights and Responsibilities Journal, 2,* 121-139.

Rousseau, D. M., & Wade-Benzoni, K. A. (1994). Linking strategy and human resource practices: How employee and customer contracts are created. *Human Resource Management, 33,* 463-489.

Schwartz, S. H. (1992). Universals in the content and structure of values: Theoretical advances and empirical tests in 20 countries. In M. P. Zanna (Ed.), *Advances in experimental social psychology* (pp. 1-65). Orlando, FL: Academic Press.

Schwartz, S. H. (1994). Beyond individualism and collectivism: New cultural dimensions of values. In U. Kim, H. C. Triandis, C. Kagitcibasi, S. C. Choi, & G. Yoon (Eds.), *Individualism and collectivism: Theory, methods, and application* (pp. 85-119). Thousand Oaks, CA: Sage.

Smith, R. (1993). *Politics in Australia.* Sydney, Australia: Allen & Unwin.

Stretton, H. (1985). The quality of leading Australians in Australia: Terra incognita? *Daedalus, 114,* 197-230.

3

Belgium

A Culture of Compromise

Luc Sels
Maddy Janssens
Inge Van den Brande
Bert Overlaet

"Sire, il n'y a pas de Belges" ("There are no Belgians, Sire"). These words of a senator addressing King Albert I in 1911 expressively capture the institutional complexity of Belgium. First, there is no Belgian language: The Flemish part of the country speaks Dutch, and the Walloon part of the country speaks French. The complexity of Belgium as a federal state is even more astonishing to outsiders. Because linguistic communities do not exactly match the Flemish and Walloon regions, and because of the special position of Brussels as a bilingual capital, the country has six different governments for a population of only 10 million people. On the other hand, the country's central position and openness to different traditions have brought prosperity and wealth to most of its inhabitants.

The case of Belgium shows that the central question of this book—What is "emic" and what is "etic" in psychological contracts?—is important not only in international but also in intranational research. In an attempt to simplify Belgian complexity, we will concentrate as much as possible on the etic aspects of psychological contracts that are generalizable across the country's cultural and linguistic boundaries. For although there is no such thing as a "Belgian ethnicity" to serve as a frame of reference, employers and employees in Belgium share the same historical, social, and legal context.

Some elements of this shared history may be relevant to the discussions in this chapter. First, the embryo of the Belgian state emerged from the medieval "Low Countries" when Holland successfully seceded from Spain, leaving Belgium under an oppressive Catholic reign. The Catholic culture institutionalized in Spain, Italy, and France is very different from the Protestant culture that dominates German and Anglo-Saxon countries. Its emphasis on dogma and centralized control and its inherent antirevolutionary nature have promoted the culture of large power distance in Belgium (Hofstede, 1980). But although Catholicism has been associated with external oppression throughout European history, it offers much more internal freedom of thought and action than its Protestant counterpart. Instead of being built on effort, consistency, and virtue, the Catholic ethic is built on sin and redemption, leading to a culture of enjoying life in the seclusion of one's private sphere. It is no surprise, therefore, that when the Low Countries were reunited after the battle of Waterloo, the union with the Netherlands failed, and the new state of Belgium turned to France for support and inspiration.

Another historical observation, equally important in understanding Belgian labor relations, is the fact that Belgium was a pioneer in the second industrial revolution. It was the first country on the European continent to build railroads and to operate machines in its important textile industry. This led to severe outbursts of social conflict, illustrated by the complaints of Pierre Lafargue (1883/1975), son-in-law of Karl Marx, that the Belgian army was famous for fighting its own laborers.[1] Such social outbursts were aggravated by the existing dividing lines between Catholics and liberals, Flemish and Walloons.

We identify five basic characteristics of psychological contracts in Belgium. Psychological contracting in this country seems driven by attitudes and behaviors of high loyalty and low exit; respect for authority combined with the value of equality; strong work and salary orientation as driving motivators; a culture of compromise grounded in an institutional basis of rules and regulations; and a paradoxical mix between the need to belong to a group and an individualistic perspective on work. To understand the origins of these characteristics, we first discuss the legal and institutional context in which employment relationships take shape. We present the differences between a contract in the private sector and a statute in the public sector as well as the juridical distinctions between blue-collar workers and white-collar workers. After introducing these basic forms of employment relationships, we focus on employment contracts in the private sector.

Often, employment contracts are only membership certificates, with little room for free negotiation of the terms and conditions of employment. This discussion of the Belgian model of collective bargaining and the country's continuing reliance on standard employment contracts leads us to a first indication of the values, expectations, and obligations that are important in Belgium (e.g., compromises, job security, company-employee bonding, continuity, and

TABLE 3.1 Important Distinctions in Employment Conditions for Public/Private and Blue-Collar/White-Collar Workers in Belgium

	Public Sector	*Private Sector*
Regulation of employment relationship	Personnel statute governs employment relationship for most employees	Employment relationship formalized in employment contract
Striking differences between categories of employment		
White-collar workers	Employed by statute Government-employer may unilaterally determine terms and conditions of employment Job security (loyalty) Highly structured internal labor market	Paid monthly High protection from dismissal (loyalty)
Blue-collar workers	Employment by contract (cf. private sector) Mainly fixed-term contracts	Paid hourly Low protection from dismissal System of temporary unemployment

industrial peace). These contextual features then bring us to a more focused discussion of the five main characteristics of psychological contracts. We conclude by introducing two major trends that are currently changing the employment relationships in Belgium and are likely to influence psychological contracting in the future. These trends point to an increasing reliance by companies on legal remedies in crisis situations and the devaluation of the existing model of collective bargaining.

THE DIFFERENT FORMS OF EMPLOYMENT RELATIONSHIPS

A first important distinction is that between contract and statute, two different mechanisms of formalizing the employment relationship. A second distinction still very much present in Belgium is that between blue-collar and white-collar workers. The employment contract contains very different provisions depending on whether you belong to the first or to the second group. We will briefly sketch these two differences because they are important background information for understanding the meaning of psychological contracts in Belgium (see Table 3.1).

Contract Versus Statute

Employment relationships in the private sector are formalized in employment contracts. People become members of companies by signing a contract in which they promise to obey the orders of their employers, work under their control, and follow their instructions. Employers, in turn, are obliged to reward employees according to the terms and conditions of their contracts. In principle, the parties to the contract are regarded as equals. They have, even if only "in principle" (as we will discuss below), the possibility of free negotiation with respect to the content of the contract.

In the literature on employment relationships in Western economies, these forms of contractual arrangements are regarded as self-evident. However, this overlooks the fact that in Belgium and other countries, large groups of employees do not have freedom of negotiation. This is the case in the Belgian public sector, where approximately 30% of the labor force is employed (Steunpunt WAV, 1998). For the majority of these individuals, a statute takes the place of an employment contract. A statute can be described as a regulation of the relationship between the government and its employees, as established by general administrative order. The content of this statute is unilaterally determined by the government-employer. There is no question of "autonomous expression of will," as in a contractual relationship. Individuals entering into a statute subject, so to speak, their individual will to the general interest. Employment by statute even allows the government-employer—in the "general interest" and for the sake of the "ever changing requirements of the civil service"—to change the content of a personnel statute unilaterally (Déom, 1990, p. 292).

Two convergent trends, however, make the difference between contract and statute less clear-cut than the foregoing remarks might suggest. In the private sector, the freedom to negotiate the content of employment relationships has been limited over time. This is the result of extensive standardization of working conditions, as we will discuss later. In the public sector, the process of collective bargaining between government and trade unions has grown in importance. This leads to more joint consultation between the government-employer and the trade unions than unilateral determination by the government (Sels, 1996).

One of the most striking differences between contract and statute that still remains widespread concerns the degree of job security. Employment under a statute implies that the government may proceed to dismissal only in restrictively defined cases, and "lifetime employment" is the rule. However, this is just one side of the picture. Statutory employment also implies that employees may not quit the organization except under strictly defined conditions because the government views mass exit as a threat to the stability and continuity of the civil service. It is precisely for this reason that government bureaucracies have turned their doors into one-way valves. Members get in, but once inside, it is sometimes difficult for them to get out. The government desires such security because it wants the ability to impose unilateral measures on its personnel in order to ensure that its policies are carried out without provoking employees' exit en masse.

Blue-Collar Versus White-Collar Workers

The private sector draws important distinctions between blue-collar workers and white-collar workers. Labor law treats these two categories differently for issues such as salary arrangements, the probationary period, guaranteed income, temporary unemployment, and annual vacations. The distinction between white-collar and blue-collar workers also is reflected in collective industrial relations. In the majority of cases, there are separate administrative structures (i.e., joint committees) for blue-collar and white-collar workers employed within the same industry. Even the trade union structure itself is based on this distinction: These two groups of workers have separate unions. The distinction also exists in the labor courts, and so on.

This juridical distinction was introduced in 1900 to reflect the different position of the two groups in the organizing process. White-collar workers were traditionally seen as employer confidants who were closely involved in the company's objectives and policies. Over time, this view was reflected in higher pay, stronger protection against dismissal, longer annual vacations, and other distinctions. Historically, the legislature assumed that only the interests of manual or blue-collar workers that opposed those of management required legal protection. Although the improvement of blue-collar workers' rights has been at the center of collective trade union action throughout the 20th century, blue-collar workers still lag behind with respect to terms and conditions of employment.

In comparing the formal contracts of blue-collar and white-collar workers, the most striking difference is the degree of employment security. The law governing dismissal contains three types of regulations, for blue-collar workers, lower white-collar workers, and higher white-collar workers (mostly management positions). The differences in degree of protection from dismissal are striking. After finishing a probationary period, white-collar workers are entitled to 3 months' notice after 18 years of service. Blue-collar workers with 18 years of seniority, on the other hand, are entitled to only 28 days' notice. To mitigate this difference, labor law has installed the principle barring arbitrary dismissal for blue-collar workers. This means that employers must be able to show that the dismissal is connected to the behavior of the worker or the operations of the company. If this is not the case, an employer must compensate the worker for wrongful dismissal. Although this principle seems fair, it is seldom applied in practice.

Differences in employment security are not only reflected in longer periods of notice for white-collar workers. Blue-collar workers also receive far less unemployment compensation after dismissal, even in comparison with other members of the European Union. In Europe, the average compensation for blue-collar workers was the equivalent of 16.7 weeks' pay in 1990—more than three times the level in Belgium (Mosley, 1994).

THE EMPLOYMENT CONTRACT: NO MORE THAN A "MEMBERSHIP CERTIFICATE?"

Individual employment contracts reflect two central principles of Belgian labor law that seem contradictory but are not. On one hand, the labor law states that an employment contract is by definition a relationship of authority. This authority not only implies that employers have full discretion or decision-making power on strategic, marketing, or cost-related issues but also gives them the right to direct work, give orders, and control the performance of the work. Trade unions may challenge this principle from time to time, but they generally accept the authority of the employer.

On the other hand, the same labor law was developed as a reaction toward the individualistic principles of individual contract law. Because the continuity of the employment relationship and a guaranteed income were central concerns (Blanpain & Vanachter, 1996), labor law emphasized solidarity instead of individualism. Pay and working conditions are mainly determined by law, collective agreements, and labor regulations. Consequently, in most cases the individual parties do not arrange the content of individual employment contracts, which are reduced to "membership certificates" with little room for negotiation. Because so much is predetermined for large groups of workers, the contract becomes a shared normative belief rather than an individual psychological contract per se.

In this section, to fully explain the effects that "membership certificates" have on psychological contracts in Belgium, we discuss two characteristics of this type of employment contract. The first is the collective regulation of membership certificates, prompted by a tradition of social negotiation and consultation. The second important characteristic is the continuing use of standard employment contracts instead of more flexible contracts. This durability of standard employment relationships indicates the importance of company-employee bonding.

A Socially Regulated Employment Relationship

Belgium has a long tradition of social consultation and negotiation at the national, industry, and company levels between employers' associations and trade unions, which originated in the Social Pact of 1944. In this agreement, employers' associations and trade unions recognized that "the smooth running of the businesses, which is linked to the general prosperity of the country, can only take place through loyal cooperation (*Het sociaal overleg op interprofessioneel vlak,* 1974, p. 27). The two parties acknowledged each other as social partners, and employers accepted the presence of trade unions where unions accepted the employers' authority. As stated in the pact, "The workers respect the legal authority of the owners of the businesses [and] show their respect through the loyal and dutiful execution of their work" (*Het sociaal overleg op interprofessioneel vlak,* 1974, p. 28).

Further elaboration of the Social Pact created a system of national multi-industry bargaining, resulting in social planning agreements covering the entire private sector. These agreements, which constitute the frame for the social and economic policy, are renewed every 2 years. The issues settled in these agreements not only include topics such as minimum wages, working hours, and holiday arrangements but also deal with practices to fight unemployment, interventions in pension schemes, and the family allowance system. Hence, social consultation has played a leading role in the development of the welfare state.

This negotiation and consultation system has a pyramid shape (Vilrokx & Van Leemput, 1998). The signing of a multi-industry social planning agreement typically triggers a top-down succession of negotiations, resulting in a hierarchical structure of multi-industry, industrywide, and company-level collective labor agreements (CLAs).[2] Although these multi-industry agreements do not go beyond relatively general provisions, more detailed provisions are filled in by joint committees at the level of each industry. A CLA negotiated at the industry level automatically applies to all companies in that industry. This general binding declaration of CLAs explains the high percentage of workers falling within the scope of industrywide CLAs. In 1983 and 1984, 66% of employees were covered by a collective agreement concluded at industrywide level. More recently, the figure was 90%. The negotiation pyramid is completed at company level. In recent years, there has been a sharp rise in the number of collective agreements entered into at the company level. These CLAs take shape after negotiation between management and trade union delegation, which is further discussed below.

Outsiders often wonder about the relative durability of this consultation and negotiation pyramid. It seems to contradict the increasing demands for flexibility at the company level. However, it is important to consider that employers' associations still strongly believe that they gain from central (or at least industrywide) agreements. For them, the main advantage is keeping social peace in their companies. With the 1968 collective labor agreement law, the trade unions acquiesced to the obligation to keep social peace for the duration of an agreement. Giving their assent to collective agreements is thus one way in which employers can "buy" industrial peace.

A second explanation for the continuing durability of the social consultation process can be found in the content of the Social Pact, which was established at the end of World War II. This pact clearly defines the boundaries of negotiation. The most important rule of the game is the noninterference of trade unions in production affairs. Employers receive exclusive rights in the areas of economic, financial, and strategic policy and in organizing the production process. Social consultation and negotiating are limited to the distribution of productivity profits (pay) and social security. Issues about work itself and the organization of the production process seldom get onto the agenda. When this does happen, the negotiations focus on the consequences of work reorganizations such as pay, job classification, and working conditions.

Employers' readiness to enter into collective labor agreements still does not explain why they continue to support the broad application of such agreements (termed the *general binding declaration*). Although the general binding declaration is debated in other European countries, this is not the case in Belgium, which can be explained by the fact that employers and trade unions see sufficient advantages in transcorporate regulation of the terms and conditions of employment. For trade unions, central consultation implies that personnel in small companies where unions are weak also enjoy the fruits of these social agreements. For employers, one advantage of central agreements is that they prevent the dumping practices of small, nonunionized companies. Belgian employers probably would not accept central agreements without the attached guarantee that identical standards were being applied to "union-busting" companies. A second advantage is that central agreements enable industries to avoid snowball effects, runaway wage increases that spread from one company to the next. Third, central consultation is perceived as an effective means of keeping conflict between employers and trade unions away from the shop floor (Sels, 1996).

The Stability of the "Standard Employment Relationship"

As in surrounding countries, employment relationships in Belgium are confronted with an ever-increasing demand for flexibility. This puts pressure not only on the collective regulation of the employment relationship but also on the principles of security and continuity of the relationship, once so important for the general orientation of Belgian labor law. What might be considered a typically Belgian response to this push for flexibility is the relative stability of the standard employment relationship. The following table shows the different forms and use of standard and contingent work (Table 3.2). Standard work is here defined as a steady, full-time job that is not carried out in a shift system and follows a fixed timetable (Sels & Van Hootegem, 1997). Forms of contingent work include temporary, part-time, shift, and flexi-hour work. We draw a comparison with the Netherlands—like Belgium, a small country with an export-oriented economy—to identify the peculiar "Belgian" quality of employment relationships.

In Belgium, 62.2% of the labor force is engaged in regular employment, a decrease of 7.1% from 1989. However, the Belgian trend toward greater flexibility is remarkable because it cannot be ascribed to an undermining of the permanent employment relationship. The share of temporary work rose only from

TABLE 3.2 Contingent Workers in Belgium and the Netherlands (Percentage of the Labor Force), 1996

	Belgium (Percentage)	Netherlands (Percentage)
Regular workers	62.2	55.6
Contingent workers	37.8	44.4
Temporary workers	5.9	13.3
Part-time workers	15.9	36.7
Shift workers	18.6	5.6
Flexi-hour workers	4.5	1.7

SOURCE: Adaptation of Labor Force Survey data.

5.4% in 1989 to 5.9% in 1996; it is part-time and shift work that have most rapidly increased. In comparison, the standard employment relationship is common for only 55% of Dutch employees. Contractual flexibility is much greater in the Netherlands, as well as in the other EU member states.

Numerous reasons can be cited for the slow growth of temporary employment, but the allegedly too-strict regulation of flexible contracts is too often cited as an explanation (for an overview, see Delsen, 1995; European Commission, 1994; Organization for Economic Cooperation and Development, 1993; Siau, 1995). This argument loses its power when it is considered that successive fixed-term contracts have been possible in Belgium since 1994 and that the regulation of temporary employment has become more flexible in recent years. Interestingly, these deregulations have had relatively little impact.

A second, more accurate explanation for the slow implementation of temporary work is the relative flexibility of the law governing dismissal in Belgium, especially for blue-collar workers. Strict protection from dismissal goes hand in hand with the intensive use of temporary labor (Delsen, 1997). Employers who perceive the dismissal arrangements as too restrictive tend to rely on temporary contracts to achieve staffing fluctuation (Mosley, 1994). European comparisons indicate that countries with restrictive dismissal systems have relaxed their regulation of flexible contracts.

A third plausible explanation is that Belgian employers attach importance to company-employee bonding and are cautious in their use of fixed-term contracts for precisely that reason. The importance of this bonding is further supported by the fact that, despite the long required notice periods for white-collar workers, certain industries and companies offer additional job security guarantees. When agreeing to a job security proviso in a collective labor agreement, employers promise that they will try out all other measures before initiating dismissal proceedings. They may even relinquish their right to dismissal for a set period or propose other practices to mitigate dismissal (e.g., employers can give priority to dismissed persons in new recruitment drives) (Rigaux,

1993). The reason for including this extra job security guarantee in collective agreements is to increase workers' readiness to constantly adapt to new situations. Employers in Belgium generally assume that workers will react more flexibly if their job security is guaranteed.

On this last point, it is interesting to note that during bargaining, relative job security is often exchanged for flexible working hours (see the relatively high percentages of workers opting for temporal variants in work in Table 3.2). This brings us to a fourth explanation—namely, the function of relative job security as "flexible rigidity" such that employment practices permit dismissal and flexibility in scheduling workers while supporting stable incomes (Dore, 1986). A striking feature of flexibility in Belgium is that it has more to do with working hours and time of working than with the duration of the contract. Furthermore, this is mainly a matter of "negotiated flexibility." This expression indicates that flexibility practices are usually negotiated at the industrywide and company levels. The case of Belgium, with its negotiated flexibility, shows that increased flexibility need not always entail the individualization of industrial relations and that trade unions often win relative job security by accepting temporal flexibility. One saying in Belgium, which is not so far off the mark, is that anything goes regarding flexible hours—as long as it is regulated in an agreement between the social partners.

Psychological Contracts and the Culture of Compromise

The legal and institutional contexts in which employment relationships are negotiated encompass the most important values and characteristics of psychological contracts. The company-employee bonding and job security reflected in the continuing use of standard employment contracts mirror the psychological contract form of *high loyalty, low exit.* The second characteristic, *authority and equality,* is found in the two apparently contradictory principles of labor law, a relationship of authority and an emphasis on solidarity. The *culture of compromise* is grounded in the long tradition of social consultation and negotiation, the institutional web of laws and rules, and the search for continuity. As we mentioned earlier, the Social Pact creates a strong focus on "distributive" issues in negotiation and consultation. This causes economic expectations to be central to psychological contracts. Finally, the paradoxical mix between the need to belong to a group and an individualistic perspective on work is the consequence of a continuing search for a balance between security and social peace, as well as the belief in the principle of private ownership and the achievement society.

High Loyalty, Low Exit

One characteristic of psychological contracts in Belgium is that they reflect high company-employee bonding. This is due to the behavior and expectations of both employees and employers, supported by institutionalized work systems. From 1996 to 1997, an estimated 96% of employees who continued their employment in trade and industry stayed in the same job position. Belgians prefer high job stability and can be very much seen as the "stay-at-home" type. Job hopping is not in Belgian workers' blood, although certain industries with a high need for skilled people (e.g., information technology) or poor working conditions (e.g., textiles or construction) do show relatively high turnover figures.

Most Belgian employers also favor long-term relationships. Contracts are generally open-ended, with unspecified durations, though they are expected to be fairly long term. Moreover, the continuity of employment relationships is strongly supported on an institutional basis in Belgium. For example, the temporary unemployment system allows employers to temporarily dismiss blue-collar workers, who then receive increased unemployment benefits at the expense of the social security system for the term of their inactivity. This system enables employers to limit labor costs without terminating employment and is seen as an important instrument for managing capacity. In 1996, temporary unemployment was equivalent to 3.51% of the total hours worked by blue-collar employees (Sels & Van Hootegem, 1997).

One advantage of the temporary unemployment system is that companies confronted with economic downcycles need not immediately cut personnel, only to recruit them back once the business cycle picks up. One can retain company-specific human capital and save the cost of recruitment, selection, dismissal, and training. Moreover, the system makes it possible to invest in company-employee bonding and relational contracting. Temporary unemployment can be regarded as a functional equivalent of the large-scale introduction of flexible contracts. The number of "standard" employees can be geared to the average or maximum production capacity. Whenever this capacity is not achieved, the company can fall back on the system of temporary unemployment. Lacking such a system, more companies would have to gear the number of standard employees to their minimum capacity, with peak production times taken care of through the use of temporary workers.[3]

Authority and Equality

A second characteristic of psychological contracts is the paradoxical combination of acceptance of authority relationships yet valuing of equality. The acceptance of authority relationships is a cultural value of Belgium, as shown in Hofstede's (1980) typology. Belgium approximates the high French score on the dimension of "power distance." Subordinates recognize authority and are prepared to do as they are told. They find it natural that differences in hierarchical position should correspond to differences of status. The Flemish people in particular accept and support total private ownership and the autonomy of owners and executives to manage their company (Mok & Van Goethem,

1990). In the work environment—as in any social setting—communication follows rather formal channels. Although informal language is present in many companies, formal titles are usually a safer bet.

Despite the acceptance of status differences, equality is still a touchstone for understanding individual psychological contracts (possibly even more so than equity). The collective regulation of the employment relationship also gives human resources management a rather collectivist slant. It is striking, for example, that job and pay classifications negotiated for the entire industry are followed in the majority of companies (Seghers & Van der Hallen, 1994). In addition, employees are seldom rewarded for their individual performance or effort; cooperation among colleagues is considered to be more important. Moreover, workers find it important to be treated equally with members of specific reference groups (e.g., colleagues in the same job or pay classification, department, or work group). This expectation of equal treatment is important for psychological contracting in Belgium.

Economic Expectations

Belgians are strongly oriented toward work and the compensation they obtain from it. Even though Belgians have typically spent less time at work over the last decade, work has lost little of its motivating force (Mok & Van Goethem, 1990), and the country's citizens have a profound belief that people both need and want to work. To illustrate this, Belgium is noted for its high productivity (the country has the highest per capita output of all European countries). Gannon (1994) described this complex country as a "doing society" that is "busy all day long" (p. 55). Nearly half of all Belgians claim that they always do their best, regardless of their level of salary (Mok & Van Goethem, 1990). When asked what they would do if they had a winning lottery ticket, a large majority indicated that they would simply go on working (though perhaps under different conditions) (Claes et al., 1984).

If work remains so important, one must ask what the Belgians are looking for in their work. The findings of the longitudinal European Values Study (EVS) provide some insight into employees' expectations of work. Comparing the EVS results of 1981 with those of 1990, we note that employees have greater expectations with respect to the quality of work (Mok & Van Goethem, 1990). Here, the Belgians fall in line with the general trend toward more expressive work orientations such as autonomy, self-realization, and ability to contribute in a useful way (Yankelovich, 1985). These days, much greater value is attached to showing initiative and drawing on one's own capabilities at work. More than before, these characteristics are being related to the prestige or status of particular jobs, prestige that is important to both Flemish and Walloons. Given the unchanged strong work ethic, this development also involves risks. The gap between the ever-growing expectations regarding the quality of work and the reality in work organizations is threatening to increase (Huys,

Sels, Van Hootegem, Bundervoet, & Henderickx, 1999). An unfortunately large majority of Belgians are therefore of the opinion that their skills are underutilized.

The stronger emphasis on the quality of work does not change the fact that Belgians are in the first place working for money. The emphasis on job security seems to have decreased significantly in the early 1990s compared with the early 1980s, perhaps due to the recovery of the economy in the late 1980s. Moreover, it seems that Belgians regard relative security of employment as an acquired right. Another striking fact is that having good prospects for promotion is a relatively less important work motive for Belgians—just 30% find this "somewhat" important, implying that vertical mobility is not a must. What does matter is having a good working relationship with colleagues. After being paid a good salary, this is the second-highest job expectation and is steadily growing in importance.

The Culture of Compromise

Another striking characteristic of psychological contracts is the extensive use of compromises grounded in institutions and regulations. This feature goes back to Hofstede's dimension of uncertainty avoidance, on which Belgium is ranked fifth. According to Mok (1993), the development of the social consultation model as a complex web of institutions, rules, and rituals is to be understood precisely as a response to this experience of uncertainty. Security is highly prized in the collective agreements, and considerable time is spent on continuity, status quo, and balance. Or, as Gannon (1994) put it, "The moderate climate seems to reflect their [Belgians'] approach to life: the middle road between extremes" (p. 157).

This "middle road" points to Belgians' willingness to compromise, a survival strategy in a country full of potentially explosive conflicts. The society is split along three lines that maintain a shaky equilibrium of ideology (Catholic vs. Protestant), linguistics (French vs. Flemish), and economics (labor vs. capital). Despite the potential for conflict, open conflicts are the exception rather than the rule. Conflicting interests are usually swiftly neutralized in negotiation processes that favor compromise over consensus. Compromise is possible only if each of the parties is willing to compensate the others for any loss sustained and, in turn, to ease up on some of its own principles. This is so typical of the Belgian style of conflict management that one sometimes speaks of Belgium as a "compensation democracy" or "culture of compromise" (Hees, 1995; Vilrokx & Van Leemput, 1992).

The readiness to strike a bargain explains why the number of industrial conflicts remains limited, even in the 1990s, a decade marked by rationalization and mass dismissals. Compensation democracy is at work here too. Most rationalizations and mass redundancies are "bought off" with dismissal settlements that can be lucrative. This is possible because of a union strategy that is geared toward acquiring the most attractive material compensations rather than maintaining the maximum possible number of jobs (Vilrokx, 1996). As a result, a huge number of workers have benefited from early retirement systems over the past 10 years.

The example shows that even in crisis situations, the players involved in employment relationships try to avoid breaking the psychological contracts of the "survivors." Continuity is the goal to be pursued and compensation the preferred means to that end. In Belgium, this compromise-oriented negotiation method often takes the form of a positive-sum (instead of zero-sum) arrangement because the parties involved can always fall back on a government that, for the purpose of continuity and keeping the industrial peace, regularly bears the financial costs of the compensation game.

Balancing Individualism and Collectivism

A last characteristic of psychological contracts reflects the image of Belgians as resourceful survivors and staunch individualists (Mok, 1993). Here the "Belgian paradox" becomes apparent. On one hand, Belgians have a strong need to belong to a group; they comply with social rules relatively easily and cultivate family ties. On the other hand, Belgians often score high in the area of "individualism" on cross-cultural surveys. This ambivalence is an expression of the constant tension between freedom and individualism (symbolized in the high value placed on owning one's own home) and the certainty of compromise, observance of rules, and recognition of authority. The following examples illustrate this paradox:

- Belgian citizens talk sarcastically about their "state," make fun of the gendarmerie and police, and oppose state control of the economy. Yet to ensure the security of the "established order," the majority of Belgians are willing to tolerate the interference of these public powers (Gannon, 1994).

- Most Belgians (62%) and a majority of blue-collar workers say they have little or no confidence in the trade unions, but at the same time about 70% of wage earners are willing to reap the benefits of compensation democracy through their trade union membership (Mok & Van Goethem, 1990).

- Belgians accept the principles of the "achievement society," provided that these do not encroach on certain forms of security. Accordingly, the majority of employees find the principle of "pay for performance" the most fair. However, they are willing to increase their efforts even if these are not translated into higher pay, and the majority continue to opt for a guaranteed wage increase linked to seniority.

- Employers will claim conspiratorially (and preferably in private circles) that the trade unions are the ruination of the economy; the next minute, out of respect for the order of done deals, they will be perfect diplomats, playing by the rules of the game of compensation democracy.

This confusing mix of freedom, individualism, the need for security, and the respect for agreements and rules also explains why the web of institutions and rules manages not to get in the way of flexibility. Most of these rules were instituted through compromise, and it is worth noting that rules are never put before a sense of pragmatism, which overrules principles and enables the rules to be applied flexibly. Though rules are something to fall back on in times of uncertainty, they seldom stand in the way of a flexible solution to the problem.

Pragmatism and the spirit of negotiation are sometimes characterized as Belgian talents, developed as defense mechanisms in a land that had to cope with one invasion after the other (successively by Austria, Spain, France, the Netherlands, and—twice—Germany). In the Flemish subsidiaries of multinationals such as Volkswagen, Monsanto, or Samsonite, we find a Flemish management style characterized by a flexible approach to people and their problems, a pragmatic attitude, and openness to reaching a compromise. Even where laws and collective rules stand in the way, solutions can be negotiated, usually in an atmosphere of mutual understanding.

TRENDS

In this final section, we illustrate a trend that strikes at the heart of the existing social contract and also affects the content of psychological contracts: the increasing subjection of labor relations to legal remedies and the "devaluation" of social consultation.

There are signs of worsening labor relations within some companies. The list of company cases, symbolic of this deterioration of the social climate, grows longer each year: in 1992, the closure of the Delacre biscuit factory (a profitable production site of a French multinational company), followed by worker plant takeover for 2 months with no results (highly exceptional in the compensation democracy); in 1995, the unilateral termination of all collective agreements by the management of Sabena; in 1996, the announcement by telephone of a mass dismissal by Caterpillar; in 1997, the violent reaction of workers following the reorganization of Forges de Clabecq; also in 1997, the closure of Renault-Vilvoorde, which to some extent created a rift in Franco-Belgian relations; and in 1998, the closing of four production sites of Lévi-Strauss, where trade unions negotiated wage restrictions and flexibility for job security.

It is striking that in this recent wave of company-level conflicts, employers have taken their cases to civil rather than labor courts (Stroobant, 1994). In these cases, the courts have been petitioned to impose penalties on anyone preventing access to the plant or unlawfully occupying the factory. The referral of collective conflicts to courts of law is a more common practice in the Netherlands, Germany, and Great Britain, and it represents a break with the Belgian tradition of social consultation. The consultation model focuses on striving for compromise between social partners. The model is aimed at solving conflicts through different forms of social mediation, with little outside intervention. Court rulings undermine this model.

It is unknown whether this trend toward managing conflicts in the civil courts is a symptom of an imminent collapse of the social consultation model. Social consultation has undeniably been on the defensive in recent years, sharing in the institutional crisis of the country as a whole that is symbolized by a succession of political shock waves—ranging from political murder to slush-money affairs, illegal party funding, and pedophilia cases—that have struck at the heart of Belgian politics. Confidence in the "pillars" of the national state—among which negotiation and consultation must certainly be included—has reached an all-time low.

It is notable that in 1996 the social partners (for the first time in 10 years) failed to reach a national multi-industry collective agreement. The problem does not lie so much in a reduced willingness to carry on with social consultation but is a direct result of the limitations of the compromise between the social partners. Central negotiation, which is designed to play a redistributive role, cannot work when there is not much left to distribute. The government instituted a pay freeze from 1995 through 1996, making it difficult for central negotiation to fulfill its historic role as a redistributor of wealth. This pay freeze was followed by the introduction of a wage standard that linked the growth of wages in Belgium to the wage growth of the country's main trading partners. This government intervention in wage determination reduces social consultation to a "game without marbles" (De Swert, 1994).

The Belgian model of industrial relations may be at a turning point. As early as the 1980s, various commentators saw a possible movement toward a system with fewer central and industrywide agreements and a larger role for flexible company consultation (Blanpain, 1984). If statistics are any indication, the importance of collective labor agreements at the company level has grown. The number of these agreements increased from 38 in 1970 to 2,187 in 1996 (Vilrokx & Van Leemput, 1998). This increase may reflect an increasing need for more company-specific regulatory frameworks. Organizations that are required to adapt ever faster to the whims of the sales market can no longer let their employment relationships ossify as a result of external, central regulation.

Nonetheless, it seems premature to announce the demise of the consultation economy. In the first place, we should note that fewer than half of all collective labor agreements embody a more company-specific interpretation of the employment relationship. Second, company consultation usually does not take the place of industry level consultation but rather is added on top of it.[4] Third, and perhaps most important, there is no indication that company-specific agreements will supplant industrywide agreements, which reached 834 in 1995 (the highest number since 1991). In this period of wage restraint, the areas open for negotiation have been reduced to issues relating to employment and the redistribution of work. But the gap is partially filled by additional responsibilities in the organization of training and education—since 1988, successive collective agreements at industry level have made financial provisions for a training policy (Denys, 1995).

Finally, despite all speculations about individualized terms of employment, trade unions continue to play a central role in companies throughout Belgium. Despite a rather radical economic reorganization, the size of union membership grew by 12% between 1990 and 1995 (Vilrokx & Van Leemput, 1998). The persistently high proportion of union membership can be explained in part by the fact that trade unions act as "subcontractors" for the state in a number of areas, assuming responsibility for the administration of unemployment benefits. This can also be seen as a good example of the manner in which the social partners in postwar Belgium have collaboratively developed the welfare state.

CONCLUSION

In this chapter, we have identified five basic characteristics of psychological contracts in Belgium. Notwithstanding the country's complexity, these characteristics seem to be sufficiently generalizable across the different linguistic boundaries. Evidence for the emic character of the Belgian psychological contract stems from the fact that its characteristics result directly from the Belgian culture and value system as well as from the legal and institutional context in which employment relationships in Belgium take form. Overall, these characteristics indicate that the Belgian psychological contract is relational. The emphasis on loyalty and job security, for example, results from the Belgians' preference for high job stability and from their continuing use of the standard employment contract. Respect for authority reflects the high power distance in Belgian labor relations. The emphasis on equality rather than on equity is mainly due to the tradition of collective regulation that emphasizes cooperation and solidarity. The culture of compromise is grounded in a long tradition of social consultation and negotiation and in the institutional web of laws and rules. It also reflects Belgians' high uncertainty avoidance and their focus on collectivism.

On the other hand, Belgian psychological contracts carry a few transactional elements. Belgians' strong orientation toward compensation is a consequence of their focus on distributive issues when negotiating. Their desire for freedom and individualism while maintaining collectively negotiated rules and laws results from their continual search for balance between the principle of private ownership and the need for security, social peace, and belonging.

From this, we can infer that psychological contracts in Belgium do not seem to fit with any one of the specific types that are found in American research. We wonder whether this finding only illustrates the complexity of Belgian employment relationships or whether we can conclude that typologies of psychological contracts always are determined by culture and are therefore context specific. At any rate, our text shows that the historical, social, and legal contexts in which psychological contracts occur are important contract makers.

These factors affect how workers and employers understand the terms of their agreements.

The process of writing this chapter confronted us with the emic character of the Belgian psychological contract. Internal terms referring to commonly used Belgian legal and institutional practices do not seem to have the same meaning for outsiders. A few examples are *statute,* referring to the employment relationship in the public sector; the principle of loyal cooperation at the national, industry, and company levels between employers' associations and trade unions, called the *social partners;* and the reduction of the individual employment contract to a *membership certificate.*

One consequence of emic psychological contracts is that measures of labor market regulation should fit the existing institutional context. The flexibility debate is a good example. Belgium has often been criticized by the Organization of Economic Cooperation and Development because its labor market lacks flexibility, and it has been suggested that the country make individual dismissal easier and increase the use of contingent work contracts. Our analysis, however, shows that the historical context and institutional characteristics present in Belgium generate flexibility in a different way. In Belgium, *flexibility* refers to flexible working hours, the formal temporary unemployment system, and the acceptance of collective layoffs. Job security is relative in that employment practices permit dismissal and flexibility in scheduling workers while supporting stable incomes—a system of "flexible rigidity." Any advice regarding labor market policy should take into account that in Belgium flexibility is a matter of collective flexibility, which is different from—but functionally equivalent to—the more individual forms of flexibility that are common in English-speaking countries.

From these observations, we conclude that future research on psychological contracts should pay more attention to institutional and contextual factors, not only at the international level but also at the national, industry, and company levels.

NOTES

1. "We mention the army of Belgium, that paradise of capitalism. Its neutrality is guaranteed by the European powers, and nevertheless its army is one of the strongest in proportion to its population. The glorious battlefields of the brave Belgian army are the plains of the Borinage and of Charleroi. It is in the blood of the unarmed miners and laborers that the Belgian officers temper their swords and win their epaulets" (Lafargue, 1883/1975, p. 55).

2. The social planning agreements are elaborated in multi-industry CLAs within the context of the National Labor Council (NAR). The best-known examples are CLA 5 on union representation in companies, CLA 39 on technology agreements, CLA 42 on regulations governing working hours, and CLA 62 on the European Workers' Council.

3. The system has a downside: It frustrates vocational training. The ideal time for training is when there is an overcapacity and surplus workers can be quietly "packed off to school." Training in times of recession is the proven recipe by which Japanese companies manage their lifetime employment. But not their Belgian colleagues. Less work? "Send them home, not to school!"

4. One exception was the so-called "company plans for redistribution of the available work," introduced in 1994 and financially supported by the government. These company plans broke with the logic of the "pyramid" (see above), under which bargaining follows a hierarchical path. Some observers saw this as a legitimization of the decentralization of labor relations and a recognition of the company level as being a relatively autonomous level of negotiation.

REFERENCES

Blanpain, R. (1984). Les tendances récentes de la négociation collective en Belgique. *Revue International du Travail,* pp. 347-354.

Blanpain, R., & Vanachter, O. (1996). *Schets van het Belgisch Arbeidsrecht.* Bruges: Die Keure.

Claes, R., Coetsier, P., Quintanilla, A. R., Wilpert, B., Andriessen, J., Drenth, P., & Van der Kooy, R. (1984). Meaning of working: A comparison between Flanders, Germany and the Netherlands. In A. M. Koopman-Iwema & R. A. Roe (Eds.), *Work and organizational psychology: European perspectives* (pp. 57-76). Lisse, Belgium: Swets & Zeitlinger.

De Swert, G. (1994). Het verweduwd overleg. *De Gids op Maatschappelijk Gebied, 85,* 145-156.

Delsen, L. (1995). *Atypical employment: An international perspective.* Groningen, the Netherlands: Wolters-Noordhoff.

Delsen, L. (1997). Flexibilisering van de arbeid in Europa. *Tijdschrift voor Arbeidsvraagstukken, 13*(1), 23-37.

Denys, J. (1995). *Sectorale opleidingsinitiatieven in Vlaanderen.* Leuven, Belgium: Hoger Instituut voor de Arbeid.

Déom, D. (1990). *Le statut juridique des entreprises publiques.* Brussels, Belgium: Story-Scientia.

Dore, R. (1986). *Flexible rigidities.* London: Athlone.

European Commission. (1994). Fixed-term contracts in the European Union. *Employment Observatory, 47,* 30-39.

Gannon, M. J. (1994). *Understanding global cultures: metaphorical journeys through 17 countries.* Thousand Oaks, CA: Sage.

Hees, M. (1995). Belgium. In J. Brunstein (Ed.), *Human resource management in western Europe* (pp. 9-29). Berlin: de Gruyter.

Het sociaal overleg op interprofessioneel vlak 1936-1947 (1974). Brussels: Verbond van Belgische Ondernemurgen.

Hofstede, G. (1980). *Culture's consequences: International differences in work-related values.* Beverly Hills, CA: Sage.

Huys, R., Sels, L., Van Hootegem, G., Bundervoet, J., & Henderickx, E. (1999). Towards less division of labour? *Human Relations, 52*(1), 67-94.

Lafargue, P. (1883/1975). *The right to be lazy.* Chicago: Charles Kerr.

Mok, A. (1993). Belgium: Management and culture in a pillared society. In D. J. Hickson (Ed.), *Management in western Europe* (pp. 9-25). Berlin: De Gruyter.

Mok, A. L., & Van Goethem, W. (1990). Werken in de prestatie-maatschappij. In J. Kerkhofs, J. Kerkhofs, K. Dobbelaere, & L. Voyé. (Eds.), *De Versnelde Ommekeer* (pp. 69-92). Tielt, Belgium: Lannoo.

Mosley, H. G. (1994). Employment protection and labor force adjustment in EC countries. In G. Schmid (Ed.), *Labor market institutions in Europe* (pp. 59-82). Armonk, NY: M. E. Sharpe.

Organization for Economic Cooperation and Development. (1993). *Employment outlook.* Paris: Author.

Rigaux, M. (1993). Werkzekerheidsbedingen in collectieve arbeidsovereenkomsten. *Actuele problemen van het arbeidsrecht* (pp. 441-503). Antwerp, Belgium: Maklu.

Seghers, N., & Van der Hallen, P. (1994). *Functieclassificatie: Supernova of uitdovende ster?* Brussels, Belgium: Stichting Technologie Vlaanderen.

Sels, L. (1996). Statuut versus contract. *Tijdschrift voor Arbeidsvraagstukken, 12,* 325-337.

Sels, L., & Van Hootegem, G. (1997, September). *België-Nederland: Strijd om de meeste flexibiliteit.* Paper presented at the Stichting Interuniversitair Instituut voor Sociaal-Wetenschappelijk Onderzoek. Labor Market Conference "In Banen Geleid?" Rotterdam, the Netherlands.

Siau, B. (1995). *Le travail temporaire en droit comparé européen et international.* Montpelier, France: Université de Montpelier.

Steunpunt Werkgelegenheid, Arbeid, Vorming. (1998). *De arbeidsmarkt in Vlaanderen.* Leuven, Belgium: Author.

Stroobant, M. (1994). De waarde van het sociaal overleg. *Samenleving en Politiek, 1*(3), 23-26.

Vilrokx, J. (1996). Trade unions in a post-representative society. In P. Leisink, J. Van Leemput, & J. Vilrokx (Eds.), *The challenges to trade unions in Europe: Innovation or adaptation* (pp. 31-51). Cheltenham, UK: Edward Elgar.

Vilrokx, J., & Van Leemput, J. (1992). Belgium: A new stability in industrial relations. In A. Ferner & R. Hyman (Eds.), *Industrial relations in the new Europe* (pp. 357-392). Oxford, UK: Blackwell.

Vilrokx, J., & Van Leemput, J. (1998). Belgium: The great transformation. In A. Ferner & R. Hyman (Eds.), *Changing industrial relations in Europe* (pp. 315-347). Oxford, UK: Blackwell Business.

Yankelovich, D. (1985). *The world at work.* New York: Octagon.

4

Does Psychological Contract Theory Work in France?

Loïc Cadin

Honor is not so much something you owe to others, but something you owe to yourself.
> Montesquieu, *De l'esprit des lois* (1748/1951, Book 4, Chapter 2)

Psychological contract theory has been widely studied in the United States and other countries for several decades (Roehling, 1996), but French scholars to date have been silent on the subject. Organizational scholars in France are well aware of the concept and the related research. Nonetheless, the conventional ways in which non-French scholars have conceptualized psychological contracts may be at odds with the way that the French think about the employment relationship. This chapter addresses the essential question of whether the construct of a psychological contract coincides with the representation of the employment relationship in the minds of French people.

Psychological contract theory did not originate in the United States by chance. In the United States, the concept of contracts forms the basis of the larger society. However, contracts are only one of many ways to enable cooperation between people, and from one country to another, the meaning of contracts varies. Importantly, the degree of trust associated with contracting may be less in those societies that do not have the concept of contracts as the foundation of their social pact. I will show that France prefers the *rule*[1] to the contract as the building block of society. Rule is defined by laws and statutes stipulating appropriate and inappropriate conduct. Note that the French are not necessarily respectful of the rule. Rather, they spend their lives playing games with it, and these games produce social relationships that are uniquely French. Nonetheless, I will argue that psychological contract theory provides us with useful concepts that can be applied to the French context, even though the contract model is not the dominant basis for social relations in France.

IS CONTRACTING A UNIVERSAL CONCEPT?

The concept of contracting may be universal. In each country, it is possible to identify forms of mutual obligations and exchanges that could be thought of as contracts. But the idea that the contract is a desirable and virtuous way to build cooperation is less universally shared. It is unlikely that the French would universally agree with the words of Henry James Sumner Maine that serve as one of the opening quotes for Chapter 1. If the "contract model"[2] is representative of American culture, which model is the French equivalent?

First, let me state that French social relations are not based on the contract model. *Social relations* refers to the tacit norms of life in society: what is acceptable, tolerable, reasonable, or taken for granted in social life. Particularly helpful to elucidate alternative views of social relations is the work of d'Iribarne (1985, 1989). In several plants of the same company operating in different countries, he studied hierarchical relations, relations between peers, and the collective behaviors that made each plant work. Contrasting styles of collective behavior were evident across countries, which led d'Iribarne to some conclusions about societal effects on workers and people in general.

According to d'Iribarne (1985), each society develops its own solutions to fundamental universal questions such as

- Which type and which forms of liberty will individuals enjoy?
- Which type and which forms of security will individuals have?
- How will respect for rules be sustained?
- Which forms of authority are legitimate?
- Which mix of authority, morality, and social pressures is tolerable?

Societies answer these fundamental questions throughout the course of their history; critical events can become founding moments in a society's social pact. D'Iribarne's contribution is to raise awareness of how fundamental features of the social pact play a role at every level of a society, even at the very local or ordinary level. This homothetic[3] view of the local compared to the national level has been criticized. However, rather than reopen this debate, we will simply accept that it is legitimate and necessary to increase our understanding of psychological contracts by considering broader societal perspectives.

Compared to France, the American system provides a relatively great rule security (i.e., the country's rules typically are clear and respected), with reasonable protection from arbitrary laws. However, it also tends to generate insecurity because it exposes people to significant risks: One can win big or lose a lot. The French system yields greater security socially and economically: When a person obtains a job or other social position, the system tends to guarantee it. In France, insecurity arises from a lack of clarity in the rules themselves (i.e., too many rules increase the risk of contradictions among them) and the weight of arbitrary laws.

The American Pact, or the "Contract Model"

The American social pact is labeled a contract model because it views the relations between people as those of parties to a contract. D'Iribarne (1989) found the seminal writings of Tocqueville (1835) particularly elucidating. One and a half centuries after Toqueville's observations on the United States, d'Iribarne identified in the daily life of the American plant observations consistent with those of Tocqueville: "We see the same emphasis on the exchange between equals, the same combination of sophisticated procedures, of moral references, and of social pressures to enable 'free' relations between the strong and the weak" (p. 161).

The immigrants who landed in 1620 on the coasts of New England dreamed of a society based on a free association of equal citizens bound by a "social contract." They established a pact in the form of a contract that set up the society. This society was based on a solemn agreement to build political institutions. According to d'Iribarne (1989), one can imagine that from the American point of view nothing could be higher than an agreement between those who commit mutually. The contract is not only a formal agreement but something sacred and, in the immigrants' own words, made "before God." The celebrated freedom is based on a religious vision ("Make without fear what is fair and good"). D'Iribarne concluded that the legacy of the pious merchants who founded the United States continues to influence American reality (p. 162).

In the logic of merchant relations, working for an equal and receiving money from him or her do not reduce the status of the worker. This logic is tempered by the concept of fair exchange, where each gains the respect of the other by fulfilling obligations. The familiar performance management technique of management by objectives (MBO) is a typical application of this philosophy.

The French Model, or the "Logic of Honor"

The logic of honor is the foundation of the French social pact, as illustrated by d'Iribarne's observations (1985, 1989). The plants d'Iribarne visited used a process that could not be interrupted without harming the equipment. Occasionally, problems occurred at night when fewer staff were on duty. In the

American plant, procedures specified that the first worker who observed an incident was to call the foreman, who was supposed to have the requisite expertise to deal with the problem. The worker was not supposed to try to solve the problem, a stipulation that was respected. Although similar procedures existed in the French plant, they were not respected. To explain this, d'Iribarne (1989) theorized that French workers have a different concept of job and responsibility. French workers think first of their duty, which takes precedence over the application of a procedure. Their sense of their professional status dictates that they should do whatever is necessary to deal with a problem. In effect, each French worker has a concept of his or her duties as well as the privileges of his or her profession. Note that d'Iribarne did not use the term *profession* as it is meant in English; rather, he referred to the worker's social status, which is based on the job's prestige in society. Although France celebrates "equality" in all circumstances, it has never entirely relinquished the hierarchies of the ancien régime with its arguments over issues of etiquette and ceremony.

The Concept of Honor

Montesquieu (1689-1755) characterized the concept of honor in 1748 with the publication of *l'Esprit des lois* (1748/1951) ("The Spirit of Laws"). This work highlighted the principles underlying the main forms of government: democracy, aristocracy, despotism, and monarchy. The underlying principle of democracy is respect of the law; the principle of aristocracy is moderation (tempering the fundamental inequity of this form of government); the principle of despotism is fear. Honor is the principle of monarchy: This virtue reigns like a monarch, ruling the prince as well as the people. Montesquieu (1748/1951) defined honor as each person's prejudice or predisposition to view his or her social standing in a particular way. Prejudice is not the result of law, reason, or the prince, but of tradition. Honor is pride in one's own rank and fear of losing it: It is "not so much something you owe to others, but something you owe to yourself" (Book 4, Chapter 2). A person acting honorably would never do anything that could be interpreted as a behavior beneath that rank.

Key to understanding this principle of honor is the idea of a *societé d'ordres,* or a society based on division. In 1789, France abolished traditional privilege and ended the traditional division of society into three orders: the clergy, nobility, and the third estate. (This division comes from the Indo-European tradition, which distinguishes in society and mythology among priests, warriors, and peasants.) These three orders fit into a hierarchy of purity, from those who are very near the sky (thanks to their spiritual activities) to those who spend their days bent to the earth. Each order is divided into subgroups, which can be numerous: Tocqueville (1856/1952) identified 36 different categories among the notables of one little town. Each category differentiates itself through small privileges and disputes over precedence. Tocqueville related the refusal of the wig manufacturers in the town of La Fleche to participate in the city council because of a preference given to the bakers!

Honor and the Revolution

The idea of equality in France is not an idea born in the 18th century. The debate about equality was already active in the 10th century. The revolution of 1789 abolished privileges and declared equality, but the old concept of order in society remains, albeit in renewed forms. Much more recently, the French press frequently accused President Francois Mitterand of harboring a monarchic conception of his function—a classic example of how the concept of societal orders continues to play out in modern France.

The sources of legitimacy for societal orders have changed. Today, the diploma has taken the place of nobility titles. The French elite reproduces itself by maintaining features of nobility. The comparison of the career paths of the CEOs at the top 200 companies in France and Germany is revealing (Bauer & Bertin-Mourot, 1997). Half of the French CEOs originated from one of two schools.[4] In German firms, the role of experience and success within the company is three times as important to attaining the CEO role as in France. Advancement potential in France derives from the education system, where admission to a grande école is a trump card for life.

Education plays a similar role in both the pay trajectory of workers and the construction of elites. French-German comparative research conducted by Maurice, Sellier, and Silvestre (1982) showed that the pay and career systems in both countries can only be understood through the interactions among the educational, organizational (work division inside the firms), and industrial relations (IR) systems. In France, increases in workers' pay are largely explained by their level of general education. In Germany, the more powerful explanatory variable is the level of vocational education. In effect, education contributes to a broad social contract regarding opportunities for employment advancement and economic earnings, as well as to social status.

In the United States, professional roles influence social status, but loss of a professional position does not necessarily ruin a person's social status. In France, social status and professional position are so closely connected that a professional misfortune results in a loss of one's identity.

The logic of honor has consequences for hierarchical relations between workers and managers. A subordinate dislikes having the boss supervise him or her too closely because such behavior is seen as a lack of trust or as an insult to the subordinate's professionalism. The subordinate does not feel obliged to follow the injunctions of the boss, who is not supposed to know the situation as well as the subordinate. However, there is a paradox. Under routine conditions, the boss is supposed to leave the subordinate alone to do his or her job. During a crisis when neither the workers nor their foremen are more likely to solve the problem, the boss is supposed to make all decisions, even in the smallest details. The boss will be judged on the basis of his or her decisions in a crisis. When the crisis is over, the routine restarts, and each goes about his or her own business.

Hierarchical relations are further complicated when the logic of honor is applied to the workplace because an honorable boss must not give orders that place the subordinate in a servile position or suggest a loss of dignity. It also explains why France has been slow to develop a service orientation in business: The French enjoy helping someone but cannot tolerate being in the service of anyone. To a French person, defending one's rank is more important than defending one's business interests.

PSYCHOLOGICAL CONTRACTS AND FUNDAMENTAL SOCIAL PACTS

The terms that illustrate psychological contract theory—*promises, obligations, contracts, fairness, performance*—originate from the vocabulary of the fundamental American social pact, as viewed by d'Iribarne and Tocqueville. This overlap between psychological contract theory and the American pact was evidenced by Rousseau (1995): "The contract is a mental model," (p. 27) and "Contracts provide an intuitively appealing and culturally acceptable way to describe employment relationships" (p. 2). Rousseau also proposed a homothetic typology of contracts: The psychological contract is at the individual level what the social contract is at the level of the society (p. 15).

The universes of psychological contract theory and the societal contract model are so intertwined that they share common management practices. D'Iribarne (1989) saw MBO practices as an illustration of the contract model at the company level. He tried to explain the difficulties of this management method in the French context. When Rousseau (1995) made suggestions for the management of the psychological contract, she also referred to MBO, suggesting that this approach to performance appraisal could help maintain a psychological contract with employees (p. 151).

Although MBO might be effective in France, it is generally difficult to make performance appraisals work in that country. Therefore, MBO would be a risky starting place for psychological contract management. The words Rousseau (1995) used to describe a well-managed relationship based on psychological contracts (*mutual adjustment, reframing, creativity*) make a French reader think of the vocabulary often associated to the concept of a project (p. 172). This is consistent with D'Iribarne (1989), who argued that large, innovative projects such as Concorde, TGV, and Minitel can arouse enthusiasm and energy (p. 175). In France, the period when a company project and the role an employee might play in it are under discussion would be an ideal time for career counseling and planning to clarify the terms of the psychological contract, better than performance appraisal meetings.

Although there are clear similarities between the vocabulary and assumptions of psychological contract theory and the contractual model of American society, I am not arguing that psychological contract theory is irrelevant outside the United States. Rather, we can learn a great deal from applying the concept of psychological contracts to a context where the logic of honor dominates (and from applying the logic of honor to the concept of a psychological contract). Consider d'Iribarne's (1989) recommendations:

- Never deride honor.
- Avoid servile submission.
- Avoid a close supervision.
- Respect the dignity of the worker.
- Don't interfere with the worker carrying out the duties of his or her professional role.
- Respect precedence. (p. 99)

These explicit prescriptions articulate the implicit expectations underlying cooperation in a French context. They provide useful concepts for interpreting the "game" that makes French psychological contracts dynamic.

Progress Need Not End With Contract

When Tocqueville recalled the founding moment in American society, he helped us to understand the value given to contracts in the United States. However, the historical perspective in France, and more generally in Europe, is quite different. Contract is considered only as one moment in history and as a form that has been improved on.

Law historians offer key concepts that can help explain the structure of the psychological contract in France and perhaps in Europe, as well. The different legislations of employment relations in Europe have had to find a way to combine divergent legal traditions (Supiot, 1994). The Romanist tradition, originating from Roman law, maintained that free people could not accept subordination. However, for exceptional circumstances, the Romans developed the concept of *locatio hominis,* in which the free man rents himself in the same way as the master rents his slave. The Napoleonic Code incorporated a service rental concept of *locatio hominis* that was copied from objects rental contracts. In this conception, a labor contract did not differ from a commercial contract.

An opposing tradition, called Germanist, derives from feudal law and is founded on the relation of vassality between persons. The employment relation is viewed as a reciprocal tie of faithfulness, something similar to a family tie. This tradition dominated the guilds, where belonging to the work community generated mutual obligations (based on duties and not the will of the members).

TABLE 4.1 Legal Traditions of Employment Relations

	Romanist	*Germanist*
Philosophical origin	Commercial law	Feudal law
Central concept	Contract	Statute
View of the parties of the labor relation	Free and equal individuals	A "work community" providing protection against subordination

Nineteenth-century European employment was dominated by the Romanist tradition, an approach with a particular emphasis on the principle of individual liberty. At the end of the 19th century, criticism began in Germany regarding the individualist and contractual conceptions inherited from the Romanist tradition. The concept of work community was reevaluated, and the employment relationship re-emerged as the main community tie. In England, unions gained legal status, and collective bargaining took precedence over individual contracting (see Table 4.1).

The Balance of French Employment Relations

The contractual approach assumes equality between contracting parties. In contrast, socialists assume that real equality does not yet exist.[5] The concept of statute emerged from the German tradition as a means of creating equality between contracting parties. Statutes specify a set of duties and rights that can be neither given nor taken away by the employer or the employee.

The French have implemented the concept of statute in a distinctive way that involves the intervention of the state through the law. Statute creates "social public order" by introducing a legal hierarchy with law at the top, collective bargaining next, and individual contracts last. Individual contracts cannot depart from legal rules and collective conventions. The individual contract endows the employee with a statute. The statute is the set of provisions provided by law and collective conventions that specify the fundamental guarantees granted to a group of workers or collective. The employment relation not only is a contract of exchange but also involves cooperation, in the frame of an institution of the French society. Duties and rights are not defined by individuals but are designed collectively by the state. Inserting a statute within each employment contract contributes to the formation of the collective identity of workers. In all cases, statutes restrict considerably individual workers' zones of negotiation (see Table 4.2).

At the heart of the French employment relationship is the assumption that the state is supposed to compensate for any imbalances in this relationship. In effect, the psychological contract in France is not only between one individual

TABLE 4.2 The French Compromise: Statute Plus Contract

The central concept: social public order
The concept's meaning:
The freedom of the parties is restricted.
The state defines the basic framework of the contract.
The collective bargaining can fill in the framework.
The parties cannot break the dispositions of state and collective bargaining.

and his or her employer; it also includes a third party (the state), represented in the form of a statute. In shifting from discussion of a legal contract to a psychological one, it is important to note that French law is both a party to the legal contract and a mechanism in the creation of individual psychological contracts. This concept of statute is not only a legal construction but also a norm or a position in the French hierarchy of values. French people distinguish between "good" and "bad" statutes: The statute governing civil service would be considered the best statute, whereas statutes governing contingent work would be bad statutes.

THE LAW'S PRESTIGE

State intervention in the employment contract to rebalance the employment relationship is characteristically French, in comparison to the English or German emphasis on collective bargaining. Yet there is a fundamental paradox in the French orientation toward law and the state. The French demand more regulation and state intervention to address social problems, yet French people are often disrespectful of the law. In effect, the law does not inherently command respect, but it seems to exist in order to play a different role.

The Law Symbolizes Social Progress

This heading might be surprising to readers who prefer collective bargaining to state intervention, but we explain it through the structure of the French system of IR. IR regulation was introduced late in France,[6] especially as compared to England (see Table 4.3).

In France, major social milestones tend to coincide with political events of national importance. For example, the first law introducing collective bargaining was passed in 1919 just after the First World War. At the end of the Second World War (1945), the workers' council was created. Labor strikes in 1937 and 1968 coincided with the respective creation of the "worker representative"

TABLE 4.3 Milestones in English and French Labor History

	England	France
Trade unions legalized	1824	1884
The right to strike is granted	1825	1864
Trade unions federate at the national level	1851	1886
Creation of trade union congress	1868	1895

and the legalization of company-level trade unions. In 1982, when leftist parties governed France, an obligation of annual collective bargaining on salaries and work duration was introduced by law.

The State Dominates the French IR System

In this chapter, we explicitly refer to the concept of an IR system as defined by Dunlop (1958), who argued that such a system is shaped by (a) the relations among employers, employees, and the government; (b) the distinction between procedural and substantive rules; (c) the creation of rules through collective bargaining, laws, and customs; and (d) the pressures of political, social, economical, and technological environments. This concept is useful for identifying the methods of creating rules within the IR systems of different nations. In the French IR system, firms and unions adjust their strategies around the state's central position. Firms and unions always manage to bring the state into the mix, ensuring that the game has three players. French trade unions traditionally have low membership and do not collaborate with each other, except during very limited historical periods. They are composed of militants rather than having a broader membership, as German unions do.[7] They also tend to lack money and expertise. Union efforts are focused on putting pressure on the state, by such means as organizing national demonstrations before elections (*journées nationales d'action*) to increase employer regulation. Companies have been reluctant to accept local unionism (only legalized in 1968), reflecting a deep-rooted discomfort with direct negotiations with unions. Employers prefer to deal with the state and its representatives rather than with representatives of the workers. In France, the economic elite and the state elite are sociologically very close: They share the same schools, career paths, and family connections (Bauer & Bertin-Mourot, 1997). The system favors labor management relations that are focused on the state, leaving the government issues that would be addressed in other countries through collective bargaining. Note, for example, that the French minimum wage is decided at the ministers' council.

Three explanations for the state's centrality in employment are Jacobinism, Colbertism, and Gaullism.

Jacobinism was inherited from the Revolution of 1789, when the state's mission was to prevent the return of the ancien régime. The Club des Jacobins, a sort of political party, supported centralization as a strategy to implement the revolution. Long experience with monarchy had already paved the way for continued centralization.

Colbertism symbolizes the tradition of state intervention in economic activities, as illustrated by the "royal manufacturers." Colbert[8] hired civil servants to implement quality standards, thus enabling French products to be better positioned in international markets. The extension of the nationalized sector can be considered as a continuation of this interventionism tradition. The 20th century amplified the size of the public sector to the extent that one third of the working population is employed by the public and nationalized sector. The state is an economic actor, but it also claims to promote means of social progress. The public sector is expected to experiment with ideas, approaches, and systems that can be applied to companies through the law or interprofessional agreements.

Finally, Gaullism implemented a program of reforms elaborated by the Conseil National de la Resistance, which endowed the state with a strong interventionist mission. During World War II, unions were actively engaged in the Resistance, and socialist, communist, and Christian sympathizers were far more influential than employers. (In 1945, De Gaulle pointed out to employers that they were not present in London, where the Resistance was based.) Gaullism views the law as a force behind social reforms, with a more powerful role in employment relations than collective bargaining. The 30 years that followed the Second World War implemented the Gaullist vision.

This IR system was pervasive in France until the beginning of the 1980s. Subsequently, efforts have been made to promote a more decentralized operation of the system. However, crises within the unions have undercut these efforts, so the state often ends up as the central player.

The demand for state intervention remains great, spurring a proliferation of laws and rules. Note however, that this does not imply respect for the law. Laffer asserted that "too much tax kills the tax," and something similar could be proposed in the area of rules: "Too many laws kill the law."[9] Freyssinet (1997) showed that in the field of work duration rules are so numerous and contradictory that confusion results. Freyssinet suggested that this effect may be the result of deliberate attempts to sabotage change or may be the cumulative effect of many actors working at cross-purposes.

D'Iribarne (1989) maintained the importance of the English tradition of respect for legal forms in his presentation of the American contract model (p. 165). The social role of the law and rules more generally differs between France and the United States. This difference must be analyzed to understand the dynamics of psychological contract.

Rules of the Game Versus Games With the Rules

D'Iribarne's (1989) anecdote regarding the different responses of American and French workers to a night-shift crisis suggests that where U.S. workers consider a rule to be binding, the French see it as optional. D'Iribarne gave a cultural interpretation of this statement and explained that identity is more important than the rule in France.[10] Further insight into the role of rules in society is provided by the sociological research stream of what is called the sociology of regulation.

Our most familiar representation of the contract is as a negotiation. Its main features include an interactive process of communication (which does not exclude information manipulation) and an exchange of concessions that creates a win-win situation for both parties.

Political science scholars (Perlman, 1936; Walton & McKersie, 1965; Webb & Webb, 1897)[11] maintain the plurality of conceptions of negotiation, including a noncontractual model in which negotiation is a means of providing pressure to obtain compensation without concessions. Henry Kissinger encountered this model when negotiating with the Vietnamese at the time of the Paris peace talks. The Vietnamese delegation used the sessions to publicize their position and repeatedly state their requirements, a way to block communication. Viewing negotiation as a means to create political pressure is helpful in understanding how French unions behave (Morel, 1994). Morel has labeled this technique "demonstration-negotiation" (negotiation manifestation), characterizing the use of discussion as a means of exerting pressure, resisting compromise, and trying to win without making concessions. Several French practices illustrate this concept, including

- Attempts to transform the negotiation into a demonstration (e.g., numerous delegates, verbal aggression, frequent change in delegates)
- Use of rules as a mean of pressure (e.g., working to rule)
- Demands far above what is likely ever to be accepted

This negotiation strategy can be efficient in situations with widely unequal power. When the weak adopt this strategy, they can significantly improve their bargaining clout. True negotiations in which mutual give and take occurs may actually occur only where there is a relative balance of power between the parties.

Demonstration-negotiation is not the general model of IR in France. However, it illustrates the role of power strategies in playing games with the rules. Abundance of rules can be transformed into pressure. This logic can be summed up as "Require a rule, and you shall always find an opportunity to profit from it or to turn it into a weapon."

Negotiation should not be thought of only in terms of a specific interaction or bargaining process that results in a final agreement. The demonstration-negotiation concept views negotiation as an ongoing, permanent process. Revolutionary unions, for instance, see any compromise as a temporary truce because the contradictions of capitalism and society will sooner or later revive the conflict.

In the sociology of regulation, playing games with the rules is not viewed as an anomaly or a sign of perversity of actors without faith or law.[12] The metaphor of the "game" (which plays with the variety of meanings of the word *game* because in French, *game* and *play* have the same root, *jeu*) is central in the different French streams of the interactionist sociology. Let us take some of the most spontaneously associated images with the metaphor of the game/play or *jeu:*

- The artist plays (interprets) a character, and the musician plays (interprets) a score. Even with strict indications from the author, the interpreter works her own intentions into the text.

- Engineers speak of interplay between the different gear wheels of an engine. A space must remain between the different parts to provide the necessary fluidity.

- Lawyers spend their time discussing the spirit and the letter of the law. The barrister plays with the procedures, adapts the legal text, proposes a new interpretation of the law, and uses the inevitable incompleteness of the law.

These images illustrate the view of interactionist sociology, which can be summed up with a few proposals:

- The actors of a situation have to deal with a set of rules (laws, traditions, etc.) that restrict their possible behaviors. The rules of the social game can be viewed at least in a first approximation as the rules of any sport or parlor game. To understand the behavior of the actor, one must identify the rules he or she must deal with.

- The liberty of an actor can never be completely eliminated. Even in the most unbalanced power situation, an actor's freedom cannot be totally annihilated.

- The actor retains the capacity to negotiate his or her participation. The actor is rational, even if boundedly so, and political. He or she builds alliances, develops tensions and tricks, and can create conflicts while trying to transform the rules to improve his or her situation.

Interactionist sociologists try to explain behavior by examining the constraints that influence people and the rational activities they choose in particular situations. These researchers reject the explanations of determinist sociologists, who would endow the actors with the benefit of experience and the normative behaviors learned in past social relations.

Interactionist sociology decodes the behaviors in terms of negotiation. Faced with control regulation originating from management or the top of the firm, subordinates develop their own autonomous rules based on what they consider as indispensable to the accomplishment of their work.[13] The regulations observed within a work unit are called joint regulations, resulting from somewhat formal negotiations between managers and their subordinates to balance control regulation and the autonomous regulation. For example, de Terssac (1992) described how the workers of a cement factory produced far more than the specified standards during the course of an hour. They achieved their quotas at the end of the day. Then they played cards conspicuously in the presence of the foreman. By this behavior, the workers proved that they were able to organize themselves as efficiently as the method department claimed to organize them. They demonstrated that the control regulation could not foresee everything and that they had the most relevant skills to adapt to the situation and its requirements. This behavior asserted their autonomy regarding work accomplishment.

The sociologists who have studied the most prescriptive forms of Taylorism have often observed these clandestine organizations and can quote numerous examples of autonomous rules (the production rate is the most obvious one). The search for autonomy is not defiance in the French context but a means by which a collective actor expresses power and identity.[14]

The sociology of regulation is not only valid in the French context. However, it has been developed in the context of French realities and thus can help interpret seemingly paradoxical French behaviors. As psychological contract theory is symbolic of the American context, the sociology of regulation is symbolic of the French context.

To formulate these points in terms of national models, the U.S. model is based on the assumption of a free actor who enters into mutual obligations with an organization. This pact between the parties is used to compare actual experience with expectations. The French model presents an individual actor who exposes him- or herself to the fundamental asymmetry between employer and employee. The rules are viewed as the result of the anterior balance of power. The game with the rules is a form of permanent ongoing negotiation and generates identity and autonomy. Autonomy is the departure point of the American pattern and is the arrival point of the French pattern.

THE ROLE OF PSYCHOLOGICAL
CONTRACT THEORY IN FRANCE

The first two parts of this chapter might seem to discourage the application of psychological contract theory in the French context. This section summarizes

TABLE 4.4 Cooperation Models

	Contract Model	*Rule Model*
Balance of the parties	Symmetrical	Asymmetrical
Products of the negotiation	Mutual commitments	Rules of the game (substantive and procedural)
Behaviors	Respect or violation of the playing rules	Playing games with the rules
Foundations	Confidence	Power relations
Vision of the society	Consensus	Conflict

the main discrepancies and assesses their significance by referring to the issues addressed in Chapter 1 of this book. This will provide an answer to the question raised regarding distinctively French features (emic features) of psychological contracts. The issue of generalities (etic features) will be addressed by examining what the introduction of psychological contract theory can bring to France.

Contract or Rules of the Game?

How relevant is the concept of contracts to cooperative employment relations in France? Psychological contract theory refers to a model of contract based on assumptions not shared by the French, as shown by this chapter's review of the history and theories that dominate the French intellectual scene.

The assumptions that underlie psychological contract theory relate to voluntary commitments made by the actors and the symmetry of stakeholders who are considered to be legally equal. In contrast, the French tradition is based on asymmetrical stakeholders (legally equal but viewed by French society as fundamentally unequal in reality), negotiations that rely on strategies and games, and state intervention to compensate for the imbalance between stakeholders, such that the state has become an obligated third party—visible or invisible—in the negotiations.

The features of French employment relations characterize an alternative model that can be called "the model of rules and games with the rules." This model downplays contracts, instead resting on the rules of the game (and the game itself overshadows any respect for the rules). These two models are further contrasted in Table 4.4.

Consequences of the French Sociological Background

With the help of law historians, we have tried to show how labor legislation introduced the institution of social public order, or statute, into the employment contract. Statute symbolizes an implicit norm of employment relations in France: the statute of civil service. We do not pretend that legislation was designed to pull private law in the direction of public law, but in the minds of French people, the employment security and career path associated with civil service are used as points of reference—perhaps even an ideal. Half of French households have no member employed in the private sector. Employment security and seniority-based promotion are public sector practices copied in many parts of the private sector. Standardized career paths are features of the French model that have been accentuated since the end of the Second World War. The French variation of the Fordist compromise[15] is an exchange of loyalty to the company for employment security.

France is one of those societies, as described by the Meaning of Work International Research Team (1987), where the prevailing belief is that society has to provide work. One indicator of this belief is the continually high demand for state intervention in employment. Another indicator is the growth of public sector employment in response to public pressure.

However, there are some signs of change in French employment relations. In terms of the typology that Rousseau and Wade-Benzoni (1994) have proposed, French employment remains largely relational (open-ended and with weak performance-reward connections) today and into the foreseeable future. However, contingent work and transactional contracts have increased in recent years. The gap between insiders and outsiders has broadened, but insiders do not feel ready to share their statutory advantages with (contingent workers) outsiders.

The Zone of Negotiation

Labor laws are more developed in France than in English-speaking countries, giving the state greater say over employment relations. In contrast, collective bargaining in France is far less developed than in countries such as England or Germany. The space left to individual negotiation is relatively limited.

The zone of negotiation is narrow, but in another sense, it is expandable because of the games that French workers and employers play with the rules. Reynaud (1989) elaborated the concept of joint regulation to stress the permanent development of the autonomous rule and the unending negotiation. Although frustrating for foreigners not familiar with these behaviors, this permanent negotiation is not synonymous with anarchy. The tension between joint and autonomous rules delimits the range within which any adjustments are made.

CONCLUSION: PSYCHOLOGICAL CONTRACT THEORY HAS A ROLE TO PLAY IN FRANCE

We hope we have demonstrated that the psychological contract theory is embedded in a model of social life that does not fit the French reality. This raises the question of whether the theory is at all applicable to France and whether it can help us understand the employment situation in France today.

In psychological contract theory, promises not only are based on verbal or written obligations but also arise through inferences made in the course of daily interactions. Psychological contract theory addresses not only an explicit contract but also any construction arising from interpretations regarding employee/employer behavior. Its focus goes beyond rhetoric to include the meanings given to actions.

Playing games with the rules, so central to the French way of cooperation, makes the French very sensitive to any discrepancy between declarations and acts. The French are so used to ineffective rules that they view employer and government statements and policies with a skeptical eye. Concrete actions and facts prevail over mere words. Psychological contract theory does not ignore actions or how they are interpreted, an important link to research issues arising in French employment relations. Moreover, because psychological contract theory addresses not only how one party views a promise from another but also what that party believes his or her own obligations to be, French scholarship would consider a party's sense of his or her own obligations as an autonomous promise (in the terms of the sociology of joint regulation described earlier). The concept of promise is the bridge between the contract model and the regulation approach to the study of employment relations.[16]

We have emphasized in this chapter the dominant orientations within the French model of employment relations. But we have also made allusions to the crisis affecting this model. Unemployment is currently very high in France, as is the proportion of people who are unemployed over the long term. French assumptions regarding the state are being questioned because of the weight of its bureaucracy and the inefficiency of its interventions. The IR crisis (Groux, 1996) has been widely acknowledged, with a further decline in unionism a primary symptom (the French membership rate is one of the lowest among industrialized countries).

Such changes arouse extreme reactions in many segments of French society. One common fear is the loss of entitlements, for employers increasingly declare that they can no longer be accountable for their traditional obligations due to economic uncertainty and volatile markets. The rhetoric of "employability" has met with employee skepticism and a sense that this term is mere window dressing as companies attempt to disguise their abandonment of historical responsibilities.

Psychological contract theory provides concepts that are essential to understanding these transformations. It explains that between guaranteed employment for life and no commitment at all is a space to imagine mutual obligations that are acceptable to both parties. Between relational and transactional contracts lies a range of alternative possibilities. Psychological contract theory explains that a promise does not necessarily require absolute certainty: It is possible to articulate promises that incorporate risk and unpredictability. Promises can create obligations of results or obligations of means (employability is an obligation of means, whereas life employment is an obligation of results). Either can be attractive to workers. Finally, psychological contract theory helps us to imagine a diversification of psychological contracts that adapt to and potentially integrate the interests of both parties. Just as companies progress toward individualized compensation and hire individuals through very different legal contracts, they can create more diverse and flexible psychological contracts.

In France, the silence regarding psychological contract theory is being broken. On one side, companies have begun to diversify the psychological contracts they propose. Individuals have not waited for the diffusion of the concept to develop nontraditional organizational career paths. Nonetheless, just as French research in management sciences has much to learn from psychological contract theory, we think that psychological contract theory can develop through exchanges with different intellectual traditions beyond those that supported its birth.

NOTES

1. "The rule" here has a very broad meaning, including legal rules, informal rules, and norms. We will define this concept more precisely in the rest of the text.

2. *Contract model* is the literal translation of the expression *modèle du contrat,* developed by D'Iribarne (1989). *Modèle* means a "stylized" representation of reality.

3. *Homothetic* means that the social pact created at the level of the society works at a more local level, such as the level of a company. There is a difference of scale but not a different logic.

4. After the A level, students have the choice between attending a university or attending a *grande école*. Admission to the university does not depend on any entrance criteria (the A level is enough). Admission in a *grande école* is very selective, and each school offers a limited number of admissions. After 2 years in a preparatory school, the candidates take exams. The schools are ranked according to their prestige; the best are the most selective.

5. The employer and the employee are formally equal in the labor market, but the employee is obliged to sell his or her labor power if he wants to eat. The employer is less obliged to hire the employee because his or her survival does not depend on a single worker.

6. The French Revolution abolished guilds, and the law (called Le Chapelier; June 14, 1791) forbade any form of association. This law has delayed the elaboration of an industrial relations system.

7. German unions offer services to their members, who can evaluate the advantages they draw from their membership fees. French unions do not view themselves as service agencies but more as political parties in charge of ideological positions.

8. Jean-Baptiste Colbert (1619-1683) was a minister of Louis XIV who focused on the development of exports.

9. The issue of work duration is very typical of this inertia of the IR system, as illustrated by Freyssinet (1997).

10. D'Iribarne also cited Montesquieu, who developed the concept of moderation that influences interindividual adjustments in the French culture.

11. And also political actors such as Henry Kissinger (1979).

12. This is the direct translation of the French expression *sans foi ni loi,* commonly associated with bandits.

13. Roethlisberger and Dickson (1939) and Mayo (1949) had already observed that groups create informal norms. The sociologists have reelaborated this activity in terms of rule production.

14. Sociologists do not define a collective by a common situation but by its action. A collective exists when it is able to produce rules and to impose them.

15. Economists use this term to describe the social compromise that has prevailed during the postwar growth period: gaining salary increases at the cost of poor working conditions.

16. We borrow this way to look at promises from F. Dany (1997). She rejected the concept of psychological contract and prefers the concept of career promise, which she elaborated in the framework of joint regulation theory in a way that supports the message of this chapter.

REFERENCES

Bauer, M., & Bertin-Mourot, B. (1997). *Radiographie des grands patrons français: Les conditions d'accès au pouvoir.* Paris: L'Harmattan.

Dany, F. (1997). *La promesse d'employabilité: Un substitut possible à la promesse de carrière? Construction d'un cadre d'analyse de l'évolution des pratiques de gestion de carrière des cadres.* Lyon: Université Jean Moulin, Institut d'Administration des Entreprises.

de Terssac, G. (1992). *Autonomie dans le travail.* Paris: Presses Universitaires de France.

d'Iribarne, P. (1985). La gestion à la française. *Revue Française de Gestion, 50,* 5-13.

d'Iribarne, P. (1989). *La logique de l'honneur: Gestion des entreprises et traditions nationales.* Paris: Editions du Semil.

Dunlop, J. J. (1958). *Industrial relations systems.* Boston: Harvard Business School Press.

Freyssinet, J. (1997). *Le temps de travail en miettes: 20 ans de politique de l'emploi et de negociation collective.* Paris: Editions de l'Atelier.

Groux, G. (1996). Régulation de la crise, crise de la régulation. In G. La Chaise (Ed.), *Crise de l'emploi et fractures politiques.* Paris: Presses de Sciences Politiques.

Kissinger, H. (1979). *A la maison blanche 1968-1973.* Paris: Fayard.

Maurice, M., Sellier, F., & Silvestre, J. J. (1982). *Politique d'education et organisation industrielle en France et an Allemagne.* Paris: Presses Universitaires de France.

Mayo, E. (1949). *The social problems of an industrial civilisation.* London: Routledge & Kegan Paul.

Meaning of Work International Research Team. (1987). *The resuming of work.* New York: Academic Press.

Montesquieu, Baron de. (1951). De l'esprit des lois. In R. Caillois (Ed.), *Oeuvres completes de Montesquieu.* Paris: Gallimard. (Original work published 1748)

Morel, C. (1994). *La grève froide.* Toulouse, France: Editions Octares.

Perlman, S. (1936, March). The principle of collective bargaining. *Annals of the American Academy of Political and Social Sciences, 184,* 154.

Reynaud, J. D. (1989). *Les règles du jeu: L'action collective et la régulation sociale.* Paris: Armand Colin.

Roehling, M. K. (1996). The origins and early development of the psychological construct. In J. B. Keys & L. N. Dosier (Eds.), *Academy of Management best papers proceedings* (pp. 202-206). Statesboro: Georgia Southern University.

Roethlisberger, F. J., & Dickson, W. J. (1939). *Management and the worker.* Cambridge, MA: Harvard University Press.

Rousseau, D. M. (1995). *Psychological contracts in organizations: Understanding written and unwritten agreements.* Thousand Oaks, CA: Sage.

Rousseau, D. M., & Wade-Benzoni, K. A. (1994). Linking strategy and human resource practices: How employee and customer contracts are created. *Human Resource Management, 33,* 463-490.

Supiot, A. (1994). *Critique du droit du travail.* Paris: Presses Universitaires de France.

Tocqueville, A. de. (1835). *De la démocratie en Amérique.* Paris: Gallimard.

Tocqueville, A. de. (1952). Etat social et politique de la France. In *Oeuvres complètes* (Vol. 2). Paris: Gallimard. (Original work published 1856)

Walton, R. E., & McKersie, R. B. (1965). *A behavioral theory of labor negotiations.* New York: McGraw Hill.

Webb, S., & Webb, B. (1897). *Industrial democracy* (2 vols.). London: Longmans, Green.

5

Psychological and Normative Contracts of Work Group Members in the United States and Hong Kong

Cynthia Lee
Catherine H. Tinsley
George Zhen Xiong Chen

The city of Hong Kong is at the crossroads of the East and West, mingling Eastern collectivism, hierarchy, and tradition with Western individualism, competition, and a free-market orientation. This chapter compares psychological contracts in Hong Kong with those in the United States to address how Eastern and Western influences shape employment relations in Hong Kong.

THE HISTORICAL CONTEXT OF HONG KONG

Although Hong Kong is a Chinese city, it was ruled by Britain for much of the 20th century. The island was ceded to Britain in 1842 and returned to Chinese sovereignty on July 1, 1997. More than 98% of the city's 6.5 million residents are ethnic Chinese, some of whom migrated from mainland China in the 1950s. Throughout its history, Hong Kong has been influenced by Chinese philosophies, British governance, and its unique position as the gateway for East/West trade and commerce. As is perhaps fitting for a city at the crossroads, Hong Kong developed through commerce, its port allowing large ships to deliver

AUTHORS' NOTE: A portion of Cynthia Lee's work on this manuscript was conducted while she was a visiting professor in the Department of Management of Organizations at the Hong Kong University of Science and Technology.

merchandise bound for Asia and transport products from Asia to the rest of the world. The city profited from the two-way exchange of goods and picked up intangible philosophies from both sides of this rich exchange along the way.

Traditional Hong Kong businesses were structured around a familial model. Whether an organization was actually family owned or not, the work relations had a familial quality and the management was paternalistic. However, familial workplace relationships were not as strong in Hong Kong as they were in China, where collective work groups served as the basis for both employment and social structure. This difference was caused by the heavy westernization of Hong Kong citizens due to British governance of the city. In 1968, for example, Hong Kong established a labor contract to protect employee wages, regulate general employment conditions, and address related issues.[1] In contrast, mainland China historically offered no employment contracts entailing mutual obligations that parties could enter into and exit at will. Prior to 1978, communist China adopted the planned economic system used in the former Soviet Union, in which the majority of businesses were state owned, a small portion were collectively owned, and no private enterprise existed. The country had no job market because its people did not choose their jobs; rather, government agencies allocated human resources to the various organizations. The government also set wages and welfare payments at fixed monthly amounts that were unrelated to performance.

More recently, multinational corporations have entered Hong Kong, replacing some of the more familial organizations and "mom-and-pop" operations. The Western orientation of these corporations has pushed the city toward a capitalistic society more typical of the United States or western Europe, with competitive, free-market economies. At the same time, however, opposing forces are pushing Hong Kong toward a more traditional Chinese orientation. When China and Britain signed a joint declaration in December 1984 stipulating that Hong Kong would return to Chinese rule on July 1, 1997, the resulting population exodus created labor shortages throughout the city. The unemployment rate dropped from 3.9% in 1984 to a historic low of 1.1% in 1989. In response, the Hong Kong government launched the General Labor Importation Scheme in 1990, which allowed employers to hire workers from outside the country, particularly from China, on a contractual basis. The Labor Importation Scheme worked, and the government successfully attracted Chinese workers from overseas. In the third quarter of 1997, the unemployment rate was still relatively low at 2.2%, but the Asian financial situation has since caused the rate to rise back to the pre-1984 level.[2]

As a consequence of its Labor Importation Scheme, Hong Kong developed a labor contract that more closely resembled the Chinese employment relationship. One reflection of this more Chinese orientation can be seen in the lack of formal rules put forth by the Hong Kong Labor Department, which defines a contract of employment as an oral or written agreement between an employer and employee that may include both explicit and implicit agreements but need not be written, signed, and officially authorized to be valid. This informal structure is not surprising in a high-context culture where rules are suggested rather than set in stone. As in mainland China, both parties to an employment contract seem willing to rely on mutual trust in establishing and maintaining their employment relationship. Similarly, as one might expect in a culture that values harmony, the Labor Department guidelines give employers and employees a great deal of latitude. In Hong Kong, both parties to the employment contract seem to value flexibility, and as a result, employee turnover can be quite high.

CURRENT EVENTS IN HONG KONG

The two most salient events affecting employment contracts in Hong Kong have been its change in status from a British territory to a special administration region (SAR) of greater China and the economic crisis that devastated much of Asia during 1997 and 1998. Though they were significant, these events do not seem to have significantly altered Hong Kong's position as a crossroads of Eastern and Western culture. Rather, the two events may have counteracted each other, enabling Hong Kong to remain a city-state influenced by both the East and West.

Although the labor shortages associated with the impending transition to Chinese rule seemed to push Hong Kong toward a more Chinese-influenced orientation, it might have been expected that the formal end of British governance structures would propel the city even further in this direction. However, the Chinese government recognized Hong Kong's special status, history, and climate and—perhaps understanding the imbalance that the transition to Chinese rule would create—declared that the city's employment systems, which were based in part on the British structures, would not change for 50 years. This promise was included in the Basic Law governing the Hong Kong SAR.

The handover from Britain to China created an apparent backlash against socialist China among the younger Chinese residents of Hong Kong, who were educated under the British system and tend to espouse more Western values. Public opinion polls conducted in 1996 and 1997 by two Hong Kong universities found that most citizens disapproved of the hard-line civil rights position of the new chief executive-to-be, Tung Che Wah, who indicated that the needs of the community should come before those of individuals (Frankenstein, 1998). These polls do not mean that Western values dominate Hong Kong society, but they do illustrate the delicate balance that Hong Kong citizens wish to maintain. The pro-Western backlash against the new government came in response to environmental changes that shifted the country toward a more Chinese orientation. In the face of this Chinese influence, the people of Hong Kong may feel obliged to reaffirm the Western part of their identity.

But at the same time that they reaffirm their Western heritage, citizens also seem obliged to reaffirm the Eastern part of their identity—especially in light of the recent economic downturn in Hong Kong, which has forced employers to reduce wages, bonuses, year-end payments, fringe benefits, and other compensation. As a result of the Asian financial crisis, employment contracts in Hong Kong have become more transactional and short term, more closely resembling contracts in many Western firms. In response to this shift, the Labor Department issued informal guidelines advising employers to discuss contracting changes with their employees in order to help maintain collective welfare and harmony. This action was decidedly more Eastern than Western, again illustrating the delicate balance that characterizes employment contracts in Hong Kong.

CHARACTERISTICS OF THE EMPLOYMENT CONTRACT

Given the historical context of employment contracts in Hong Kong, we would expect them to reflect a mixture of Eastern and Western beliefs, values, and practices. To gain a deeper understanding of the components of these contracts, we must first understand the nature of employment contracts in general. It is useful to start with a review of U.S. research on Western employment contracts and then use our understanding of Hong Kong's beliefs, values, and social structures to examine how its employment contracts might differ.

Components of the U.S. Contract

Research has found that psychological contract terms are multidimensional, often characterized along two dimensions: relational/affective and transactional/"instrumental" (Lincoln & Miller, 1979). However, psychological contracts arising out of various combination of terms take many forms. Rousseau and Tijoriwala (1996) observed three forms of psychological contract in a sample of American registered nurses: (a) relational, reflecting open-ended obligations without clear performance measures; (b) transactional, reflecting an obligation to provide a prescribed level of performance without a specified time frame or any involvement with the organization; and (c) "team player," combining obligations that involve highly specified performance levels with broader commitment to the organization.[3]

Components of Contracts in Hong Kong

Although we argue that similar underlying dimensions of the psychological contract are relevant in both Hong Kong and the United States, those of Hong Kong may differ from those of the United States due to divergent beliefs, values, and social structures. Ambler (1995) noted that negotiations related to Sino-Western joint ventures may fail because each party places different priorities on specific aspects of the psychological contract. He argued that the

Chinese believe in building successful relationships that will lead to successful transactions. On the other hand, Westerners attempt to build successful transactions, from which relationships may follow.

On the basis of this contrast between East and West, we propose that the relational component of a psychological contract is more important to establishing a cooperative work arrangement in Hong Kong than in the United States. These differences arise in part from the differing social structures that are part of each country's historical legacy. In the West, personal relationships have historically had less effect on behavior, leading to the enactment of legal sanctions to ensure that obligations are met. For example, 18th-century European contract law was intended to give traders a reasonable assurance that deals would be honored. Business deals typically started with a standard formal contract, which was altered to fit the circumstances, was signed, and—if successfully carried out—led to a relationship. On the other hand, the Chinese believed that having a personal relationship, or *guanxi,* ensured that an obligation would be met. Obligations based on relationships have traditionally meant more than terms written on a piece of paper (Yang, 1993); until January 1995, when the national labor law in the People's Republic of China took effect, commercial law barely existed in China, and a legal, written contract was a sign of bad faith. The quality of the relationship was always more important than any particular transaction, and any problems that did arise would be worked out to the long-term benefit of both parties (as long as each continued to monitor the state of the relationship) (Redding, 1990). On the basis of the differences in social structure between China and the West, one can argue that the relational aspect of the psychological contract would be more important for the Chinese.

Chinese beliefs and values also suggest that the relational issues are more important to Hong Kong workers than to Western workers. China can be characterized as a society dominated by "personalism," defined as the tendency to allow personal preferences and relationships to influence decision making and action (Redding, 1990). Western societies tend to institutionalize power in explicit rules of conduct, whereas the Chinese have traditionally relied on individual morality, interpersonal trust, and relationships to maintain social order. In addition, psychologists find Hong Kong's culture to be more collective and traditional than Western cultures (Schwartz, 1994). Because Hong Kong Chinese are taught to value social harmony and affinity and to strive for smooth social interactions, we propose that they consider it their duty to actively develop the social or relational components of work contracts (Bond, 1988; Ho, 1993; Leung, 1997; Leung & Bond, 1989; Yang, 1993). Hong Kong Chinese are socialized to make sure that everyone involved in a social interaction is emotionally comfortable and to help each other "save face" in awkward situations (Ho, 1993). Thus, they not only feel obligated to develop relational contracts but also expect others—particularly the members of their work group—to devote energy to the development of relational contracts as well.

Proposition 1: The relational component will be a more important part of psychological contracts in Hong Kong than in the United States.

The team player component of employment contracts appears to be important in both Hong Kong and America. On one hand, there is evidence that people in collective, traditional cultures define themselves less as autonomous units and more as members of specific groups (Markus & Kitayama, 1991; Triandis, 1982). This type of culture emphasizes obligations to the group and the alignment of individual goals with those of the group (Triandis, McCusker, & Hui, 1990; Yang, 1993), and it allows for less social loafing than in individualistic cultures (Earley, 1989, 1993). These observations suggest that a team player orientation would be important for the collective, traditional Hong Kong culture.

At the same time, the emphasis on self-mastery and egalitarianism in the United States may lead Americans to embrace the team player orientation as well. The term *self-mastery* refers to active efforts to succeed through self-assertion, implying that people from cultures that score high on this dimension will actively pursue whatever is required to achieve their desired goals (Schwartz, 1994). This need for achievement—the desire to "master" a project—impels individuals beyond basic levels of performance (i.e., the transactional component) toward higher levels of commitment (i.e., the team player component). In addition, the U.S. culture's egalitarian nature suggests that when group members feel that everyone has made an equal contribution, all are free to actively engage in high-commitment behavior. These sentiments are echoed in recent American management literature, which has increasingly embraced teamwork over the past decade and, as a result, has perhaps given team players important status in American organizations (Sundstrom, DeMeuse, & Futrell, 1990). These aspects of American culture indicate that the team player component will be important for the United States as well. Therefore, we put forth another proposition.

Proposition 2: The team player component is an important part of psychological contracts in both Hong Kong and the United States.

Relationships Among Psychological Contract Components

Although we have generally compared Hong Kong employment contracts with those in the United States, we also assume that the importance and relevance of various components will vary within Hong Kong. Some situations or circumstances may give rise to a transactional contract rather than a relational or team player contract. In the unskilled labor force, for example, many companies offer relatively simple contracts that are usually transactional in nature. These contracts spell out the work to be done, the working hours, salary, and benefits. In contrast, contracts for professional staff may be geared more toward the team player dimension, including terms such as confidentiality, management responsibilities, training, and staff development. Overall, we believe that the type of employment contract a Hong Kong worker will develop depends on two factors: the nature of the other party (i.e., the type of organization with which a worker enters into a contract) and the nature of the work that is being performed.

Yang (1993) characterized Chinese society as having four major orientations: familistic, relationship, authoritarian, and other. The Chinese social orientation, according to Yang, is a product of the country's traditional agrarian economy and social structure. This history may not be as relevant in Hong Kong, which has moved from an agricultural society to an industrial and commercial society (perhaps losing some of its original intensity and characteristics in the process). For example, traditional Chinese society extended the attitudes and behaviors toward the head of the family (the authority) to the heads of larger social groups or organizations. These leaders were thought to be incapable of making mistakes, or their mistakes were excused as permissible due to their positions of authority. In Hong Kong, the influence of Western education and exposure is eroding this authoritarian orientation, and authorities are being held more accountable for their actions than they were in the past.

Despite these changes to Hong Kong society, some of Yang's orientations seem to still be relevant. The Hong Kong Chinese may have used these orientations as a means of adjusting to British rule and the influences of Western cultures. Especially relevant is the "other" orientation of the Chinese, which refers to their tendency to be influenced by other people on both a psychological and behavioral level (Yang, 1993). This gives rise to an important feature of collective cultures such as China, the tendency to characterize other people as either insiders or outsiders. This ability may have enabled the Hong Kong Chinese to incorporate outside influences (those of Britain and other Western nations) as long as these influences could be viewed as part of the outside world.

In China, family members are the ultimate insiders. Yang's familial orientation dictates that individuals should subordinate their personal goals, interests, and well-being to their family's goals and interests. This orientation leads Chinese to be especially loyal to their primary group members, which is one source of competitive advantage in the business empires built by overseas Chinese families. Coupled with the "other" orientation that distinguishes between insiders and outsiders, the familial orientation implies that nonfamilial organizations such as the British government or foreign citizens are not owed as much as those bound to an individual through family ties. In employment contracts, transactional forms may take precedence over relational forms when a person is dealing with nonfamilial organizations, but relational or team player contracts will be seen as a given when the other party is family or some other insider.

By observing the patterns of workplace interactions, one can see in-group versus out-group tendencies in practice. The lunch hour is typically an in-group function, where insiders gather at restaurants, picnic areas, basketball courts, and soccer fields. In addition, when insiders have a conflict with people outside their group—such as management—it is common for members of the in-group to sabotage managerial actions or even resign as a group. Therefore, we propose:

> Proposition 3: Hong Kong Chinese will be more likely to form relational contracts when they are working with in-group members and more likely to form transactional contracts when they are working with people outside the group.

Another factor influencing the type of contract that will be made is the nature of the work itself. We believe that when there is high task identification and demand, Hong Kong workers will espouse a team player contract. Yang suggested that those who have a high "other" orientation will constantly worry about others' opinions, conform to other people's views, have a deep concern about social norms, and hold reputation in high regard. Other-oriented people will attempt to avoid criticism, ridicule, rejection, and punishment at all costs and will do their best to win the approval, acceptance, help, and appreciation of others.

The roles prescribed by a given social network dictate what members should and should not do. In circumstances where high effort is the norm, conforming to these prescribed roles means that workers will do as much as they can to fulfill their duties, in effect employing a team player approach to the contract. Thus, when employees identify highly with a task and others also show a great team effort, Hong Kong Chinese should display this teamwork attitude as well, whether or not they are working with in-group or out-group members. Thus, we propose:

> Proposition 4: When Hong Kong Chinese workers identify highly with particular tasks and work, the team player component of the contract will become more salient for them.

Figure 5.1 contrasts Propositions 3 and 4, showing that the psychological contract that is emphasized depends on the status of the other entity (in-group or out-group) and the nature of the task to be performed (whether a worker has high or low identification with the job).

Empirical Verifications of the Propositions

We studied the types of contracts that employees form over time with the members of their work groups. Although it was beyond the scope of this chapter to fully test all of the propositions presented here, the data we gathered provide insight into the relative importance of each contract dimension in

Out-group obligations:	In-group obligations: loyalty and affection	
	Low	*High*
identification with task and work		
Low	Transactional	Relational
High	Team player	Team player

Figure 5.1. Proposed Psychological Contract Dimensions in Hong Kong

Hong Kong as opposed to the United States. We conducted some preliminary tests to determine whether the contract dimensions identified in the U.S. literature were relevant in Hong Kong. Work groups are common in Hong Kong and increasingly prevalent in America, indicating that this context would offer an employment setting that was common in both cultures.

Methods

We sought to study participants' perceptions of their contract with the work group. We defined the contract as a set of mutual obligations that each party (in this case, the member and the work group) is expected to fulfill. To develop measures of the psychological contract components (transactional, relational, and team player), we modified measures that have been developed for use in the United States. We also asked a work group of 20 students from each country (United States and Hong Kong) to generate items relevant to group work. Students were asked to think of a class where they were required to participate in a group project and to explain their expectations of the group members as well as their obligations to the group.

Students generally gave three to four responses for each open-ended question. Two of the authors tabulated responses and eliminated the redundancies to come up with a total of 15 items that measured the obligations that members expected others in the group to fulfill toward themselves and 16 items to measure their anticipated obligations to others. (These measures are listed in the appendix to this chapter.)

After generating these 31 items, we collected data from 175 second-year undergraduate students in Hong Kong and 104 third-year undergraduate students in the United States. The universities in Hong Kong follow the British system, in which students attend a 3-year university program. Therefore, the second-year students were roughly equivalent to our third-year American students. The average age of the students from both countries was 20 years. There were twice as many women (as men) in the Hong Kong sample but twice as many men in the United States sample. Students in both samples were required to work together on two group projects during the semester to receive course credit. There were 27 Hong Kong groups and 18 United States groups. We asked participants to refer to their experiences with these groups when filling out the survey.

Although there is little reason to expect group initial perceptions of the work group contract to be identical, it is logical to expect similar responses from students in the same culture compared to students from another culture. The way participants perceived their exchange relationships was shaped by their previous work group experiences as well as their knowledge of other people's work group experiences, both of which are a function of the cultural environment in which they have been socialized. Therefore, it was valid, at least as a preliminary test of work group contracts, to ask members what they perceived to be their exchange obligations with their work groups. Moreover, because we did not anticipate convergence within groups but simply tested for differences between cultures, all analyses were conducted at the individual level rather than at the group level.

Results

To examine the differences between survey answers across the Hong Kong and U.S. cultures, we used the standardization method created by Bond and Leung (Bond, 1988; Leung, 1997; Leung & Bond, 1989), which controls for cultural differences among means and standard deviations by standardizing the scores within each culture (also known as *deculturing*). This method retains the correlation matrix within each culture but allows comparisons to be made from one culture to another without the confounding effects that would have been caused by differences between cultural means. We performed factor analysis on the standardized scores for members' initial obligations and expectations, which resulted in four dimensions for both obligations and expectations. The four-dimensional structure was the same for both Hong Kong and the United States, and three of the dimensions—relational, transactional, and team player—paralleled those of Rousseau and Tijoriwala (1996). In addition, we found what we call a "broader context" dimension, which reflected the anticipated expectations and obligations among the students and a larger organizational environment (in this context, either the class or the course as a whole). In an employment contract, the broader context dimension might reflect a worker's exchange relationship with a union or professional group; we found this dimension less useful for the purposes of this chapter than the other three. The items included in each factor are listed in the appendix.

The items that made up the four factors were averaged for each student, creating a score on each of the contract dimensions: group transactional (GT),

TABLE 5.1 Cultural Differences on Contract Dimensions in Hong Kong and the United States

Contract Dimension	United States		Hong Kong		F (1,275)	p
	Mean	SD	Mean	SD		
Expectations						
Group transactional (GT)	−.03	1.5	−.30	1.5	2.07	*ns*
Class transactional (CT)	−2.60	2.8	−1.20	2.3	20.67	.001
Relational (RLN)	−.08	1.7	.77	1.4	21.6	<.001
Team player (TEAM)	.46	1.5	.35	1.5	.33	*ns*
Obligations						
Group transactional (GT)	4.4	1.5	4.0	1.6	3.4	*ns*
Class transactional (CT)	3.6	2.9	3.7	2.4	.11	*ns*
Relational (RLN)	.73	2.0	2.9	1.6	102.6	<.001
Team player (TEAM)	2.2	2.3	1.6	2.1	4.45	.03

broader context or class transactional (CT), relational (RLN), and team player (TEAM). This led to a total of eight factor measures—four for initial obligations and four for expectations. To test for cultural differences in these contract components, the individual-level scores on each of the eight measures were subjected to ANOVA, with culture as the independent variable.

As shown in Table 5.1, the relational component was stronger in Hong Kong than in the United States (for obligations, $F = 102.57$, $df = 1, 263$, $p < .001$; for expectations, $F = 21.65$, $df = 1, 275$, $p < .001$). These results provide strong support for the first proposition, that the relational component will be a more important part of psychological contracts in Hong Kong than in the United States. Results for the team player component were less consistent. The United States had a higher mean for TEAM expectations, but this difference was not significant ($F = .32$, $df = 1, 274$, *ns*). However, the United States had significantly higher scores than Hong Kong on the TEAM factor for initial obligations ($F = 4.45$, $df = 1, 264$, $p < .05$). Therefore, Proposition 2—that the team player component is an important part of psychological contracts in both Hong Kong and the United States—is only partially supported.

Table 5.1 shows one other significant difference: The CT dimension for expectations was significantly weaker in the United States than in Hong Kong ($F = 20.67$, $df = 1, 273$, $p < .001$). Moreover, each culture had negative means for this measure, implying that the broader context dimension was not a major aspect of psychological contracts for either culture relative to the other three components.

Discussion

Although this preliminary analysis is clearly limited, it does lend support to our theory that both the Hong Kong and U.S. cultures form work group contracts that feature transactional, relational, and team player components. Because we formulated measures with the help of representatives from both cultures and measured the three dimensions using the same survey items in both Hong Kong and the United States, it seems reasonable to believe that these dimensions have similar meanings across the two cultures. The questionnaire items relating to the transactional component (be available to meet with group members, be prompt, complete projects as assigned) suggest that this component reflects basic levels of commitment to a group and the performance of routine tasks that can be monitored. The relational component items (affinity, attachment) reflect obligations toward the group's emotional health rather than explicit task performance. Items related to the team player component (sharing ideas and opinions, communicating problems and questions) reflect higher levels of commitment to the group and the performance of more complex, challenging cognitive tasks.

Moreover, our limited study did support the proposition that the relative importance of these dimensions differs across cultures. People from Hong Kong appear to place more importance on the relational component, whereas Americans tend to place a greater emphasis on the team player component. Given these and other cultural differences, Hong Kong Chinese may initially feel uncomfortable when working in mixed-culture groups if they are not able to spend enough time and effort developing the group's emotional health. On the other hand, Americans may worry that too much time is being spent on activities that appear unrelated to the task at hand. Although both cultures may need to adjust their approaches when working in mixed culture groups, Americans should keep in mind that positive benefits accrue to groups that meet members' relational expectations—regardless of the culture in which they function.

CURRENT AND FUTURE STATUS OF CONTRACTING IN HONG KONG

As noted above, written employment contracts are not compulsory in Hong Kong. Many of the country's smaller, family owned businesses, which have no formal human resources policies, rely on oral contracts instead of written ones. Like the enterprises in mainland China, both parties to the contract are willing to rely on their mutual trust in establishing and maintaining their employment relationship. However, in contrast to mainland China, employees who believe that their employers have violated their basic rights can seek legal protection based on the Hong Kong Employment Ordinance. This is another indication of the balance between East and West. The legal system in Hong Kong is well established, and the people have a better sense of law and know how to protect their rights.

Hong Kong's labor market is again in turmoil, as it was in the mid-1980s with the labor exodus. This time, however, there is a labor surplus. In 1998, the country experienced a rising unemployment rate heightened by the economic downturn throughout Asia. Both family businesses (e.g., Shui Hing department stores, Maria's Bakery) and multinational corporations (e.g., Diamaru, Yoham) went out of business, declared bankruptcy, or downsized drastically (e.g., Theme, Wing On department stores). A logical question is whether these changes in the labor market will change the nature of employees' labor contracts. One hypothesis is that the longer time frame associated with relational contracts may turn into a shorter term emphasis on transactional contracts as a result of the labor surplus and the inability of businesses to find work for all of their employees. Currently, organizations in Hong Kong are willing to employ independent contractors, though they rarely use permanent part-time or contingent workers.[4] It may be interesting to observe whether these shorter term, transactional employment arrangements will increase in Hong Kong over the years to come.

Another equally logical hypothesis regarding the effects of changing labor markets on employment contracts in Hong Kong is that in-groups may become even more cohesive in the face of external threats such as the "Asian flu." As work group members bond together to fight these threats, the already strong relational component of Hong Kong psychological contracts may become even more pronounced.

We can look at the changing nature of the employment contract in the United States—which recently experienced a similar period of downsizing and bankruptcies—for some guidance on the possible outcomes of such turbulent times in Hong Kong. Rousseau (1995) has argued that downsizing and restructuring spurred U.S. employment contracts to shift from long term and relational to shorter term and transactional. Employees had fewer expectations of a long-term relationship with a single company and became concerned instead with ensuring compliance to performance standards through short-term transactional contracts. On the other hand, Hall and Moss (1998) have argued that some organizations during this time period initiated a continuous learning process that slowly changed the old contract into a self-focused, "protean" contract that is entered into with oneself and one's work. The measurement of success for such a contract takes place internally or psychologically rather than externally, as signified through upward mobility or status. Employers are obliged to provide the resources and opportunities for core employees to learn new skills and develop their careers; in other words, the employers enable continuous learning on the part of their employees. The view of Hall and Moss suggests that the employment contract is changing, but not toward a shorter term transactional contract; instead, organizations value the ongoing relationships they have with employees and take a long-term view in their employment practices.

Since the July 1, 1997, changeover from British to Chinese sovereignty, employment contracts in Hong Kong have remained enormously flexible. Because labor contracts in China are in their infancy, it is unlikely that Hong Kong will propose formal changes to the flexible contract guidelines that exist in the country, and it also appears unlikely that China will impose contract changes on Hong Kong employers. It is more likely that change, in whatever form it may take, will come as a result of the new economic environment.

The flexibility of psychological contracts in Hong Kong may prove to be both a blessing and a curse, for organizations are on their own as far as establishing mutually rewarding employment arrangements. Research suggests that relational and team player contracts are critical to developing solid work group relationships. These components may be important to group performance regardless of the culture. Our Propositions 3 and 4 give some ideas for developing these important contract components. Future research should test these ideas in order to offer managers a prescription for building durable contracts that lead to high organizational performance.

NOTES

1. See http://www.justice.gov.hk/blis.nsf/d2769881999f47b3482564840019d2 f9/ Chapter57: The Hong Kong Employment Ordinance.

2. The unemployment rate and employment trends were published in Information Services Department (1998, pp. 114-126).

3. A detailed description of the contract types can be found in Rousseau (1995).

4. Contingency workers were defined by Polivka and Nardone (1989) as individuals who do not have "an explicit or implicit contract for long-term employment or have one in which the minimum hours of work can vary in a nonsystematic way." This definition excludes permanent part-time and independent contractors.

REFERENCES

Ambler, T. (1995). Reflections in China: Re-orienting images of marketing. *Marketing Management, 23,* 23-30.

Bond, M. H. (1988). Finding universal dimensions of individual variation in multicultural studies of values: The Rokeach and Chinese value surveys. *Journal of Personality and Social Psychology, 55,* 1009-1015.

Earley, P. C. (1989). Social loafing and collectivism. *Administrative Science Quarterly, 34,* 565-581.

Earley, P. C. (1993). East meets West meets Mideast: Further explorations of collectivistic and individualistic work groups. *Academy of Management Journal, 36,* 319-348.

Frankenstein, J. (1998). Hong Kong 1997: A look back at Hong Kong's future. *Thunderbird International Business Review, 40,* 31-53.

Hall, D. T., & Moss, J. E. (1998, Winter). The new protean career contract: Helping organizations and employees adapt. *Organizational Dynamics, 26,* 22-26.

Ho, D. Y. (1993). Relational orientation in Asian social psychology. In U. Kim & J. W. Berry (Eds.), *Indigenous psychology: Research and experiences in cultural context.* Newbury Park, CA: Sage.

Information Services Department, Government of the Hong Kong Special Administrative Region. (1998). *1998 Hong Kong: A new era.* Hong Kong: Hong Kong Government Press.

Leung, K. (1997). Negotiation and reward allocations across cultures. In P. C. Earley & M. Erez (Eds.), *New perspectives on I/O psychology* (pp. 640-675). San Francisco: New Lexington Press.

Leung, K., & Bond, M. H. (1989). On the empirical identification of dimensions for cross-cultural comparisons. *Journal of Cross-cultural Psychology, 20,* 133-151.

Lincoln, J. R., & Miller, J. (1979). Work and friendship ties in organizations: A comparative analysis of relational networks. *Administrative Sciences Quarterly, 24,* 181-199.

Markus, H. R., & Kitayama, S. (1991). Culture and the self: Implications for cognition, emotion, and motivation. *Psychological Review, 98,* 224-253.

Polivka, A. E., & Nardone, T. (1989). The definition of contingent work. *Monthly Labor Review, 112,* 9-16.

Redding, S. D. (1990). *The spirit of Chinese capitalism.* Berlin: Walter De Gruyter.

Rousseau, D. M. (1995). *Psychological contracts in organizations.* Thousand Oaks, CA: Sage.

Rousseau, D. M., & Tijoriwala, S. (1996, April). *Perceived legitimacy and unilateral contract changes: It takes a good reason to change a psychological contract.* Symposium at the Society for Industrial and Organizational Psychology meetings, San Diego, CA.

Schwartz, S. H. (1994). Beyond individualism/collectivism: New cultural dimensions of values. In U. Kim, H. C. Triandis, C. Kagitcibasi, S. C. Choi, & G. Yoon (Eds.), *Individualism and collectivism: Theory, method, and applications* (pp. 85-122). Newbury Park, CA: Sage.

Sundstrom, E., DeMeuse, K. P., & Futrell, D. (1990). Work teams: Applications and effectiveness. *American Psychologist, 45,* 120-133.

Triandis, H. C. (1982). Dimensions of cultural variations as parameters of organizational theories. *International Studies of Management and Organization, 12,* 139-169.

Triandis, H. C., McCusker, C., & Hui, C. H. (1990). Multimethod probes of individualism and collectivism. *Journal of Personality and Social Psychology, 59,* 1006-1020.

Yang, K.-S. (1993). Chinese social orientation: An integrative analysis. In L. Y. Cheng, F. M. C. Cheung, & C. N. Chen (Eds.), *Psychotherapy for the Chinese: Selected papers from the first international conference.* Hong Kong: Chinese University of Hong Kong.

APPENDIX

Exploratory Factor Structures for Psychological Contracts: Expectations and Obligations (Both Time Periods) With Items That Had Factor Loadings Greater Than .40

Expectations

1. **TRANSACTIONAL (TRANS) component:**

   a. The **GROUP TRANSACTIONAL component** represents obligations to provide a basic level of performance without any specification of time frame or commitment to the group (Items 1-4, 12; alphas = .73 and .72 for Times 1 and 2, respectively):

      - I expect group members to be available to meet as often as necessary.
      - I expect each member to participate equally.
      - I expect members to complete, on time, all jobs assigned to them.
      - I expect them to put a priority on our joint projects.
      - I expect them to be prompt and punctual.

   b. The **CLASS TRANSACTIONAL component** represents the individual's exchange relationship with the larger social environment. In this case, it is the class; in an organizational context, it might be the organization or a professional group rather than a division or work group (Items 14, 15; alphas = .81 and .69 for Times 1 and 2, respectively):

      - I expect them to attend class.
      - I expect them to study and receive a good grade.

2. The **RELATIONAL component** represents obligations focusing on attachment to the group, with open-ended contract terms without clear performance specifications (Items 8, 9, 10, 11, 16; alphas = .82 and .74 for Times 1 and 2, respectively):

   - I expect them to help each other.
   - I expect them to be friendly.
   - I expect them to respect each other's opinion.
   - I expect them to get along with each other.
   - I expect them to be motivated.

3. The **TEAM PLAYER component** represents obligations involving both high levels of performance and broader commitment to the group (Items 5, 6, 13; alphas = .79 and .77 for Times 1 and 2, respectively):

   - I expect them to freely share all of their opinions and ideas.
   - I expect them to create an open environment for idea generation.
   - I expect them to communicate problems and questions.

Obligations

1. **TRANSACTIONAL (TRANS) component:**

    a. The **GROUP TRANSACTIONAL component** represents obligations to provide a basic level of performance without any specification of time frame or commitment to the group (Items 1, 3, 4, 14; alphas = .67 and .69 for Times 1 and 2, respectively):

    - I should do my portion of the work.
    - I should complete my work on time.
    - I should be available to meet as often as necessary.
    - I should be prompt to all meetings.

    b. The **CLASS TRANSACTIONAL component** represents the individual's exchange relationship with the larger social environment. In this case, it is the class; in an organizational context, it might be the organization or a professional group rather than a division or work group (Items 13, 15; alphas = .74 and .69 for Times 1 and 2, respectively):

    - I should attend class.
    - I should study and receive a good grade in this class.

2. The **RELATIONAL component** represents obligations focusing on attachment to the group, with open-ended contract terms without clear performance specifications OBLIGATIONS (Items 2, 7-11, 16; alphas = .83 and .78 for Times 1 and 2, respectively):

    - I should make others enjoy their work.
    - I should help other members when they cannot finish their portion.
    - I should try to get agreement from every member of the group.
    - I should suggest improvements to others' work.
    - I should be friendly toward other members.
    - I should compromise my own personal feelings when the group disagrees.
    - I should get along with all other members.

3. The **TEAM PLAYER component** represents obligations involving both high levels of performance and broader commitment to the group (Items 5, 6, 12; alphas = .60 and .62 for Times 1 and 2, respectively):

    - I should help to coordinate the group.
    - I should be the leader and director of the group.
    - I should do as much as I possibly can for this group.

6

India

Caste, Commitments, and Change

Snehal Shah

Prana jaye per vachan ne jaye. "(I can) let go of my life but not of my promise."
Indian Proverb

The words *promise* and *fulfillment of promise* have immense significance in Indian society, as indicated in Indian mythology and religious Hindu and Islamic texts. One of the most revered epics, the *Ramayana,* was written to document the life of Lord Rama, a Hindu deity who spent 12 years in exile to fulfill his father's promise to his stepmother. The Koran, the Islamic religious text, narrates the story of how Prophet Mohammed was willing to sacrifice the life of his only son to fulfill his implicit promise to God. The importance of promise and fulfillment is also evident in Indian history, which is replete with instances that describe vividly how the emperors and moguls of India waged great wars, witnessed the rise and fall of their dynasties, and lost their empires in order to keep their word. The heroic tales of warriors who sacrificed their lives to keep their promises have been passed on from generation to generation.

AUTHOR'S NOTE: I would like to thank the editors for inviting me to write this chapter. I am also grateful to Vijay Reddy, Sridhar Sarathy, and Sudhakar Shah for insightful comments on the earlier drafts of the chapter. Thanks are also due to Dilip Shah and Kannan Srinivasan for useful discussions and to the interviewees for sharing their experiences.

In fact, when kings, emperors, and princes ruled India, keeping one's word was viewed as a defining characteristic of manhood, dignity, and royal upbringing.

Traces of these historical and religious roots are still found in the personal and professional lives of many Indians today. The focus of this chapter is on how promises and mutual obligations, conceptualized in organizational research as psychological contracts, play out in the Indian work environment. It is important to note here that as is true in many countries, the work environments in India are very diverse. Different types of employer-employee relationships exist depending on whether an organization is publicly owned, privately managed, or an entrepreneurial undertaking. Further, these employment relationships are shaped by different laws prevalent in India. Recognizing this diversity, the chapter first gives a brief background of the different types of work environments that exist in India. Next, it describes the relevant social, legal, and political climates and how they influence employment relationships within a particular work environment. Finally, the chapter enumerates some current trends in work practices and their implications for future employer-employee relationships.

With its religious and cultural diversity, India presents a varied context in which to study the employer-employee relationship. India is a huge country whose more than 900 million people practice a range of religions such as Hinduism, Islam, Christianity, Buddhism, Sikhism, and Judaism. It is a formidable task to capture this diversity within the framework of this chapter. Because about 75% of the Indian population is Hindu, the chapter studies the employment relationship primarily from a Hindu perspective.

One of the main objectives of this book is to elicit features of the employment relationship that are shaped by the sociopolitical and cultural milieu unique to a country. For a country like India that is increasingly participating in a global market, private sector white-collar professionals and managers' employment relationships tend to be flexible, open-ended, and the least restricted by sociopolitical and legal systems. On the other hand, the sociopolitical environment exerts greater influence on the employment relationships of public sector and blue-collar workers. Keeping the above-mentioned objective of the book in mind, this chapter examines the effects of the sociopolitical/legal environments on the employer-employee relationship across different segments of the workforce.

INDIA'S EMPLOYMENT STRUCTURE

When India gained freedom from British rule in 1947, the Indian political leaders faced the great challenge of leading a huge country on the path of growth, development, and self-reliance. To achieve this difficult goal, the economy's planners focused their attention on developing industries and infrastructure, despite the fact that India was primarily an agriculture-based economy.

The Indian workforce both then and now can be broadly classified as working in two main sectors: organized and unorganized. The organized sector is composed of public and private enterprises that either are registered or come under the purview of any of the acts and/or are maintaining annual accounts and balance sheets. This sector includes departmental and nondepartmental public enterprises; registered manufacturing, mining, and private transport companies; the service industry and private, corporate sector companies; registered schools, colleges, and hospitals; and corporate trading activities and services (Reserve Bank of India, 1979).[1] In contrast, the unorganized sector includes private sector employment that is marginally affected or regulated by labor or industrial laws. Unorganized sector enterprises are usually very small (typically fewer than 10 persons). Occupations such as agriculture, carpentry, weaving, and other skill-based activities fall in this category. The wages in this sector are generally considered to be low, and the working conditions can be harsh and unsafe. Though less than 10% of the workforce is employed in the organized sector, these organizations contribute nearly 50% of the gross national product (Ratnam, 1995).

The organized sector can be classified into two main categories: public sector units (PSUs) and private sector industries (PSIs). The public sector units are owned and managed by the government. Heavy industries such as iron, steel, cement, and chemicals and infrastructure industries such as railways, postal, telecommunications, banks, utilities, and aviation fall under this category. The private sector industries can be further classified into the private corporate sector (PCS) and small-scale industries (SSIs) and traders. The PCS includes primarily organizations that have a significant equity stake from family houses, stockholders, or international parent firms. This chapter will focus on the two main components of the PCS: family-owned/professionally managed businesses and multinational companies. Family-owned businesses have a stronghold in textiles and high-end household products such as refrigerators and other appliances (Reserve Bank of India, 1979). The strength of multinational corporations lies in manufacturing, marketing, and distributing consumer products, particularly in the international market. Trading and SSIs span a wide range of products and services from manufacturing and selling activities to serving as agents to the government and the multinationals. (See Figure 6.1.)

This book's introduction emphasizes the importance of the social and national-level context that shapes the psychological contracts between employers and employees. These macro-level issues are very relevant in India because they exert a significant influence on how employer-employee relationships are formed. In the next section, we give a historical perspective of the nature of employment practices against the backdrop of the social and legal/political climate in India. Then we discuss the specific features of this climate as they shape the implicit and the explicit features of the employer-employee relationship.

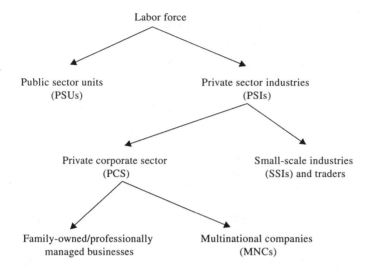

Figure 6.1. Employment Structure

SOURCE: Sridhar Sarathy, deputy manager, Tata International Limited, personal communication, June 20, 1999.

EMPLOYMENT AND EARLY SOCIAL CLIMATE

Centuries ago, work practices in India bore no semblance to what we understand as "employment" today. Indian society was primarily divided into two main classes, the feudal lords who possessed the vast majority of land and wealth and the landless laborers who worked these lands. These laborers were typically poor and were paid mainly in food and clothing. There was little likelihood that a laborer would accumulate wealth or alter his social standing in his lifetime.

Employment during the preindustrialized era was determined by the particular social class a person belonged to by birth. Indian society is traditionally divided into four main social classes that are hierarchical. Those who belong to the first class in the hierarchy are known as *Brahmins.* Considered to be a part of an elite class, traditionally, the Brahmins were responsible to preach and protect the Hindu religion. The warrior community belongs to the second class, known as the *kshatriyas,* responsible for fighting wars and protecting the country. Traders and entrepreneurs belong to the third class, the *vaishyas,* and are known for their business acumen, willingness to take risks, and love of money. Those who clean the streets, sweep the floors, and perform other menial jobs belong to the fourth class and are known as *shudras.* This class is at the bottom of the hierarchy in terms of power, wealth, and status. Together, these four classes make up what is known as the caste system.

During the preindustrialized era, one's occupation was determined largely by birth. Usually, those who belonged to higher castes employed persons who belonged to lower castes. Also, the power and status of the upper-class members determined the rules and set the guidelines for a "master-servant" type of relationship.

Employment and Political/Legal Climate

The kind of voluntary employer-employee relationship known today emerged in India with the advent of industrialization in the mid- to late 19th century. Individuals from different castes, backgrounds, and social strata found employment as factory workers in what signaled a departure from their traditional roles. In most cases, these factory workers belonged to the lower caste (i.e., shudras), whereas mill owners belonged to the higher caste (i.e., Brahmins, kshtriyas, and vaishyas). Relations between workers and employers have been marked with conflict since the beginning of industrialization (Sharma, 1987). One notable exception to this conflicting relationship was the Gandhian notion of "trusteeship." In 1918, when the textile workers of Ahmedabad went on strike and demanded a 50% increase in wages, Mahatma Gandhi intervened and settled the dispute amicably by advocating a new method of dispute resolution (now known as the Gandhian labor ideology). The key to Gandhi's approach was his emphasis on truth and fairness in the formulation of demands and the avoidance of bitterness during the negotiations. The industrial copartnership was based on equal status, dignified work, and mutual interests between labor and management. The Gandhian concept of "trusteeship" provides a means of transforming the capitalist order of society into an egalitarian one (Sharma, 1987). However, British rule in India and the sociocultural gap between the employers and the employees during those times proved to be the greatest hindrance to adopting the Gandhian philosophy nationwide. Nonetheless, trusteeship forms part of the mission of many contemporary Indian firms (including TISCO and Eicher, described later in this chapter).

The emergence of industries and factories also coincided with the long British rule in India. At that time, many Indians worked as laborers in the factories that were established and run by the British. In most cases, managers and supervisors also were British, although some factories promoted Indians who had become followers of the British. During the early stages of industrialization and British rule, there were weak efforts to unite workers into unions that would champion their rights. However, the organized labor movement did not take hold in India until the beginning of the 20th century. In 1920, following in the footsteps of the International Labor Organization (ILO), which India had helped to found, the All India Trade Union Congress (AITUC) was established as a national-level organization. At its inception, 64 unions were affiliated with AITUC, including workers from railroads, shipping, and other industries. The most significant milestone of the labor movement's history was the passage of the Indian Trade Union Act in 1926. This act gave legal status to registered unions and provided them a certain degree of immunity from civil suits and criminal prosecution.

The growing movement for independence from British rule also had a major impact on the development of the labor movement. Because Indian industries were predominantly owned by the British by the beginning of the 20th century, union activities and the independence movement became increasingly difficult to separate. Union members were also in most cases members of a specific group fighting for independence from the British. After gaining independence, some of these groups formed the basis of political parties. Thus, labor unions are strongly associated with political parties in modern India (Venkatchalam & Singh, 1982).

Industrial development emerged after the country gained its independence, as a means to achieve growth and prosperity. The architects of the Indian economy emphasized a synergistic interaction among the government, management, and organized labor to provide momentum for industrialization (Myers & Kannappan, 1970). Many policies and legislation were enacted to realize this goal. Therefore, it may be appropriate to say that in the Indian context, the formal legal/political system and organized labor unions representing the blue-collar workforce have developed almost in parallel. It should be noted that because of the close ties between the labor union movement and the struggle for national independence, the labor laws that existed prior to independence favored employers and sought to curb the labor movement. To correct for this imbalance, the Indian constitution charted after independence tends to favor employees. The constitution contains directives such as equal pay for equal work between men and women and decent wages and working conditions for blue-collar workers. However, the scope of this labor legislation is limited in practice to blue-collar workers in the organized sector.

National Policies Concerning the Employer-Employee Relationship

An important piece of legislation relevant to our discussion of employment relationships is the Industrial Employment Act of 1946, commonly referred to as the "Standing Orders." This act seeks to regulate recruiting and other facets of employment in industrial establishments with 100 or more workers. It also addresses the termination of employment and the means of redress available for workers. These rules can, in a sense, be interpreted as the terms of an employment contract between the employers and the workers.

The legal and the political machinery of the Indian government can powerfully shape employment terms and conditions. However, its jurisdiction is largely limited to blue-collar workers of the organized sector, who constitute less than 10% of the Indian workforce. Because labor unions representing blue-collar workers have strong ties to political parties, unionized employers appear to have limited flexibility in negotiating idiosyncratic employment agreements. Legal factors play less of a role in the relationship between white-collar workers and the employers.

The concept of employees who are willing to cooperate in order to achieve the overall objectives of the firm is at the heart of practices such as "participative management," which are advocated by the Indian constitution. The constitution directs the state to secure the participation of workers in the management of organizations and establishments (Sharma, 1987). The Sachar Committee[2] (1978) suggested a variety of measures to promote worker participation and social responsibilities of management. It recommended the provision of safe working conditions, an agreeable work relations program, and training programs to develop employees' talents.

Shifting Policies Regarding the
Employer-Employee Relationship

After independence, many traditional employment practices persisted. The status of one's father or another relative in the society or a recommendation from a political leader could secure a job more readily than personal merits and accomplishments (Lambert, 1963; Sharma, 1973; Vaid, 1968). The favoritism that employers showed at the time of hiring and promotions, the general absence of any consistent rules, lack of appreciation for merit-based achievement, and lack of condemnation of lethargy and neglect were obstacles to a good employer-employee relationship (Mukharji, 1969). However, there has been a considerable change in these practices since the reform process that began in the early 1990s, beginning with a government initiative to deregulate core industries such as banking, telecommunications, and airlines. Since then, initiatives have encouraged foreign investments and have given more autonomy to public and private sector companies. Now in these sectors, hiring practices have seen a marked shift from nepotism and favoritism to hiring based on merits and suitability to the job.

The Gandhian concept of trusteeship has persisted. Over the last several decades, the conventional profit-seeking motive of organizations has increasingly been questioned. The notion that business and industry should reconcile their desire to reap profits with social responsibilities toward their employees, customers, and the larger community has permeated the traditional management mind-set. Eicher, a large manufacturer of automotive vehicles, includes in its mission statement the goal of promoting the education of the female children of the poor. The firm's leadership (and many of its employees) spend a considerable amount of personal time in the villages promoting the education of girls in the hope that the children that these girls will raise will be literate and educated themselves. In the same vein, in 1965, the Seminar in Delhi, a distinguished gathering of businessmen, management experts, economists, and administrators, identified certain key obligations of the management toward their employees: Provide secure employment, pay fair wages, and provide the opportunity for growth and development. These measures were considered necessary not only because they contributed to organizational efficiency but also because justice and fair play demanded such actions (Sharma, 1987).

Employment and Education:
The Rise of Employer Training

The planners of the newly independent Indian economy committed a vast amount of resources to the promotion of industrialization. They made huge investments in infrastructure by building factories and buying machinery and created an administrative system at the state and national levels to ensure appropriate use of the resources and adequate return on investment. As new factories were established and service industries such as banking and telecommunications continued to expand, the country faced an acute shortage of skilled, educated labor. To tackle this shortfall, the planners focused resources on the educational system in an attempt to provide the skills required by the burgeoning industries. Unfortunately, even today the Indian educational system has difficulty in promoting skills that match employers' needs. Contemporary Indian firms seeking to compete in the global market find themselves needing to make substantial investments in worker training.

The traditional view regarding education of female and male children in agricultural households is that education is irrelevant for girls, whose traditional role in society is to bear children and manage the household. On the other hand, educating a boy who is born and raised in a farmer's household means one less pair of hands to do the work if that boy migrates to a city in search of a job off the farm. With more than 70% of households employed in agriculture-related activities holding such beliefs about education, it has been difficult to spread the new work ethics and market economy principles through educational channels. Finally, the mismatch between formal education and employment is accentuated by the fact that even if the market conveys a signal that it demands a particular skill, the more or less rigid educational system is not able to adapt quickly (Johri, 1992).

The weak link between the formal education system and employability has necessitated substantial investments in training among private sector firms located in India. One prominent example is TISCO, founded by the Tata family, producing products and services for a variety of industrial sectors. TISCO leadership has mandated that managers must spend their training budgets on training, and in one branch of TISCO, Tata International, there are currently 54 internal training programs for workers at all levels (S. Sarathy, Deputy Manager, Tata International Limited, personal communication, June 20, 1999).

PSYCHOLOGICAL CONTRACTS IN INDIA

Psychological contracts are defined as individual systems of beliefs shaped by organizations regarding the terms of a mutual exchange agreement (Rousseau, 1995). These systems are beliefs about the mutual obligations regarding the terms of an employment arrangement. In discussing psychological contract issues in India, I would like to highlight two key features that are conspicuous by their limited applicability to employment relationships between blue-collar workers and their employers. The first feature is that psychological contracts are fundamentally idiosyncratic. Their premise is that each organization and each employee have the flexibility to create their own unique relationship. As discussed in the following sections, many Indian companies negotiate employment contracts with unions, creating a collective or group-level agreement rather than a distinctive individual one. The second feature is that psychological contracts are voluntarily entered into where commitments are freely made. Though the postindependent employment relationships in India have many voluntary aspects, the social and legal/political environments in which Indian organizations operate can severely limit choices for broad segments of the Indian workforce.

Because of the historic influence of British rule and because many pre-independence factories were owned by the British and employed Indians as laborers, the attitudes of subservience and respect for authorities persist in the Indian psyche. These attitudes are manifested in the work environment as formalities (such as referring to one's boss as "sir" or "madam") and following bureaucratic processes. Stratification of the society into different castes, and the power differential this creates, creates hierarchical reporting structures. The last names of individuals signify social status, and those whose last names belong to the privileged classes consider it below their dignity to work as a clerk, waiter, or janitor. Finally, the existence of a male-dominated culture makes it difficult for male employees to take orders from female bosses and for women to climb up the corporate ladder (Reddy, 1998). However, as mentioned earlier, due to the deregulation of the economy, these aspects of the Indian work environment have undergone significant transformations. Formalities continue to exist, but an undercurrent of defiance of authority is emerging. However, respect for one's seniors, especially elders, persists in Indian society.

The following sections address the applicability of the concept of psychological contracts in India's public and private employment sectors.

Psychological Contracts and the Public Sector

Postindependence India is a democratic country, based on the political ideology of socialism, that essentially advocates the concept of egalitarianism. This concept strives to reduce the inequality between the rich and the poor, the landed class and laborers, and employers and employees. The decision to include the philosophy of socialism as an important part of the national agenda was driven by India's socioeconomic history. Rigid social norms and deeply entrenched cultural dogmas about status and hierarchy heightened the feelings of inequality and injustice. Socialism came to be seen as panacea for all evils, leading to the creation of PSUs as a means of implementing the socialistic agenda of the postindependence government.

PSU employment after independence was intended to help build the Indian industrial and social infrastructure and, in particular, to redress social inequalities. Typically, PSUs promote equality by reserving slots in educational institutions and jobs for the underprivileged classes of society. The policy governing PSUs stipulated that a certain percentage of positions in government-owned or -managed educational institutions and industries would be reserved for specific tribes and castes identified as underprivileged in a list or schedule announced by the government. Because the names appeared in a schedule, these entities are commonly referred to as schedule castes and schedule tribes. This policy is controversial nationwide because it has essentially provided a legal birthright for employment. The underlying premise behind this policy was to rectify historical socioeconomic deprivation.

The introduction to this chapter described the value of implicit promises within Indian society. However, the employment relationship in the PSUs is not reflective of this spirit. Industrial laws, the existence of strong labor unions, and the social divide between employers and employees have limited the scope of the employment relationship to just an explicit legal contract between employers and groups of workers.

Labor unions in PSUs and other government agencies spend a great deal of time, effort, and resources in negotiating explicit procedures for settling employee grievances, pay raises, better working conditions, and so on. Such activities give rise to very explicit, transactional employment contracts that are short term and specific and that engender limited loyalty from workers (Rousseau, 1995). Because unions negotiate these contracts with management on behalf of the workers as a collective group, there is little room for management and individual workers to negotiate idiosyncratic contracts. For example, the typical Indian labor union expects its workers to be promoted on the basis of seniority. Therefore, it is extremely difficult for a unionized employer to promote a star performer solely on the basis of his or her merits if he or she does not have sufficient experience for the more senior position.

The social principle of welfare is also reflected in labor laws regarding retrenchment. With regard to the termination of an employee, the legislation enacted after India gained independence requires both public and private sector employers to serve notice in writing and provide a layoff and/or retrenchment compensation as a proportion of the employee's basic salary. Especially for government employees, the laws give a "cradle-to-grave employment" promise regardless of performance, productivity, or the worker's attitude toward the job.

The employer-employee relationship in the public sector is characterized by low productivity, low job satisfaction, and strong influence of labor unions and politics. Though the employment relationship between employers and unionized workers appears to be one of consensus, this consensus is brought about by law. Unfortunately, in reality, the employer-employee relationship in India is often strained. The labor laws alone cannot bridge the socioeconomic and attitudinal divide between the employers and the workers. The key problem seems to be a lack of trust. Employees frequently consider employers to be *paisa chor,* or "money thieves." Balance sheets are sometimes considered to be pieces of fiction. On the other hand, employers consider employees as *kam chor* ("work thieves"—i.e., lazy people who avoid work) (Ratnam, 1995).

There are signs that public sector enterprises are moving toward the more participative practices used in the private sector. Maruti Udyog Limited, a successful government-managed car manufacturing company formed in collaboration with the Suzuki Company of Japan, follows some Japanese work and management practices. To foster participative management at all levels, employees are encouraged to solve problems in groups and form quality circles. To develop a sense of oneness and promote interaction among employees at all levels, workers, regardless of their status, are expected to wear the same uniforms provided by the company, travel in the same bus, sit in the same office space, eat in the same cafeteria, work the same hours, use the same medical facilities, and abide by the same leave-of-absence rules. Thus, Maruti's work culture is based on principles of equality and emphasizes the importance of a robust work environment for higher productivity and unwavering loyalty (Sharma, 1987).

Psychological Contracts and the Private Sector

Private sector employment in India involves the corporate sector, which is made up of family businesses (often founded by families but also including nonfamily stockholders) and multinational companies and the traders and SSIs (e.g., textile, consumer products, and service industries). This section discusses psychological contract issues with respect to different types of private organizations and makes the distinction between issues related to blue-collar and white-collar workers wherever applicable.

Blue-Collar Workers and Family-Owned Companies

Whereas the employment relationship in the PSUs has tended to be one of "cradle-to-grave" employment, the employer-employee relationship in the textile industry from 1900 to 1960 tended to be one of "generation-to-generation" employment. The grandfather, father, and son in the same family would work at the same textile mill. From the psychological contract perspective, the difference between the two models is enormous in the sense that "cradle-to-grave employment" in the public sector to a large extent is shaped by the policy directives, whereas "generation-to-generation employment" in the textile industries owned by veteran family houses (e.g., the Mafatlal group of companies) is shaped by a supportive, long-standing relationship that attracts generations to the same firm.

The employer-employee relationship in family businesses during those days epitomized the societal importance accorded to promises and their fulfillment. The relationship went beyond job-related reciprocity. A blue-collar worker in the textile factory and his entire household became a part of the large extended family of the employer, who unconditionally gave huge sums of money to the worker on the occasion of his daughter's marriage or when other needs arose. Such gestures were reciprocated by the worker through lifetime loyalty and the commitment that his son or another person from the household would work for the same employer to repay the obligation. During economic hardships, retrenchment was not considered, and workers were willing to take pay cuts or receive no pay for a couple of months until the factory saw better days. During festivals such as *Diwali* (Festival of Lights), it was customary for the workers and their families to visit their employer's house to pay their respects. After the mid-20th century, these traditional relational psychological contracts shared between blue-collar workers and their employers slowly eroded as some of the major textile firms folded.

For the past several decades in the area of engineering and consumer products, big businesses owned by such families as the Tatas, the Birlas, and the Godrejs have dominated the scene. Tata Iron and Steel Company (TISCO), a subsidiary of the Tata group, has been a good example of a company with less mobile and more relationship-oriented workers who are loyal to management. The workers are viewed as a long-term investment that should be nurtured. In return, management can expect adequate return on the investments it makes on training and development. In addition to providing safe working conditions, relative secure employment, and attractive facilities for employees and their families, TISCO has successfully implemented systems such as participatory management, grievance handling, and two-way communication.

White-Collar Workers and Family-Owned Companies

The description of the bygone era of relational psychological contracts between blue-collar workers and their employers in the textile industry and, until recently, at TISCO is somewhat different from the experiences of white-collar workers in family-owned organizations. Though loyalty and commitment to the employer are important features of white-collar workers' psychological contracts, other features reflect the unwritten, implicit nature of their jobs. First, personal favors such as taking the owner's family members to the airport or fulfilling other personal favors and errands are an unwritten part of their job description. Second, and more importantly, the implicit understanding is that the employee will never be at the top of the organization. As one senior non-family member employee of a family business said to me, "In a few years, I may get close to the top, but since my last name is not _____, I will *not* be *at* the top." In the same vein, Dhawan (1998) has stated that in a family-run organization, the father is the chairman, the sons and in some cases the wives and daughters are the board of directors, and nephews and other more distant relatives and nonrelatives of the same caste form the central groups of divisions of the same organization. Professional management in such businesses is of recent origin and peripheral in influence and often is only a sign of a family running out of sons and nephews.

To summarize, white-collar workers in privately owned organizations as described above have a distinct type of psychological contract, which can be thought of as a "qualified" relational contract. This contract is relational due to its open-ended terms, long-term relationship, and presence of loyalty and trust. In some cases, this relationship entails acceptance of two implicit rules coming from traditional Indian social structure: (a) Valued employees are those who are willing to perform personal favors, and (b) successful workers accept nepotism as part of the deal. However, the more global the market of the firm, the less likely it is that such traditional norms will predominate.

Since the early 1990s, India has liberalized its economy and encouraged private and foreign investment in the utility, telecommunication, and financial sectors, which either were the exclusive realm of the public sector or were dominated by the private sector until a few years ago (Ratnam, 1995). The implication of having many foreign companies in India is that foreign cultures are challenging the traditional work ethics and social values of the Indian society, and private family-owned companies are forced to become more professional as they face fierce competition from their foreign counterparts. Layoffs of employees, especially white-collar workers, are steadily on the rise.

One way to illustrate this phenomenon is through the story of India's largest business group, the House of Tatas (TISCO). The 129-year-old, $8-billion company has a presence in as many as 25 industries, ranging from information technology to atomic research to knitwear (Sachar Committee, 1978). Historically, Tata's strength has been its size—it has never been split apart or fragmented. With the liberalization of the economy, however, CEO Ratan Tata faces the biggest challenge of his career: keeping the company as a homogenized unit but at the same time developing a flexible organizational structure that can adapt to intense competition and the changed environment. In the last 5 years, Ratan Tata ousted a number of business heads and brought in outsiders who were not family members or did not have previous employment history with the company. Industry observers wondered whether Tata was a professional CEO with the heart of a family patriarch. Due to liberalization and subsequent slump in the economy, TISCO reduced its workforce by approximately 9,500; 15% of those downsized were executives (Aiyar, Abreu, Jain, & Rekhi, 1997).

As a result, the axe has fallen heavily on the white-collar middle and top management executives. Observing this trend, the industry experts Aiyar et al. (1997) remarked that "while the [laid-off] blue-collar workers enjoy legal and union protection against retrenchment, executive jobs are a lot more vulnerable."

Psychological Contracts and Multinational Corporations

The multinational companies that have entered the Indian markets usually are subsidiaries of parent companies from the United States, Japan, Germany, Sweden, and other European countries. The work culture, work ethics, and issues related to the employer-employee relationships of these subsidiaries are fairly similar to those of the parent companies. The Indian subsidiaries still must comply with the "law of the land" and modify their activities to fit the Indian environment and social values. Some features that set them apart from PSUs and privately run companies include pay based on performance, merit-based promotions, the promise of challenging jobs, opportunities to travel abroad, and—most of all—the promise of high salaries.

The market forces and the work culture prevalent in the multinational companies operating in the United States and other countries give them the flexibility to fire white- or blue-collar employees when faced with market fluctuations or economic downturns or when employees do not perform up to expectations. Indian culture places great importance on the notions of stability and job security, giving the Indian multinationals less flexibility to fire employees, especially blue-collar workers. However, other, softer options are available to multinational companies, such as offering a "golden handshake" and other voluntary retirement schemes to reduce dead weight and excess staffing.

White-Collar Workers and the Multinationals

For white-collar workers in multinational companies, the trends suggest a different story. Financial institutions that took a beating in Southeast Asia during the late 1990s typically curtailed their operations in India, causing a significant number of elite and highly qualified professionals to lose their jobs. Business magazines referred to the layoffs as a "bloodbath" and noted that the streets of India were "littered" with the resumes of executives seeking work ("Resumes on the Street," 1997, p. 205). *Business India* remarked that as difficult as the layoffs were "for those rendered jobless, it has been no less nerve-rattling for the employers giving out the pink slip(s)" (Bhardwaj, 1998, p. 138).

Though the working community was generally shocked by the mass down-sizings, those who lost their jobs received little sympathy, a reaction that is somewhat surprising and peculiar to the Indian culture. The reason attributed for this indifference was jealousy—those who were laid off from foreign institutional investor banks were on average earning about 20 times more than their former colleagues ("No Sympathy," 1997). After being downsized, many of these formerly highly paid elites became desperate and accepted jobs that entailed major salary reductions. Human resource directors at these companies were skeptical of their new employees' intentions to remain with a company that could not pay them half of what they had made at the foreign institutional investor banks.

Psychological Contracts and SSIs

The Indian trading community mainly includes wholesalers, retailers, and distributors of consumer products, garments, fresh produce, packaged foods and spices, machinery parts, and other goods. Psychological contracts in this sector of the market are not confined to the typical employer-employee or supervisor-subordinate relationship but are relevant to this chapter nevertheless. The way trade is carried out is reminiscent of the unconditional importance given to promise and its fulfillment by the Hindu/Islamic gods and the great Indian emperors of historic times. In the trading community, millions of dollars worth of trade takes place on the basis of a trader's *bol* (words) or a *vachan* (promise), and professional relationships develop over time among traders. For example, without exchanging money, formal documents, or collateral, a retailer of food grains can receive 100 tons of wheat from the wholesaler and delay payment until a later date. The only insurance that the wholesaler has is the reputation of the retailer. If the retailer does not keep his oral promise to pay back, the cheated wholesaler and most other grain wholesalers will ostracize the defaulting retailer. Keeping one's word can make or break the business in a trader's market.

The Indian government has consciously encouraged the creation of SSIs through tax breaks and flexible labor laws. SSIs generally employ fewer than 100 employees and include government contractors, agents, and companies that contract with public sector units, large private sector organizations, and multinational companies for various outsourced functions. Though SSI workers may not be unionized, the employers do feel the subtle pressure of the power that is bestowed on Indian blue-collar workers as a group. For example, I interviewed one of the partners of an SSI about how one of the partners had decided to retire and withdraw her share from a firm that had had 28 years of successful operation. She stated that the partners had to fulfill most of the non-union workforce's demands due to the sheer strength of their numbers. Workers could have resorted to making personal and physical threats against the partners and their families if their demands were not met adequately.

Another aspect to note here is the dominance of caste-specific employment in SSIs within rural and urban regions. For most of the migratory labor force, friends and relatives are the only source of job market opportunities. Therefore, workers employed at an SSI tend to suggest family or caste members as prospective workers. As a result, blue-collar workers in a company often are predominantly from the same caste community. This particular phenomenon can also be observed in the factories of PSUs and privately run organizations. Kannappan (1983) described the labor market of Calcutta (an east Indian town and capital of the state of West Bengal) as follows:

> In jute manufacturing in Bihar and Uttar Pradesh [two states adjoining West Bengal], Muslims are dominant in the manual worker category while Bengalis [natives of West Bengal] are dominant in the white-collar [engineering] and technical categories. Engineering, chemicals, rubber, printing, banking, and insurance are also dominated by Bengalis. (p. 63)

Zone of Negotiability and Indian Work Environment

The importance of an oral promise, subtle labor influences on the SSI sector, and caste-specific job searches and employment are distinctive features related to employment in the trading community and the SSIs' freedom to negotiate contract terms. To get a better understanding of the employment relationship as it exists in the Indian work environment, it is important to know the zone of negotiability in other private sector and public undertakings. Broadly speaking, given the strong influence of labor unions in shaping the employment contracts of blue-collar workers, there is little freedom to negotiate idiosyncratic contracts. In contrast, because white-collar jobs, especially those in the private sector, are not regulated by stringent labor laws, managers and workers have a broader zone for negotiating individualized contracts. In the past, this freedom was of limited usefulness as a "fair" motivating mechanism due to (as discussed in the earlier sections) the presence of nepotism, favoritism, subjectivity, and ad hocism in management's hiring, promotion, and day-to-day activities. However, it was in the private sector industries, especially the family businesses, trading communities, that relationship-oriented, idiosyncratic psychological contracts emerged in the past and still exist to some extent. These psychological contracts reflect some of the key features of the Indian socioeconomic milieu in which the employment relationship is embedded. (Please refer to Table 6.1.).

Employment Relationships in the Unorganized Sector

Approximately 90% of the Indian workforce is employed in the unorganized sector, which consists of primarily private sector companies employing fewer than 10 workers (Venkatchalam & Singh, 1982). This sector covers occupations such as agriculture, carpentry, weaving, and other skill-based crafts. As very few labor laws govern employment in the unorganized sector, the employer-employee relationship is often parochial and imbalanced. In extreme cases, work relationships resemble oppressive practices of the past, in which the landless laborers and the lower-caste members were exploited by

TABLE 6.1 Psychological Contracts and the Indian Work Environment

India-Specific Psychological Contract Issues	Public Sector Units	Family Businesses	Private Sector Units		
			Trading and SSIs	MNCs	
Blue-collar workers	Hiring based on "reservation policy" for underprivileged classes; "employment by birth" Labor unions negotiate the contract on behalf of workers Labor and industrial laws exert a strong shaping influence on employer-employee relations Promise of "cradle-to-grave" employment Narrow zone of negotiability	Till mid-20th century: Feeling of being part of a big family "Generation-to-generation employment" Relations going beyond job-related reciprocity Long-term relational contract From mid-20th century to date: Trend toward less relational contract Sense of belongingness still existent Narrow zone of negotiability	Trading community: Trading based on "oral promise" and trader's reputation SSIs: Workers not unionized, but their sheer strength shapes employment relations Evidence of communal employment (i.e., job searach through employed relatives)	Management has limited freedom to fire workers due to legal protection given to workers by law	

India-Specific Psychological Contract Issues	Public Sector Units	Private Sector Units		
		Family Businesses	Trading and SSIs	MNCs
White-collar workers	Gradual promotion; pay based on seniority Strong job security Quid pro quo attitude Explicit, formal transactional type of contract Limited influence of unions Narrow zone of negotiability	Nepotism exists Non-family members cannot reach the top Implicit, open-ended relational contract Non-work-related activities an implicit part of job description Not unionized in most companies Wider zone of negotiability but limited applicability due to biased management practices	Not applicable	Culture similar to parent MNC but modified to suit local social climate

rich farmers, feudal lords, and the socially elite class. On average, workers in the unorganized sector have very little power—legal, social, or economic—to influence their employment relationships, so they tolerate the terms and conditions set forth by the employers to sustain themselves and their families.

EMPLOYMENT RELATIONSHIPS

A large-scale, quantitative study undertaken by Sharma (1987) supports this chapter's description of psychological contracts in India's public and private sectors. The study focused on how different personnel policies and practices (which Sharma referred to as the overall "organizational climate") affected supervisor-management relationships and labor-management relationships.

Results from the 51 organizations studied indicated that Indian employers and managers were willing to provide adequate security and attractive monetary benefits to their employees but that participative management and training and education were relatively neglected. Supervisors perceived management to be relatively objective but not strong in handling grievances. In the case of workers, the results regarding grievance procedures were just the opposite. Sharma speculated that workers' perception of good grievance procedures might be due to statutory mandates and the presence of fairly strong labor unions.

The trend described above is also found in separate analyses of private and public sector organizations. However, the extent to which different organizational climate dimensions matter is different. In the case of security, welfare, and monetary benefits, the public and private sectors fared the same, but on the other dimensions, such as advancement and participatory management, the public sector companies consistently rated lower than their private counterparts.

This research indicates that employers pay attention to such aspects as welfare, safety, and money but that both sectors—especially the public sector—neglect employees' social and psychological needs. In the context of Maslow's (1943) hierarchy of motivation theory, this finding implies that the Indian firms have done a good job of fulfilling employees' basic needs but more effort is needed when it comes to fulfilling higher-order needs such as affiliation and self-actualization.

PSYCHOLOGICAL CONTRACT
VIOLATION IN INDIA

The concept of violating the psychological contracts of blue-collar workers in the organized sector is not very relevant in India. Labor unions negotiate collective agreements on behalf of groups of workers. Therefore, the notion of idiosyncratic, voluntary, or implicit promises exchanged between an individual worker and the management—the defining characteristic of a psychological contract between an employer and an employee—is almost nonexistent for blue-collar workers in India. Note that employment relationships in some family-owned businesses and some SSIs would be an exception.

White-collar workers employed in PSUs and private firms, even if they feel that their employers have not kept their side of the deal, are less likely to express their perceptions of violation due to their low mobility, low market-ability, and preference for stability. White-collar workers employed in multi-nationals, especially in the financial sector, tell a different story regarding violations. The recent downsizing described earlier left many workers disappointed. Promises of recognition, challenging jobs, and unmatched salaries are now perceived as empty. An interview with one laid-off stockbroker revealed that his overwhelming feelings were of betrayal and embarrassment. He felt betrayed because he had given up a stable, prestigious job to join an investment bank that had laid him off just 4 months after promising him a dream job, and he felt embarrassed because friends and ex-colleagues mocked him once he was no longer a sought-after employee earning 20 times more than what they were earning.

CONCLUSION

Employment history and the prevailing social and legal climate influence employer-employee relationships in India today. Due to the exploitative nature of employment in the formerly caste-ruled society and the subsequent formulation of protective labor policies, the employment relationship has taken on a meaning that is untrue as compared to the concepts of psychological contracts and their violation that are common in organizational research. The main objective of this chapter was to highlight those unique features of the Indian employment relationship as shaped by the socioeconomic and legal climate and thus to make the study of international psychological contracts more varied and insightful.

NOTES

1. A report by the Reserve Bank of India (1979) outlined the Indian employment structure and the economic development of the country since independence.

2. A committee formed by the government to study the employment climate in India.

REFERENCES

Aiyar, V. S., Abreu, R., Jain, S., & Rekhi, S. (1997, September 8). In the firing lane. *India Today.*

Bhardwaj, N. (1998, December 29-January 11). Dealing with the downside. *Business India,* pp. 138-140.

Dhawan, R. (1998, January 7-February 6). Can Tata survive? *India Today,* Business section.

Johri, C. K. (1992). *Industrialism and employment system in India.* New York: Oxford University Press.

Kannappan, S. (1983). *Employment problems and urban labor market in developing nations.* Ann Arbor: University of Michigan, Graduate School of Business Administration.

Lambert, R. D. (1963). *Workers, factories and social change in India.* Bombay: Asia Publishing House.

Maslow, A. H. (1943). A theory of human motivation. *Psychology Review, 50,* 370-396.

Mukharji, P. B. (1969). *Social responsibilities of business: Report of the Study Group of the Calcutta Seminar.* New York: Oxford University Press.

Myers, C. A., & Kannappan, S. (1970). *Industrial relations in India.* New York: Asia Publishing House.

No sympathy [Editorial]. (1997, December 23). *Times of India.*

Ratnam, C. S. V. (1995). Economic liberalization and the transformation of industrial relations policies in India. In A. Verma, T. A. Kochan, & L. D. Russel (Eds.), *Employment relations in the growing Asian economies* (Chap. 8). New York: Routledge.

Reddy, V. (1998). *Psychological contracts in India.* Unpublished class presentation, Carnegie Mellon University.

Reserve Bank of India. (1979). New Delhi: Author.

Resumes on the street. (1997, December 15-28). *Business India,* "Executive Track" section, p. 205.

Rousseau, D. M. (1995). *Psychological contracts in organizations: Understanding written and unwritten agreements.* Thousand Oaks, CA: Sage.

Sachar Committee. (1978). Report.

Sharma, B. R. (1973). The Indian industrial worker: His origin, experience, and destiny. *Economic and Political Weekly, 8*(23), M38-M43.

Sharma, B. R. (1987). *Not by bread alone: A study of organizational climate and employer-employee relations in India.* New Delhi: Shree Ram Center for Industrial Relations and Human Resources.

Vaid, K. N. (1968). *The new worker.* Bombay: Asia Publishing House.

Venkatchalam, V., & Singh, R. (1982). *The political and labor climate in India* (Multinational Industrial Relations Series, No. 8, Asian Series).

7

Psychological Contracts in Israel

Moshe Krausz

People are the image of their homeland's landscape.
Tchernichovksy (1990)

Human beings are close to themselves [see their own good first].
Talmud, Sanhedrin

The unasked question posed to the writers of each chapter can be phrased as "Are there unique characteristics of psychological work contracts in your country?" The attempt to answer this question in this chapter is not straightforward. Like any other nation, Israel has many unique features, but at the same time, it shares many traits with other nations and cultures. The Israelis, as individuals, also share various traits with each other and with people around the world, but like any other individuals, all of them are "universes in their own right" and have their own peculiarities that render them different from anybody in their own country as well as from any individual elsewhere in the world. If a contract has at least two parties, the complex interactions between each pair of partners are further multiplied. Therefore, although this chapter attempts to present commonalties, it also points out subgroup and individual differences. Any attempt to draw generalized conclusions about psychological work contracts in Israel must bear in mind these cautions.

ISRAEL: NATION, RELIGION, AND STATE

Israel is a small country located on the boundary between Asia and Europe. This location was appealing and strategically important to ancient empires and remains so to more modern powers. In addition, it is a religious center for three major religions, Judaism, Christianity, and Islam. The country is encircled by Arab nations that, despite some recent changes, are still essentially hostile to Israel. Even Egypt and Jordan, the two Arab nations that have signed a peace treaty with Israel maintain what Israelis refer to as a "cold peace."

Although the state was established in its current form just 50 years ago, Israelites had lived in the region for many years until they were exiled and scattered in numerous locations around the globe for close to 2,000 years. The geographical location itself has been a politically important territory over which nations have fought throughout the ages. From a cultural perspective, both Europe and Asia have played an important role in shaping the unique characteristics of the modern state. Influences from European, Asian, and African cultures are visible, and the social and cultural framework includes both Western and Eastern elements.

The element of "promise," which is considered to be a key aspect of psychological contracts, was rooted in this nation from its beginning. We may say that the very existence of the nation began as a psychological contract: Israelis live in the "Promised Land," a divine promise to this nation, as described in the Bible and in both ancient and more recent scholarly writings. Accordingly, Israel has a long history as a nation but a very short presence as a modern, reborn state. The nearly 2,000 years when Israel's people were dispersed among other nations and religions have shaped the current state and the heterogeneity of Israel. Thus, its social and cultural heritage has accumulated throughout several millennia. Any discussion of Israeli psychological contracts cannot overlook that heterogeneity.

The impact of history on Israel's culture has been dramatic in all respects. Although this chapter does not purport to present a comprehensive and representative historical account of the nation, some additional historical and sociological notes are needed to understand the nature of today's realities of promises and psychological contracts.

Cultural Diversity

Life in widely separated communities among different nations and religions led to the absorption of diverse values, patterns of thought, life outlooks, and habits from the different communities where Jews had lived. The return of large numbers of their ancestors to the historical Promised Land began in the second half of the 19th century and continued following the establishment of the renewed state in 1948. Some of the most extreme differences within Israel today are between Jews whose origins are European or American (Ashkenazi Jews) and those who lived in Arab and Muslim cultures in Africa and Asia (Sephardic Jews). Most recently, large waves of emigration to Israel came from the different cultures of former Soviet Union and from Ethiopia.

This varied cultural heritage created differences in the general perceptions, attitudes, behavioral patterns, and work values of Jews. Moreover, Jews in many countries, particularly in Europe, were barred from public sector positions, leading many of them to start trades, crafts, and small businesses. Those who resettled in Israel often faced situations they had not experienced before, such as work in unfamiliar occupations, including agricultural jobs and public sector office work. Most had never worked in an organization and therefore had to adapt their attitudes and beliefs to this new kind of occupation.

National and Religious Diversity

Another significant fact related to heterogeneity of psychological contracts in Israel is that the country is a small national and religious entity surrounded by huge Arab and Muslim nations. A state of war still prevails between Israel and most of its neighboring countries, although even as these lines are being written, massive efforts are being made to achieve agreements between Israel and the Palestinians. This has implications for psychological work contracts in at least two ways. First, a large Arab-Muslim minority has lived in Israel since its establishment. Although they are Israeli citizens, issues of dual loyalty—to their state and to the surrounding Muslim brethren—have created problems of equality and fairness with regard to their employment. Second, large numbers of Arabs live in the occupied territories that are on the current agenda for peace efforts with the Palestinians. Those Arabs are not Israeli citizens, but many of them earn their living by working in Israel. Those human resources are instrumental for both Israel and the Palestinians. In fact, Palestinian workers are very important to several Israeli industries, such as manufacturing, construction, and unskilled services. The operation of some sites and factories depends highly on their work. From the perspective of employment contracts, Israeli Arabs and the Palestinians, both of whom are mostly Muslim, are two populations that have different civic rights and different objective and subjective characteristics of the contracts under which they work.

An additional category of objective and psychological contracts in Israel pertains to the growing number of foreign workers. Although many of these foreign workers are legally staying and working in Israel, others are illegal. Under the Migrant Workers Treaty of the International Labor Organization, which Israel signed, foreign workers are entitled to all payments and benefits as local workers. They work under the labor laws that prevail in the host nation regarding such issues as holidays, working hours, health insurance, and accident insurance. On the basis of that, foreign workers who come to Israel and stay legally are entitled to all rights and benefits that the law provides to Israeli citizens. The problem lies in their relatively weak position to fend for their rights and request the provision of all entitlements. Many do not know their rights and are, in general, in an inferior position (due, in part, to weak mastery of the local language). Ironically, in some respects, illegal foreign workers are in a somewhat better position to change their workplace. The legal foreign workers are brought by labor contractors for a prespecified job and cannot change that position unless they or their contractor receive official permission.

Most foreign workers are employed in construction, domestic services, and health care jobs. They come from various places, though many are from east European and southeast Asian countries. The presence of large numbers of foreign workers affects the formal working contracts as well as the psychological contracts of many Israeli citizens. The lower pay to foreign workers and the wider flexibility afforded to their employers have an adverse affect on employment contracts for Israeli workers too; many risk losing their jobs to the cheap and easy-to-replace foreign labor force.

Judaism and Psychological Contracts

The laws of the Jewish religion, which have developed over thousands of years, are an important influence on current trends and societal structures. The Mishnah is an elaboration on Biblical laws, and the Talmud, which expands on the Mishnah, contains the scholastic debates over Jewish laws regarding most realms and stages of human life. Throughout the years, Jewish laws have been interpreted to address the changing realities of life in the Diaspora and, later, life in the reborn independent Jewish state.

Jewish law pervades all realms of life, not just the relations between man and God. It affects interpersonal and intergroup relationships as well as what in modern terminology would be called person-organization issues. These include the obligations and entitlements of employees and their employers as well as appropriate ways of conducting business transactions.

These ancient religious writings had a lot to say about the value of work itself. Any work is generally considered to be better than idleness, with the exception of work that is socially unacceptable or disrespectful. Sayings such as "Idleness is the source of lechery and boredom" (Talmud, Ketubot) and "Torah [Bible] studies that are not accompanied by work are ultimately wasted and lead to sin" (Mishnah, Avot, Chapter 2) exemplify what today are known as Judeo-Christian work values. Those normative statements were accompanied by stories of the great ancient scholars who—in addition to religious studies— also worked in crafts and menial jobs to provide the basic means of existence for their families.

Jewish laws dictate the proper conduct between employer and employee and require honesty, fairness, and prompt payment of wages. The laws describe detailed behavioral patterns when disputes arise between employers and employees. Today, work is often arranged around triangular contracts involving employees, external labor agencies, and client companies; in the times when these laws were written, God was considered, in a way, to be an additional external party to contracts between employers and employees. Exemplifying this arrangement are the laws concerning employees' entitlement to pray to their God during a workday. It is interesting to note that in some of today's industrial factories in Egypt, where the working day is extremely long, the number of paid and unpaid prayer breaks is part of the formal employment contract. In Israel, such agreements are, most likely, less formal. The issue is also less cardinal because Jewish religion requires three prayers daily as opposed to the five required by the Islam. Acknowledging that Jews lived in different countries and diverse cultural settings, the Talmud also states that employment relations are affected by specific environments and may differ: "Everything is based on the customs of the country."

The Talmud deals in breadth with breach of contract. The party violating a contract is regarded as the offender, and if the dispute comes before a Jewish court for ruling, he or she will have to compensate the other party. In addition, God, as a hidden party to all contracts, is expected to punish the violating party, particularly when protection of the socially weak and the needy is concerned.

An interesting question in our time is whether individuals accepting the Jewish religion and adhering to its laws have different work values with respect to psychological contracts. A recent study conducted in Israel (Sagie, 1993) compared the work values of religious and nonreligious youth. Although the study pertained to entitlements as well as obligations, only the latter were measured. The findings supported the hypothesis that religiosity is positively associated with perceptions of self obligations. Statistically significant differences between religious and nonreligious respondents were found mainly with respect to intrinsic variables, whereas three extrinsic items dealing with values that were not anchored in the Jewish religious law or ethic (e.g., expending of effort in the presence of idle coworkers) did not differentiate between the groups.

Socialistic Trends

Large numbers of Jewish people began returning to their historical homeland toward the end of the 19th century, and more so after World War II. Early influences on the spirit and structure of the state-to-be came from people who emigrated before and after the communist revolution, with the goal of building a society based on equality and modesty. The development of the kibbutz, a cooperative and egalitarian agricultural society, rested on socialistic values and the basic concept guiding kibbutz life: Everyone contributes as much as he or she can and is entitled to get as much as he or she needs. This was a collective psychological contract between an individual and his or her commune, which was in a sense truly a contract between the individual and him- or herself as part of the collective community. A. D. Gordon advocated a "religion of work" as a substitute for the religious values and practice against which the socialists had revolted, proclaiming that hard work is a value in and of itself rather than a means of realizing other values. Gordon's principles served as a guiding value for the kibbutz movement, which he helped to pioneer.

Since the establishment of the modern Israeli state, its culture has been strongly influenced by historic Jewish thinking and laws, as well as the more recent trends of the 19th century. These factors have influenced labor legislation, government policies, labor relations, and structural mechanisms in modern Israel, all of which will be described in the following sections.

STRUCTURAL CHARACTERISTICS OF ISRAELI LABOR RELATIONS AND PSYCHOLOGICAL CONTRACTS

In 1948, the newly established state began to absorb a large influx of Holocaust survivors from Europe and other immigrants from Asian and African countries. The nation's two most immediate concerns have been housing and financial means of survival, through work. The government enacted policies granting every person the right to a job. In addition, although labor relations were mainly governed by collective bargaining during the early years of the new state, an intricate web of labor laws developed as time went on (Ben-Israel, 1990). These laws, combined with a primarily labor party government and a strong union system (in which many unions banded together to form the Histadrut organization), created a belief that employment would last for a lifetime. Firing employees who are covered by collective agreements has always been difficult, whether a firm desires to terminate a single employee or to downsize its entire workforce. Labor laws requiring severance pay and the power of unions to negotiate even higher payments sustained the idea that everyone was safe from layoffs. This feeling—in reality, a myth—was known as *Keviut,* meaning "permanency" or "tenure." The Histadrut, which at its peak had influence over close to 90% of organized employees, was able to nurture and support the workforce's belief in *Keviut,* which prevailed until the late 1980s. At that time, the labor relations system was shattered by several massive downsizing programs in the government-owned defense industries and in some companies owned by the Histadrut itself. This indicated that the loss of job security had penetrated even the union-owned industries, not just the private and public sectors.

It should be noted that the concept of *Keviut* still is important, although its value is often psychological rather than practical; in short, employees still desire tenure even when it has no real "teeth," or is seemingly unnecessary. One example of the latter case occurred in a medium-sized organization whose employees were mostly organized in the Histadrut, in which about 10% of the labor force had never gained tenure. Although these workers were laid off near the end of their annual employment contract, the company would rehire them for another year almost immediately. Since this arrangement had prevailed for more than 13 years, it would have been logical for these employees to feel like permanent workers. Nevertheless, they constantly pressured the management to change their contract by granting them the desired *Keviut,* despite the devaluation of that concept. This behavior is explained in the psychological contract literature, which suggests that employees who believe in lifelong employment have a more relaxed attitude toward work that centers on their entitlements rather than their obligations toward their employers (Rousseau, 1995). From the employers' perspective, labor laws and strong unions create many obligations toward employees, with apparently few reciprocal obligations on the part of employees. Israeli employers have claimed that many employees are like a nail without a head: "Once in, you can never remove it."

Tenure continues to be a viable issue despite radical events and changes that have occurred since the mass layoffs of the late 1980s. Studies by Hartley, Jacobson, Klandermans, and van Vuuren (1991) indicate a marked increase in job insecurity in Israel associated with those downsizings. It should be pointed out that the dual role of the Histadrut as both an employer and an employee representative has always been an issue for debate. Several years ago, a clearer separation was made between those conflicting roles, and currently the Histadrut is mostly dealing with employee representation in collective agreements rather than as an employer itself.

Another social structure that influences psychological contracts in Israel is the country's generally high litigation rate. Litigation related to contract violation has also been on the rise over the years. The reasons for that phenomenon are not easy to untangle but probably reflect the complex historical trends noted earlier, accompanied by diminishing social solidarity and diminishing reliance on informal social mechanisms such as the resolution of disputes within families or social units. Orally expressed promises are being replaced by formally sanctioned obligations and contracts that, when breached, often require a more objective third party such as a mediator or labor court. The high number of lawyers in the country compared to many developed countries (20,000 out of a population of about 6 million, of which a high proportion consists of very young people) leads to more litigation in cases of contract violation. Informal statistics show that the number of lawyers in Israel equals the number in Japan. The rising number of court complaints also may be due to the fact that more contracts—formal as well as psychological—are violated. The declining power of labor unions and the increasing volatility of business enterprises builds pressures on organizations to violate their previous promises and obligations. However, it must be noted that despite the decline of organized labor's power, the unions are still viable, as they demonstrated several times in recent months when the Histadrut declared work stoppages in several vital industries such as electric utilities and public transportation. Strikes are an increasingly common phenomenon in Israel, and although they cause inconveniences and draw many complaints, they are accepted rather calmly by a majority of the people. When a group strikes, it expects and often receives support from nonstriking labor sectors, either verbally or through active participation on picket lines. This is a product of a norm of solidarity and expected reciprocity between striking and nonstriking sectors.

Though labor courts were initially established in response to societal needs, their very existence incites even more appeals. Statistics show that a vast majority of cases heard in labor courts are related to individual worker complaints rather than violations of collective agreements. Whereas the personal cases are introduced by employees who feel unfairly treated, the few cases related to collective agreements are brought by employers in an attempt to forestall worker strikes.

New Employment Contracts in Israel

Globalized markets, worldwide competition, high volatility, and an increased need for flexibility have affected Israel like most other countries. Organizations have been seeking employment contracts that enable them to achieve a better fit between operational demands and the size of the labor force. This has resulted in fewer collective agreements and an expansion of individually negotiated, fixed-term contracts and externalized or contingent contracts, including outsourcing, part-time work, and the use of outside labor agencies. These practices have become common even in companies and utilities where the large majority of the employees have collective agreements.

The common element in all of the practices described above is the move from relational to transactional contracts. This shift has been particularly dramatic because of the young country's historically high prevalence of collective agreements and powerful labor unions. The trend toward transactional contracts is particularly problematic in Israel, where the recent influx of immigrants from the former Soviet Union and from Ethiopia coincides with the ideal of providing work to every person. Despite this ideal, the illusory belief in lifelong employment collapsed within a relatively brief period. Moreover, unemployment has further reduced the sense of social solidarity, a crucially important factor in a nation surrounded by enemies. Achieving and maintaining social solidarity is a difficult task even in relatively stable environments; it is particularly difficult in Israel's geopolitical environment, which allows for very little stability or security. The social fabric may be at risk when individualism replaces collectivism as the leading value in society. Still, this bleak outlook has to be balanced—collectivism and individualism have existed side by side throughout the Jewish history. Though we seemingly have "one Bible and one Law," it has been long indicated that there are "70 faces to the Bible." This has always been the case when a cross-sectional outlook is adopted: Different schools and varied interpretations of Jewish laws and customs have always coexisted. From a historical perspective, different generations have adapted laws and behavioral norms to their unique needs and to the changing environments. Although each of us may be seen as a solo player, we are nevertheless part of a large orchestra, in which, according to the Talmud, "All Israelites are responsible for each other" (Shavuot).

New and emergent contracts within organizations, particularly the increasing employment of external employees, are a potential source of problems and raise issues that have not yet been sufficiently explored by empirical studies in

Israel and elsewhere. In the past, most or all employees in Israeli organizations had similar contracts, which were essentially relational. This was congruent with the socialist and collectivist preference for minimal reward differentials. The current realities create two (or more) employment statuses within organizations, including those who are part of the family—the core and permanent "internal" employees—and others who are outsiders or "externals," although Israeli studies show that external employees do not necessarily receive lower pay or fewer extrinsic and intrinsic rewards (Cohen & Haberfeld, 1993; Krausz, Brandwein, & Fox, 1995). In addition, a new division of labor has been developing within organizations. A U.S. study showed that some roles and responsibilities have shifted to the internal employees, leading to more enriched jobs, while roles that do not require the same level of knowledge have been given to external employees (Davis-Blake & Uzzi, 1993; Pearce, 1993). Although no empirical data are available to corroborate it, those changes are also a potential source of stress for the internals.

The two-tiered employee status may also create problems for internal employees with relational contracts. For these core employees, working side by side with externals threatens their own jobs, as well as presenting a constant threat of further increases in transactional contracts at the expense of relational ones. However, only anecdotal evidence can be provided for this assumption. First, local labor unions within organizations are objecting to the expectation that they will recruit contingent employees in greater numbers. The higher the proportion of contingent workers, the weaker the local union's power. The level of sensitivity and secrecy regarding the use of internal versus external employees is so high that researchers interested in examining the social and psychological effects of using contingent employees are not very welcome. Even a single survey question about workers' employment contracts raises an immediate objection and is considered a risk to the internal labor relations system.

Israeli labor relations law contains a rarely used option to employ both permanent and temporary employees under the same collective agreement. In such a case, all employees are represented by the local union. The parties to this are required to negotiate honestly and fairly; it is not a plot between the employer and the union but rather a sincere agreement dictated by the employer's operational needs. The union is held accountable to represent both groups of employees.

With regard to the employment of external employees, Israel shares more features with the European Union nations than with the United States. Europe and Israel have similar laws and regulations concerning employment. One recently enacted Israeli law regulates the operation of external human resource agencies, affecting such issues as the certification of external agencies, their obligations to their employees, and the status of the agency employees in the company that hires their services. Even prior to this legislation, state labor laws relating to benefits such as severance compensation and working hours applied to all employees, including agency employees. The new law adds protection for those employees.

The new law's effects on psychological contracts are already noticeable. First, the law prohibits firms from employing the same person through an external agency for more than 3 years. If employment is extended beyond 3 years, the external employee is entitled to become part of the internal core labor force. Thus, employers who are pleased with the work of certain individuals but have no additional permanent positions are caught in a conflict between their need to motivate external workers and their inability to reward them with permanent employment. This conflict sometimes leads management to make promises to the external employee during the 3-year period that are likely to be violated later, inconveniencing and upsetting both parties. I have encountered client companies that refuse to allow the collection of data from employees of external agencies because it might appear that they were part of the core labor force.

Are There Unique Israeli Features of Psychological Contracts?

In the Hebrew language, the root for the English word *promise* is itself very enlightening for the current contract context. It means "guaranteed" in the sense that once a promise has been explicitly or implicitly made, one may rely on its fulfillment. In that sense, a promise may be viewed as an obligation or a contractual agreement to act on what has been verbally uttered. An additional meaning of the Hebrew word for *promise* is "safe, calm, and relaxed," implying that once a promise has been made, the party to whom it was made may be safe and calm knowing that it will be performed.

In daily life, however, the context in which a promise is made is crucial. The context may determine whether the receiver of the promise truly feels safe that it will be fulfilled. Even the size of the party receiving the promise can be significant: A promise made to a single person is more personal and private and is probably weaker than a promise made to a group, a community, a nation, or the world. The larger audience can be seen as a body of witnesses to whom violation of a promise would be more difficult and offensive. An additional important factor in determining whether a promise may be perceived as a guarantee or obligation is the quality of the ongoing relationship between the parties. A history of trust and fairness or a perception of trustworthiness that has not yet been tested may be crucial.

The answer to the question presented in this section's title is not straightforward. It is unrealistic to expect any nation to have a single common psychological contract. The unique features of psychological contracts are affected by at least three layers of influence: national/cultural, subcultural/subgroup, and individual.

The first and most fundamental layer is national, in which common cultural and religious features affect the expectations of employees and employers and their interpretations of promises, obligations, and entitlements. Attempts to characterize the Israeli people in general and employees in particular as sharing certain features face the risk of superficiality. Nevertheless, such efforts are common and quite natural attempts to gain understanding of a country's people. Values are conceptualized and measured in varied ways, some pertaining to the general importance of life values for individuals and others focusing on work-related values. Accordingly, it is difficult to describe Israelis in terms of major values that motivate them for two reasons. First is the great diversity of concepts, approaches, and methodologies that have been used, and second is the apparent lack of empirical studies using a representative sample of the Israeli population. Even if such studies had been conducted, the differences among subgroups and subcultures would probably be as large as the similarities. Studies of general life values as well as the work values of Israelis (Abu-Saad & Isralowitz, 1998; Elizur & Sagie, 1999; Prince-Gibson & Schwartz, 1998; Sagy, 1997; Schwartz, Verkasalo, Anotonovsky, & Sagiv, 1997) provide only a rough idea of what one might define as "Israeli values." With those caveats in mind, the findings of some empirical studies are still of interest.

Several studies have used the Schwartz Value Scale, which measures 10 values. Five emphasize harmony, such as conformity, security, and benevolence, and five challenge harmony, such as achievement, hedonism, and self-direction. On average, Israelis were found to be relatively high in self-direction, benevolence, hedonism, security, and achievement and to be lowest on the tradition and power values. Other studies found that health, happiness, love, and security topped the list of general life values and that most of the highest work value ratings were given to intrinsic values such as job interest, responsibility, fair supervision, growth, and independent use of skills and abilities. The studies reported no gender differences in value importance or in work values and no culture-based differences in work values between young native-born Israelis and Russian immigrants.

Despite indications of growing individualism and a decline in national solidarity, a sense of sharing is still strong in Israel. The following anecdote from the employment realm is an illustration of that. Several years ago, a small high-tech company changed from a system of universally defined levels of payment to individually negotiated personal contracts. The company's president asked employees to keep their contracts and reward packages confidential. However, minutes after employees received envelopes containing the details of their deals, a long line formed at the president's office. Each individual wanted to know why they received lower wages than some of their colleagues. This anecdote highlights a sense of sharing and solidarity in which coworkers disclose their income level to one another. The norm of sharing with others still prevails to some extent. In fact, open and detailed discussions of personal rewards and benefits are a favorite topic at informal social meetings both within and away from the workplace and between friends who work in different companies.

This social solidarity and sense of togetherness are also expressed in low power distances and high informality operating even within seemingly formal relations. People queuing in line will often open a discussion with somebody they have never met before or make a personal comment to a perfect stranger. The direct appeal to a company's president is another indication of those relationships. For good or bad, the creeping of the informal into the formal is characteristic of Israeli society. Even under collective contracts and universalistic norms, many Israelis will seek ways to establish their unique aspects, often with some success.

An additional national feature of employment contracts pertains to the role of the family in employment relations. Either through legislation or via collective agreements, firms may treat employees' families as "partial employees" and take their needs into consideration. The family has always occupied an important role in Jewish religion and heritage and still plays a strong role today, despite some recent changes. The decline of the world Jewish population due to the millions who perished in the Holocaust spurred many to raise larger families on average, a trend that is now on the decline, although it is still higher, on average, than that of most Western countries. Labor legislation provides various benefits for women who give birth. First, they are entitled to 3 months' paid maternity leave. Moreover, if they choose to, they are entitled to an additional 9 months of unpaid leave with guaranteed return to the same job level. More recent legislation allows the transfer of these rights to the father. Laws and collective contracts also permit mothers of children younger than 6 years old to work slightly shorter hours.

Those benefits sometimes create problems. Because they demand extra effort and energies from employers and create discontinuities in the work flow, employers often seek ways to curb or avoid them, even if their tactics are illegal. One way of violating the requirements is through the process of employee recruitment—for example, by asking female candidates whether they are pregnant or intend to become pregnant in the near future. A positive answer may harm their chances of being hired. It is important to reiterate that such practices clearly violate the laws governing equal hiring and employment.

The second layer affecting Israeli psychological contracts consists of the unique influences of subcultures and subgroups. Values and perceptions shared by subgroup members may supplement more universal national perceptions or may at times deviate from or even negate certain elements on the broader national level. The number of such subgroups or subcultures is huge. A few Israeli examples include kibbutz members, people sharing military experiences, those who share a country of birth (Israel, Russia, Ethiopia, United States, Iraq, Morocco, etc.), ultra-orthodox groups, businesspeople in the diamond industry, graduates of the same class, and handicapped war veterans. Each of those groups shares certain features that affect members' attitudes, behavior, mutual expectations, and perceived obligations. One example that highlights these effects can be found in Israel's large and prominent diamond industry. In this industry, business transactions of tens or hundreds of thousands of dollars are closed by shaking hands and uttering two words: *mazal* and *bracha* (actually pronounced as "mazel" and "bruche"). The meanings of those two Hebrew words are "luck" and "blessing," but in their unique pronunciation they are actually the Yiddish equivalent words (Yiddish is a unique mix of Hebrew and German that developed and has been used for many years in eastern Europe). The utterance of those two words is considered better and more binding that any written or legal contract, and violation of those spoken words is sanctioned by unwritten rules shared only by businesspeople within such trades. Another example of subgroup-level characteristics is the attempts of some groups, such as kibbutz members or emigrants from the same country, to settle incidents of disagreement, offense, or even criminal behavior within the group rather than submitting the case to legal authorities.

Common subcultures also create shared perceptions of time and expectations and a shared feeling of being offended when promises are violated. A common behavioral pattern observed among Jewish Ethiopian people who settled in Israel in recent years is their unique interpretation of spoken agreements. For example, an employer of non-Ethiopian origin may say to an employee, "I want to meet with you this coming Monday at 10 a.m." The employee may know that he is unable to make the appointment, but the code of respect to people in authority positions requires that he or she not object (apparently, the word *no* is nonexistent in the Amhara language). Instead, the Ethiopian person may show up at 10 a.m. on a different day without saying anything; in his or her view, he or she has fulfilled the obligation despite changing the terms in accordance to his or her perceptions or needs. Another example comes from the subculture of ultra-orthodox communities, which have particularly interesting expectations and obligations. Some of these groups live and work as semiclosed communities. Among themselves, verbal promises are as good as formal or legal contracts, and the communities have mechanisms to enforce compliance and punish violations. In relations with the majority culture or other subcultures, similar promises are much less binding.

The third—and the least shared—layer of influence on psychological contracts is the individual level. People are affected by hereditary factors, early family experiences, social experiences, and labor market experiences. All of these things are unique to a particular individual and are not shared with members of the nation, the subculture, or any social groups to which they belong. The various factors influence individuals' perceptions of their employment obligations and entitlements, and each person has a unique threshold for perceiving what constitutes a breach of his or her psychological contract.

Commitment and Organizational Citizenship Behavior

Today's employment and organizational realities have interesting implications for psychological contracts. The traditional outlook on organizations assumed the existence of a two-way commitment: Employers fulfilled their obligations to employees and expected that the employees would reciprocate by showing loyalty and commitment to the organization. Anecdotally, it seems that many of today's Israeli employees feel that organizations expect them not only to fulfill their basic job obligations but also to demonstrate extrarole and organizational citizenship behavior. At the same time, employers seem to demonstrate little loyalty to their employees.

Two recent articles pertaining to the U.S. labor market echo this transition. In the first, a consultant and experienced company manager declares the end of loyalty (Carbone, 1997). Loyalty, in his experience and opinion, has become self-loyalty rather than faithfulness to agreements with others and should be replaced by enlightened self-interest. A second article asserts that forced overtime is an increasing, problematic trend in various U.S. industries (Babbar & Aspelin, 1997). Employees feel that they are coerced to give more hours to their organization than they would like. Many Israeli employees feel the same way; these workers would prefer to spend more time with their families or friends than at work, but they feel powerless to rebel. Working long hours is often a social norm and an undeclared contractual expectation that does not necessarily represent a real need. Instead, the tendency to work long hours may be part of an organizational culture that seeks to transmit the message that "we are working hard." Ironically, this expectation of high employee loyalty occurs mainly in high-tech industries, which, due to vigorous global competition and highly volatile markets, are the least loyal to their employees.

The expanding use of transactional contracts has been especially pronounced in the kibbutz—a former bastion of relational contracts. The idea of the kibbutz was to reorient human and social relationships both inside and outside work through a cooperative and egalitarian community. Profits were never a declared or desired goal. However, this has changed in recent years. Though kibbutz members do not lose their jobs nor membership rights when economic problems abound, as would happen in most organizations, the entire kibbutz concept has taken a dramatic turn. Economic pressures have caused the *kibbutzim* (plural of *kibbutz*) to function as profit-oriented organizations. In sharp contrast with previous years, jobs are now being measured and evaluated in a manner similar to practices in capitalistic companies. This is being done informally as well as formally. The major changes are still taking shape, but the trend is toward evaluating the different contributions of each job (agricultural, industrial, administrative, education, etc.) to the economic welfare of the kibbutz. In the near future, this change is likely to lead to differential pay structures. Most kibbutz settlements have been changing from egalitarian communities into businesses that must compete in a tough economy. Such transitions have dramatic effects on role-related interactions as well as on informal friendships within each kibbutz. Loyalty and commitment to the kibbutz is bound to change as a result.

Implications

The changes occurring in the kibbutzim may be seen as a reflection of the social changes taking place within the country as a whole. Although informal promises have historically been enough to "seal the deal" between parties, today there is a growing reliance on formal contracts and legal arrangements. As a result, psychological employment contracts in Israeli organizations have changed from the traditional relational agreements to more transactional agreements. The increasing prevalence of these transactional employment relationships can be seen as a significant change within the general Israeli society.

REFERENCES

Abu-Saad, I., & Isralowitz, R. E. (1998). Gender as a determinant of work values among university students in Israel. *Journal of Social Psychology, 137,* 749-763.

Babbar, S., & Aspelin, D. J. (1997). The overtime rebellion: Symptom of a bigger problem? *Academy of Management Executive, 11,* 68-76.

Ben-Israel, R. (1990). Temporary help employment in Israel: The legal dimension. In A. Galin & O. Carmi (Eds.), *Management 2000: Flexible management.* Tel Aviv, Israel: Management Library (In Hebrew).

Carbone, J. H. (1997). Loyalty: Subversive doctrine? *Academy of Management Executive, 11,* 80-86.

Cohen, Y., & Haberfeld, I. (1993). Temporary help service workers: Employment characteristics and wage determination. *Industrial Relations, 32,* 272-287.

Davis-Blake, A., & Uzzi, B. (1993). Determinants of employment externalization: A study of temporary workers and independent contractors. *Administrative Science Quarterly, 38,* 195-223.

Elizur, D., & Sagie, A. (1999). Facets of job values: A structural analysis of life and work values. *Psychology: An International Review, 48,* 73-87.

Hartley, J., Jacobson, D., Klandermans, C., & van Vuuren, T. (1991). *Job insecurity: Coping with jobs at risk.* Newbury Park, CA: Sage.

Krausz, M., Brandwein, T., & Fox, S. (1995). Work attitudes and emotional responses of permanent, voluntary, and involuntary temporary-help employees: An exploratory study. *Applied Psychology: An International Review, 44,* 217-232.

Pearce, J. L. (1993). Toward an organizational behavior of contract laborers: Their psychological involvement and effects on employee co-workers. *Academy of Management Journal, 36,* 1082-1096.

Prince-Gibson, E., & Schwartz, S. H. (1998). Value priorities and gender. *Social Psychology Quarterly, 61,* 49-67.

Rousseau, D. M. (1995). *Psychological contracts in organizations.* Thousand Oaks, CA: Sage.

Sagie, A. (1993). Measurement of religiosity and work organizations among Israeli youth. *Journal of Social Psychology, 133,* 529-537.

Sagy, S. (1997). Work values: Comparing Russian immigrants and Israeli students. *Journal of Career Development, 23,* 231-243.

Schwartz, S. H., Verkasalo, M., Anotonovsky, A., & Sagiv, L. (1997). Value priority and social desirability: Much substance, some style. *British Journal of Social Psychology, 36,* 3-18.

Tchernichovsky, S. (1990). Human beings are nothing but. . . . In S. Tchernichovsky, *Poems and ballads.* Tel Aviv, Israel: Am-Oved.

8

A Break With Tradition

Negotiating New
Psychological Contracts in Japan

Motohiro Morishima

Traditional Japanese employment contracts were based on a special set of employment practices, characterized by open-ended employment and the evaluation of employees' competence and skill development (Morishima, 1995). Employment relationships were expected to be long term, though the exact duration was unspecified, and the exchange of contributions and rewards was expected to balance over the life of a relationship. In these exchanges, employers evaluated and rewarded employees not only for their actual contributions but also on the basis of their potential contributions to the organization over the long term, including their willingness to develop firm-specific skills that would make them more valuable. In sum, employees were assumed to commit themselves to their employers, and those organizations were in turn expected to secure employment and reward employees' long-term contributions.

During this period, the most common Japanese psychological contracts were strongly relational, as opposed to transactional (Rousseau, 1989). After 30 years of economic growth, however, the Japanese economy progressed to the next stage. This stage was marked by the disappearance of the continuous growth that would have enabled firms to maintain long-term employment and stable career advancement for nearly all employees. An extremely strong yen and the bursting of the so-called "bubble economy" in the early 1990s drove Japanese employers to attack existing management practices. Companies faced with slow growth, fierce domestic and international competition, bloated bureaucracies, and expensive human and capital investments resorted to a number of cost-cutting measures, including significant changes in the human resource management strategies related to such fundamental areas as staffing, employee development, employment security, pay determination, and performance standards.

Because human resource management practices signal employers' expectations of the employment relationship and act as the mechanism through which employees come to understand the terms of their employment contracts, changes in these practices have significant implications for the psychological contracts that employees develop. In this chapter, I argue that the recent changes in Japanese human resource management practices are likely to modify the psychological relationship between employers and employees and diminish the relational nature of the psychological contract. Rousseau (1989) has theorized that psychological contracts lie along a continuum ranging from the relational, characterized by both economic and social resources, an indefinite duration, and diffuse obligations, to the transactional, characterized by monetizable resources, short time frames, and specifically delineated obligations. Another important distinction is that relational contracts are often implicit whereas transactional contracts are explicit; thus, relational contracts are open to interpretation by the parties and subject to dynamic processes of change. I argue that the introduction of pay-for-performance schemes and an increased use of externalized employment arrangements are likely to alter the basis of psychological contracts in Japan. These practices make reward-contribution exchanges more specific and dictate a short-term time frame for employment. Consequently, the balance that existed in traditional relational psychological contracts has begun to be destroyed, negatively affecting employees' attitudes toward their employers and creating contracts that are more transactional.

PSYCHOLOGICAL CONTRACTS IN JAPAN UP TO 1990

A psychological contract is a set of beliefs and perceptions that an individual holds regarding the terms and conditions of a reciprocal exchange agreement. In employment relationships, employees' psychological contracts specify the contributions that they owe to their employer and the contributions and rewards that they believe are owed to them in return. The characteristics of these inducements and contributions define the type of psychological contracts that exist between employees and employers. In particular, psychological contract theorists have argued that among the many elements involved in defining the two types of psychological contracts, two dimensions appear to have the strongest discriminating power: the time horizon of the contract and the specificity of the transaction (Rousseau & Wade-Benzoni, 1994).

Time horizon refers to the expected duration of employment, ranging from short term to long term. *Specificity of the transaction* refers to the employer-employee understanding of what is to be exchanged in the employment contract. It ranges from an explicit situation in which employers expect specified performance standards to be met and employees expect to receive corresponding (mostly pecuniary) rewards to an implicit situation in which employers simply expect dedication and loyalty from employees and employees expect to receive such general rewards as paternalistic treatment by employers. Along both of these dimensions, Japanese employment contracts have traditionally been relational.

The long-term nature of Japanese employment contracts (for core employees) is not unintended. The duration of Japanese employment contracts is often open-ended, and exchanges are assumed to balance over an unspecified span of time. When employees are hired into the core workforce of a firm, they receive a contract that carries an implicit promise of guaranteed employment until a point (such as the forced retirement age) at which both parties agree to terminate the relationship (Koshiro, 1993). Two important consequences follow from the intended long-term nature of Japanese employment contracts. First, both employees and employers are expected to balance their exchanges over the course of an employee's entire career, a period that may cover more than 35 years (Shimada, 1994). Second, open-ended contracts enable firms to invest in their employees' long-term skill development. As noted by a number of researchers, one of the most important implications of long-term employment practices in Japan is their ability to encourage firms to begin internal training programs (Cole, 1992). Because employers are not likely to lose their investment in human capital, they are motivated to provide more intensive in-house training to their workers. Long-term employment practices have also promoted learning on the job by employees, which in turn has allowed Japanese firms to develop organizational technologies that use employee inputs and involvement, aspects represented by such practices as continuous improvement and total quality management.

The other important aspect of current Japanese employment contracts is that reciprocal obligations are extremely general and underspecified. Because terms are only generally specified, details are worked out as circumstances change over time. Details are also subject to constant reinterpretation and clarification. From the employee's point of view, concepts such as jobs and roles have very different meanings in Japanese organizations. Even when jobs are created for individual employees, those individuals are implicitly expected to "be flexible in their role behavior and take an 'expansionist' view of [their] work" (Ishida, 1991). Always going beyond the basic role requirements is a built-in component of Japanese employees' behavior.

Japanese organizations are also designed to take advantage of the organizational citizenship behavior that is fostered by relational contracts (Morishima, 1996b; Parks & Kidder, 1994). Research shows that Japanese job classifications are much simpler and broader, and job assignments much more fluid and flexible, than those in Western bureaucracies (Aoki, 1988; Lincoln, Hanada, & McBride, 1986). One important consequence of this flexible organizational structure is the way Japanese employees are evaluated. In most Japanese firms, employees' pay and promotions are determined through a "skill-grade" system that uses a set of very detailed criteria to assess each employee as to what he or she is *capable* of performing, not what he or she actually performs (Koike, 1991). Supervisors' assessments of employee competence and potential, known as *satei,* play a crucial role in the evaluation process (Endo, 1994). In this scheme, employees' capabilities are considered to be based on cumulative on-the-job experience and internal training and are therefore strongly related to their tenure in the company. The skill-grade pay system also encourages learning throughout one's career in a corporation. Because there are on average seven to eight skill grades for each occupational category and because it takes a few years for an employee to complete a skill grade, advancing through the entire skill-grade hierarchy may take more than 25 years.

The skill-grade system is very similar to the system of skill-based pay or pay for knowledge. Because of broadly designed job structures, however, there is a much larger number of skills to be learned in a Japanese skill grade than in a typical skill grade in U.S. workplaces (Koike, 1994). A survey conducted by the Japanese Ministry of Labour (1990) shows that 79.6% of the approximately 6,000 firms with 30 or more employees used the skill-grade system to determine at least some portion of their employees' take-home pay. This system was used by almost 100% of the firms with 1,000 or more employees. Most firms reported that they used the skill-grade system to determine the pay of white-collar workers as well as blue-collar workers.

Foundations of Japanese Relational Contracts

Japanese psychological contracts represent an exchange of obligations and rewards on two levels, a deeper level and a surface level. The deeper level includes agreement over the basic principle of employment security and corresponding employee obligations, similar to what economists might refer to as "trust" in exchange relationships. Both parties assume that the implicit terms of the agreement will not be violated because violation of the contract terms would result in an unstable system in which no further exchanges were possible. In Japan, employers have historically maintained the deeper level of psychological contracts—as well as employee trust—by providing employment security to their core employees, even when this security entailed some cost to the employer.

As long as the deeper level of a psychological contract remains stable, such contracts can be extremely fluid at the surface level. Contract terms related to the exchange of contributions and rewards can be altered without difficult negotiations between the parties as long as major violations do not occur at the deeper level. In Japan, major violations occur when one party perceives that the other is abandoning the implicit assumption of long-term employment. By maintaining this assumption, Japanese employers have maintained substantial freedom to change their employment terms and human resource management practices as circumstances have demanded, a phenomenon often called "flexible rigidity" (Dore, 1986).

The stability of the deeper level of Japanese psychological contracts has been helped by cultural norms that emphasize the importance of "belonging," or being a member of a larger entity such as a group or organization. The idea of belonging is similar to collectivism, in which members of an in-group are expected to align their goals with those of the larger organization, emphasizing larger social obligations rather than the pursuit of individual needs (Brett & Okumura, 1998). In contrast with collectivism, however, Japanese culture also emphasizes equality among the members of a group. The key aspect of "belonging" is being a member of a group, not assuming a particular role or achieving status within that group. Psychological contracts that are consistent with the cultural notion of belonging—contracts that are relational, providing long-term employment security—can be a critical component of Japanese employment relationships. The implications of this must be examined to understand the changes in Japanese human resource management practices.

Development of Relational Contracts in Japan

Relational psychological contracts may be embedded in Japanese cultural norms, but these norms were not the only basis for the development of relational employment contracts in Japanese firms. Efforts by both employers and employees during the period immediately following World War II produced long-term, relational employment contracts. Although the relational nature of Japanese employment relations is often highlighted, such relations reflect the outcome of continuous negotiations between employers and employees, as well as the interdependence of employers who rely on employees' skills and decision-making abilities and of employees who need stable jobs to maintain the value of their hard-learned skills. This interdependence is created because Japanese work organizations promote employee involvement, and firms' decision-making structures derive their vitality and adaptability from employee inputs. In this context, employers have demanded (and obtained) full control over the skill development process, including supervisory assessments of employee learning, frequent changes of assignment, and the use of the skill-grade system in reward determination. By taking almost exclusive control over these items, management obviously gains strong power in the determination of employment conditions for individual employees.

From the employees' perspective, this system gives them a stake in making sure that employers uphold the implicit understanding that the development of organization-specific skills will be rewarded throughout an employee's career.

Firm-specific skills are not likely to be valued as highly by other employers offering similar levels of employment conditions. Thus, employees have a strong incentive to keep their firm in business and help it be profitable in order to maintain their employment status.

Since the end of World War II, Japanese unions have generally engaged in bargaining focused on employment security and skill development, whereby core employees—those whose skills and decision-making abilities are most often relied on by employers—win employment security in return for management's almost unilateral influence on the allocation of rewards and training opportunities to individual employees. Enterprise unions in large Japanese firms have always put employment security for their regular-status members, the core employees of those firms, as the top item on their bargaining agendas. When employment security has been threatened, the unions have historically engaged in tough and often violent negotiations. The unions' strong insistence on employment security for core employees precluded Japanese employers from competing on the basis of low wages and employment cuts, a policy that was unsuccessfully attempted during the 1950s (Gordon, 1985). Japanese unions engaged in violent strikes during that time, and even today most labor conflicts involve disagreements over how to handle employment redundancy. By protecting employees' job security, union strategies have served as a strong impetus for the development and maintenance of relational employment contracts in Japan.

CHANGES IN JAPANESE HUMAN RESOURCE MANAGEMENT PRACTICES

The circumstances that helped create these formal arrangements for managing core employees in large Japanese firms—often referred to as internal labor markets—have changed. Although Japanese employers have engaged in a series of adjustments to the Japanese employment system over the past three decades, two aspects are most important in their recent efforts to modify employment practices: the introduction of pay-for-performance schemes and the introduction of externalized employment arrangements within the firm workforce (for details, see Morishima, 1996a).

Pay-for-Performance Schemes

A shift away from basing employee evaluation and rewards on criteria related to seniority and skill development has resulted in an increased emphasis on employee contributions to the organization through such practices as performance-based evaluation and management by objectives. The change is most visible in the compensation arrangements of middle and senior managers, although a number of firms have introduced similar measures for a range of nonmanagerial workers. According to a survey conducted in 1995 by the

Japanese Ministry of Labour (1996), approximately 7.9% of large firms (those with more than 1,000 employees) had built some type of pay-for-performance criteria into their compensation practices. Another 11.6% reported that they were considering doing so over the next 5 years.

When the sample is restricted to firms that play major roles in the Japanese economy, however, the proportion adopting pay-for-performance schemes increases substantially. In a 1997 survey of 450 large firms whose stocks are traded in the Tokyo public stock exchange, 54.0% had instituted pay-for-performance schemes for at least some portion of their workforce (Tsuru, Morishima, & Okunishi, 1998). The prevalence is even higher for larger firms (65.8% of those with more than 5,000 employees) and manufacturing firms (61%).

Another emerging practice is the assignment of employees who have only recently joined the firm to managerial and supervisory positions on the basis of their performance records. This finding goes against the accepted practice of advancing employees in the same cohort (as defined by year of entry and occupational grouping) en masse for 7 to 10 years with little individual differentiation. This traditional approach to promotion and employee advancement was considered necessary to carefully identify employees with managerial talent.

Two surveys conducted 6 years apart (summarized in Ministry of Labour, 1996) suggest that firms may be introducing status differentiation earlier in employees' careers than previously was the case. In a 1987 Ministry of Labour survey, more than 20% of firms reported that they introduced status and pay differentials more than 10 years after the cohort entered the firm. Another 40% introduced such differentials after 5 to 10 years. In a Japan Institute of Labour survey conducted in 1993, the proportion of firms introducing such differentials after 10 years dropped to 7.6%. Similarly, the proportion of firms introducing differentials after the cohort had been employed 5 to 10 years dropped to 33.1%. In this survey, the largest proportion of firms (46.3%) reported that they would introduce large status and pay differentials after the cohort had been employed for 3 to 5 years. The same survey also indicated that these "early career" differentials were introduced on the basis of employees' current performance and career potential.

Externalized Employment Relations

The externalization of employment has been proceeding in Japan much as it has in other industrialized nations. In particular, Japanese firms have begun to externalize core positions not only through the increased use of part-time and temporary workers (Osawa & Kingston, 1996) but also through the hiring of limited-contract employees. The goal has been to introduce staffing flexibility and to better match employees with jobs. This goal is accomplished by reducing the likelihood of long-term employment relationships and giving employees and employers more flexibility to choose the "right" partners.

Some Japanese firms have also begun to sort core workers into categories with different levels of employment protection. According to the Ministry of Labour, the percentage of firms offering multiple career tracks increased from 6.3% in 1990 to 11.5% in 1996. Firms requiring employees to "retire" from managerial positions at a preset age increased from 11.8% to 15.8% during the same period. Finally, "specialist" career tracks were used in 19.9% of the firms in 1996, compared to 16.2% in 1990. "Specialists" usually have weaker employment protection, and their careers often have lower ceilings. In addition, many firms have begun practices that remove senior employees from the company payroll by temporarily or permanently lending them to other companies. Some transfer destinations are affiliated with the original firm in terms of capital or business transactions; others have no such affiliation (Sato, 1996). As a result of these approaches, Japanese core workers now find themselves in various places along the continuum from being strongly protected to being weakly protected.

In sum, Japanese employment practices are changing in two ways: (a) replacement of appraisal and reward criteria based on ability progression and seniority with criteria based on performance and career potential and (b) a decreasing proportion of core employees protected by strong employment security. Overall, the diffusion of increasingly performance-based reward practices and the growing use of externalized employment arrangements represent Japanese employers' attempts to increase the flexibility of employment systems and to control the costs of managing their core employees.

Psychological Impacts of
Changes in Employment Practices

Employees in large Japanese corporations are increasingly evaluated on the basis of specific role behavior (performance) instead of generalized commitment to the company. Similarly, employers are changing the expected length of the employment relationship from open-ended, long-term employment to more specified, limited-term contracts. These changes are moving Japanese employment contracts from the relational end of the continuum to the transactional end.

Since these changes began to be discussed most seriously in the early 1990s, their impact on employee perceptions of psychological contracts and, consequently, on employee behavior has not been examined empirically. One issue that needs to be examined is the effects of changing human resource management practices on employees' psychological relationships with their employing organizations. One way to approach this issue is through the concept of "functional complementarity" or internal fit among the human resource management dimensions (Milgrom & Roberts, 1995).

My argument is based on the "duality principle" idea within Japanese human resource management.[1] According to Aoki (1994), effective Japanese practices are based on the long-term, internal development of firm-specific skills that enable employees to participate effectively in the workplace, as well as on a reward system that motivates employees to compete for promotions and pay increases. However, assessment based on competence or skill development will not be effective unless employee development is cultivated over a long period and employment is relatively secure (Aoki, 1994; Morishima, 1995). In turn, long-term employment will be dysfunctional unless the value of employees as assets is assessed constantly over their careers. Thus, the two dimensions that were observed in the traditional Japanese human resource management system were complementary and provided an internal fit. As noted earlier, this fit also produced a stable relational psychological contract between employees and employers.

Extending this argument, one might posit that short-term employment and assessment based on explicit output can also be complementary and internally consistent. If firms want to base their evaluation of employees on short-term outcomes and reward them for explicit changes in productivity, employment practices need not be long term. Here, the maximization of human resource value depends on the maximization of short-term output by employees, not the level of skills acquired over the long-term employee-development process. Employers, therefore, have incentives to also design short-term employment arrangements in order to determine the value of their human resources over a relatively limited period of time. These employers do not have incentives to offer long-term employment to employees. Because employers evaluate their employees on the basis of short-term performance, human resource management practices that are designed to raise the level of employee skills are also not economically feasible.

Moreover, employees may prefer short-term contractual arrangements because those whose performance is not up to the standards set by the firm may be motivated to leave that firm and seek employment in firms where their performance might be evaluated more favorably. In sum, the short-term assessment of human resource value based on output is congruent with employment arrangements that offer employees limited-term security. This second kind of internal fit is predicted to produce another type of stable psychological contract, namely the transactional.

Applying these arguments to the current Japanese employment scene, one may hypothesize that firms have internally consistent human resource management systems when they are either maintaining long-term employment and assessment based on capabilities or advancing employee appraisal based on performance and externalization of employment. In Figure 8.1, firms that fall into Quadrants 1 and 4 have internally consistent human resource management systems. Employees in these firms are likely to have stable psychological contracts and positive attitudes toward their employing organizations. However, the contents of the psychological relationship between employers and employees may be opposite.

	Assessment Based on Competence Development	Assessment Based on Output/Performance
Long-term, internalized employment arrangements with internal human resource development	Quadrant 1	Quadrant 2
Limited-term, externalized employment arrangements with no preference for internal human resource development	Quadrant 3	Quadrant 4

Figure 8.1. Possible Combinations of Human Resource Management Dimensions

In contrast, firms in Quadrants 2 and 3 have internally inconsistent human resource management systems. In Quadrant 2, employee assessment is based on output or performance, but the employment arrangements are long term, with a strong preference for internal skill development. Inconsistency in this quadrant exists because employees are evaluated on the basis of short-term performance outcomes but develop their skills over a long period of time. Employees have few incentives to engage in long-term learning if they are not evaluated on the development of their competence. Similarly, employers have no incentives to invest in skill development if their interests are in maximizing employees' short-term performance.

Similarly, firms in Quadrant 3 are expected to have an internally inconsistent human resource management system because employee evaluation is based on competence or ability development, but employment arrangements are short term, with no explicit preference for internal human resource development. With short-term employment arrangements, employers have very few incentives to invest in human resource development. Thus, although employees are expected to develop their competence, they get very little help from their employers. The skills employees possess are likely to be general, as opposed to firm specific, thus reducing the overall value of human resources to the firm. Assessment of employees in terms of skill development is not likely to work unless employees are trained over some time span.

In Japan, there are some indications that firms may be quickly adopting employee appraisal based on performance but that the degree to which they are incorporating employment externalization is more limited (at least for core or regular-status employees). Previous research indicated that about one third of sampled firms had internally inconsistent HRM systems (Morishima, 1996a). These firms tended to have highly competitive, performance-based appraisal systems but limited employment. In addition, the comparison of large-scale surveys conducted in the 1980s and 1990s indicates that fewer firms are willing to modify long-term employment practices but that, at the same time, more are willing to change their appraisal system to more output-based evaluation practices (Morishima, 1992). Employee attitudes toward these internally inconsistent organizations are predicted to be negative.

Systems and Employee Attitudes

Some support for the above argument is provided by data from a survey conducted by the Japan Productivity Center for Socio-Economic Development through its Joint Labor-Management Commission. I participated as one of the principal investigators of the commission, which examined trends in the human resource management policies and practices of Japanese firms. The target employee group covered in this survey was the core, regular-status white-collar employees in middle-management positions, known as *kachos*.

Methodology

The survey was conducted in June 1997. Questionnaires were distributed to approximately 3,000 managers in 63 firms in the Tokyo and Osaka metropolitan areas. With a response rate of about 40%, 1,192 usable questionnaires were received. The questionnaires were distributed through firms' personnel departments (usually with their endorsement) and were returned via regular mail. All the respondents were in middle-management positions, with 68% in line manager positions as opposed to staff manager positions. The average age of respondents was 47 years, and the average tenure was 24 years. About three quarters of the respondents (76%) had at least bachelor's degrees, and the average annual income was approximately 10 million yen. Ninety percent had worked for the same employer throughout their careers. About 29% of the employees worked in firms employing 5,000 or more regular-status employees; the minimum size of the sample firm was 1,112 regular-status employees. Women constituted less than 2% of the sample (Japan Productivity Center, 1997).

Human Resource Management System Clusters. The type of human resource management practice changes experienced by employers was measured using two items that correspond to the two dimensions in Figure 8.1. The item corresponding to the appraisal dimension asked employees whether there had been an increase in the emphasis on concrete output and performance in employee appraisal. The other item asked employees whether the firm in which they worked had shifted away from the policy of long-term employment. These answers were dummy-coded (1 = yes, 0 = no). Using these items, employees were classified into the following four groups:

- *Group 1* (Quadrant 1 in Figure 8.1): No to both questions, 19.9% of the sample (N = 237)
- *Group 2* (Quadrant 2 in Figure 8.1): Yes to appraisal change, no to employment practice change, 52.9% (N = 630)
- *Group 3* (Quadrant 3 in Figure 8.1): No to appraisal change, yes to employment practice change, 6.3% (N = 75)
- *Group 4* (Quadrant 4 in Figure 8.1): Yes to both questions, 17.1% (N = 204)

Consistent with prior research, the largest proportion of employees fell in Group 2, where firms' human resource management policies include the adoption of output-based appraisal but the continuance of long-term employment policies (Morishima, 1996a). The smallest proportion fell in Group 3, whose employees reported human resource management policies opposite to those in Group 2.

Differences in Employee Attitudes. Employee attitudes toward their employing organizations were measured by one item scale that asked about their organizational satisfaction. This measure used a 3-point scale, with 1 indicating the lowest satisfaction and 3 indicating the highest satisfaction. In addition, the survey attempted to capture the type of psychological contract that employees had with their employing organizations by asking employees whether they would like to develop the rest of their careers in the current organization. Answers were again coded using a 3-point scale, with higher values indicating a stronger desire to develop one's career within the current organization. Higher values were thus interpreted as indicating the presence of relational psychological contracts.

The averages of the four groups are shown in Figure 8.2.

First, employees in Groups 2 and 3—the groups with mixed yes-no answers—showed lower levels of organizational satisfaction than those in Groups 1 and 4. The averages for Groups 1 and 4 were not significantly different from one another. In this sample, employees had relatively positive attitudes toward their employing organizations when they experienced either (a) a shift to output-based appraisal *and* a shift away from long-term employment or (b) no shift to output-based appraisal *and* no shift away from long-term employment. According to the duality model, these two types of human resource management systems are internally consistent and are thus likely to create balanced psychological contracts and relatively positive attitudes toward employing organizations. In contrast, employees in Groups 2 and 3 showed lower satisfaction due to the lack of balance in their firms' human resource management practices. The internally inconsistent human resource management systems may have produced these negative attitudes.

Also shown in Figure 8.2 is that employees in Group 1 reported a significantly higher desire to develop their careers internally than employees in the remaining three groups. Group 1 was the group of employees whose firms had

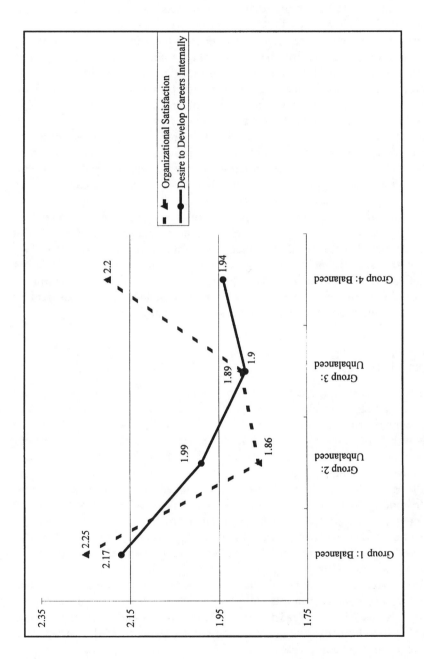

Figure 8.2. Human Resource Management System and Employee Attitudes

153

made no changes in appraisal or employment practices and who would therefore be expected to have more relational contracts. One way to interpret this finding is that when employers adopt either output-based appraisal or externalized employment practices, change in either dimension is powerful enough to create transactional psychological contracts between employers and employees. Thus, employees in Group 1 showed a relatively strong desire to develop internal careers because they were the only employees whose firms maintained the traditional human resource management system. This finding lends partial support to this hypothesis.

One caveat is that the variable used in this analysis (employees' desire to develop careers internally) may not be a good indicator of the type of their psychological contract. Employees in Group 1 may be expressing their expectations (not necessarily their desires) that they will develop their careers in the current firms. Because firms in Group 1 are likely to have maintained the traditional pattern of employment, employees in this group may feel relatively secure regarding the prospect of developing their careers inside their present organizations. Employees in the other groups may feel less certain that their careers will remain internal because their firms have already started to adopt more flexible human resource management practices. If this interpretation is correct, the finding may be a direct outcome of human resource management practice changes rather than being mediated by a change in psychological contract types.

CONCLUSIONS

Previous research indicated that only about 10% of Japanese firms showed both substantial weakening of employment security and employee assessment based on specific performance standards (Morishima, 1996a). The rest of the firms were almost evenly divided into those with both long-term employment security and development-based assessment (traditional firms) and those with long-term employment security and assessment based on specific performance standards (transformed firms). Thus, although Japanese employers are attempting to modify their human resource management policies and practices and break away from tradition, a substantial number still appear to preserve the long-term, open-ended nature of the traditional employment relationship. The distribution of respondents among the four types of human resource management systems in this study (Groups 1 through 4) shows even more strongly that employers are changing their appraisal practices more quickly than the employment practices. The data used in this study indicated that the largest proportion of employees (40.1%) belonged to Group 2, in which employees experienced appraisal based on concrete performance but relatively little shift away from long-term employment practices.

Evidence presented in this chapter shows that psychological contracts in Groups 2 and 3 may not be balanced and may therefore lead to negative attitudes toward employing organizations. The level of organizational satisfaction was lower for employees in Groups 2 and 3 than for those in Groups 1 and 4, the two balanced groups. These differences are naturally only *relative* in the sense that they are comparisons across the four groups used in this study and must be corroborated by further research. However, these findings indicate that if employers continue to make only partial modifications to their human resource management systems, primarily placing themselves in Group 2, the overall psychological well-being of the Japanese employees may deteriorate over time. Either a complete switch to the Group 4 system or a commitment to the traditional Group 1 system is likely to have a more positive impact on employee attitudes.

There was also some evidence, although not as strong, that the level of loyalty and commitment to organizations will change from the traditional pattern of long-term attachment to firms and internal career development to more short-term attachment and career development by switching companies. Even more surprising, the data indicated that this shift in psychological contracts might reveal itself even when firms engage in only partial modification of their human resource management systems. Psychological contracts became more transactional in nature when firms either changed their appraisal practices or moved away from long-term employment practices.

Changes in the human resource management practices of Japanese firms are likely to continue in the future, and so is the renegotiation of psychological contracts between employees and employers. The directions that these changes will take will depend on a variety of factors. Currently, government regulations concerning Japanese labor markets and societal expectations of long-term attachment to a single firm still make it quite difficult for Japanese firms to completely overhaul their human resource management systems to introduce flexibility in employment contracts. From a psychological standpoint, however, these developments are not likely to produce stable psychological contracts based on the transactional exchanges between employees and employers. Changes are needed in Japanese employment practices to increase employment flexibility. Otherwise, the effectiveness of Japanese organizations will be at risk.

NOTE

1. This concept was originally developed by Aoki (1994).

REFERENCES

Aoki, M. (1988). *Information, incentives, and bargaining in the Japanese economy.* New York: Cambridge University Press.

Aoki, M. (1994). The Japanese firm as a system of attributes: A survey and research agenda. In M. Aoki & R. Dore (Eds.), *The Japanese firm: Sources of competitive strength* (pp. 11-40). New York: Oxford University Press.

Brett, J. M., & Okumura, T. (1998). Inter- and intracultural negotiation: U. S. and Japanese negotiators. *Academy of Management Journal, 41,* 495-510.

Cole, R. (1992). Issues in skill formation in Japanese approaches to automation. In P. S. Adler (Ed.), *Technology and the future of work* (pp. 187-209). New York: Oxford University Press.

Dore, R. (1986). *Flexible rigidities: Industrial policy and structural adjustment in the Japanese economy, 1970-80.* London: Athlone.

Endo, K. (1994). Satei (personal assessment) and interworker competition in Japanese firms. *Industrial Relations, 33,* 70-82.

Gordon, A. (1985). *The evolution of labor relations in Japan: Heavy industry, 1853-1955.* Cambridge, MA: Harvard University Press.

Ishida, H. (1991, February). *Flexibility in Japanese management.* Paper presented at the Workshop on Labor in Japan: An Approach to Labor-Management Cooperation, Manila, Philippines.

Japan Productivity Center for Socio-Economic Development. (1997). *Roshi Kankei Jonin Iinkai Chosa Kenkyu Hokokuho: Kobetsuka No Shinten To Roshi Kankei* [Survey report on the changes in employment practices: A preliminary report of the JPC Labor-Management Commission]. Tokyo: Japan Productivity Center for Socio-Economic Development.

Koike, K. (Ed.). (1991). *Daisotsu White-Collar No Jinzai Kaihatsu* [Human resource development of white-collar employees]. Tokyo: Toyo Keizai.

Koike, K. (1994). Learning and incentive systems in Japanese industry. In M. Aoki & R. Dore (Eds.), *The Japanese firm: Sources of competitive strength* (pp. 41-65). New York: Oxford University Press.

Koshiro, K. (1993, October). *Comment on "Aging Population and Human Resource Management" by M. Ito.* Paper presented at the Japan Institute of Labour-University of Illinois Institute of Labor and Industrial Relations Conference on the Change of Employment Environment and Human Resource Management in the U.S. and Japanese Labor Markets, Tokyo.

Lincoln, J. R., Hanada, M., & McBride, K. (1986). Organizational structure in Japanese and U.S. manufacturing. *Administrative Science Quarterly, 31,* 338-364.

Milgrom, P., & Roberts, J. (1995). Complementarities and fit: Strategy, structure and organizational change in manufacturing. *Journal of Accounting and Economics, 19,* 179-208.

Ministry of Labour. (1990). *Heisei Ni Nendo Koyo Kanri Chosa Kekka Sokuho* [Comprehensive survey on pay and working hours]. Tokyo: Ministry of Finance Printing Office.

Ministry of Labour. (1996). *Heisei Hachi Nenban Rodo Hakusho* [1996 white paper on labour.] Tokyo: Japan Institute of Labour.

Morishima, M. (1992). Japanese employees' attitudes toward changes in traditional employment practices. *Industrial Relations, 31,* 433-454.

Morishima, M. (1995). The Japanese human resource management system: A learning bureaucracy. In J. D. Jennings & L. Moore (Eds.), *HRM in the Pacific Rim: Institutions, practices, and values* (pp. 119-150). New York: Walter de Gruyter.

Morishima, M. (1996a). Evolution of white-collar HRM in Japan. In D. Lewin, B. E. Kaufman, & D. Sockell (Eds.), *Advances in Industrial and Labor Relations, 7,* 145-176.

Morishima, M. (1996b). Renegotiating psychological contracts: Japanese style. In C. L. Cooper & D. M. Rousseau (Eds.), *Trends in organizational behavior* (Vol. 3, pp. 139-158). New York: John Wiley.

Osawa, M., & Kingston, J. (1996, January 1). Flexibility and inspiration: Restructuring and the Japanese labor market. *Japan Labor Bulletin,* pp. 4-8.

Parks, J. M., & Kidder, D. L. (1994). "Till death us do part. . .": Changing work relationships in the 1990s. In C. L. Cooper & D. M. Rousseau (Eds.), *Trends in organizational behavior* (Vol. 1, pp. 111-136). New York: John Wiley.

Rousseau, D. M. (1989). Psychological and implied contracts in organizations. *Employee Responsibilities and Rights Journal, 2,* 121-139.

Rousseau, D. M., & Wade-Benzoni, K. A. (1994). Linking strategy and human resource practices: How employee and customer contracts are created. *Human Resource Management, 33,* 463-489.

Sato, H. (1996, December 1). Keeping employees employed: *Shukko* and *tenseki* job transfers: Formation of a labor market within corporate groups. *Japan Labor Bulletin,* pp. 5-8.

Shimada, H. (1994). *Nihon No Koyo* [Employment in Japan]. Tokyo: Chikura.

Tsuru, T., Morishima, M., & Okunishi, Y. (1998, January). *Niju Isseiki No Jinteki Shigen Kanri Sisutemu Ni Mukete No Kiso Chosa Kekka Sokuho* [Press release on the 1997 survey on the assessment and evaluation practices of large Japanese firms]. Unpublished manuscript, Hitotsubashi University, Tokyo.

9

Psychological Contracts in Mexico

Historical, Familial, and Contemporary Influences on Work Relationships

Hector R. Diaz-Saenz
Patricia D. Witherspoon

> *Las palabras se las lleva el viento. (Spoken words are blown away by the wind [but words on paper are permanent].)*
>
> Popular saying

Mexico is a land of contrasts, woven together in a socioeconomic, political, and cultural fabric. It is a land of cosmopolitan and rural people, of well-educated citizens and those with little formal education, of the very poor and the very wealthy. It is a land with a growing middle class, seeking social changes for its people and new markets for its products. It is a land rich in history, and its people take pride in that history.

AUTHORS' NOTE: We want to thank the human resources managers who provided valuable information for the development of this chapter through questionnaires or interviews. Special thanks to Hugo Flores Tamez of HYLSA and President of Ejecutivos de Relaciones Industriales A.C, ERIAC; Eduardo López Pérez, President of Confederación Mexicana de Asociaciones de Relaciones Industriales, COMARI; and Lauro Cesar Rodríguez-González of Organización Benavides.

The Mexican people are descendants of Spanish explorers and Indian natives, a mix of those who sought a new world and those who valued staying in one place. Mexican employees increasingly work in urban corporations and companies. As a result, psychological contracts—the beliefs and expectations that workers and employers hold regarding their mutual obligations in organizations—are particularly important. In Mexico, psychological contracts are creations, and reflections, of the country's culture and community, as well as its history and contemporary environmental influences.

Mexican employees base their job decisions and expectations on the needs of their families, who are central to their lives. A job is seen as a means to a single important end: providing a good standard of living for one's family. Workers' expectations of benefits for their families are one component of psychological contracts in Mexico. For example, large Mexican corporations often sponsor sports teams and recreational clubs for the families of their employees. Such largesse did not always exist in Mexico, especially when industrialization was just beginning. The current features of psychological contracts are the result of social upheaval among the working class, who experienced only limited privileges before the Revolution of 1910. Not even after its war of independence from Spain, or its revolution a century later, as Octavio Paz observed in *The Labyrinth of Solitude,* did the country achieve modernization. Wealth continued to be in the hands of a few people, and there was little ideological or structural change in society, only transfers of power within the same social class.

Traditionally, workers and employers viewed one another as enemies. Top management rarely shared information with workers. The lack of trust between employees and employers was embedded in their respective belief systems and has characterized their relationship for much of the time since the beginnings of the nation's industrialization. Recently, competition has put Mexican companies and jobs in jeopardy. As a result, workers and employers sometimes have joined together to fight common enemies, such as foreign companies with better products, manufactured with newer technology and offered at lower prices. Some companies now share information with their employees to ensure that they take care of the organization together.

Contrasts are evident in the predominant forms of Mexican psychological contracts. Federal law limits an employer's ability to cut wages or fire an employee, creating a stable employment relationship for many workers. However, more dynamic employment arrangements exist among well-educated professionals. Moreover, the globalization of Mexico's economy has prompted its companies to outsource human resources and look for flexible and competitive organizational structures and processes, further changing the traditional psychological contract.

Mexico's past has greatly influenced its current economy, as well as its political and social life. Understanding psychological contracts in Mexico, now and in the future, requires a look at the nation's economic history.

HISTORICAL PERSPECTIVE

Industrialization in Mexico began in the second half of the 19th century when the country began to evolve slowly from an agricultural economy. The evolution of Mexican labor-management relations can be traced through three distinct periods. The first period was associated with the *hacienda* agricultural model, based on the feudal model in Europe and inherited from the occupation of Mexico by the Spaniards. The next period developed in postrevolution Mexico (after 1920) and laid the foundation for the institutionalization of federal law that continues to regulate employment relations. Finally, the third period was initiated after World War II, when increasing numbers of Mexicans migrated from rural to urban areas. This period continued with the globalization of Mexico's economy in 1986, the year Mexico opened its borders through participation in the General Agreement on Tariffs and Trade (GATT). This globalization reshapes the labor-management relationship, and resultant psychological contracts, in the country today.

The Hacienda Period

The earliest industry, textiles, had its origins in 1829, when an initiative developed in the city of Puebla (Novelo, 1991). In this earliest stage, fabrics were produced by craftsmen who owned small shops. The craftsmen were key to the production system because they had the skill and knowledge to produce fabrics. However, as soon as the capital was available to invest in the industry, these individuals had to compete against new factories and wholesalers who were allowed to import higher-quality fabrics from outside the country at better prices. Many of those factories were established in the haciendas (similar to fiefdoms or feudal kingdoms) in rural Mexico. At some point in the middle of the 19th century, the textile industry was the second most important one in Mexico, surpassed only by mining, in terms of tax collection. As a result of the capital invested in textiles, the factory production system began to change from a craftsman-based system to a modern production system using salaried workers. The textile industry fostered production systems that were predominant for a time in Mexico (Novelo, 1991).

Along with the evolution of the production system, the working class emerged, establishing the foundations for labor management. Factories began to dominate the market, changing the craftsman-based production system to one of mass production using machines. Craftsmen had to submit to new labor conditions, such as wages that were based on the quality and quantity of pieces made, number of hours worked, and rules and regulations imposed by contractors. Production volumes and requirements were determined by managers and machines instead of individuals with a craft. Thus, craftsmen lost ownership of the process and had no influence on decisions related to it.

They worked long shifts of at least 12 hours each. They were obligated to live in rented houses near the factories, provided by the companies. They were required to purchase their household goods and food in company-owned stores. In addition, they were punished for insubordination. All of these conditions allowed owners to control a "captive" labor force. The authoritarian and paternalistic treatment of workers was similar to the treatment of peasants on the haciendas (Novelo, 1991). Less favorable conditions were experienced by temporary workers, who had to tolerate meager payment and were sometimes whipped for making mistakes. According to Novelo (1991), the labor force was part of an exploitation system, a modern slavery practice, used in agriculture before the country's independence. Thus, the industrialization of Mexico emerged with a capitalistic perspective but with cultural practices borrowed from the haciendas.

The working class evolved with a strong culture characterized by rural values and an appreciation of craftsmanship. It is important to understand that "the land" had an important meaning for generations of peasants before the Spaniards took their land from them. When the Indians ruled the rural regions, the *calpully,* a piece of tribal common land, was assigned to those who promised to farm it. Now, during the industrialization, land increasingly was taken by a few individuals who were, in many instances, the developers of the factories as well.

A group identity emerged among the workers who viewed themselves as sharing the same sufferings. They saw themselves as bound to an exploitative system. Having the same antagonists helped them develop a sense of support for each other (Adleson & Camarena, 1991).

On September 16, 1871, a number of diverse groups of workers established the Gran Circulo de Obreros de Mexico (the "Great Circle of Mexican Workers") or GCOM. This association was intended to better defend workers' job interests and emancipate them from hardships imposed by management (Novelo, 1991). The strike was proposed as the main device to enter negotiations with employers. However, GCOM could not develop enough support to face the financial and political pressures of the time, and it disappeared in 1876 (Novelo, 1991).

In this industrial setting, managers intensified the creation of a new work culture as a framework for labor relations. Rules were established to regulate behavior in the workplace, in an attempt to replace preindustrial views with industrial ones (Novelo, 1991). In the meantime, workers wanted purchasing alternatives to the factory stores in which they were obligated to buy. They wanted themselves and their families to be less bound to the factories in every aspect of their lives (Novelo, 1991).

San Rafael, a paper factory, located in the state of Mexico, serves as an example of employment relations of the region during the 1890s. These relations mainly were established by oral agreement, resulting in high turnover, especially for workers with peasant backgrounds (Méndez & Huerta, 1991).

Many peasants viewed the job as a way to generate some income when there was not time to work the land. Labor relations in the factory were regulated by a type of contract used in the haciendas called *de servidumbre* ("of servants"). Such contracts stipulated workers' obligations to the company, delineating their required tasks and work schedules. However, the company's obligations to workers were not stipulated in the contract. As a result, workers were easily fired when they were not needed (Méndez & Huerta, 1991).

As the country grew more industrialized, workers became increasingly unhappy about their employment arrangements and began to demand better conditions, social justice, a dignified work life, and equality. These ideals led to the Mexican Revolution, which focused on social, economic, and political changes (Peña, 1984).

Unions did not receive legal recognition until the Constitution of 1917, when the right to organize unions and the right to strike were granted. Since then, clashes have occurred between the state, which tries to subordinate unions, and workers who wish to keep their unions independent from the state (Laurell, 1984).

Government-led agrarian reform emerged after the revolution, when the haciendas were dissolved and divided into *ejidos,* or land given to people to work without ownership (Méndez & Huerta, 1991). New production technologies and the conditions created during the postrevolutionary period led to changes in labor management. For example, two ways to gain employment at the San Rafael paper factory emerged: through the union or through a contractor (Méndez & Huerta, 1991). Contractors offered management greater control over the labor force because contract workers, as opposed to the unionized workers, had no rights. They were also paid less than their unionized counterparts because the contractors kept part of their salaries.

Federal Involvement in Labor Management

A new framework for employment relations emerged in 1931. A collective legal agreement prompted by the Federal Work Law evolved with the establishment of unions, which pursued permanent jobs for their members (Rodríguez-González, 1997). As a juridical instrument, this contract continues to regulate labor relations between the unions and employers. In 1934, the union movement made substantial progress with the establishment of the Confederation of Mexican Workers (CTM) (Laurell, 1984).

Workers and employers continued to have antagonistic relationships during the early decades of the 20th century. They sporadically enjoyed the favor of the government, which tended to support the interest of one party at the expense of the other. In 1938, President Plutarco Elias Calles unified the most important worker unions from each industrial sector, as well as the unions of peasants and politicians, under the umbrella of the official party, PNR (National Revolutionary Party), now called PRI (Institutional Revolutionary

Party) (Laurell, 1984). In 1965, 95% of all unionized workers in Mexico belonged to the PRI. Employers, on the other hand, enjoyed the support of a protective government that closed its borders to external products and services in order to help the country modernize. In 1941, the Federal Employment Law was modified to restrict the right to strike, specifying procedures for unions to follow before taking such an action. At the same time, the state increased its jurisdiction to mediate conflicts between workers and employers.

Effects of Geography

Labor relations historically differ across the regions of Mexico. During the transition to a modernized industrial economy, accelerated growth and change have occurred in northern Mexico, especially the state of Nuevo Leon. Mexico can be divided into three distinct regions, northern, central, and southern, each with its own characteristics. The deserts and mountains in the northern part of the country presented continuous challenges to their Indian inhabitants. In contrast, the Indians of central and southern Mexico had rich land and found whatever they needed within reach. This difference may be why people in southern Mexico feel that the environment provides plentiful opportunities for making a living, whereas the Mexicans in the north have had to conquer the environment in order to survive (Gutiérrez-Vivó, 1998).

For most of the country, the model of work relationships evolved from agricultural traditions. In the northern state of Nuevo Leon, however, such relationships evolved from a different business philosophy. The vision of the people of Monterrey, in conjunction with their state government, fostered important industrial development that has had a strong influence on the country and the economy (Cerruti, 1984). This philosophy was developed by a group of wealthy families who invested in industries such as beer and steel at the end of the 19th century. Unique to the business vision in Monterrey was a compensation system that paid people salaries more than three times those of other workers in other regions in the country. This system, and the state's geographical proximity to the United States, have helped Nuevo Leon enjoy more rapid industrial development than the rest of the country.

Monterrey was entrepreneurial in comparison to central and southern Mexico, whose traditions opposed change. The industrial development of Monterrey and its surrounding region and the comparatively high salaries attracted a great number of people to the labor force, and in turn, Monterrey's relatively high density of population may have facilitated the development of an industrial culture.

Another interesting distinction about Monterrey is that its people are socially mobile. It is not uncommon to find an executive or professional who is the son of a blue-collar worker. A key reason for this has been the awareness that educational preparation is important, an awareness that may have developed from the presence of several major universities in the city.

A Global Economy and the New Work Culture

For a long time, Mexican companies enjoyed the protections of the country's closed economy. Over the last 15 years, however, drastic changes have compelled companies to manage their businesses in new ways and to create flexible working relationships in order to survive. The factors influencing these changes range from an increasing exchange of goods and services with other nations, initiated when Mexico entered GATT, to major crises in the Mexican economy. As a result of these challenges, a new work culture emerged in Mexican corporations. This new culture is having a major impact on psychological contracts in the country.

The culture that is developing in Mexican companies promotes cooperation among the individuals who affect the organization's productivity. It creates commitment from employers, workers, and unions. The representatives of workers and employers collaborate to create and maintain dignified jobs and satisfy workers' needs. The participants in this process also work toward social justice and respect for all employees in the workplace. The notions of "union" and "solidarity" are important principles. For instance, in HYLSA, a steel company, union workers and management have been collaborating to encourage productivity as well as a positive organizational climate. Representatives from Mexico's industrial sectors signed a document reflecting this new culture, *La Nueva Cultura Laboral* (1996), with the president of Mexico as a witness.

The main objective of the new work culture is to satisfy the material, social, and cultural needs of workers and their families—the center of Mexican life—in order to achieve higher levels of productivity and competitiveness (Abascal-Carranza, 1998). Fair salaries—those that cover basic needs, grow at least as quickly as the rate of inflation, and are comparable to compensation in other companies for similar work—promote harmony between workers and management and reward individual and group efforts in the organization. Training is used to expand capabilities and facilitate individuals' professional and personal development. Safety and hygiene, as well as overall organizational well-being, are the main objectives of the new work culture. Effective communication is viewed as the key to maintaining harmonious relations (La Nueva Cultura Laboral, 1996).

The two work cultures characterizing Mexico's economy developed during two important stages in the country's history. The *competitive, production-focused culture* emerged at the end of the 19th century during a peak in industrialization. This culture aimed to boost productivity by teaching workers from a peasant background how to work in a factory setting. It laid the foundation for the confrontational tradition of labor relations. On the other hand, the *collaborative, international culture,* as it is being promoted at the beginning of the 21st century, is intended to bring workers and managers together in a collaborative approach to the challenges inherent in a globalized economy. These characteristics of Mexico's work culture, as well as other components of life in corporate organizations, are molded largely by the culture of the larger society.

CULTURAL PERSPECTIVE

According to de Buen (cited in Gutiérrez-Vivó, 1998), Mexicans are productive and loyal employees when their working conditions are adequate and when they receive the necessary incentives to satisfy their personal concerns. A love of work is integral to the belief systems of Mexicans, and employees are apt to work more if they will share in the benefits of extra work. If the value of their extra tasks accrues only to company owners, however, employees may work only the required number of hours each day.

It is important to understand the Mexican perspective on work, considering the heritage of the population. The European economic view of the world is different than that of the Indian, the original inhabitant of Mexico. The Indian lives for today, values family life, substitutes personal satisfaction for economic ambition, and embraces a spiritual approach to living that is sometimes enhanced by religion (Gutiérrez-Vivó, 1998). In this view, work is not as important as it is to the European because it is not the means to achieve what is fundamental in life.

In general, the population of Mexico is composed of *mestizos* (those of Spanish and Indian descent) and *criollos* (Creoles or Spaniards born in Mexico). To the latter, work is a fundamental commitment. For *mestizos,* work is accomplished because it is viewed as a necessity, as a means to provide for one's family; however, the workplace is also important for the Mexican as a social setting. Indeed, good social relationships are a priority (Gutiérrez-Vivó, 1998). Mexican culture is collectivistic, and the well-being of the group is greatly valued. One story that illustrates this observation is the example of the fruit seller who did not want to sell all of her fruit to one person at once because she would not have anything left to sell for the rest of the day (Gutiérrez-Vivó, 1998).

The family is considered the building block of Mexican society and as such is a very valued social unit. According to one survey, a family's mother and father deserve the most respect in the Mexican culture (Alducin-Abitia, 1986). In the same study, the reasons for working were listed in the following order: to support the family, to have money, to satisfy aspirations, to educate children, and as a way to eat and live (Alducin-Abitia, 1986). Weekend leisure time is invested in recreational activities with the family, including the extended family of grandparents and cousins (Kras, 1986). Even job attendance is influenced by family issues. Because of the importance of family to most Mexicans, if a child is sick or a special family need arises, work is of secondary importance.

Some Mexican companies view a phone call from home as so important that employees are allowed to take the call even if it means interrupting a meeting. In other organizations, every employee may be a member of a recreational and social club that provides a wide variety of family services, including health care and scholarships. Providing this environment for families allows employees to focus on their work. Further, it is not uncommon for someone to recommend a relative when there is a position open in the organization. For some Mexicans, it is not easy to accept a higher position in the organization if it means changing cities because that change might mean leaving one's extended family (Kras, 1986).

The notion of living for work, as seen in American culture, is not reflected in Mexican culture, where social interaction and friendship are very important, even in the workplace. Courtesy and politeness are valued during workplace interactions. Managers who show interest for the well-being of employees' families are much appreciated.

Another component of Mexican culture affecting psychological contracts is the view that cooperation is more efficient than competition (Alducin-Abitia, 1993). Mexican managers are skillful in the art of diplomacy as a means to diminish the possibility of confrontation (Kras, 1986). They are expected to share the responsibility for job initiatives such as new tasks and projects with the general manager. Workers and their managers generally are not very independent. One seeks input from a superior because that person is responsible for work outcomes (Kras, 1986).

Both Mexican executives and workers have traditionally had great respect for authority figures, perhaps enhanced by the tradition of the autocratic father in the Mexican family. The delegation of authority was once nonexistent in the workplace. However, changes in this component of the work culture have been prompted by employee training (Kras, 1986), as well as by the increasing number of women with academic degrees who work in organizations. As notions of authority and paternalism change in the country, companies increasingly recognize the value of employee ideas.

Mexican culture also is reflected in organizational staffing, in which networking is considered an important way to identify desirable professionals or supervisors, as well as good employees (Flynn, 1984). Job referrals more often arise from one's social network than from one's technical prowess or knowledge.

Mexican employees express their loyalty differently than in some cultures. Employees are often more loyal to their supervisors than to the company. It is not uncommon for subordinates to follow an executive who switches companies. As a result, an organization may lose not only the executive but also some of the employees that the executive supervises (Flynn, 1984).

The Mexican work culture also affects the reward systems that recognize performance. A worker receiving increased pay as a reward may be viewed as a "favorite" of management, thereby creating psychosocial distance between him or her and other workers. One executive observed:

> It's much more important for a Mexican person to have a congenial working environment than it is to make more money. There have been cases where very good workers, ones who have performed well and received pay recognition for that, have left the company because they felt ostracized by their co-workers. (Flynn, 1994, p. 44)

As a result, merit pay or individual bonuses are best given with little fanfare.

As in other countries, Mexico's history and culture have combined to affect the social construction of psychological contracts. We turn now to a discussion of some of them.

SOCIAL CONTRACTS IN THE WORKPLACE

Social contracts, shared beliefs regarding duties and obligations, abound in Mexico. Federal law stipulates many terms of the Mexican employment relationship. For instance, under the "acquired rights" law, if an employer provides a benefit, bonus, or other term of employment for two consecutive years, employees have a right to continue receiving it. This is true even if the employer has not formally agreed on these continued provisions. As one executive has commented, "You can't reduce salary, you can't take away benefits. You simply cannot. To do so would be considered a breach of contract, unless each individual employee's contract is renegotiated" (Flynn, 1994, p. 39).

Under Mexican labor law, employee pay includes compensation for holidays and weekends, and the concept of an hourly wage is unknown. As a result, comparisons between hourly pay in the United States and Mexico can understate Mexican wages by 40%. To support employees, Mexican companies must also give 5% of the salary to INFONAVIT, a governmental institution that administers a fund to provide employees with houses and credit for purchasing houses.

Seniority is recognized in the Mexican work culture, which counts the number of years worked for the organization and adds longevity funds to the severance packages of workers who are dismissed. Those who are fired must be given written notice, never merely oral notification. Otherwise, an assumption is established that an unjustified action may have been taken. The principle behind this practice is to provide a stable working environment and encourage stable labor-management relations.

An interesting use of strikes as devices to send a message to an organization is a "strike by solidarity." This is observed when workers show support for their peers who are on strike at other companies. Workers at various companies strike to put pressure on the target company if they are part of the same union. If a strike takes place in Mexico, employers must enter arbitration, but the union is not required to do so. Arbitration is designed to analyze the situation and reasons that prompted the strike.

Religion also affects employment practices in Mexico, reflecting the influence of Roman Catholicism in the country (although there is no official religion in Mexico). During Holy Week, all organizations are expected to give employees Thursday and Friday off, if not the entire week, in recognition of custom. During the month of December, some employees receive support from their companies to attend "peregrination," a pilgrimage to visit the Shrine of the Virgin of Guadalupe, the patron saint of Mexico, whose apparition is said to have appeared on December 12. Some religious holidays are celebrated only by companies in certain cities. In Guadalajara, for instance, October 12 is a holiday for employees to celebrate the Zapopan Virgin. Instead of Halloween, Mexicans commemorate the "Day of the Dead," or *Dia de los Muertos,* on November 2. Every employee is given a half-day off to visit cemeteries and lay flowers on the graves of relatives. Mother's Day, Children's Day, and Secretaries' Day are also celebrated, and companies may hold parties to honor these individuals.

ECONOMIC FACTORS AFFECTING
PSYCHOLOGICAL CONTRACTS

The acceptance of Mexico into GATT in 1986 and the 1994 enactment of the North American Free Trade Agreement (NAFTA) altered the environmental factors that influence the way business is conducted in Mexico. New factors include political reforms, major crises in the Mexican economy, and the interchange of services and goods within international markets. Before 1986, consumers frequently complained about prices, quality, and the availability of products. Today, products and services have improved, and consumers have access to a greater variety due to the presence of foreign competition.

This change process has not been easy. Organizations have invested great effort to adapt to the new conditions, not always with positive results. The globalization of markets in Mexico has facilitated a change in the nation's business paradigm. Many companies have gone out of business due to their inability to adapt to the new business environment. Others have been transformed through acquisitions, mergers, or strategic alliances.

Unions understand that Mexican companies must be competitive in order to survive and are becoming more flexible in their relations with management. The two parties are collaborating to identify tasks, facilitate work, and develop reward systems. More specifically, employees work with management to set work schedules and change production processes. In turn, companies are changing the way they approach unions, sharing information on their productivity, finances, and competitors. In this way, the new Mexican work culture is trying to overcome old assumptions and values. In addition, new organizational processes are emerging, such as a focus on core activities and the subcontracting of the other jobs to service companies, thereby increasing manufacturing output. The outsourcing of employees is increasing, with even some executives being employed on a project basis. A growing number of professionals conduct work from their homes.

COMPONENTS OF PSYCHOLOGICAL
CONTRACTS IN MEXICO: SELECTED EXAMPLES

Psychological contracts in Mexico are going through a series of organizational and psychological changes, altering many of the elements that shaped traditional working relationships, guided the establishment of work relations, and prompted formal and informal contract negotiations. Companies in Mexico manage the challenges prompted by economic factors in different ways. One example illustrates the clash of old and new assumptions in the workplace during the nation's economic transition in the last 10 years. Union workers in the public services division of a municipality in the state of Mexico went on strike because the assignment of new garbage collection vehicles was based not on seniority but on workers' participation in a job improvement training program (Tapia-Covarruvias, 1997). The unions argued that those who had spent more years in the organization deserved to be rewarded with new equipment. The management decision to reward training rather than seniority reflected a change in its own values underlying psychological contracts in organizations. Workers are beginning to adapt to the shift. Although seniority has traditionally been an important value in the workplace, companies today also value productivity, as measured by how much the workers do for the organization to offer better services or products.

Another example of a Mexican company adapting to environmental challenges is the case of FRISA, a world-class producer of industrial goods, which has a plant in Monterrey. This Mexican corporation has been able to respond successfully to several current, critical factors affecting companies throughout the world, such as global competition, new technologies, price competition, and service demands. Because of its relatively small size and flat structure, FRISA has conducted its business differently than bigger Mexican companies, which traditionally have had a more rigid hierarchical structure. Workers at FRISA are able to help their managers find solutions that improve their way of doing things. The company fosters a working climate featuring open communication, incentives for employees to upgrade their educational level, and a reward system that recognizes workers' accomplishments. Despite the low educational level of many Mexican workers, their natural creativity and willingness to improve their work comes to the fore when given the right encouragement. When the company began selling its products in the United States, its biggest challenge was developing the trust of American customers. Learning their customers' needs developed this trust, as well as consistency in fulfilling commitments. The FRISA case is an excellent illustration of how Mexican workers respond when they are motivated to make a difference in their workplace and their lives.

Ultimately, FRISA's success prompted management to buy a plant in Detroit. The contrasting experiences of the workers in the Monterrey and Detroit plants indicate some cultural differences. For instance, Mexican workers received more guidance from supervisors because of their perceived lack of educational preparation and because Mexican culture tends to favor a "command and control" style of management. The management has exchanged workers between Monterrey and Detroit plants so that employees may learn from one another. The workers in Detroit were typically viewed as more independent and self-confident in their abilities. Some of these individuals had gone to college and entered the workplace prepared to develop solutions to problems and improve work processes. After their visits to the United States, Mexican workers made changes quickly because they were eager to improve their skills and grow professionally. They tended to be more receptive to change, more willing to contribute to organizational learning, and more interested in personal and professional development. They were interested in self-improvement for the sake of their children, who they hoped would have a better standard of living than their parents. They used opportunities given by the company to finish elementary school or high school and to help their children do well in school. In contrast, the workers in the Detroit plant displayed less flexibility and willingness to learn. FRISA sponsors a party every time a Mexican employee graduates from elementary or high school to acknowledge and reward this accomplishment.

Another difference between the two plants is that in the Detroit plant there is a division between management and workers due to status differences. At the Monterrey plant, in a break with tradition, this division does not exist. Managers and workers see themselves on the same side and share a variety of information. The president of FRISA indicates that the company's business philosophy is open to organizational change and that the input of employees is welcome. If something needs to be changed in the Mexican plant, management asks for input from those who will be affected by that change. The company values employees greatly, and meetings are scheduled to talk about sales and profits so that everyone is informed, and involved, in matters related to company performance.

One human resource manager in HYLSA (Hojalata y Lámina S.A.) has discussed the company's model for labor relations as a unique one. Indeed, other companies have shown interest in adopting it. One unique feature offered to workers is its recreational and social center. This center has as part of its mission the integral development of the worker and his/her family into the organization. The club has an Olympic-size pool, a diving area, 12 tennis

courts, soccer fields, basketball courts, a gym, a theater, and all of these facilities are for the employees and their families. The center also includes a hospi-
tal, which offers complete medical services to workers and their families. The
way workers are treated in this company, as reflected in the center, allows them
to identify with the company and develop loyalty to it. Additionally, part of the
company's success relates to the fact that department heads have a close relationship with their direct reports. They are expected to be mentors as well as
supervisors, to know the employees and their families. In HYLSA, supervisors
also manage benefits packages. For instance, if a worker wishes to request a
scholarship for a child, there is a standard procedure administered by the
supervisor who will explain the procedure to the applicant. HYLSA's excellent
relationships with the union, as well as with the workers directly, ensure that
both parties are interested in the welfare of the company.

These three examples suggest that a shift is occurring in fundamental assumptions about employment in Mexico. Status, though still important, means
less than in the past, and contributions to firm performance mean more. The
attitude toward work relations as an extension of family ties occurs along with
a focus on employment as a means to develop in ways that provide workers'
families with security and opportunities for the future.

PSYCHOLOGICAL CONTRACTS IN MEXICO:
A SURVEY AND A LOOK AT THE FUTURE

We have indicated throughout this chapter that historical and contemporary
influences have shaped Mexican labor relations. At the end of the 19th century
and the beginning of the 20th, the production of goods changed from a system of
individual hand-crafting to one of mass production. A working class emerged,
and unions were established to protect employees from mistreatment by management. Labor relations focused on the creation and maintenance of loyalty
and stability in the workplace. In the last years of the 20th century, organizations
have experienced dynamic environments where change is a constant influence,
stimulated in great part by foreign competition.

The expansion of the Mexican economy has influenced greatly the way
business is conducted in the country. Increased interaction between management and unions has enhanced the trust between them. Their mutual interest in
collaboration facilitates company competitiveness and a better standard of living for employees. A recent study indicates that NAFTA has led Mexican firms
to offer more innovative benefit packages to employees, even though certain
included benefits may not be required by law. These new benefits range from
increased pay, such as production bonuses, to health services and day care centers (Peek, 1998).

The lead author recently surveyed 26 human resource managers in Mexico
to ascertain their opinions on psychological contracts in past, current, and
future business organizations. These individuals represented 26 companies

located in different cities throughout the country. There was no consensus among those surveyed regarding whether relational (long-term and open-ended) or transactional (short-term with explicit requirements) contracts are more likely to be found in Mexican organizations. Ten years ago, they reported, contracts were more relational than transactional. Although relational contracts still predominate slightly, it is expected that transactional contracts will increase and that for the next 10 years a combination of the two will be found in companies. These responses are consistent with the changes Mexico is experiencing as a result of its entrance into the international market. The survey results also provide evidence for greater use of written contracts specifying working hours and the type of work to be done by employees. Workers in Mexico believe that a written contract protects their individual interests; as one Spanish saying has it, *Las palabras se las lleva el viento* ("Spoken words are blown away by the wind [but words on paper are permanent].")

Respondents consistently identified the globalization of markets as the main source of new human resource management and business strategies in Mexico. This factor was considered more significant than any economic crises or political changes experienced in the country to date. The human resource managers reported that employees were generally flexible in adapting to organizational changes. They emphasized the positive attitudes of most workers toward Mexico's new work culture. Workers support organizational changes that are believed to help the organization be successful. In the last 10 years, according to survey results, there have been significant changes in business and human resource management strategies. For example, in the case of HYLSA, as a result of the business strategy change from domestic to international markets, human resources strategies were altered. Changes included a shift from a hierarchical communication system to a collaborative relationship with the union, from specific to multitask worker profiles, and from a seniority to a training reward system. Interestingly, HYLSA also manifests the traditional emphasis that Mexicans place on family but does so to produce high performance. HYLSA promises employment for workers' children. However, if a father recommends a son for a job, the father signs a letter guaranteeing his son's good performance and agrees to be his tutor. If the son becomes a problem, the father assists in his improvement or is responsible for firing him. HYLSA pays above-market wages and employs whole families, promoting high performance and a supportive work climate. Such a firm is a model of a global strategy built on Mexican values.

What do employees want from their jobs now and during the beginning of the 21st century? "Career opportunity" is the predominant answer these human resource managers give. A decade ago, employment security was the expected answer; today, a competitive salary and training to enhance professional growth are the main desires. Organizational expectations related to preferred qualities in employees also have changed. The survey indicates that loyalty was the most important quality 10 years ago, followed by ethical behavior and hard work. Now, teamwork skills and goal achievement are the desired characteristics. The presence of learning skills has emerged as another important employee quality. During the next 10 years, teamwork, creativity, and communication skills will be increasingly viewed as desired employee qualities.

The human resource managers participating in the survey anticipate that organizations will offer employees several advantages during the next 10 years, including increased job satisfaction, a better quality of life, flexible working schedules, greater challenges, opportunities to develop skills useful for any position, a larger share of profits, professional development, competitive salaries, and variable compensation in relation to productivity.

Implications for Psychological Contracts

In general, psychological contract theory as understood in the United States is applicable in the Mexican context, due to the proliferation of American management practices in Mexican organizations and the great influence of American companies operating in Mexico. Yet there are specific cultural issues that make features of psychological contracts unique in Mexico. As we have discussed, the family is very influential in shaping labor relations in Mexico. In one company we visited, foreign competition is forcing the use of new technologies in place of human workers. The families of these workers are encouraging them to do whatever is necessary to remain with the organization, including moving out of management positions and taking salary cuts. Motivating these actions are the benefits and working conditions given to employees and their families. The duty to support one's family creates special terms in the Mexican psychological contract between firms and workers.

Several human resource managers contacted during the writing of this chapter agreed that globalization of the economy is the main cause of organizational change in Mexico. Before this development, the government viewed employment as one of its primary functions. It owned 1,500 corporations, including the nation's telephone company, steel corporations, train system, banks, and some television stations. Employee loyalty was expected in these organizations, in return for which employees expected opportunities for career advancement and employment security.

As the Mexican economy became globalized during the late 1980s, the government sold many corporations to private owners/investors, and within a few years its 1,500 companies decreased to 150. This privatization increased competition among Mexican companies and greatly influenced labor relations in the country. Employee loyalty has been affected by restructuring and a decreased emphasis on long-term employment security. In addition, training (rather than seniority) has emerged as a primary way to ensure employability.

Loyalty may be linked to career opportunities, but only if the company offers those opportunities. Indeed, employees have come to realize that migration from one company to another is part of a new working environment. *Maquiladora* employees assembling products along the U.S. border, for example, now migrate from one company to another in search of better salaries. The structure of *maquiladoras* makes it difficult for companies to retain good workers because these organizations are perceived as assembly line units that offer good salaries to employees but little else. Other Mexican companies are now engaged in organizational renewal, part of which is designed to reward employees who are team players with creativity and communication skills instead of loyal and hard-working laborers.

Foreign competition and domestic economic crises create opportunities to renegotiate psychological contracts. Tolerance for breaking promises can be higher, depending on the situation—employees are more accepting of unfulfilled commitments for which the company is not responsible than agreements that are broken by management. When their psychological contracts are breached, employees often retaliate in nonconfrontational ways. A group of employees from different divisions of the same glass corporation decided to work the minimum number of hours required on their shifts and exert little effort in response to the closing of one of the company's plants. Protesting is also seen in early retirements and resignations. If a breach of contract affects union workers, a strike can be imminent.

New psychological contracts are affected by experiences in the hiring process. To compete in a single, worldwide market requires the upgrading of employee credentials. Those who do not meet the new job requirements face difficult times finding work, which poses a challenge for the educational system in Mexico. Moreover, because supply and demand in the labor market is continually changing, there is increased room for qualified workers at many levels to negotiate their salary and benefits.

CONCLUSION

The history and culture of Mexico greatly affect psychological contracts within its business organizations, and economic factors increasingly influence labor/management relationships. Realizing that they are part of a global society, Mexicans have witnessed the dramatic development of other countries, and many have wondered why their nation has grown more slowly. As a result, they have sought more citizen participation in government, more education for their children, and better treatment from the management of organizations in which they work. As the Mexican middle class increases, so do its expectations concerning employment and resultant psychological contracts. In a country where the word *promise* has been marred by years of governmental breaches of commitments to the citizenry, *fairness* and *justice* are the words that motivate new generations of employees.

REFERENCES

Abascal-Carranza, C. M. (1998, August). La Nueva Cultura Laboral. *COMARI, 10,* 3-5.

Adleson, S., & Camarena, M. (1991). Presentación. In Instituto Nacional de Antropología e Historia (Ed.), *Comunidad, cultura y vida social: Ensayos sobre la formación de la clase obrera: Seminario de Movimiento Obrero y Revolución Mexicana* (pp. 7-13). Mexico City: Instituto Nacional de Antropología e Historia.

Alducin-Abitia, E. (1986). *Los valores de los Mexicanos: México entre la tradición y la modernidad* (Vol. 1). Mexico City: Fomento Cultural Banamex.

Alducin-Abitia, E. (1993). *Los valores de los Mexicanos: En busca de una escencia* (Vol. 3). Mexico City: Fomento Cultural Banamex.

Cerruti, M. (1984). Desarrollo capitalista y fuerza de trabajo en Monterrey, 1890-1910. In Universidad Autónoma de Puebla (Eds.), *Memorias del encuentro sobre historia del movimiento obrero* (Vol. 1, pp. 167-195). Puebla, Mexico: Universidad Autónoma de Puebla.

Flynn, G. (1994). HR in Mexico: What you should know. *Personnel Journal, 73*(8), 34.

Gutiérrez-Vivó, J. (1998). *El otro yo del Mexicano.* Mexico City: Editorial Oceano.

Kras, E. S. (1986). *Cultura gerencial México-Estados Unidos.* Guadalajara, Mexico: Impresora Analco.

Laurell, A. C. (1984). Proceso de trabajo y salud. In Universidad Autónoma de Puebla (Eds.), *Memorias del encuentro sobre historia del movimiento obrero* (Vol. 1, pp. 289-327). Puebla, Mexico: Universidad Autónoma de Puebla.

Méndez, C., & Huerta, R. (1991). La vida social de los trabajadores de la fábrica de papel San Rafael, 1890-1930. In Instituto Nacional de Antropología e Historia (Eds.), *Comunidad, cultura y vida social: Ensayos sobre la formación de la clase obrera: Seminario de Movimiento Obrero y Revolución Mexicana* (pp. 75-92). Mexico City: Instituto Nacional de Antropología e Historia.

Novelo, V. (1991). Los trabajadores Mexicanos en el siglo XIX: ¿Obreros o artesanos? In Instituto Nacional de Antropología e Historia (Eds.), *Comunidad, cultura y vida social: Ensayos sobre la formación de la clase obrera: Seminario de Movimiento Obrero y Revolución Mexicana* (pp. 15-52). Mexico City: Instituto Nacional de Antropología e Historia.

La Nueva Cultura Laboral. (1996). Unpublished document.

Paz, O. (1994). *El laberinto de la soledad/Posdata/ Vuelta a el laberinto de la soledad.* Mexico City: Fondo de Cultura Económica.

Peek, B. C. (1998, August). *Current benefits in a post-NAFTA Mexico.* Paper presented at the Ronald E. MacNair Research Conference, Pittsburgh, PA.

Peña, S. (1984). La clase obrera en la historia de México. In Siglo Veintiuno Editores (Eds.), *Trabajadores y sociedad en el siglo XX.* Mexico City: Siglo Veintiuno Editores.

Rodríguez-González, L. C. (1997). *Manual de políticas y prácticas de administración de recursos humanos.* Monterrey, Mexico.

Tapia-Covarruvias, S. (1997, October). Panorama laboral. *Revista COMARI, 5,* 18-19.

10

Psychological Contracts in the Netherlands

Dualism, Flexibility, and Security

Charissa Freese
René Schalk

Negotiating is reaching compromises.
Dutch Saying

Psychological contracts in the Netherlands can be described as "dual" in nature. The country places a premium on employees' freedom of choice but also strongly values security and stability in the workplace. Finding a balance between flexibility and security is the core issue in psychological contracting in the Netherlands today. The use of temporary and flexible work arrangements is increasing and becoming more accepted by Dutch society, and the promise of lifelong employment is decreasing.

Dual messages are sent to employees with respect to the need for flexibility and the provision of job security. The case of the Unilever corporation provides an example of this. When the company released its most recent annual results, shareholders received an unexpected return of 16 billion guilders. Even after the surplus was paid out, the board of directors indicated that the company had enough money left to buy any company it wished to take over. Viewed in isolation, this show of confidence might have led employees to view the company's strong financial position as a signal of ample job security for workers.

In reality, however, Unilever management stressed that a reorganization of the company still was necessary to improve efficiency and competitiveness.

This chapter traces the evolution of psychological contracts in the Netherlands by examining the country's history and culture, tracing recent developments in the Dutch labor market, and, finally, discussing how those changes affect human resource management practices and psychological contracts in the Netherlands.

THE NETHERLANDS

To gain a full understanding of how certain aspects of psychological contracts develop, it is necessary to first introduce the Netherlands, its culture and labor market. The Netherlands is a very small, densely populated country (16 million inhabitants) situated in the northwestern part of Europe. Although the country is a constitutional monarchy, with Queen Beatrix as head of the government, the queen has no official political power. Since 1994, a so-called "purple" government, a coalition in which both left ("red"), right ("blue"), and center parties are present, has led the Netherlands.

The Netherlands is a member of the European Community and faces many changes in the forthcoming years due to European unification and the introduction of a common form of currency, the Euro. Banks began using the Euro in January 1999, and the hard currency is due to be introduced in 2002. Dutch society tends to have an international orientation, which began centuries ago with international trade. Newspapers and broadcasts present a great deal of international news, and most Dutch citizens speak one or more foreign languages. Some Dutch university programs are given entirely in English.

The Dutch economy is currently a successful example of what has been called the Poldermodel (named after a typical Dutch landscape). The basis of this model is the way the Dutch resolve conflicts: by negotiation. Divergent views are taken into consideration, all parties are heard, and usually a compromise is found that keeps all parties satisfied. This leads to the Poldermodel of consensus policy making, in which the government, employers, and trade unions negotiate frequently about actions that will keep the Dutch economy healthy. The Organization for Economic Cooperation and Development (OECD) recently noted that decisions made by the Poldermodel negotiating parties are incorporated remarkably quickly into Dutch organizations. Social unrest is rare in the Netherlands; although strikes do sometimes occur, they are usually seen as a last resort and are seldom organized in a socially disruptive fashion. Unions usually choose actions that they call "public friendly" that do not inconvenience citizens. An example of this would be the police going on strike by refusing to hand out parking tickets.

Consensus policy making has created a generous social welfare system. Every citizen is able to access health insurance and all forms of education (including universities). Social security, general family allowances, unemployment benefits, old age pensions, and general disability benefits are all regulated by law. Nonetheless, in changing circumstances—for example, because of the aging of the population (both Dutch men and women have on average one of the world's highest life expectancies)—this system has continuously been revised, generally tending toward reductions in benefits.

History of Employment

Dutch employment developed much like employment in other European countries. Before the industrial revolution, farming and trade were important sources of income. During the industrial revolution, unions were created. Both Protestants and Catholics had their own organizations and unions, which were similar in scope, goals, and hierarchies despite different religious traditions. The Netherlands has a colonial past, starting with the "golden age" in the 17th century. Dutch economic supremacy, with trade spanning the world, led to the foundation of colonies in Asia (Indonesia) and the Caribbean (the Dutch Antilles) and the exchange between England and the Netherlands of New York (then called "New Amsterdam") for Surinam. Today, only the Dutch Antilles are still part of the Kingdom of the Netherlands. Because of this colonial past and a shortage of labor in the period around 1970 that led to the recruiting of foreign workers (mainly Turks and Moroccans), the Netherlands became a multicultural society. However, working life has not become a multicultural experience. Successful employees from ethnic groups in Dutch organizations usually have adapted to Dutch culture. There are many foreign shops, restaurants, and travel agencies (mostly Turkish), but they usually have their own banks, customers, and suppliers. The Dutch and foreign cultures do not really mix; they coexist. This means that in the vast majority of workers and companies the Dutch psychological contract predominates.

Culture

"The difficulty in defining the values held by countries is whether or not it should be assumed that the values are actually shared" (Roe & Ester, 1999, p. 4). This remark is typically Dutch: The Dutch find it difficult to generalize. In this section, however, some general conclusions are drawn by using the outcomes of value research. First, the Dutch decision-making style is further discussed, followed by elaboration on the cultural values of power, equality, and achievement.

Decision Making

As previously mentioned, decision making in the Netherlands is achieved through negotiation processes that encourage open communication among all parties as a compromise is formed. This practice extends to legal procedures, where a typical Dutch strategy (*gedoogbeleid*) can be observed. This strategy entails the tolerance for certain behaviors that technically are illegal. Drug use, euthanasia, and prostitution are illegal in the Netherlands, but Dutch courts have condoned these practices when certain norms are adhered to. An example of the *gedoogbeleid* is the policy of testing of Ecstasy pills at "house" parties. Ecstasy is illegal in the Netherlands, but because their use at "house" parties is generally known, these pills are tested with consent of the police at the entrance to ensure that nobody is endangered by taking highly toxic, even lethal versions of the drug. Behind the combination of strict rules but flexible enforcement is the high value that the Dutch place on individual freedom. Personal circumstances are taken into account, and definitive, generalized statements are seldom made.

The *gedoogbeleid* leads to misconceptions abroad—and even some Dutch people do not know exactly what is legal and what is not. A foreigner once said, "If you ask a Dutchman if something is legal in the Netherlands, the reply will not be simply 'yes' or 'no,' but 'I am not sure, I will have to look it up.'" Despite these uncertainties about the legality of various behaviors, the Dutch tend to be law-abiding citizens. Laws and procedures are followed, and procedural justice is very important. In working life, this is reflected by a strict following of procedures. Many organizations today—concerned with "company ethics"—formulate rules that define the conditions under which an employee can accept business gifts in order to minimize the risk of bribery. The Netherlands, in fact, is one of the least corrupt nations in the world.

Power

Two multinational investigations concluded that the Netherlands is highly egalitarian with respect to power (Hofstede, 1980; Thierry, Den Hartog, Koopman, & Wilderom, in press). Dutch organizations have a relatively flat structure. There is a general questioning of authority; police officers and the elderly are not treated with much respect in the Netherlands. In Dutch culture, outstanding individuals are usually not identified as heroes: "It runs counter to important values and habits to attribute unusual performance mainly, let alone exclusively, to individual characteristics" (Thierry et al., in press). The scarcity of statues of historical figures in Dutch society can be attributed to these values.

Equality

Dutch society tends to seek the minimization of inequality. In one poll, 80% agreed that everyone should have equal opportunities. In 1997, 64% of Dutch said that income differences in their country were too large, an increase of 10 percentage points in 2 years (Sociaal Cultureel Planbureau [SCP], 1998). Because income differences did not increase significantly over that time period, it appears that more Dutch have become sensitive to the issue of equality. This taste for equality is a mix of valuing equal opportunities and equal results. Education, for example, is freely accessible (equal opportunities), and income differences are relatively small in the Netherlands (equal results). Societal groups that are relatively less fortunate are viewed as deserving of help, a value that is reflected in the solid social security system established in the Netherlands. This value reflects the preference for certainty and security. To describe Dutch culture in this way means that Dutch value freedom but also want to believe that security and a feeling of freedom are available to all citizens. Research indicates that two of the issues people value most are security and safety (i.e., employment and low crime) (SCP, 1998).

Achievement

The Netherlands score moderate on achievement orientation (Thierry et al., in press), caused by the fact that although businesses tend to be oriented toward achievement, the Dutch taste for equality tends to lower aspirations for rewards differing from their peers'. Employees want to be recognized for their performance, but outstanding performers are also vulnerable to social sanctions and must strive to be better than others in an inconspicuous way. In the Netherlands, the Calvinistic moral of sobriety is common, and the Dutch tend to frown on those who lead a luxurious, extravagant lifestyle. "Acting normal" is very important in the Netherlands, and the biggest compliment a successful manager, politician, actor, or scientist can get is to be considered down to earth despite his or her success. Nonetheless, employees attach great importance to jobs that are challenging and also allow freedom in the workplace. Career planning is important, especially for young, well-educated workers. Because it is difficult to both raise children and have a career, young, well-educated Dutch women tend to pursue a career prior to having children. Dutch women have their first child at an average age of 29, the highest in the world.

Perceived pressure at work is the highest in Europe (Centraal Bureau voor de Statistiek [CBS], 1998b). Although official working hours are short (a 37-hour workweek on average), employees commonly work overtime. Despite this, Dutch employees value their personal lives, and there is a strict boundary between work and private life. For example, employees are called at home for business reasons only in emergency situations or when they have given explicit permission to do so. In addition, companies do not interfere in the social lives of their employees. The Dutch place great weight on family life—according to one poll, it is the second most valued aspect of life in the Netherlands, second only to one's health (SCP, 1998).

Cultural values affect the expectations employees have regarding proper workplace behavior. For example, the Dutch egalitarian culture may lead employees to believe that a supervisor should have lunch at the same table as his or her subordinates. Recently, lower-paid employees at Tilburg University were given the ability to travel first class on business trips to treat them the same as their higher-paid counterparts. In the same vein, individualism may lead to the expectation of an autonomous job in which one is recognized for one's achievements.

Economy

Most people are employed in service sector occupations such as insurance, accounting, banking, and government. Trade and transportation are important sectors as well, especially because Rotterdam is the largest seaport in the world. Industry, focused mainly on the production of basic products, employs fewer people. Although Dutch agricultural products (primarily tulips and cheese) are a trademark abroad and are thus important for export reasons, relatively few people work in this sector. Agricultural and industry businesses are becoming larger, but large scale and more efficient production are achieved with fewer people because of the increased use of machinery. As one Dutch manager stated, "The Netherlands does not create anything anymore. Only 6 or 7 percent of our national income consists of physical output. The Netherlands pushes paper" (quoted in *De Volkskrant,* March 27, 1999). The Dutch economy is growing at 3.5% a year, and inflation is at about 2%. The public sector deficit has decreased from 4% to 1.5% in the last 4 years. The unemployment rate in the fourth quarter of 1998 was 3.6% in the Netherlands as opposed to an average of 10.2% in the European Union (CBS, 1998a, p. 5). Nearly a quarter of the Dutch population under age 65 is inactive (defined here as not having a paid full-time job). This veritable army of inactives consists of unemployed people, part-time employees, early retirees, and individuals on leave due to illness or disability. This places the low unemployment figures in a somewhat different context (*Economist,* May 2, 1998). However, after years of declining participation among older employees (55 to 64 years old), the participation of this category in the labor force is again increasing (CBS, 1998a).

Education

The educational level in the Netherlands is high. Almost 100% of the population are literate, and a great deal of value is placed on foreign-language education. Young people tend to go to secondary schools and institutions for higher education more often and to enter the labor market at a high age. In the academic year 1994-95, 25% of young people leaving the school system were graduating from professional schools or universities. On average, Dutch men have a higher educational level than women; however, this is due to the higher educational level of men over 45 years of age. Young women (aged 15 to 24) tend to have more education than their male peers (SCP, 1996).

DEVELOPMENTS IN THE DUTCH LABOR MARKET

The Dutch labor market has changed completely in recent years. The SCP, the country's social cultural research bureau (SCP, 1998) described the changes as a small revolution in the living situation of the Dutch. These changes are a consequence not only of economic and demographic trends but also of changing opinions regarding who should work. The opinion of the public and the government has changed on participation in the labor market by the elderly, mothers, chronically ill people, and people with disabilities. Here, the developments in the labor market are described with respect to working hours, temporary and flexible work, mobility and labor supply, part-time work, gender and multicultural issues, and rewards.

Working Hours

The economic climate has had a profound influence on working hours and the way in which organizational commitment is appraised. In an excellent review article, Tijdens (1998) described how working hours have changed along with the economy. In 1919, the Dutch Labor Law was passed. At that time, employers were prohibited from offering working days longer than 8 hours and could provide a maximum of 48 hours per week (Saturday was still a regular working day). After World War II, the rebuilding of the national economy made it necessary to oblige employees to work at least 48 hours per week. Beginning in 1959, employees worked fewer hours (45 hours a week at first) and received paid vacations (1 week). Near the end of the 1970s, as the country experienced increased unemployment, unions pleaded for shorter working hours in order to reallocate labor. This reallocation was achieved mainly through early retirement schemes. By 1982, this was considered to be too expensive, and very few older employees were still employed. Collective reduction of working hours (ADV; *arbeids duur verkorting* in Dutch) was introduced, in which extra vacation days were offered every year. Collective reduction of working hours was seen as a way to reduce the labor force without mass dismissals. After 1985, the economy blossomed. Between 1986 and 1994, no further measures to reduce working hours were requested by the unions because employees could not afford to take further days off due to work pressures. Subsequently, several factors led to the extension of opening hours for shops: just-in-time delivery schedules, consumer behavior (more two-income households requiring service outside of regular office hours), and congestion on the Dutch highways. The opening hours were extended in 1996 to run from 6 a.m. until 10 p.m. Labor during these irregular hours had to become cheaper, so reduction of working hours was traded against lower irregular wages and was offered on a weekly basis. Also in 1996, the 36-hour workweek was introduced in several collective labor agreements (Tijdens, 1998).

In the Netherlands, there was much concern that the extension of working hours and the opening of shops on Sundays would create a 24-hour economy. Politicians, unions, and the Catholic Church warned about the negative consequences. However, the 24-hour economy is an illusion. A 16-hour economy would be a more correct term (*Intermediair,* June 18, 1998). This new work schedule applies mostly to highly educated employees who voluntarily work irregular hours during evenings and weekends (no nights and more time at home). Highly educated employees do have an influence on their work hours, whereas lower-educated employees do not. Statistics report that in the last 20 years the number of employees working irregular hours has increased only slightly. In 1975, 12.7% of the employees worked irregular hours, as opposed to 14.2% in 1995 (CBS, 1998a). Worker psychological contracts are affected considerably by these trends in working hours. For many years, older employees knew that they could retire early; today, retirement depends on individual choices, including whether individuals have saved and planned for it. Overall, employees have become more responsible for their own careers and have a greater responsibility for what formerly were employment benefits.

Temporary and Flexible Work

Within Europe, temporary work is most prevalent in the United Kingdom, where 3.9% of total employment is temporary. The Netherlands is second in Europe, with a 3.7% prevalence rate. Other countries with a booming temporary labor market include France, Belgium, and Luxembourg. In contrast, in the Scandinavian countries, temporary work agencies are rare (*Intermediair,* June 23, 1998). Labor unions in the Netherlands have recently stopped objecting to temporary work, and the number of job contracts with a duration of less than 1 year or without a fixed number of hours ("on-call contracts") is growing—approximately one half of all new jobs have these characteristics. On-call contracts are contracts in which employees are only called when needed and are only paid if they actually worked (De Nederlandse Bank [DNB], 1996). The government has also assumed responsibility for making the labor market more flexible by altering rules regarding the renewal of temporary contracts and dismissal procedures. At the same time, long-term temporary workers are obtaining more secure positions and are entitled to social security benefits paid by the employment agencies when there is no work.

Mobility and Labor Supply

External mobility (the ability to take a position outside one's organization) is quite low in the Netherlands. Many employees stay in the same organization for many years. In collective bargaining agreements, mobility is an issue. Organizations must attempt to enhance internal mobility (mobility within the organization) to ensure that employees are better equipped if they have to look for a job outside the organization. Employees who have a higher educational level or work in sectors such as information technology or the hotel and catering industry have on average a greater mobility. Careers are no longer vertical, and *promotion* no longer refers solely to acquiring a higher position in the same organization. Building a career involves finding a sequence of challenging jobs, inside or outside the organization. Employees who leave organizations for jobs elsewhere are viewed more positively than they were 15 years ago. Among younger employees in particular, turnover and mobility are encouraged and in some cases even required—for example, in law firms.

Dutch organizations are changing their human resource policies to conform to the changes taking place on the larger labor market. For example, mothers and older employees increasingly participate in the labor market and influence human resource practices. In 1997, the number of jobs grew sharply, and there was a shortage of employees across several sectors, mainly in the areas of health care, education, information technology, commercial services, and real estate (CBS, 1998a). Temporary work agencies also experienced a shortage. As a result of this labor shortage, some organizations began to retool their human resource management strategies in an attempt to attract new employees and commit valuable employees to the organization. One home-help organization offered established employees a trip to Spain as a reward for recruiting new employees to the company (*Intermediair*, June 4, 1998). One accounting firm launched an advertising campaign to change the image of its profession and attract new workers (*Intermediair*, June 18, 1998). The Dutch postal service, KPN, aired television commercials in which two employees—one of them a member of the board of directors—presented their background and family life, stating at the end: "I am KPN." These commercials, which attempt to identify the company with specific individuals, are most certainly a product of their times.

Part-Time Work

The proportion of part-time work in the Netherlands is the highest of the 29 countries participating in OECD and twice as high as the average of the European Union; every third employee (38%) works part time in the Netherlands versus one in six employees (16%) in the European Union (DNB, 1996). The Netherlands has such a high prevalence of part-time workers because most women work part time. Until recently, many women stopped working after their first child was born. Today, women often continue to work, but Dutch society still does not really approve of children being raised by people other than their parents. Most couples with children now opt for one-and-a-half jobs. In 1996, women worked an average of 25.8 hours per week, whereas men worked an average 38.6 hours (Ministerie van Sociale Zaken en Werkgelegenheid/CBS, 1998).

Research by the largest Dutch Labor Union indicates that 25% of the working population wants to work fewer hours, yet 75% of these employees do not request a reduction of hours. The reasons given are loss of income, negative consequences for pension benefits, lower promotion opportunities, and a perception that the employer objects to part-time work. Twelve percent of employees who started working part time did report that they were demoted.[1]

The increased percentages of female and part-time workers in the labor force have shaped the issues that are addressed by unions and politicians. In 1998, for example, the government enacted a law giving employees the right to work part time if they wished, although the company can deny this right if it cannot find a substitute. Parental leave has also been enacted into law; employees who have worked for a company for more than 1 year are permitted (by law) to reduce their working hours by a maximum of half of their work hours, for 6 months, if they become parents.

Women in the Dutch Labor Force

In 1976, a law was passed that prohibited the automatic discharge of women who married or became pregnant (Fokkema & Van Solinge, 1998). Dutch women still make up one of the smallest proportions of the European labor force (*Economist,* May 2, 1998). However, the participation of women in the labor market is increasing faster than in other European countries (SCP, 1996). For example, the percentage of Dutch mothers who were working increased from 25% in 1988 to 45% in 1997. In 1998, 70% of all households in the Netherlands consisted of two incomes; in 1986, only 30% could be described as such. Opinions on working mothers have become more positive in recent years, but 34% of the population still disapprove of putting children in day care centers (SCP, 1998). Paid work was not common for women in the Netherlands for many years, but most young women today enter the labor force and remain employed even after they start a family.

Young female employees (and also young male employees who wish to take care of their children) will have different career experiences than older employees. They are confronted with problems that their older male colleagues probably have never experienced. Many young women expect to build careers early, then take some time off to raise children or work part time in an interesting job (with flexible working hours or child care provided by the organizations) before returning to their careers again. This is a completely different career path from that of their senior male colleagues.

Multicultural Workplaces

Although the Netherlands can be considered a multicultural society, the country's different cultures are far from integrated in the workplace. Unemployment rates are much higher for foreigners than for the native Dutch. The government has recognized this problem and is seeking to solve it by requiring foreigners who move to the Netherlands to participate in an integration course. The Dutch government also provides financial support to schools that have many foreign students in order to improve the education these children receive. Furthermore, organizations are obliged to report the number of foreign employees working at their organization as well as to implement measures increasing employment of foreigners. Employer and employee organizations have recommended laws that would guarantee foreign employees the right to celebrate their own holidays and obey their religious principles (e.g., by providing space for prayer or the opportunity to wear head shawls) (De Wit, 1995). Foreign employees often participate in less skilled, lower-paying jobs than the native Dutch.

Rewards

Labor unions historically opposed performance-based compensation, which is not in keeping with the Dutch egalitarian culture. Nowadays, however, performance-based compensation is accepted by most employees, and labor unions have stopped objecting to such practices. As these changes have occurred, rewards have become increasingly individualized, with organizations offering a range of benefits from so-called "cafeteria plans" to the ability to trade reduced working hours for computers, early retirement, sabbatical leave, or extra days off. This shift in opinions regarding rewards has taken place gradually, along with changes in society, such as labor market shortages and the different needs of two-income households, that have made individualized rewards acceptable to many employees. Employees today feel comfortable with the broader negotiation range of contract conditions. On the other hand, employees who have worked for a company for many years sometimes feel they have been treated inequitably compared to new employees who have negotiated better conditions. These labor market tendencies could be reflected in the fact that the number of Dutch people who agreed with the statement that income differences were too large in the Netherlands increased by 10% in only 2 years (SCP, 1998).

Male and female employees are on average rewarded differently in the Netherlands. The income differences between men and women are among the largest in Europe. Only Greece has a larger income differential between men and women performing the same kind of work. Female employees earn on average 30% less than their male counterparts (*Intermediair,* June 9, 1999).

These developments in the Dutch labor market are creating changing expectations on the part of employees. For example, shortages in the labor market led many organizations to abandon their early retirement programs. Thus, as "new" employees age, they probably will not automatically expect to retire early unless they have made provisions of their own in a cafeteria plan.

Because many more women stay in the labor force after their first child is born, new parents may expect organizations to provide flexible working hours or child care facilities. As temporary work becomes a regular arrangement, this may lead to divergent forms of commitment and feelings of "belonging" to the organization across the Dutch labor force. Finally, because of labor shortages, valued employees may expect bonuses or performance-based pay in order to commit them to the organization.

Until now, we have described cultural values and labor market developments that influence expectations held by employers and employees: in other words, cultural values and societal factors that can influence the psychological contract. The next section describes how the key concepts of psychological contract theory apply to the Dutch situation.

PSYCHOLOGICAL CONTRACT THEORY IN THE NETHERLANDS

This section applies psychological contract theory to the Dutch labor market situation by explaining the context of Dutch labor law and how the key concepts of this theory—contracts, promises and obligations, and the zone of negotiability—are manifested in the Netherlands.

Many aspects of Dutch labor contracts are regulated, either by law or through collective bargaining agreements. A number of the features of these contracts (e.g., probation periods, advance notice of contract termination, minimum wages, maximum hours, minimum number of vacation days) are covered by rules and laws. Even aspects that are informal and not part of a written contract are covered by broad legislation called the "good employer" law (Burgerlijk Wetboek, Artikel 7A: 1638Z; see Wessels, 1991). This law defines "good employers" vaguely, leaving the definition open to interpretation. It does, however, hold employers responsible if they do not protect employees against an unhealthy environment. This responsibility implies that if discrimination, sexual harassment, or bullying, among other things, occurs in the workplace, the employer will be held responsible and will be obliged to find a solution. Many labor contract features are covered by law or collective bargaining agreements. This applies to all employees, unionized and nonunionized. Both groups of employees are entitled to similar benefits and are not treated differently. Therefore, most employees do not feel a real need to be a member of a union. As a result, the percentage of unionized employees in the Netherlands is low.

The word *contract* is defined in the Dutch dictionary as a written agreement describing mutual obligations (Geerts, Den Boon, Geeraerts, & Van der Suijs, 1999), which resembles the definition of a psychological contract given by Rousseau (1989). A labor contract specifies the position an employee holds, provisions for pay, and other job-related provisions. Most organizations provide employees with a manual containing information on working hours, training and other professional development opportunities, holidays, job security, sick leave, and other issues. In the Netherlands, many of these aspects (such as working hours, minimum vacation time, and child care benefits) are regulated by law or collective bargaining agreements. Those that are not regulated may be negotiated by individual employees.

Note, though, that the *zone of negotiability* is broadest for young, highly educated workers who have a lot to offer to organizations. Because these employees are highly sought after and are relatively rare, they have more power to negotiate advantageous contracts. Older or less educated or skilled workers have limited power to negotiate idiosyncratic employment conditions.

Promises about mutual obligations are indeed the basis for Dutch psychological contracts. But because the Dutch words *belofte* ("promise") and *verplichting* ("obligation") have a special distinctive meaning, the outcome in terms of specific work-related expectations is considered to be the core issue in psychological contracts in the Netherlands.

In the Netherlands, the word for "promise" has strong meaning: One common Dutch saying is that "a promise creates a debt." The Dutch believe that a promise should be kept and never broken. Breaking a promise is a serious matter and not easily done. A promise concerns serious matters and is undertaken explicitly. The word for "obligation" has a bit of a moral connotation, referring to things one really ought to do—perhaps closer in meaning to the word *duty* in English. Therefore, using the Dutch words for *promises* and *obligations* to describe Dutch psychological contracts would be too strong.

In Dutch psychological contracting, explicit promise making seldom takes place. The implicit promises based on employee manuals and other such communications lead to specific expectations (*verwachtingen*) that employees have in their psychological contract. Note that the word *verwachting* in Dutch has a stronger and more specific connotation than the English term *expectation*. Note, too, that employees are well protected by law when organizations cannot meet their commitments related to those expectations. This is true even for conditions that are not written in an employee manual due to the "good employer law" described earlier.

"THE" DUTCH PSYCHOLOGICAL CONTRACT

Dutch society is a culture of compromise. Interpersonal relationships are valued. Equality is important: It is thought that everybody should be treated in the same way, from blue-collar employee to CEO of an organization. Yet one arena where this is less true is gender. Women are still struggling to find jobs in higher positions and often earn less than men. Because of low power distance and the low level of respect for authority, and a highly educated society with high social security and protection, demands that employees make are high. Because the unemployment rate is currently extremely low, it is possible for many workers to find a good job. Employees are expected to "do the best they can," but at the same time high achievers are expected to act unobtrusively. There is a strict boundary between work and private life. We will describe psychological contracts in the Netherlands more specifically, using a feature and a content approach (Rousseau & Tijoriwala, 1998).

Features of Dutch Psychological Contracts

Five categories of features of the psychological contract are commonly used to categorize contracts as more transactional or relational contracts: focus, time frame, range, stability, and tangibility (MacNeil, 1985). To describe the general features of Dutch psychological contracts, we will discuss only focus, time frame, and range because stability and tangibility are highly dependent on the employees' profession and specific contract.

Focus

The focus of Dutch psychological contracts is broadly social-economic. Because the service sector is the most important supplier of labor, and low-level jobs are becoming scarce, few jobs have only an economic focus. The level and content of most jobs in the Netherlands require a social-economic focus. As has been discussed before, the Netherlands has a unique position in Europe, with many temporary work agencies. Working for a temporary work agency has in principle a more economic focus. However, an increasing number of temporary work agencies in the Netherlands specialize in higher-level work, and some of those specialize in providing jobs and organizations that match the applicant's social life. Young, highly educated employees tend to be more calculating in their relationship with employers, and loyalty is no longer a virtue for them.

Time Frame

Because most new labor contracts have or at least start with a fixed time frame (probation period), they can be characterized as more transactional in nature. In the past, this was not standard. But today, even tenure does not automatically imply security, whereas temporary employment has become less insecure. In addition, the government and society are slowly accepting temporary work as a normal form of employment. For example, although it is still difficult, it is possible for a worker on a temporary contract to get a mortgage. Temporary work is now a more common form of a working arrangement, and most temporary employees are considered by the labor force to be part of the organization ("one of us").

Range

Most Dutch employees do not mix work life and private life. In the 1960s, some large companies built houses and sports facilities for their employees. In Eindhoven, certain parts of the city are called Philips Village or Bata Village, referring to the companies who built these neighborhoods for their employees, and the city's Philips Sports Association is also named after the company that started it. This invasion into the employee's life is now a part of history, but it may be expected that in the future work life will invade private life in other ways. Because the Netherlands is a very densely populated country, traffic congestion is a major social problem. Working at home and working flexible hours are both solutions to this problem and are becoming more acceptable forms of employment. The government is also stimulating this by, for example, giving employees a tax reduction if they buy a personal computer for use at home. This is one example of work life spilling over in to the employee's private life. Other examples are participation in the social activities arranged by organizations, a social hour on Friday afternoon, or sporting events that are used to meet with customers.

The Content of Dutch Psychological Contracts

Employer Obligations

The content of psychological contracts in the Netherlands with respect to *employer obligations* can be described in terms of five categories: job content, opportunities for personal development, social aspects, human resource management policy, and rewards (Freese & Schalk, 1996).

Job Content. In the service professions, providing quality goods and services is becoming more important, work pressure is high, and the organizational structure is flat. Supervisors have broad control, though employees are involved in decision making.

Personal Development. The Netherlands is characterized by lifelong education, an increasing educational level, and greater participation of women and an expected increase of older employees in the labor market. Organizations are making significant investments in training and development programs, primarily for young and talented employees.

Social Aspects. Good working relations are considered to be important. Behavior is informal toward colleagues and bosses, who typically refer to one another on a first-name basis. Despite the informal behavior, the dress code is formal in most companies. Birthdays and other events are celebrated with cake or drinks at work. Open communication is highly valued and usually not considered as a threat to an employee's or supervisor's dignity. However, the Dutch do not appreciate an open show of emotions at work; this is considered to be unprofessional.

Human Resource Management Practices. Many aspects of human resource strategies are regulated by law or collective bargaining agreements. Part-time work and temporary work are also regulated by law. Despite these collective regulations, the application of specific human resource practices tends to become more individualized.

Rewards. Dutch employees draw some distinctions regarding the rewards they may receive at work. To gain a higher-status title with no other changes is not considered to be a reward, whereas a new company car or an extra salary increase is—even if it is not accompanied by a higher-status title. The Polder-model mentioned above regulated a slow pay increase to support economic growth and lower unemployment. Because of labor supply shortages in some sectors, pay has tended to increase much faster in the recent past. Income differences are relatively small in the Netherlands. Cafeteria plans are new in the reward system. Young and talented employees tend to be highly rewarded so that they will be committed to the organization, which leads other employees to believe they are being treated unfairly.

Employee Obligations

The other side of the deal is the obligations that employees feel toward the organization (*employee obligations*). We will first give a specific Dutch example and then describe different aspects of employee obligations.

A company in the western part of the Netherlands gives new employees and customers a linen-bound document, signed by the management team, containing the organization's mission and goals. According to this document, the company's primary goal is "to offer its employees a lasting and fine job with good benefits." The document also outlines key aspects of the company's culture, which include highly committed and motivated employees; a strong team spirit; top-quality products and service; a high standard of business ethics; the delegation of responsibility whenever possible; consideration of the environment when making decisions; "fine frugality" (unnecessary luxury is not the organization's style); and communication based on truth, openness, friendliness, and respect for the viewpoints of others. Every employee can explain the content of this document, and actions on the part of this company reveal genuine commitment to this document.

In the Netherlands, many organizational obligations are regulated by law or by a collective bargaining agreement, but the obligations of employees are rather vague. Employees must be present at work, but little else is put down in writing. Although the document described above is certainly not representative of the viewpoints of all managers in modern businesses, it illustrates well what many Dutch employers consider to be important issues included in the psychological contract of their employees.

Here, we describe employee obligations by using the framework established by Robinson, Kraatz, and Rousseau (1994).

Working Overtime. As mentioned in the first section of this chapter, work pressure in the Netherlands is the highest in Europe. Although standard working hours are short (37 hours per week on average), most people tend to work overtime. Given the shortage of labor in many sectors, overtime will probably increase in the future.

Loyalty. Opinions on loyalty have changed. Young people tend to be loyal to their career rather than loyal to the organization. In this respect, they respond to the message many organizations have preached for years.

Extrarole Behavior. This is a difficult aspect because behavior considered as extrarole (e.g., exceeding standard performance) in other countries such as the United States is felt in the Netherlands to be a responsibility and is thus performed. The distinction between loyalty to the organization and to one's own work is important here as well.

Notice. The time frame of notice is regulated by law.

Transfers. This aspect depends on the position of the employee. High-level employees tend to feel obliged to accept a transfer, whereas low-level ones tend not to. Although the Netherlands is small geographically, many people are attached to their own community and consider accepting a transfer to be a major contribution to the organization.

Competitor Support. Most employees do not feel obliged to avoid supporting competitors. In fact, home-help employees, for example, sometimes advise their clients to buy competitors' products because they are cheaper. They do not even consider this to be disloyal to their organization; rather, they perceive this as being loyal to their work, advising their client in the best way they can.[2]

Proprietary Protection. This obligation is felt strongly by virtually every employee. There is a strong shared ethical norm concerning it, which is enforced by law.

Minimum Stay. Almost nobody feels obliged to stay with the organization for a certain time; most people desire the freedom to change employers if this is in their best interest, and it is generally accepted that employees do this.

CONCLUSION

Despite the many changes taking place in the Dutch labor market and popular opinions on the growing flexibility of the labor market, the Dutch labor market is in transition. Employees holding a flexible contract (e.g., those who have temporary contracts, work for temporary work agencies, or work "on call") and those with tenure and a flexible working arrangement, such as flexible hours or flexible tasks, are still in the minority. However, it must be noted that the "standard" employee who has the security of lifetime employment is no longer the norm (SCP, 1998). Mobility is quite low. Many employees prefer to work many years for the same organization. However, with all the recent developments in the labor market and new laws, flexibility is becoming more common.

This chapter started with the statement that Dutch psychological contracts are characterized by dualism. This dualism is reflected in many aspects. Freedom is very important in the Netherlands, as evidenced by the country's freedom of self-determination concerning the human body (e.g., through euthanasia, drug use, and abortion). On the other hand, the Dutch also value security and stability. This is reflected in the Netherlands' history of generous social security, which still largely holds true today. In addition, "weaker" parties are well protected by law. Employees are protected from the organization, and tenants are protected against their landlords. Equality is important, but compared to neighboring countries, very few Dutch women participate in the management layer of organizations. The participation of women in the labor market is the lowest in Europe. Income differences between men and women performing the same kind of work are among the largest in Europe.

The government itself is also dual in its approach to employer-employee relations. On the one hand, the government acknowledges that employees are free to make choices; on the other hand, temporary workers are given more security, protecting them from employers. The dualism of flexibility and stability leads to the typical Dutch form of psychological contracts described in this chapter. As a result of societal developments, psychological contracts in the Netherlands are shifting from a more collective or group level to become more individualized. We expect that this trend will continue.

NOTES

1. Research by the Federatie van Nederlandse Vakverenigingen (FNV), quoted in *Intermediair,* October 1, 1998.
2. This example is based on interviews with employees of home-help organizations by the first author.

REFERENCES

Centraal Bureau voor de Statistiek. (1998a, August). *Sociaal Economische Maandstatistiek*. Voorburg/Heerlen, the Netherlands: Author.

Centraal Bureau voor Statistiek. (1998b). [Untitled.] *Index, 5*(6), 5.

De Nederlandse Bank. (1996). *Jaarverslag 1996*. Amsterdam: Author.

De Wit, M. A. C. (Ed.). (1995). *Aanbevolen arbeidsrecht: aanbevelingen van de Stichting van de Arbeid*. The Hague: Sdu Juridische & Fiscale Uitgeverij.

Fokkema, T., & Van Solinge, H. (1998). Loopbanen van vrouwen steeds langer. *Demos, 14,* 57-58.

Freese, C., & Schalk, R. (1996). Implications of differences in psychological contracts for human resource management. *European Journal of Work and Organizational Psychology, 5,* 501-509.

Geerts, G., Den Boon, T., Geeraerts, D., & Van der Suijs, N. (1999). *Groot woordenboek der Nederlandse taal*. Utrecht, the Netherlands: Van Dale Lexicografie.

Hofstede, G. (1980). *Culture's consequences: International differences in work-related values*. Beverly Hills, CA: Sage.

MacNeil, I. R. (1985). Relational contract: Why we do what we do. *Wisconsin Law Review, 3,* 483-525.

Ministerie van Sociale Zaken en Werkgelegenheid/Centraal Bureau voor de Statistiek. (1998). *Jaarboek emancipatie 1998: Tijd en ruimte voor arbeid en zorg*. The Hague: VUGA Uitgeverij.

Robinson, S. L., Kraatz, M. S., & Rousseau, D. M. (1994). Changing obligations and the psychological contract: A longitudinal study. *Academy of Management Journal, 37,* 137-152.

Roe, R. A., & Ester, P. (1999). Values and work: Empirical findings and theoretical perspective. *Applied Psychology: An International Review, 48*(1), 1-21.

Rousseau, D. M. (1989). Psychological and implied contracts in organizations. *Employee Rights and Responsibilities Journal, 2,* 121-139.

Rousseau, D. M., & Tijoriwala, S. A. (1998). Assessing psychological contracts: Issues, alternatives and measures. *Journal of Organizational Behavior, 19,* 679-695.

Sociaal Cultureel Planbureau. (1996). *Sociaal en Cultureel Rapport 1996*. Rijswijk, the Netherlands: Author.

Sociaal Cultureel Planbureau. (1998). *Sociaal en Cultureel Rapport 1998: 25 jaar sociale verandering*. Rijswijk, the Netherlands: Author.

Thierry, H., Den Hartog, D., Koopman, P., & Wilderom, C. (in press). Leadership, politics and culture in the Netherlands. In R. J. House & J. Chhokar (Eds.), *Cultures of the world: A Globe anthology of in-depth descriptions of the cultures of 14 countries* (Vol. 1). Thousand Oaks, CA: Sage.

Tijdens, K. G. (1998). De balans van twee ronden arbeidsduurverkorting, 1982-1985 en 1994-1997. *Tijdschrift voor Arbeidsvraagstukken, 14,* 212-225.

Wessels, B. (Ed.). (1991). *Burgelijk Wetboek* (10th ed.). Lelystad, the Netherlands: Koninklijke Vermande.

11

Economic Deregulation and Psychological Contracts

The New Zealand Experience[1]

Simon Peel
Kerr Inkson

New Zealand, a small island state 1,500 miles to the east of Australia, has often been a pioneer. New Zealand was the first country, in 1895, to bring in full women's suffrage. In the period between 1936 and 1949, New Zealand's Labour government pioneered the modern welfare state, creating, through the nationalization of key industries, the socialization of the medical sector and low-cost housing and the introduction of welfare benefits for all in need, a model for many subsequent European systems. In recent years, New Zealand has again been a crucible for change and a laboratory for the developed world.[2] For since 1984, successive governments have changed dramatically the economic frameworks within which its citizens live, quickly changing what was possibly the most protected, regulated welfare economy in the world (outside the Communist bloc) into one of the most unprotected, deregulated market economies.

The change for ordinary New Zealanders has been enormous. In the context of this book, this has special importance. In essence, the social contract (between citizens and government) has been changed and replaced by an invitation to New Zealanders to rely on the government less and less and to put their faith instead in a series of "transactional" contracts with others, including employers.

In this chapter, we focus specifically on employment relations and their effects on psychological contracts. We seek to show how the efforts of reforming, deregulating governments (referred to above) have disrupted long-standing arrangements for employment relations and in so doing have dramatically altered the operation of psychological contracts in New Zealand organizations.

For many years, contractual relationships governing employment and work in New Zealand were framed in the context of centralized contract-setting institutions, particularly those sponsored by the state. The late 1980s and the 1990s have seen the dramatic emergence in New Zealand of a transaction-oriented business culture and an increasingly transactional approach to employment relations. Not surprisingly, the complete abandonment of a "state regulation of relationships" model and its replacement by a "one-to-one negotiation of transactions" model has produced dramatic changes in employment relations. The framework within which psychological contracts are constructed has a major impact on the contract types that emerge. These changes, along with some of the distinctive characteristics of New Zealand workers generally, have interesting consequences when viewed from a psychological contracts perspective.

THE EARLY HISTORY OF CONTRACTS

The nature of contractual relationships—psychological as well as legal—between employers and employees is framed in part by historical forces. In New Zealand, three rather contradictory forces may be identified. The first was a climate of individualistic egalitarianism fostered by New Zealand's colonial and economic history. The second was an exceptionally strong welfare state ethos fostered by successful experiments between the 1930s and the 1950s. The third was an enduring system of protective centralized legislation that originated in the 1890s and governed employment relationships on an enduring basis.

Individualism and Egalitarianism

The psychological pressure toward individualism was created by New Zealand's 19th-century history. Settlers, largely from the United Kingdom, sought a better and richer future based on New Zealand's land resources and their suitability for the cheap production of agricultural products such as meat, wool, and butter for the distant British market. The land was systematically bought or stolen from its native Maori owners, who were quickly reduced to an underprivileged minority. Rural individualism was prized, whereas secondary industry was of minor importance. Many of the settlers had left Britain to escape its stifling class structure, and despite obvious inequalities in wealth, an ethos of egalitarianism grew. The relative masculinity, individualism, and egalitarianism of the New Zealand working culture have apparently been preserved

(Hofstede, 1984). New Zealand is a small country, and firm sizes are relatively small. This means that personal contact in the workplace is common, and relationships tend to be friendly and informal (Hines, 1974a).

Welfare Statism

Following the privations of a severe depression in the 1930s, New Zealand elected a Labour government that held strong Keynesian beliefs and enacted what was arguably the world's first full-blown welfare state. By the time the Labour government fell in 1949, the state had assumed an importance in the everyday lives of citizens to a degree possibly unique among countries outside the Communist bloc. Major parts of industry were still privately owned, but their prosperity was assisted—some would say ensured—by a variety of legislative devices. These included tariffs, import licensing on many products, and state export incentives. New Zealand was very much a "command" economy where the government made the key decisions and the role of managers was reduced to political lobbying. In addition, key industries were nationalized, including the health, energy, and transport sectors. The public service burgeoned, and its employees were protected by virtual "lifetime employment."

This fortunate situation was made possible by two things. The first was the high productivity of the rural sector relative to that of the United Kingdom, to which it exported nearly all its exports, and which copied its welfare state in the 1940s and 1950s. The second was the fact that from the time of the Second World War, unemployment in New Zealand was virtually zero: In fact, it remained below 1% until the late 1970s. Severe labor shortages persisted despite state-sponsored immigration from Europe. Although employees valued relationships with employers, such as those in the public sector, which had a good record of "looking after them," they were also secure in the knowledge that if, through some misfortune, they lost their jobs, there were plenty of other jobs to replace them.

Centralized Employment Relations

In 1894, a liberal government passed the Industrial Conciliation and Arbitration Act as a response to widespread public dissatisfaction with the exploitative working conditions and widespread industrial conflict of the times. This act provided a centralized, state-sponsored framework for contractual relationships that was to remain the mainstay of the New Zealand employment relations system for nearly 100 years. It encouraged the development of trade unions by providing for their formal registration, making them the legally recognized voice of the workers in that industry (Deeks & Boxall, 1989). It centralized bargaining and dispute resolution, ultimately in an arbitration court. It had little effect on the geographically fragmented rural sector but provided formal protection and a clear social role for trade unions, which grew in importance as secondary industry expanded and which provided powerful support for the Labour Party as their political arm. For nearly a century, New Zealand and Australia were the only industrialized market-oriented countries using an arbitration-based award system to resolve wage-fixing matters in preference to collective bargaining (Harbridge & Crawford, 1997).

Basic conditions of employment were determined by a system of "industrial awards" negotiated on a national basis, usually annually, between the unions representing a specific trade or occupation and the employers employing that group of workers. Awards were binding on all in the occupation and were in essence collective contracts, setting out minimum employment conditions in minute detail. Thus, the contractual basis of any employee's work was formalized in detail, yet he or she played little part in its determination. Awards were all-encompassing documents that made little allowance for such factors as regional differences, company profitability, or worker performance:

> The arbitration system divorced wage fixing from the concerns of individual enterprises and from the purview of individual workers. For employers and workers alike, basic wage rates were something established through mysterious processes in smoke filled rooms in Wellington. The limited amount of direct bargaining at the plant or enterprise level meant that bargaining and negotiation skills became largely the preserve of full-time union and employer officials. (Deeks, Parker, & Ryan, 1994, p. 64)

Although the system provided protections for weaker groups of workers and a relatively stable and predictable set of outcomes, it was unresponsive in boom and bust conditions. Peaks and troughs in business cycles were not accompanied by corresponding upward and downward movements in bargaining outcomes. In addition, the arbitration and conciliation system was undermined by the fact that the government might directly intervene, either to enforce a settlement to a particular dispute or to ensure an outcome in keeping with other economic policy. Under this system, the government, employer representatives, and unions were key players in the formation of contracts between the firm and the individual. It could be argued that both unions and governments were parties to any psychological contract.

DEREGULATION

New Zealand's inflexible centralized economy was to prove too unwieldy for a rapidly changing world. From the 1950s, productivity and GDP growth were sluggish. The terms of trade fell. New Zealand failed to keep pace with its trading partners. Inflation became a constant threat to standards of living. Desperately, the government imposed "freezes" on prices and wages. Government debt climbed, and unemployment grew through 1% and kept on rising. It appeared that the set of parameters that had provided such comfortable conditions for working New Zealanders were unsustainable.

The 1984 election of the fourth Labour government—a government that espoused strong welfare-oriented social policies but practiced strong monetarist economic policies—set in motion a series of unexpected reforms that were to have an impact on many aspects of the economy and the lives of individual New Zealanders. These included the abolition of government support and incentives to industry, the abolition of import licensing and the rapid reduction of tariffs, the floating of the currency, the privatization of much state-owned industry, the rapid downsizing and restructuring of the public service, and the encouragement of both internal and overseas competition. Within a few short years, New Zealand changed from being one of the world's most regulated economies to one of the most deregulated, laissez-faire market economies (Deeks et al., 1994).

The post-1984 reforms produced a phenomenon that has been described as the "enterprise culture" (Keat & Abercrombie, 1991). Economically, the enterprise culture is characterized by a continual process of privatization, deregulation of industries, structural reorganization of publicly funded bodies, and the attempted reduction of dependence and reliance throughout business sectors and government agencies. The competitive market organization becomes the role model for all other organizations, and there is a homogenization of organizational forms around commercial modes of operation. Many New Zealanders suddenly found that the securities of the past disappeared as private and public sector organizations restructured, downsized, and outsourced supply. The implicit, unwritten contracts of lifetime commitment were swept aside as if they had never been.

In psychological contract terms, the enterprise culture fosters transactional rather than relational thinking. At the level of the individual, the notion emerges that one should run one's own personal life as if it were a business, with economic concepts such as self-investment, opportunity cost, and competition. It draws people's attention to themselves as economic units in society. New Zealand's economic reforms are accompanied by reforms to the health system, the education system, and the social welfare system, all moving toward market rather than welfare models. Thus, citizens have been increasingly asked to pay for services that were previously free and have been encouraged to think of themselves as customers or clients rather than patients, students, or beneficiaries.

Such changes affect the psychological contracts that citizens have with the state as the government and its agencies attempt to reframe their beliefs about their reciprocal rights and obligations. The traditional contract was, at least to some extent, represented by the phrase "from each according to his ability, to each according to his need." Contribution was in the form of taxes, and benefits were notionally unlimited. The new contract is increasingly represented by the phrase, suddenly common in all sectors of New Zealand society, "user pays."

For example, a universal pension scheme paid for from taxation has been steadily eroded, and citizens are increasingly exhorted to make provision for their own pensions through saving.

LABOR MARKET DEREGULATION

The election of the fourth Labour government in 1984 saw the beginning of sweeping changes to many aspects of the New Zealand economy and further changes to the labor relations system. However, between 1984 and 1990, the formal mechanisms of employment relations changed only a little, for the Labour movement that had sponsored a Pandora's box of a government was still opposed to any major form of labor market deregulation. It was not until the defeat of the Labour government in 1990 that the changes sweeping through almost all aspects of the New Zealand economy were extended to the labor relations system.

The Employment Contracts Act (ECA), which came into force on May 15, 1991, introduced substantial deregulation (or at least altered regulation) of the labor market. It abolished the last vestiges of the award system, compulsory unionism, and monopoly coverage; promoted enterprise bargaining; and created a single legislative framework for employment matters (Rasmussen, Deeks, & Street, 1996). It sought to promote freedom of choice by allowing choice of contract types, either individual or collective, and of bargaining agents (where a bargaining agent might not necessarily be a union). It sought to promote sanctity of contract by leaving it to the parties to establish the detail and enforcement of aspects of the employment relationship, and to provide easy access to dispute resolution processes. It located responsibility for the enforcement of the employment contract at the level of the parties concerned and set out a disputes resolution procedure to facilitate this.

A PHILOSOPHICAL SHIFT

The principles and philosophy of the system historically can be "described as Keynesian, interventionist, welfarist, pluralist, collectivist or welfare corporatist" (Rasmussen et al., 1996, p. 149). The goal of the formal labor relations system was a form of tripartite pluralism that recognized the role of employers and unions and the role of government in managing the system.

The Employment Contracts Act (1991) represented an important philosophical shift. The late 1980s saw the emergence of a viable alternative to the existing system that centered on market-driven neoliberal analysis:

> The analysis packages together several key philosophical principles—the individual, freedom, choice, the market—such that collectivism in the labor market is understood simultaneously as a major barrier to the achievement of economic efficiency and a particularly offensive erosion of individual rights and freedoms.

Consequently, from a neo-liberal perspective, the deregulation of the labor market was a major, if not the major, policy issue confronting government. (Rasmussen et al., 1996, p. 149)

As it relates to the employment relationship, the new philosophy is based on several principles. The employment relationship is seen as a private contractual relationship. In this relationship, the parties sell and buy labor, and the operation of the market, free from state regulation, ensures optimal labor market outcomes (Deeks et al., 1994). An employment contract is not different from any other contract between buyer and seller (Walsh & Ryan, 1993). The role of the government is restricted to providing legislative support for fair market exchanges. Individuals should be free to choose the nature of the employment relationship. The philosophy clearly promotes an individualist perspective. It locates responsibility for an individual's employment contract squarely in the hands of the individual.

We now have an environment where considerations of the economy are seen as being of prime importance. Contracts cannot be isolated from it. It is an environment characterized by increased competitiveness and the ever-present threat of recession (Boxall, 1993). In such an environment, economic arguments for the needs of business to respond flexibly and to demand flexibility are persuasive and seem to have widespread acceptance. In such an environment "employers want to be able to link the pay and conditions of the workforce more tangibly to 'the needs of the business'" (Boxall, 1993, p. 150).

THE CHANGED DISCOURSE OF CONTRACTS

The changes described above have been accompanied by noticeable changes in the language accompanying work relations. It is interesting to note, for instance, that the ECA drops the word *worker* in favor of the word *employee,* a word less evocative of an era of conflict and industrial strife. It even drops the word *union* in favor of the more businesslike terms *employee representative* and *bargaining agent.* Implicit in the latter term is a more clearly defined and limited relationship than has historically been the case.

Most obvious is the change of the terms naming the most relevant pieces of legislation, from *industrial conciliation and arbitration* (a process for resolving conflict and preserving a relationship centrally) to *employment contracts* (immediate definitions of transactional relationships). The term *award* was much used prior to the 1980s: Workers talked about "award wages" or "award conditions." This is evocative of an era in which the public considered that working conditions were a matter for government guarantee at least as much as employer-employee negotiation. A common alternative to the term *award* was *collective agreement.* In place of *award* or *agreement,* the word *contract* has become ubiquitous. The shift in meaning is not particularly subtle. An award is

given, but a contract has to be *negotiated,* and the reciprocal rights and obligations that go with it are more readily apparent.

The term *relativities* was also dominant in the old employee relationship
and signaled the national belief that historical differences between occupational groups in wages and conditions should be preserved, possibly forever.
Equality gives way to *equity.* The term *demarcation* indicated jealously
guarded collective rights to defined types of work. Within a very few years,
these terms have disappeared, to be replaced by words such as *flexibility.* Flexibility is a key concept in human resource management and the industrial relations literature. The impact of flexibility on thinking about the employment
relationship is powerful. Some writers use its more globalized meaning, such
as offering the firm the ability to respond to changing market conditions (see,
e.g., Rousseau & Wade-Benzoni, 1994). In general discourse, however, the
word *flexibility* has become something of a rallying cry for those who support
labor market deregulation.

Another important part of the employment relations vocabulary, the word
strike, has largely disappeared from discourse as it has disappeared from
employment relations conduct. The number of work stoppages due to complete
strike has declined rapidly since the onset of labor market deregulation in the
mid-1980s. Complete strikes declined from 206 in 1986 to 126 in 1990. The
number was halved to 65 in 1991, the year of the Employment Contracts Act,
and from there down to 36 in 1997 (Statistics New Zealand, 1998). The number
of person-days lost through work stoppages shows a similarly dramatic
decline. It should be noted that the ECA imposed limits on the right to strike.

The new discourse and vocabulary of employment relationships has
become that of commercial practice. Employees are urged to make "investments" in themselves and to think more about their future employability. Education, despite its "opportunity cost," is a means to attain some "advantage" in
a "competitive" labor market that rewards those with the right skills. Elements
of this discourse explicitly and implicitly draw our attention to the transactional nature of the employment exchange.

THE WORK BELIEFS OF NEW ZEALAND WORKERS

New Zealand was largely colonized by the British in the second half of the
19th century. British emigrants saw the country as a "new frontier" especially
favorable for the cultivation of beef, lamb, wool, and dairy products. British
administrations and colonists quickly acquired land, by fair means and foul,
from the local Maori people. They divided it into freeholdings and sought to
"tame" it and make it productive. In this early history may lie keys to "national
character."

Although New Zealand inherited British laws and social attitudes, there
were some key differences that one might expect among workers in a colonial
environment. Several local characteristic values have been pointed out (Deeks

et al., 1994): desire for independence, belief in equality of opportunity, individualism, and egalitarianism. These characteristics are generally confirmed by the work of Hofstede (1984), who found New Zealanders to be well above average on individualism and power distance and above average on masculinity. By *desire for independence* is meant that an important goal of working men in the colony—the vast majority of whom were migrants who had taken a brave but risky step in pursuit of a better life—was to work their way out of wage dependency. Particularly relevant here are notions of the Protestant work ethic and achieving independence through one's own effort and the support of one's family. Collective action, even to promote collective well-being, was not part of this ethos (Deeks et al., 1994).

The belief in equality of opportunity was derived from the fact that the early settlers of this country faced fewer barriers to upward mobility, such as class, inherited wealth, and patronage. The legal master-servant relationship had been imported from England in the common law but was not given much credence in personal belief systems. In fact, the prevailing view was, and still is, that one person is as good as another. Egalitarianism was later reinforced through universal health care, government pensions, and a progressive taxation and welfare structure that acted as a barrier to acquisition of great wealth. This egalitarianism is reflected in workplace relationships through a lack of deference and servility. For instance, an American manager might be surprised not to automatically receive the level of respect and deference that he or she was accustomed to and might be surprised at the level of informality and use of first names. "In New Zealand the supervisor-subordinate relationship rests less on titles and hierarchy than on the perception of the manager as being competent, prudent in exercising authority . . . and in general being a 'good bloke'" (Hines, 1974b, p. 334). In recent years, the egalitarian tradition in society generally has been challenged by increasing levels of economic inequality.

It seems somewhat paradoxical that for much of its history New Zealand has operated with a highly collective industrial relations system but that it is a highly individualistic nation. As indicated above, the work of Hofstede (1984) indicates that like Australia and the United States, New Zealand has a highly individualistic culture. This individualism may offer an explanation as to why there seems to be little enthusiasm on the part of workers for a return to the days of compulsory union membership (Boxall, 1997). One would imagine that an individualized employment system would appeal to many workers. The high individualism noted by Hofstede may seem to be at odds with an egalitarian tradition and with the strong welfare state that has existed for much of New Zealand's postcolonial history. How can the seeming individualism of New Zealanders be reconciled with their egalitarianism, their collectivized industrial relations system, and their strong welfare state?

One of the difficulties with the Hofstede research is the monolithic treatment of the concept of individualism. Triandis (1995) proposed a distinction between vertical and horizontal individualism and collectivism. Individualism and collectivism have been reconceptualized (Singelis, Triandis, Bhawuk, & Gelfand, 1995) to suggest that vertical individualism is a pattern in which there is an autonomous self but others are seen as being different and inequality is expected. Competition and self-reliance are seen as being important. On the other hand, horizontal individualism seems to more closely match with the New Zealand experience. Here the individual is seen as being autonomous, but others are seen as being more or less equal in status. Therefore, New Zealanders do not necessarily link self-reliance with competition and do not necessarily see the helping of others as being illegitimate. Horizontal individualism may also provide an explanation for what has been labeled the "tall poppy syndrome" (Feather, 1996), whereby individuals who are seen as overachievers are victimized or belittled in various ways to bring them to the same level as everyone else.

The effects of individualism are also mitigated by the sections of the population who are not of European stock. Over 20% of the population are of Maori origin or are immigrants from Pacific Islands such as Samoa and Tonga. Increasing numbers of recent immigrants come from Asian countries such as Taiwan, Malaysia, Hong Kong, and Korea. All these groups may be expected to have more collectivized, family-oriented approaches to employment relations.

An individualist approach to the employment relationship can be seen to most closely map to a transactional psychological contract. According to Hofstede (1984), "In the individualist value pattern, the relationship between the individual and the organization is calculative; it is based on enlightened self-interest" (p. 284). This can be contrasted with more collectivist societies. "In such societies, free-market capitalism, with the supremacy of the profit motive which considers the labor contract between employer and employee as a calculative bargain, is an alien element" (p. 269).

Among individualist societies, social behavior is often determined by internal processes and contracts made by individuals, rather than by norms, perceived duties, and obligations (Singelis et al., 1995). According to Hofstede, individualist societies are likely to be more accepting of employment practices such as the "hire and fire" or employment "at will" principle found in the United States. However, this has not been the case in New Zealand. Even under the more market-oriented employment contracts regime, the expectation remains of ongoing employment or an open-ended employment relationship. Employment cannot be terminated without reason, and such an action by an employer would leave room for legal recourse. Further, such an action would run contrary to cultural norms of fairness.

The cultural norm of fairness is an important one worth expanding on. The concept of fair treatment, that everyone should get a "fair go," is well established throughout New Zealand society. This point is illustrated by the popularity of the long-running and consistently top-rated television program *Fair Go*. This consumer affairs show features the stories of persons who have been treated in a less than fair manner and thrives on the sense of outrage thus created.

Research evidence about the work beliefs of New Zealanders is sketchy, but it has been argued that work is not a central life interest of New Zealanders (Twinn, 1977). It is suggested that New Zealanders are not deeply committed to their jobs and view work as a means to an end rather than an end in itself. This would tend to indicate a relatively simple transactional contract whereby the employment relationship is based upon an exchange of time and effort for money with which to finance one's other life interests. It has been argued that such a passive orientation to work was furthered by the strong welfare state and low levels of unemployment (Deeks et al., 1994). A major social survey conducted in 1989 indicated that only 20% of workers believe work is central to their lives. "Interesting work" was rated more highly by most of the respondents (Gold & Webster, 1990). A study testing motivator-hygiene theory on New Zealand workers reported that interpersonal relations and supervision are critical factors in job satisfaction (Hines, 1974a). The same research found support for the notion that the social, or affiliative, motive is a strong influence on work behavior.

More recent research using the beliefs about work framework developed by Buchholz (1977) found that New Zealanders strongly endorse the humanistic belief system (Toulson, 1990). According to the humanistic belief system, people find fulfillment through the process of work. This means that even though work is seen as an indispensable human activity, what happens to people in the workplace is more important than productivity (confirming previous findings on the importance of the social side of work). This research did not support the notion that New Zealanders have an overly high leisure ethic and found similarity between New Zealand and overseas countries in this respect. It is apparent that even if work is not a central life interest to most New Zealanders, they still value its quality, and particularly the quality of workplace relationships. These are likely to be key factors in the psychological contracts of many workers.

The possible humanist orientation of New Zealanders has some interesting implications for their employment in a deregulated environment. The humanist orientation implies that individuals seek growth and development through their work and see themselves as being more important than the work itself (Toulson & Sayers, 1995). They have expectations of opportunities for development and learning. In the past, enlightened employers have played a major role in encouraging and providing such opportunities.

The humanist orientation has some strong parallels to the relational psychological contract. In a relational contract, self-interest is moderated by the acknowledgment of the value of the relationship itself, and thus the interests of the other party are of concern (Parks & Kidder, 1994). According to Rousseau (1995), transactional and relational psychological contracts differ with regard to focus (whether the exchange is purely economic), inclusiveness (whether there is concern for the person and his or her development), and scope (whether the relationship includes other aspects of one's life). To meet the needs of a humanistically oriented worker, an employer would need to offer an exchange that was wider in scope, showed concern for individual development, and included the person's wider welfare. One can conclude that firms that operate on a transactional basis of "buying" rather than "making" or "building" are going to fail to meet the needs of a significant number of New Zealand workers. Likewise, the increasingly managerial, accountability-driven approaches to human resource management apparent in many workplaces seem to run counter to what we know about the work beliefs of many New Zealanders.

EFFECTS OF THE CHANGING EMPLOYMENT RELATIONS ENVIRONMENT ON PSYCHOLOGICAL CONTRACTS

Decentralization of Wage Bargaining and Emergence of Individual Contracting

A major impact of labor market deregulation has been the shift to enterprise-based and individualized employment and contracting. As a result of the ECA, collective bargaining collapsed (Hince & Harbridge, 1994). Enterprise bargaining and individual contracting are now widespread. Prior to the act, around 60% of employees were covered by collective agreements. By 1997, 75% of employees were covered by individual contracts and only 25% by collective agreements (Boxall, 1997). The increasing individualization of employment contracting is in keeping with the philosophy of labor market deregulation. However, there is a minor trend back toward collective employment contracting, driven not by worker concerns but by employers' attempts to reduce the transaction costs associated with individual contracting (Harbridge & Crawford, 1997). The decentralization of bargaining and other aspects of the employment relationship has created pressures for both employers and employees to educate themselves on employment matters in order to better deal with these issues.

Individualizing the bargaining process has served to widen the zone of negotiability of contracts. There is a platform of minimum conditions of employment, such as minimum wages, holidays, parental leave, and employment protection, that cannot be bargained away. However, in the absence of the award structure, employees and employers have more scope to negotiate over issues such as working hours.

One of the most obvious implications for psychological contracts comes from the decentralization of wage bargaining. As a result of the act, many workers were for the first time presented with a document representing their employment contract. The realities of the new environment were thus driven home by a tangible document, whereas previously such matters were removed from everyday consciousness or represented only in informal relationships with supervisors, workmates, and/or trade union representatives. In 1991, the "awards" of many workers lapsed, at which point workers were deemed to be covered by individual employment contracts based on the terms and conditions of the expired document. Many were asked to sign an actual contract document based on those terms and conditions. In smaller firms that lack the resources or inclination to develop a contract document, contractual arrangements remain somewhat informal, and no formal documentation exists. However, these informal arrangements still have legal status as employment contracts.

Not surprisingly, these changes have led to an increasing awareness, by both parties to the employment relationship, of each other's rights and responsibilities (New Zealand Institute of Economic Research, 1996). Much of the bargaining in the new environment is face to face. This heightens the awareness. The focus of the new framework is more clearly on the parties directly involved in the employment relationship.

The emergence of individual employment contracting has many similarities to the shift from relational contracts to transactional contracts described by Rousseau (1995). It is characteristic of a relational psychological contract that it is relatively less tangible and less formalized, less focused, and more open-ended. Since the introduction of the ECA, a significant number of employers have offered employees formal written individual contracts (e.g., 34% of employees by 1993; Hector & Hobby, 1997). As noted earlier, such documents were not a feature of the employment relations scene historically. Even those who could be described as being on an individual employment contract would have nothing more than a letter of appointment and a set of customs and practices as tangible evidence of an employment relationship. This emergence of high levels of formalization and explicitness suggests a heightening of awareness of the transactional nature of the employment exchange.

The declining role of unions provides further evidence for the decollectivization of employment relations. The ECA does not contain a single reference to trade unionism. This more than anything symbolizes how fundamental, and how sudden, the change has been. Of course, it was quite possible from 1991 for any worker to choose to retain his or her union membership and to select the union to be his or her "bargaining agent" under the terms of the act. However, it is also clear that given the freedom to do so, many workers choose not to retain union membership and instead do their own bargaining or employ a nonunion agent. There is evidence of a dramatic decline in the number of unions and in union membership since the act came into force (e.g., Boxall, 1997; Hince & Harbridge, 1994). Union membership dropped from 41% to 23% (of the workforce) in the first 5 years (Rasmussen et al., 1996). The declining role of unions is another factor that creates more focus on the exchange between the individual and the firm. Furthermore, focusing on unions as mere "bargaining agents" ignores the broad influence that unions have had over employment relations for much of the last century.

Diversity of Work Arrangements and High Turnover

As in many parts of the world, a key trend has been the rise in the numbers of self-employed persons, part-timers, and persons holding multiple jobs. In recent years, the number of self-employed workers has risen markedly. Census figures show that the "self-employed workers not employing others" category steadily declined throughout the middle part of the century. Expressed as a proportion of wage and salary earners, it reached a low in 1971 of 7.01%. However, the proportion of self-employed has increased in the last two census figures to 12.48% in 1991 and 13.25% in 1996. Part-time work, often taken as an indicator of the casualization or externalization of work, has shown particularly dramatic increases. This is evident from Household Labour Force Survey (Statistics New Zealand, 1998) data expressed as a ratio of full-timers to part-timers. In December of 1985, there were 5.04 full-time workers for every part-time worker. By March of 1991, that ratio had fallen to 4.01; by September of 1996, it was 3.21. The most recent figures for March 1998 show a slight increase to 3.5. Also increasing is the number of employees holding multiple jobs: In 1997, 14% of workers reported holding two or more jobs (Department of Labour, 1997).

There is a growing diversity of work arrangements along with the growing diversity of the workforce, as discussed in an earlier section. Not only are nonstandard forms of employment becoming more common, but New Zealand has an extremely high rate of labor turnover. According to recent survey statistics, 31% of employees report being in a different job or different organization from the one they held 12 months previously (Department of Labour, 1997). New Zealand has had traditionally high levels of turnover, due in part to very low levels of unemployment. It is interesting that in a period of relatively high unemployment turnover continues at a high rate. Although there are few reliable figures on turnover, the available information suggests that long-term psychological contracts are absent for a large number of workers and that this is a relatively stable characteristic of the New Zealand workforce.

Performance Culture

Another key change is a move toward an output evaluation and performance culture. New Zealand firms are increasingly introducing performance-related pay schemes (McAllister, 1994). The trend toward greater focus on performance outputs and the linking of those outputs to remuneration is another reflection of how the typical contract is becoming more transactional rather than relational. According to Rousseau (1995), various human resource practices, such as performance management systems, convey messages that influence the formation of psychological contracts. Committing employees to well-specified performance outcomes and attaching economic incentives to those heightens the transactional aspect of the employment exchange. Systems evaluating employee outputs, and the organizational culture presumably engendered thereby, tend to blur the distinction between employee and contractor. Some firms have attempted to create a "contractual" or "accountability-driven" culture in order to get workers to focus more explicitly on their performance and their contribution to the firm. For example, the concept of "internal customer" is increasingly used: Employees such as accounting staff are expected to provide a measurable customer-focused service for those to whom they provide information. This can be seen as a deliberate attempt to reframe psychological contracts in a more transactional way. The end result of such initiatives is to focus on objectively measurable performance and to link pay more closely to performance—an increasingly transactional approach.

Notwithstanding any deliberate attempt to change the culture of organizations, it seems that many workplaces—driven by a rhetoric and a reality of increasing overseas competition and decreasing local protection—are more and more operating in a climate of cost containment and exhortations to increase productivity. An emphasis on productivity, efficiency, and payment by performance engenders an intensified view of work as a means to an end (Deeks et al., 1994). This increasingly instrumental view of work has strong parallels with transactional psychological contracts.

Litigation

As the employment relations system has become decollectivized, so have the means for resolution of issues surrounding contract violation. The ECA extends access to personal grievance procedures to all employees. Previously, these were open only to union members. There is evidence to suggest that workers are becoming more litigious in their approach to employment issues. Since its inception, the employment tribunal has faced a backlog of cases. Usage of the system has been high, and despite its relatively short history, evidence suggests that demand is increasing consistently (Harbridge & Crawford, 1997). Between 1992 and 1996, the number of cases outstanding in June of each year almost tripled. This increasing litigiousness in employment matters is interesting in a society where access to recourse through the courts is more tightly prescribed than in some other countries. As it relates to contract violation, the concept of "fair play" or expecting a "fair go" is important, as mentioned earlier. It would seem that New Zealand workers have not been slow to adjust to the new employment relations framework and make use of the system to seek redress for perceived or actual injustices. This increasing use of the legal system may, however, simply reflect the fact that for many workers the collectivist forms of dispute resolution are no longer available.

FURTHER RESEARCH

Existing research can provide answers to questions regarding the effects of the ECA on various parts of the employment relations system. For instance, we know what the effect has been on collective bargaining and on union membership. However, what we know little about and can only infer from other measures is what the changes have meant to workers and how their psychological contracts are changing in this environment. Generalizing about the meaning that workers ascribe to their employment is a difficult task. Certainly, several features of the contemporary employment relations scene are characteristic of a more transactional approach to contracting. It is possible that stable, long-term, committed employment relationships have never been a particularly common feature of the New Zealand scene, but they appear even less likely now. As other researchers (e.g., Boxall, 1997) have pointed out, employee responses to the government and employer initiatives in the post-ECA environment constitute a vital area for future research.

CONCLUSION

The individual contracting framework draws more attention to the rights and responsibilities of the parties and has led to more direct involvement of parties in the determination of their conditions and to an increasing emphasis on the transactional nature of the exchange. These effects are very difficult to trace empirically.

However, it is clear that the employment relations landscape is now significantly different from that which existed for most of this county's history. In its language and in the philosophical underpinning, it represents a rejection of a collectivist tradition embodied in a centralized bargaining system and a movement toward individualist mechanisms. The dramatic move by New Zealand toward free-market economic philosophies policies, and the ECA that applied those policies to the labor market, have had dramatic tangible outcomes. How well New Zealand can withstand and benefit from these changes to the long-standing philosophical and social foundations of its psyche, as well as its economy, is a question for the future.

NOTES

1. While this book was in press, in November 1999, a General Election resulted in a new center-left government of parties which had been critical of the deregulation process and which promised to repeal the Employment Contracts Act. In March 2000, the Employment Relations Bill was introduced to Parliament, once more altering the discourse of contracting in New Zealand. Among the key aims of the legislation were the encouragement of collective bargaining and the encouragement of bargaining "in good faith." The operation of this latter concept, the encouragement of fair dealing and mutual trust and confidence, so as to avoid "take it or leave it" bargaining will be of particular interest.

Only time will tell whether these changes signal a reversal to the trends described in this chapter.

2. For a critical review of the "reforms," see Kelsey (1997).

REFERENCES

Boxall, P. (1993). Management strategy and the Employment Contracts Act 1991. In R. Harbridge (Ed.), *Employment contracts: New Zealand experiences.* Wellington, New Zealand: Victoria University Press.

Boxall, P. (1997). Models of employment and labor productivity in New Zealand: An interpretation of change since the Employment Contracts Act. *New Zealand Journal of Employment Relations, 22*(1), 22-36.

Buchholz, R. A. (1977). The belief structure of managers relative to work concepts measured by a factor analytical model. *Personnel Psychology, 30*(4), 60-79.

Deeks, J., & Boxall, P. (1989). *Labour relations in New Zealand.* Auckland, New Zealand: Longman.

Deeks J., Parker, J., & Ryan, R. (1994). *Labour and employment relations in New Zealand.* Auckland, New Zealand: Longman Paul.

Department of Labour. (1997). *Survey of labour market adjustment under the Employment Contracts Act.* Wellington, New Zealand: Author.

Feather, N. T. (1996). Values, deservingness, and attitudes towards high achievers. *The Psychology of Values: The Ontario Symposium, 8,* 215-251.

Gold, H., & Webster, A. (1990). *New Zealand values today.* Palmerston North, New Zealand: Alpha.

Harbridge, R., & Crawford, A. (1997). The impact of New Zealand's Employment Contracts Act on industrial relations. *California Western International Law Journal, 28,* 235-251.

Hector, J., & Hobby, M. (1997). Labor market adjustment under the Employment Contracts Act: 1996. *New Zealand Journal of Industrial Relations, 22,* 311-327.

Hince, K., & Harbridge, R. (1994). The Employment Contracts Act: An interim assessment. *New Zealand Journal of Industrial Relations, 19,* 235-255.

Hines, G. H. (1974a). *Cultural influences on work motivation* (Occasional Paper No. 3). Palmerston North, New Zealand: Massey University, School of Business.

Hines, G. H. (1974b). Sociocultural influences on employee expectancy and participative management. *Academy of Management Journal, 17,* 334-338.

Hofstede, G. (1984). *Culture's consequences.* Beverly Hills, CA: Sage.

Keat, R., & Abercrombie, N. (Eds.). (1991). *Enterprise culture.* London: Routledge.

Kelsey, J. (1997). *The New Zealand experiment: A world model for structural adjustment.* Auckland, New Zealand: Auckland University Press.

McAllister, P. (1994). Performance pay. *Management, 41*(11), 38-45.

New Zealand Institute of Economic Research. (1996). *A preliminary report on the results of a survey on the Employment Contracts Act.* Wellington, New Zealand: Author.

Parks, J. M., & Kidder, D. (1994). "Till death us do part. . .": Changing work relationships in the 1990's. In C. L. Cooper & D. M. Rousseau (Eds.), *Trends in organizational behavior* (Vol. 1, pp. 111-136). New York: John Wiley.

Rasmussen, E., Deeks, J., & Street, M. (1996). The entrepreneurial worker: Changes to work and contractual relationships. In J. Gibson (Ed.), *Proceedings of the Third*

Annual Conference, International Employment Relations Association. Hamilton, New Zealand: Waikato University.

Rousseau, D. M. (1995). *Psychological contracts in organizations: Understanding written and unwritten agreements.* Thousand Oaks, CA: Sage.

Rousseau, D., & Wade-Benzoni, K. (1994). Linking strategy and human resource practices: How employee and customer contracts are created. *Human Resource Management, 33,* 463-489.

Singelis, T., Triandis, H., Bhawuk, D., & Gelfand, M. (1995). Horizontal and vertical dimensions of individualism and collectivism: A theoretical and measurement refinement. *Cross Cultural Research, 29,* 240-275.

Statistics New Zealand. (1998). *Key statistics.* Wellington, New Zealand: Author.

Toulson, P. K. (1990). *Perceptions, practices, and productivity: An assessment of personnel practices in New Zealand.* Unpublished doctoral thesis, Massey University.

Toulson, P., & Sayers, J. (1995). A profile of the changing workforce. In P. Boxall (Ed.), *The challenge of human resource management: Directions and debates in New Zealand.* Auckland, New Zealand: Longman.

Triandis, H. (1995). *Individualism and collectivism.* Boulder, CO: Westview.

Twinn, W. J. (1977). The Kiwi and the work ethic. *New Zealand Journal of Industrial Relations, 2,* 97-100.

Walsh, P., & Ryan, R. (1993). The making of the Employment Contracts Act. In R. Harbridge (Ed.), *Employment contracts: New Zealand experiences.* Wellington, New Zealand: Victoria University Press.

12

Psychological Contracts in Singapore

Soon Ang
Mei Ling Tan
Kok Yee Ng

The state endures only as long as it continues to excel. . . . Excellence is a constant struggle.

Singapore's Minister for Information and the Arts,
Brigadier-General George Yeo (1990, pp. 183-184)

Singapore became an independent nation in 1965. Since then, employment relations of this island nation have been shaped largely by Singapore's vision of building a world-class business infrastructure to overcome its limited physical and natural resources. This chapter explains psychological contract development in Singapore. A model is developed that focuses on the roles that macroeconomic and labor market conditions play in shaping the indigenous psychological contract and the organizational experiences of Singaporean workers.

This chapter will proceed as follows. In the next section, we present a model focusing on the role of macroeconomic and labor market conditions in shaping content of psychological contracts of workers in Singapore. Subsequent sections discuss the various components of our model: the economic realities, the labor market conditions, the Singaporean psyche, the content of psychological contracts, recourse for breach in psychological contract, the effects of workforce diversity on psychological contract, and managerial implications.

A MODEL OF PSYCHOLOGICAL
CONTRACT IN SINGAPORE

Our model of psychological contracts in Singapore (Figure 12.1) builds on the concept of psychological contracts as employees' beliefs concerning the reciprocal obligations between themselves and their employers (Rousseau, 1989; Rousseau & Tijoriwala, 1998). These beliefs are based on the perception that some promise has been made and that both parties have accepted the terms and conditions that form the basis of the promise (Robinson & Rousseau, 1994).

To distinguish between the sets of reciprocal obligations, we use the terms *employee obligations* and *organization obligations* (Herriot, Manning, & Kidd, 1997). By *employee obligations,* we mean employees' beliefs about their own obligations to their respective organizations: that is, what employees owe their organizations. In contrast, *organization obligations* refers to employees' beliefs about the organizations' obligations to them: that is, what organizations owe employees.

Our focus is on specific terms characteristic of psychological contracts in Singapore. Terms are the discrete obligations that individuals perceive themselves to owe (e.g., hard work, accepting a transfer) and the obligations that their employer owes them in return (e.g., advancement, support with personal problems) (Rousseau & Tijoriwala, 1998).

We employ clinical and ethnographic techniques in the form of in-depth interviews and observation to uncover specific terms and discrete obligations that individuals and organizations owe to each other. As depicted in Figure 12.1, we will show how employee and organization obligations have evolved from different sets of contextual variables. First, we describe the unique economic, societal, and labor market conditions of Singapore. Second, we explain how the economic and societal conditions have molded a *kiasu* psyche, characterized by high achievement and high anxiety orientation. Third, we describe the employee obligations that are shaped by the *kiasu* psyche. Fourth, we detail how labor market conditions drive organization obligations. Fifth, we explain the recourse in instances of breach in psychological contract, and last, we elaborate on the effects of workforce diversity on the psychological contract.

ECONOMIC REALITIES

There is no law of nature that provides that life will get better for Singapore next year. We have to work to make it better.
                    Prime Minister Lee Kuan Yew, May Day message, 1986

Singapore became an independent nation in 1965. Since then, it has continued to face severe economic realities for a number of reasons. Singapore has a small population. To date, it has a population of slightly over 3 million people. It has no natural resources, importing almost all of its basic subsistence of

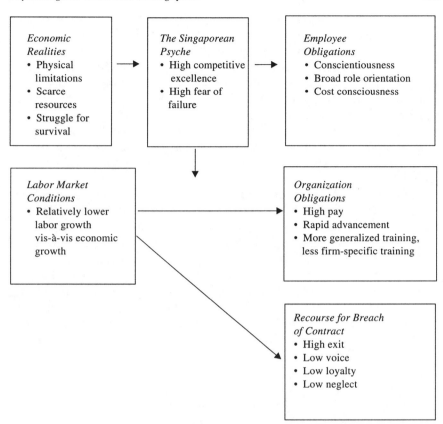

Figure 12.1. A Model of Psychological Contracts in Singapore

water and food. It is extremely tiny in terms of land mass. Geographically located at the crossroads of trade routes between the East and the West, it is approximately only 250 square miles. The physical constraints further limit Singapore's population growth and the level of economic activity it can sustain within the island state (Neo, King, & Applegate, 1995; Vogel, 1991).

In light of its physical and resource limitations, Singapore continues to struggle for survival. Singapore's strategy for generating economic wealth is to build a world-class business infrastructure—the basic framework of physical structures and socioeconomic policies that facilitate productive business activities. The objective of such a strategy is to attract multinational corporations and foreign investments in capital and technology that are vital for the nation's economic development (Knoop, Applegate, Neo, & King, 1995; Vogel, 1991).

To date, Singapore has built up a worldwide reputation for its excellent infrastructure (Sisodia, 1992). Rated as the most competitive nation in the world by the World Economic Forum (WEF) in the past 4 years (1996 to 1999), it boasts of the best airport and seaport in the world, offering sophisticated and efficient transportation and materials-handling facilities. Singapore also aims to be a world financial center and electronic commerce hub. It achieves this objective through a deliberate national information technology (IT) plan. The plan calls for the development of "an intelligent island"—the laying of an islandwide IT infrastructure to facilitate sophisticated telecommunications and information exchanges via cable and other forms of wireless information channels.

In addition to its physical infrastructure, Singapore possesses the best workforce, according to the 1998 study by the Business Environment Risk Intelligence (BERI) institution in the United States. Workers were rated on the basis of the criteria of relative productivity, technical skills, and work attitude.

Despite these accolades, Singapore realizes that it cannot take survival for granted. It faces growing competition from neighboring countries such as Malaysia, Vietnam, and China, which have developed their own air- and seaports. To continue to attract foreign capital and technology, Singapore must sustain its economic advantage by continuing to excel and develop non-imitable infrastructural resources.

LABOR MARKET CONDITIONS

Singapore's successful push for high economic growth rates has posed a problem: chronic labor shortages. The labor growth has failed to keep pace with the rapid economic expansion. Between 1983 and 1997, the Singaporean economy grew by about 7.7% per year. In the same period, total employment increased from 500,000 to 1.83 million, which is equivalent to a 2.8% annual growth rate.

Singapore has tried several measures to alleviate labor shortages. First, Singapore supplements local workers with foreign workers to fill job vacancies. Currently, foreign workers account for approximately 10% of the workforce. Second, Singapore creates new policies and programs to tap more comprehensively the nation's local workforce. For example, it promoted a "Back to Work" program to encourage the approximately 300,000 economically inactive women, primarily housewives, to return to the workforce. Third, Singapore has amended the legislation to increase the statutory retirement age from 55 to 60, and gradually to a target age of 67. This extends the economically productive years of the rapidly aging population and has strengthened the workforce by about 63,000 (Ministry of Labour, 1997).

Despite these efforts, labor supply-demand gaps exist in all sectors and at all skill levels (Bian & Ang, 1997; Lim & Associates, 1988; Verma, Kochan, & Lansbury, 1995). Abundant employment opportunities face Singaporean workers. The unemployment rate in 1997 was 1.8%. Between 1987 and 1997, the annual recruitment rate ranged from 38.4% to 56.4%, and the annual job vacancy rate ranged from 17.6% to 24.8%.

Such statistics show that an average Singaporean has little trouble finding employment. In fact, the median duration of unemployment averaged 4.1 to 7.5 weeks between 1993 and 1997. Graduates from local universities and technical institutes find employment easily, some receiving multiple job offers within months upon graduation. A favorable labor market facing workers lends itself to high turnover rates. In the last decade, the average resignation rate was about 40% per annum. As vacancy chain theory (Chase, 1990) would predict, the high turnover rate in any society augments the availability of employment, for turnover creates vacancy chains that allow considerable movement between jobs.

THE SINGAPOREAN PSYCHE

With an understanding of Singapore's economic realities and labor market conditions, we now turn to the psyche of a Singaporean worker. Singapore's struggle for survival and focal fixation on excellence has molded a *kiasu* psyche among its workforce. *Kiasu* is a Hokkien (Chinese dialect) term that encompasses two traits: a drive for competitive excellence and a fear of failure.

Kiasu corresponds well with Kanfer and Heggestad's (1997) formulation of a person-centered framework for work motivation. Their framework identifies two superordinate traits that explain individual differences in motivational levels: achievement and anxiety. Within this framework, the drive for competitive excellence and the fear of failure are subdimensions of achievement and anxiety, respectively. Both the drive for competitive excellence and the fear of failure are motivational traits that spur an individual to perform.

Singapore's economic realities and relentless struggle for survival fuel the *kiasu* psyche. As described earlier, Singapore's well-being is predicated on its ability to stay ahead of competition. In a meritocratic environment where being the best is proclaimed to be the only way to survive (Murray & Perera, 1996), the need to rival and surpass others (i.e., to achieve competitive excellence) is inevitably instilled.

The drive for competitive excellence in *kiasu*-ism manifests as positive energies in the form of diligence and hard work. The aim of this drive is to remain on top of any situation. The competitive excellence dimension of *kiasu* can therefore be interpreted as a desire to "always be number one" (Murray & Perera, 1996), "always be ahead of others" (Ho, Ang, Loh, & Ng, 1998), and "do whatever it takes to succeed" (Cunningham, 1995).

Unfortunately, *kiasu*-ism has a dark side, which manifests as high fear of failure (Ng & Ang, 1997). Because of its vulnerability, Singapore believes that if it fails to maintain its competitive advantage in business infrastructure, its survival will be in question (Knoop et al., 1995; Vogel, 1991). Therefore, failures are to be avoided at all costs.

From an individual standpoint, failures and mistakes are regarded as career-damaging events because Singapore offers no unemployment benefits (Sisodia, 1992). Singaporeans recognize that individuals, not the state, have sole responsibility for their personal success and failure. In this way, the country's struggle to survive becomes very real at the individual level, thereby creating a high fear of failure and a fear of losing out (Murray & Perera, 1996).

The desirability of workers with strong achievement and anxiety traits is mixed (Kanfer & Heggestad, 1997). Although a strong drive for success and mastery is a desirable feature of employees in any organization, the concomitant high anxiety may preclude goal accomplishment and even lead to goal avoidance. Therefore, how a worker with a *kiasu* disposition will react to work situations will depend critically on the relative strength of competitive excellence and fear-of-failure tendencies.

CONTENT OF PSYCHOLOGICAL CONTRACTS

Singapore's economic realities and labor market conditions combine with the Singaporean psyche to shape the psychological contract of a Singaporean employee.

A series of unstructured interviews regarding the content of psychological contracts were conducted with senior human resource managers in a number of local and multinational corporations in Singapore. Human resource managers were asked about employees' obligations to organizations and what employees expect from the organizations. Each interview lasted approximately 2 hours. In addition, we conducted focus group discussions with part-time MBA students. Both groups of respondents were asked to describe employees' obligations to their employers and the organizations' obligations to employees.

Employees' Obligations

We observe that the Singaporean *kiasu* psyche has influenced the perceptions of employee obligations. These perspectives reflect industries as diverse as finance, manufacturing, and human resources. The motivational traits of high drive for competitive excellence and high fear of failure have shaped three major employee obligations in the psychological contract in Singapore: conscientiousness, broad role orientation, and cost consciousness.

Conscientiousness

Conscientiousness refers to the willingness to work overtime and the drive to produce as much as a person is capable of (Van Dyne, Graham, & Dienesch, 1994). A conscientious worker often exhibits high organizational citizenship or extrarole behaviors. Discretionary in nature, these behaviors are typically not required by formal job specifications. Thus, there are no formal sanctions for failing to be conscientious (Van Dyne & Ang, 1998).

In Singapore, we observe that in-role job performance is a basic requirement that employees ordinarily fulfill. Seldom are employees sacked because of poor performance. In fact, the high achievement and high anxiety traits in Singaporean workers drive them to go beyond their in-role job specifications and exhibit high levels of organizational citizenship behaviors or extrarole behaviors. That Singaporeans are competent and conscientious at their jobs is evidenced by the consistent top ratings accorded to Singaporean workers by the Labor Force Evaluation Measure (LFEM) drawn up by BERI, which is U.S. based. Examples of conscientiousness of Singaporean workers include the following observations and comments from the director of a Singaporean executive search firm: "To us, working from 8.30 a.m. to 9.00 p.m. is normal. Sometimes, the employees work so late (after midnight), I [as their employer] have to ask them to go home," and "During busy periods, local employees take shorter lunch breaks on their own accord. . . . They eat lunch at their desks and answer phone calls even during lunch hours. Foreign employees demand the right to have un-interrupted lunch breaks."

Broad Role Orientation

Role orientation refers to the psychological boundary of a role: "the problems, tasks, and competencies an individual sees as relevant to his or her work role and effective performance of that role" (Parker, Wall, & Jackson, 1997, p. 904). Singaporean workers typically perceive a broad role orientation toward work as an important obligation they owe to organizations. Their willingness to do whatever it takes to succeed (as mentioned earlier in the discussion of *kiasu*) expands the psychological boundaries of their roles. Singaporean workers are flexible and are willing to undertake tasks and responsibilities beyond their formal job requirements because taking on such extrarole responsibilities distinguishes an excellent worker from an ordinary one. As a human resource manager in a multinational precision tools corporation comments, "[Foreign workers] have very fixed notions of what their jobs are. . . . Locals are able to think of how other departments may be linked and undertake tasks and responsibilities beyond their job scope." Similarly, the director of a Singaporean executive search firm notes that foreign workers "are very uncomfortable with a lack of clear job descriptions. Singaporean workers do not have that inflexibility."

Cost Consciousness

Cost consciousness refers to the conservation of organization resources. This is consistent with Van Dyne et al. (1994), who identified the act of conserving organizational resources as an organizational citizenship behavior. With extreme scarcity of resources in the country, Singapore has relied on high rates of productivity to excel and stay ahead. We find that Singaporean employees, to remain productive, have developed a mental schema of cost consciousness. In fact, they are so cognizant of conserving resources as a way of staying ahead of their competitors that cost-conscious behaviors become very salient. Cost-conscious behaviors prompt observations such as the remark of a general manager of a multinational oil company that "local employees are very cost-conscious. . . . When a meeting is over, local employees automatically turn off the lights as they leave the meeting room."

Organization Obligations

Whereas the *kiasu* psyche (high achievement and anxiety) shapes employee obligations, we find that labor market conditions shape organization obligations (i.e., what employees perceive to be the obligations of organizations to them). As described earlier, Singapore is experiencing a tight labor market. The chronic labor shortage and full employment situation tilts the balance of bargaining power in favor of employees. A resource dependency perspective (Pfeffer & Salancik, 1978) would predict that this makes employees relatively more powerful in specifying the terms of the employment relationship.

As powerful agents, employees can and are likely to demand more favorable employment terms from the principals (Ang, 1995). Specifically, the power differences put agents in the position of "contract makers" while relegating principals to the position of "contract takers" (Rousseau & Parks, 1993). In the case of Singapore, we find that employees, accorded high bargaining power by the chronic labor shortage climate, demand obligations from their organizations in terms of high pay, rapid advancement, and provision of generalized rather than firm-specific training.

High Pay

In an economy of chronic labor shortages, organizations compete for limited human resources. To outbid competitors, organizations often entice workers to leave their present jobs with better pay packages, causing wages to spiral upwards. Consequently, employees perceive organizations to owe them premium wages (Cappelli & Sherer, 1991). As one human resource manager of a multinational health care company lamented, "Some workers would leave their job here for just a small increase elsewhere." And in the words of a manager of personnel and training for a Singaporean stockbroking company, "The workers are a fussy and spoilt lot. We give them a 6-month bonus and that is still not enough for them."

Rapid Advancement

In addition to extracting premium wages, powerful agents also demand job advancements when labor is in short supply. In Singapore, job titles and job designations are extremely important, as they signify employees' career milestones and achievements (Murray & Perera, 1996; Vogel, 1991). Although advancement per se may not be an emic psychological contract element (i.e., although the psychological contract element of advancement may not be unique to Singapore), the notion of advancement in Singapore is unique in that it is expected to occur rapidly. Thus, besides demanding high pay, Singaporean employees also ask for rapid promotions: According to a human resource manager in a multinational precision tools company, "The [young] engineers expect to be managers in 5 years! A more realistic expectation would be for them to contribute to the company and to take on a supervisory role only in 8 to 10 years' time" and "They [the young engineers] want to be promoted to manager so that they can compare their [titles on] business cards with friends."

Provision of Generalized Training

Singaporean workers recognize the importance of training to ensure that they remain competitive and survive. However, just as is the case with job advancement, Singaporean workers demand an emic or unique dimension of training from their employing organizations. Although training is often viewed upon as an important organization obligation (Robinson, Kraatz, & Rousseau, 1994), Singaporean employees typically demand general training but not firm-specific training.

The literature on human capital has distinguished between general and specific training (Becker, 1964). This dichotomy provides a useful means of dividing the costs and benefits of training between the employer and the employee. In the case of specific training, the employer is more willing to pay training costs because the "irrelevance" of the training to other potential employers implies that market forces do not pressure them into paying a premium for the worker's higher skill and increased output (Becker, 1964). In other words, firm-specific training adds little to the "employability" of the employees, thus restricting their alternative job opportunities.

But with the greater degree of employability afforded by a tight labor market, Singaporean employees prefer general training to aid them in their next career move. An incident related by Chew and Chew (1992) shows the extent to which Singaporeans value training for its value in employability:

A group of Singaporean workers were given training in a Japanese firm. The Singaporean workers asked whether they would be given certificates of attendance. The Japanese employer enquired as to why they need the certificates of attendance and was shocked to be told that these certificates of attendance would be useful when the trainees applied for jobs with other companies. (p. 174)

In effect, the tight labor market has unwittingly promoted the concept of "boundaryless" or "protean" careers, characterized by having multiple employers in the course of an individual's career development (Arthur & Rousseau, 1996; Hall & Moss, 1998).

In a protean career orientation, loyalty to the employer is supplanted by the ability to seek better employment elsewhere. In a recent study of high-technology professionals in Singapore, Tan (1999) found that employees perceive it to be the duty of the organization to provide training only in marketable technical skills and not in those skills that benefit only the organization. Thus, with demands only for generalized training, employing organizations in Singapore are at a dilemma. According to a human resource manager in a multinational precision tools company, "We are unable to get [Singaporeans] to take part in our training course. To them, it takes too long to complete (3 years), and because it is such a specialized skill, they feel trapped." Similarly, a manager of personnel and training in a Singaporean stockbroking company reported that "in a feedback form, an employee wrote to tell us not to waste money on courses which he thought were irrelevant to his long-term career."

RECOURSE IN FACE OF BREACH IN PSYCHOLOGICAL CONTRACT

Given the typical terms of contract, what actions will a Singaporean employee undertake in face of breach of a psychological contract? Prior research has shown that when employees experience a breach of psychological contract, they undertake one of several forms of recourse: exit, voice, loyalty, or neglect (Farrell, 1983; Hirschman, 1970). In the context of Singapore, we argue that of the four forms of recourse, employees are most likely to exit and least likely to show neglect.

In a tight labor market with many employment opportunities, employees whose psychological contracts have been breached in one organization are likely to leave the firm, as they can seek easily alternative employment. This is consistent with March and Simon's (1958) conclusion that the one factor affecting voluntary employee departure is the perceived ease of movement. In other words, with a favorable labor market, employees need not endure or accept the unfavorable circumstances or wait for conditions to improve (i.e., show loyalty); nor need they invest considerable effort to change the objectionable features in the situation (i.e., voice). Rather, "exit" (quitting the company) becomes the most attractive and ready course of action.

Neglect, on the other hand, is the least likely form of recourse for Singaporean employees in face of a breach in psychological contract. Neglect, which entails passive negligence or active destruction, can range from reneging on one's duties at work to strong antisocial and counterproductive behaviors, such as vandalism, theft, and interpersonal aggression (Hirschman, 1970).

In the case of Singapore, neglect is unlikely because it runs counter to the *kiasu* mind-set. Given that the *kiasu* mind-set encourages one to contribute beyond one's duties rather than to withdraw effort, we observe that a Singaporean employee will prefer to seek alternative employment where psychological contracts can be met. In fact, the pervasiveness of "job hopping" or "career switching" attests to the fact that Singaporean employees prefer to seek alternative employment when psychological contracts are not met than to stick with the company (Khatri, 1998).

WORKFORCE DIVERSITY AND ITS EFFECTS ON PSYCHOLOGICAL CONTRACTS

Like the labor force of any nation, the Singaporean labor force is not homogeneous. Of the 1.83 million people in the labor force, over three fifths work in the services industry (comprising commerce, transport and communications, financial and business services, and community and social services), with the remaining two fifths in manufacturing and construction. About 75% have at least high school education, with the literacy rate estimated at about 92%. Thirty-nine percent of the workforce are in higher occupational status categories, including administrative, professional, and technical jobs. The remaining 61% of the workforce hold clerical, service and sales, and production and related jobs.

The workforce diversity literature shows that attitudes and behaviors of workers can vary depending on demographic and other characteristics such as age, gender, occupational status, and race (Lau & Murnigham, 1998). Therefore, we do not expect the content of psychological contracts or the form of recourse in face of breach to be the same across all Singaporean employees. Specifically, we observe that two factors, age and occupational status, affect the type of psychological contract and determine the ways in which individuals will respond to breach in psychological contract.

Age

Theoretically, age is a significant demographic variable in psychological and sociological research. Age has been examined as an antecedent to work goal importance (Hofstede, 1980), work values and job rewards (Kalleberg & Loscocco, 1983), job involvement and work experiences (Mortimer & Lorence, 1989), and job preferences (Wright & Hamilton, 1978).

Lorence (1987) offered cohort differences and the adult developmental process as reasons underlying the observed relationship between age and work attitudes. We believe these reasons to be pertinent to how age of a Singaporean worker may affect the content of, and the recourse to breach of, psychological contracts.

First, research on cohort differences shows that the job market conditions and common work arrangements that exist at the time individuals begin their work careers have an enduring impact on their work orientations. The workforce in Singapore has a median age of 36.9. On the basis of historical economic and labor market conditions, we can roughly divide the workforce into two cohorts, depending on the different job market conditions they have experienced: (a) the older cohort, who were exposed to the relatively unfavorable labor market and weak economic conditions in Singapore in the late 1960s to the mid-1970s, and (b) the younger cohort, who have been exposed only to the economic boom after the mid-1970s. In other words, whereas some of the workforce have experienced harsher economic and labor market conditions, a majority of the younger Singaporean employees are accustomed only to abundant employment opportunities. Consequently, we find the younger cohort forming higher expectations and demanding more from their employers. Comments from our interviews underscore these differences:

- "In my time, jobs were so hard to come by. We only thought of what we could give to the company. Nowadays, the fresh graduates would even ask about pay during the job interview." (human resource manager, multinational precision tools corporation)
- "The young workers all want a fast track and good pay. Those from very well-to-do families will move on if they can't achieve this [quickly] in this company." (human resource manager, multinational electronics company)
- "The younger workers are impatient [about their own success and achievement]. During job interviews, they want to know about training opportunities and overseas postings. They do not ask about or discuss their personal contributions." (human resource director, Singaporean quasi-governmental body)
- "Young workers expect more annual leave." (director, Singaporean executive search firm)

Second, research on adult development shows that job preferences shift as individuals age. Younger workers attach more importance to promotion prospects than do older workers. Older workers, on the other hand, value job security, limited work hours, and meaningful jobs (Wright & Hamilton, 1978). We found the same patterns among the Singaporean workforce. Younger workers in Singapore tend to be more ambitious, unrealistic in their expectations, and self-centered, whereas older workers are more patient and realistic:

- "Fresh graduates are ambitious and impatient. For example, they aspire to be a manager in 5 years. They do not understand what the work of a manager entails. Moreover, organizations are flattening, and opportunities of becoming a manager are diminishing." (human resource specialist, multinational telecommunications company)

- "Five years later [after they start work], employees become less money motivated. They would have stabilized by then, settled their loans. Job satisfaction becomes more important." (director, Singaporean executive search firm)
- "The older workers do not leave for the same reasons as the younger workers. The younger workers leave because of pay and promotion; the old leave because of relationship problems." (human resource manager, multinational precision tools company)

Research on adult development also shows that younger workers have higher and unrealistic expectations to begin with. These expectations are then lowered over time. For example, Wanous (1976) found that there are many aspects of jobs that younger workers cannot know at the time when they first enter the workforce. Therefore, with little work experience, younger workers inevitably form unrealistic psychological contracts and demand more of their employers than do their older colleagues at work. As the director of a Singaporean executive search firm states, "Five years into the working world, the expectations of employees become more realistic. They start to focus more on their career development and are more receptive to lateral moves, rather than remaining fixated on advancement and increasing their pay packets."

In terms of recourse in face of breach of psychological contract, we found that younger employees are more likely to leave their organizations upon experiencing breach than older workers. First, younger employees experience fewer attachments to their current employers than older employees because younger employees tend to have lower tenure in any organization. Second, younger employees are more likely to be better trained and more well educated and hence more employable. With higher levels of human capital, younger employees have more employment alternatives and are more inclined to look for alternative employment as a response to the breach:

- "The young have no qualms about leaving the organization because their friendship ties with their colleagues are not strong." (human resource manager, multinational manufacturing company)
- "Once the [young] engineers sense that they are unable to fulfill their objectives in this organization, they leave automatically." (human resource manager, multinational high-tech company)

Occupational Status

As described earlier, 39% of the Singaporean labor force occupy higher status jobs, including managers; professionals with formal accreditation, such as accountants, engineers, lawyers, and physicians; and paraprofessionals, such as technicians. Lower occupational jobs include clerical workers, production workers, craftsmen, plant and machine operators, assemblers, cleaners, and laborers.

Prior research has found a relationship between workers' occupational status and their work attitudes and behaviors. High-status employees possess a higher sense of accountability, responsibility, and obligation to their employers than low-status employees (Low, 1996). Likewise, high-status employees, with higher human capital investments, possess a greater degree of work centrality (Mannheim, Baruch, & Tal, 1997; Mannheim & Cohen, 1978). Because of work centrality among high-status workers, we observed that high-status employees possess higher aspirations and demand from employers meaningful careers and job opportunities. For example, one human resource manager in a multinational health care company stated that "production workers are mainly concerned about hygiene factors, like the type of canteen food they get and the amount of transport reimbursement they receive. Professionals and managers, on the other hand, expect good advancement opportunities and challenging jobs."

In terms of recourse in face of breach of psychological contract, we argued earlier that Singaporean workers will "vote with their feet" (i.e., exit) in light of the favorable labor market conditions. Interestingly, we observed that high-status and low-status workers differ on the aspect of voice. Specifically, it appears that low-status employees are more likely to use voice as a form of recourse to breach than high-status employees. This is because low-status employees who work in large numbers (e.g., on assembly lines) tend to experience the same breach of psychological contract simultaneously. Although psychological contracts are idiosyncratic and distinct for each individual, similar organization experiences may cause psychological contracts of different individuals to converge.

Low-status employees such as assembly line workers possess very similar psychological contracts because they work in close proximity to each other. Furthermore, verbal interaction among low-status employees coupled with similar organization experiences increases their likelihood of encountering similar experiences of breach. In our study, we found that low-status employees with similar grievances are then able to seek solidarity with each other and engage in collective bargaining via unions or informal grievance teams. In greater numbers, low-status employees are able to influence their employers to remedy the breach, so low-status employees use voice as a form of recourse to breach of contract.

DISCUSSION AND MANAGERIAL IMPLICATIONS

Examining the psychological contracts of employees from different countries poses an interesting and challenging task to researchers. It offers researchers the opportunities to explore the idiosyncratic contextual variables that lead to the formation of indigenous psychological contracts within each nation.

In characterizing the psychological contract of the Singaporean worker, we commence by elucidating the economic realities and labor market conditions facing a Singaporean worker. The vulnerable position of Singapore caused by its physical and resource limitations has produced a highly competitive national culture that spurs Singaporeans to give their best at work. Thus, although Singaporean workers are very demanding in terms of financial rewards and job status, they also feel very obligated to put in long hours and extra effort at work. Chronic labor shortage puts the Singaporean worker in a good bargaining position vis-à-vis employers. In the event of a breach of psychological contract, the Singaporean worker tends to leave for alternative employment rather than waiting for conditions to improve or attempting to change objectionable features in the organization.

From a practical viewpoint, understanding the impact of national background on psychological contracts also facilitates the implementation of international human resource practices. Specifically, in nations facing chronic labor shortages, attempts to reduce turnover rate or increase employee retention may not be practical. In such situations, firms need to consider strategies for managing high rates of employee turnover. Such alternative strategies may include (a) buffering strategies, such as creating slack human resources by hiring excess employees or creating a core of committed employees; (b) smoothing and leveling strategies, such as doing continuous recruiting and creating part-time labor pools; and (c) anticipation and prediction strategies, such as developing employee skills inventory and collecting and analyzing historical turnover data (see Mowday, 1984).

Our discussion of the nature of psychological contracts in Singapore is premised on a healthy growth in the economy and a corresponding tight labor market. Unlike the enduring nature of scarce resources and physical limitations facing Singapore, the labor market conditions favoring Singaporean employees may not be sustainable. In fact, the current Asian financial crisis beginning in the middle of 1997 is having a dampening effect on Singapore's economic growth. The economic slowdown has caused some organizations to tighten their recruitment and to even retrench some employees. With the erosion of bargaining power on the part of the workers, we would expect the pattern of psychological contract to favor employers.

We speculate that workers are less likely to demand high wages or rapid career advancement. Workers are also less likely to job-hop due to a weaker "pull" factor from the external labor market. In sum, the sudden downturn in the economy offers a valuable lesson to the cohort of younger workers who have never experienced any significant economic hardship. It also offers relief to human resource managers in Singapore, who can divert their attention away from filling vacancies to more important areas of human resource development, including reskilling of older workers for jobs requiring higher value-added knowledge, skills, and technology.

Seeking a general pattern of psychological contracts of employees across national boundaries is an interesting inquiry that deserves our attention. Through understanding the contextual environment in which employees are positioned, we may be able to better predict and explain their attitudes and behaviors at work in the global economy.

REFERENCES

Ang, S. (1995, August). *Markets and hierarchies: A powerful agent's perspective.* Paper presented at the annual meeting of the Academy of Management, Organization and Management Division, Vancouver, Canada.

Arthur, M. D., & Rousseau, D. M. (1996). *The boundaryless career.* New York: Oxford University Press.

Becker, G. S. (1964). *Human capital: A theoretical and empirical analysis, with special reference to education.* New York: Columbia University Press.

Bian, Y., & Ang, S. (1997). Guanxi networks and job mobility in China and Singapore. *Social Forces, 75,* 981-1005.

Cappelli, P., & Sherer, P. D. (1991). The missing role of context in OB: The need for a meso-level approach. *Research in Organizational Behavior, 13,* 55-110.

Chase, I. D. (1990). Vacancy chains. *Annual Review of Sociology, 17,* 133-154.

Chew, S. B., & Chew, R. (1992). *The Singapore worker.* Singapore: Oxford University Press.

Cunningham, J. B. (1995). Success in corporate and entrepreneurial organizations in Singapore. *Journal of Small Business Management, 33*(4), 80-86.

Farrell, D. (1983). Exit, voice, loyalty and neglect as responses to job dissatisfaction: A multi-dimensional scaling study. *Academy of Management Journal, 26,* 596-607.

Hall, D. T., & Moss, J. E. (1998). The new protean career contract: Helping organizations and employees adapt. *Organization Dynamics, 26*(3), 22-37.

Herriot, P., Manning, W. E. G., & Kidd, J. M. (1997). The content of the psychological contract. *British Journal of Management, 8,* 151-167.

Hirschman, A. O. (1970). *Exit, voice, and loyalty: Responses to decline in firms, organizations, and states.* Cambridge, MA: Harvard University Press.

Ho, J. T. S., Ang, C. E., Loh, J., & Ng, I. (1998). A preliminary study of kiasu behavior: Is it unique to Singapore? *Journal of Managerial Psychology, 13,* 359-370.

Hofstede, G. (1980). *Culture's consequences: International differences in work-related values.* Newbury Park, CA: Sage.

Kalleberg, A. L., & Loscocco, K. A. (1983). Aging, values, and rewards: Explaining age differences in job satisfaction. *American Sociological Review, 48,* 78-90.

Kanfer, R., & Heggestad, E. (1997). Motivational traits and skills: A person-centered approach to work motivation. *Research in Organizational Behavior, 19,* 1-56.

Khatri, N. (1998, August). *Managing human resource for competitive advantage: A study of companies in Singapore.* Paper presented at the annual meeting of the Academy of Management, San Diego, CA.

Knoop, C., Applegate, L. M., Neo, B. S., & King, J. L. (1995). *Singapore unlimited: Building the national information structure* (Harvard Business Case No. 9-196-012). Boston: Harvard Business School Publishing.

Lau, D. C., & Murnigham, J. K. (1998). Demographic diversity and faultlines: The compositional dynamics of organizational groups. *Academy of Management Review, 23*, 325-340.

Lee, K. Y. (1986, May-June). Prime Minister's May Day message 1986. *Speeches: A Bi-Monthly Selection of Ministerial Speeches*, pp. 1-3.

Lim, C. Y., & Associates. (1988). *Policy options for the Singapore economy.* Singapore: McGraw-Hill.

Lorence, J. (1987). Age differences in work involvement: Analysis of three explanations. *Work and Occupations, 14*, 533-557.

Low, L. (1996). *Professionals at the crossroads in Singapore.* Singapore: Times Academic Press.

Mannheim, B., Baruch, Y., & Tal, J. (1997). Alternative models for antecedents and outcomes of work centrality and job satisfaction of high-tech personnel. *Human Relations, 50*, 1537-1562.

Mannheim, B., & Cohen, A. (1978). Multivariate analysis of factors affecting WRC of occupational categories. *Human Relations, 31*, 525-553.

March, J. B., & Simon, H. A. (1958). *Organizations.* New York: John Wiley.

Ministry of Labour. (1997, October). The Minister for Labour's ministerial statement on the extension of the retirement age. *Labour News (Singapore)*, pp. 1-3.

Mortimer, J. T., & Lorence, J. (1989). Satisfaction and involvement: Disentangling a deceptively simple relationship. *Social Psychology Quarterly, 52*, 249-265.

Mowday, R. T. (1984). Strategies for adapting to high rates of employee turnover. *Human Resource Management, 23*, 365-380.

Murray, G., & Perera, A. (1996). *Singapore: The global city state.* New York: St. Martin's.

Neo, B. S., King, J. L., & Applegate, L. M. (1995). *Singapore TradeNet: Beyond TradeNet to the intelligent island* (Harvard Business Case No. 9-196-105). Boston: Harvard Business School Publishing.

Ng, A., & Ang, S. (1997, August 9-13). *Keeping MUM in classrooms: Feedback-seeking behaviors (or lack of) and emerging cultural antecedents of face and kiasuism in an Asian learning environment.* Paper presented at the annual meeting of the Academy of Management, Boston.

Parker, S. K., Wall, T. D., & Jackson, P. R. (1997). That's not my job: Developing flexible employee work orientations. *Academy of Management Journal, 40*, 899-929.

Pfeffer, J., & Salancik, G. (1978). *The external control of organizations.* Boston: Pitman.

Robinson, S. L., Kraatz, M. S., & Rousseau, D. M. (1994). Changing obligations and the psychological contract: A longitudinal study. *Academy of Management Journal, 37*, 137-152.

Robinson, S. L., & Rousseau, D. M. (1994). Violating the psychological contract: Not the exception but the norm. *Journal of Organizational Behavior, 15*, 245-259.

Rousseau, D. M. (1989). Psychological and implied contracts in organizations. *Employee Responsibilities and Rights Journal, 2*, 121-139.

Rousseau, D. M., & Parks, J. M. (1993). The contracts of individuals and organizations. *Research in Organizational Behavior, 15*, 1-43.

Rousseau, D. M., & Tijoriwala, S. A. (1998). Assessing psychological contracts: Issues, alternatives and types of measures. *Journal of Organizational Behavior, 19*, 679-695.

Sisodia, R. S. (1992, May-June). Singapore invests in the nation-corporation. *Harvard Business Review, 70*(3), 40-50.

Tan, M. L. (1999). *Psychological contracts of high-tech professionals.* Unpublished master's thesis, Nanyang Business School, Nanyang Technological University, Singapore.

Van Dyne, L., & Ang, S. (1998). Organizational citizenship behavior of contingent workers in Singapore. *Academy of Management Journal, 41,* 692-703.

Van Dyne, L., Graham, J. W., & Dienesch, R. M. (1994). Organization citizenship behavior: Construct redefinition, measurement, and validation. *Academy of Management Journal, 37,* 765-802.

Verma, A., Kochan, T. A., & Lansbury, R. D. (1995). Lessons from the Asian experience: A summary. In A. Verma, T. A. Kochan, & Y. R. D. Lansbury (Eds.), *Employment relations in growing Asian economies* (pp. 336-367). London: Routledge.

Vogel, E. F. (1991). *The four little dragons.* Cambridge, MA: Harvard University Press.

Wanous, J. P. (1976). Organizational entry: From naïve expectations to realistic beliefs. *Journal of Applied Psychology, 61,* 22-29.

Wright, J. D., & Hamilton, R. F. (1978). Work satisfaction and age: Some evidence for the job change hypothesis. *Social Forces, 56,* 1140-1156.

Yeo, G. (1990). Excellence. In *Singapore: Island city state.* Singapore: Times Edition.

13

The Psychological Contract in the United Kingdom

Lynne Millward
Peter Herriot

The title of this chapter makes an impossible promise. Because employment relationships in the United Kingdom are undergoing rapid changes and the labor market is increasingly fragmented, it is vain to hope to characterize "the" psychological contract in the United Kingdom. Indeed, not only is it impossible to define a particular national contract, but it is very hard to define the contracts that exist even at the organizational level of analysis. At that level, too, there are immense differences in how workers perceive their mutual obligations with their employer, especially between graduates on the fast track and front-line staff in the same organization. At the national level of analysis, all that we can hope to do is to paint a broad picture of the United Kingdom as the backdrop for an infinite variety of psychological contracts.

By avoiding generalizations about "the" psychological contract, we can maintain the distinction between the psychological contract as an analytic concept and its use for rhetorical purposes. Managerial rhetoric has seized on the concept to persuade employees to perceive their employment relationships in a particular way, insisting that the old psychological contract of security in exchange for loyalty (bad) has been replaced by a new one that trades employability for flexibility (good). However, we need to maintain the scientific construct of the psychological contract as a tool for analysis and understanding.

Everyday language provides other ways of describing the employment relationship. For example, the use of metaphors enables us to understand something foreign, in terms of other concepts with which we are more familiar. We habitually use a wide variety of metaphors to describe the employment relationship, all of them referring to other relationships that share elements with employment; common examples of this are family, club, democracy, crusade, and resource relationships. All of these draw our attention to other particular features of the employment relationship. Family encapsulates care and support; club, belonging; democracy, rights and responsibilities; crusade, vision and mission; and resource, value. But do these metaphors add to the understanding of our scientific construct of the psychological contract?

A HISTORICAL PERSPECTIVE

From a historical perspective, other metaphors have aptly expressed elements of the U.K. employment relationship. Great 18th- and 19th-century philanthropists such as Robert Owen, Cadbury, and Fry considered it their duty to concern themselves with the welfare of their employees as part of the *family.* Large U.K. organizations in the banking and finance sector or professional accounting and legal firms were archetypal *clubs,* where everyone felt they had a right to belong, provided they had the entry qualifications, knew the rules, and obeyed them. The U.K. public sector (government employment) generally had a strong element of *democracy* about it, insisting on voice and representation as rights.

However, the changing national and international context of the employment relationship has rendered these metaphors less appropriate today. Family firms owned and managed by their philanthropic founders have given way to organizations run for the benefit of pension fund shareholders. Collegial clubs of professionals have gained a hard-edged, commercial imperative. The government has subjected the public sector to private sector disciplines. Have contextual changes rendered the contract construct correspondingly *more* appropriate?

Contracting implies voluntary dealings between parties. Dealing may be free in the sense of being unconstrained except by the expectation that the other will keep to his or her side of the deal. Or it may be constrained in the sense that legal or regulatory limits are placed on what bargains are permitted or on how dealing is conducted. But it will not be true contracting if a deal is imposed by one of the parties on the other or by a third party. We should note that a free, or unregulated, labor market does not guarantee true contracting for both parties. Rather, the opposite is often true: If there is unequal power, the more powerful party may be free to impose a deal on the less powerful. Most employees fall into the latter category. Hence, regulation may, by placing a check on the unfettered use of labor market power by organizations, increase the probability of true contracting. As we will indicate, the United Kingdom, like the United States, has failed to recognize the power differences in typical employment relationships. Indeed, perhaps there has been a swing back toward 19th-century employment relationships in these countries.

THE U.K. REGULATORY CONTEXT

So we may ask to what extent the United Kingdom's context encourages true contracting in the arena of the employment relationship. In the light of our analysis above, our first question concerns the regulatory context. What is the nature and extent of regulation of the U.K. labor market, and how far does it ensure that the psychological contract is negotiated?

Although the United Kingdom has a long tradition of collective bargaining, the country's employment law has never strongly supported this tradition. For example, until the European Union (EU) Working Time Directive of 1998, there was no statutory limitation on the hours that adult workers were permitted to work. Employers have never been legally obligated to recognize trade unions. However, what legal protection U.K. employees did historically enjoy, gained largely through the efforts of their unions, was further diminished after the 1979 election of Thatcher's Conservative government.

The Thatcher government wished to encourage a free labor market as part of its adherence to a radical free-market ideology. By deregulating the labor market, the government sought to attract foreign investment, especially by Asian and American companies. Lower wages, fewer employee rights, and less protection for employees would make it more attractive to site production facilities, particularly in the United Kingdom. Wage councils were abolished, leaving no legal protection for low-paid employees. Trade unions had their wings clipped: The "closed shop," whereby only union members could be employed, was abolished, and strike action was severely limited. The EU had to insist that Britain follow its legislation ensuring equal pay for work of equal value (1984) and equal rights for part-time employees (1995).

The aim of the EU has been to harmonize employment regulations so that individual member states do not gain an advantage over the others by offering easier labor market conditions to multinational corporations. The European Community Charter of the Fundamental Social Rights of Workers (the Social Charter) of 1989 was partly aimed at this objective. However, Britain alone among the 12 EU members opted out of this and the subsequent Protocol on Social Policy (the Social Chapter) of 1992. The Labor government of Blair (1997) has promised to establish a minimum wage but is still committed to ensuring a "flexible" labor market. However, Blair's government has begun to reverse the antiunion program of the Thatcher government by passing the Fairness at Work Act, which compels companies to recognize trade unions when they can demonstrate that 50% or more of the workers within a bargaining unit are members.

In sum, the regulatory framework in the United Kingdom is minimal compared to those of continental European countries such as France and Germany (though not compared to the United States). Hence, the concept of psychological contracts is unlikely to describe employment relationships throughout the United Kingdom because the power differential between employers and employees remains largely unregulated and is usually tipped considerably in favor of the employers.

THE U.K. BUSINESS CONTEXT

In the meantime, both private and public sector organizations in the United Kingdom were preoccupied in the main with achieving cost competitiveness. The private sector faced acute competitive pressure from lower-cost products and services from abroad. With pension funds as their key shareholders, companies were also under continuous pressure to maximize dividends by cutting costs (and the quickest and most visible way to do this was to reduce the workforce). Layoffs were made even when the organization was making a handsome profit, thereby making it harder for management to claim, in accord with more traditional values, that they would not have made the layoffs if they could have helped it.

The public sector, meanwhile, was being restructured into a quasi-market (e.g., the National Health Service) or was actually being privatized (e.g., the water and power industries). The Thatcher government introduced management controls into the public sector in such a way that value for the taxpayer's money (i.e., efficiency) was held up as the core value, rather than the provision of effective services.

These structural changes were accompanied by increased managerial control, despite much managerial rhetoric about empowerment. However, because the ranks of supervisors and middle managers had dropped drastically, they were no longer able to control employees through closer personal supervision. Rather, a range of other control mechanisms was introduced, including the setting and monitoring of demanding budget targets, the introduction of performance-related pay, and a range of more psychological controls. The latter came mostly from the United States under the banner of human resource management, the "soft" version of which sought to engineer employee commitment to the organization. Initiatives such as culture change programs in general, and total quality management (TQM) in particular, were aimed at inducing commitment to statements of organizational vision, mission, and values, which had usually been created by top managers with the help of outside consultants and with little if any participation from front-line workers.

THE IMPACT ON EMPLOYEES

The widespread restructuring and increased use of management incentives had a profound effect on employees. First, restructuring required a variety of changes in the workplace. The identification of redundancies led to downsizing and expanded job descriptions for the employees who remained. As customers increasingly demanded 24-hour service 7 days a week, organizations became more flexible in order to better synchronize the supply and demand for labor.

This increased flexibility required employees to take on new functions and move from full-time contracts to part-time or shift work. In the public sector, much time was spent on administering the tight managerial controls that grew from these changes.

Productivity improved considerably as a result of restructuring, but partly as a consequence of people working longer hours. The proportion of U.K. employees working more than 48 hours per week still is the highest of any European Community nation, although productivity is still below that of France, Germany, and the United States. Work has become more intense in many cases, as evidenced by the case of so-called "emotional" labor. Employees such as supermarket checkout clerks, airline cabin crews, and fast-food restaurant staff are monitored, often secretly, to ensure that they not only display the appropriate feelings but also make those feelings seem authentic.

Management initiatives also had a considerable effect on workers, although the consequences were not always intended. The implementation of initiatives such as TQM typically required employees to work above and beyond their regular jobs. Moreover, the rhetoric with which these programs were introduced led to much cynicism when the reality failed to materialize. In particular, top management commitment was often lacking, and trust in top management's competence and reliability was dented. Each new initiative was treated by employees as evidence that top management was flailing around in search of the next quick fix. Moreover, suspicions grew that many top managers cared more about their own interests than about the organization or the employees, as their salaries and benefits increased at a rate far higher than those of others, exceeding the rate of inflation and bearing little relation to corporate performance.

It should be emphasized that these are gross generalizations. There have always been some U.K. organizations (e.g., Unilever and Glaxo Wellcome) with the resources, leadership, and management skills to ride the waves of change and stay on course. Many others learned valuable lessons from the free-market excesses of the 1980s, as evidenced by the current emphasis on recognizing the interests of stakeholders as well as those of shareholders in forming organizational policy and practice. The "balanced business scorecard," which assesses corporate performance in terms of employees, customers, and community as well as shareholders, is an attempt to recognize a broader organizational constituency. Moreover, many organizations are seeking productive working partnerships with trade unions. However, the volatility of the business environment and the threat of takeovers and mergers can rapidly divert corporate attention and resources from these good intentions.

LONG-TERM TRENDS

Finally, several underlying and long-term trends also form part of the context for the changing U.K. employment relationship. First, the workforce is on the verge of containing more women than men, although a far higher proportion of women work part time. The manufacturing sector now employs less than 20% of the U.K. workforce (although it is responsible for more than 50% of export earnings). There is a continued shift from public to private sector employment. Unskilled and semiskilled labor is less in demand, whereas technical, professional, and managerial jobs continue to increase. Small and medium-sized enterprises are employing an increasing proportion of the workforce in comparison to large organizations. The average age of the workforce is increasing as a result of a demographic trend. Unemployment moves up and down with the economic cycle but is highest among young people, especially young men. However, large numbers of potential workers have simply disappeared from the labor market and do not show up in unemployment statistics, which are based on those claiming unemployment benefit (Rousseau, 1995).

These diverse trends affect the employment relationship, particularly the question of whether the metaphor of the psychological contract is appropriate. For example, if individuals must choose between a job they don't want or the loss of their unemployment benefits, they have surely had a "contract" imposed on them. Or if women must work 12 hours a day to be promoted to senior management, what choice do many of them have, given the circumstances of the rest of their lives?

Some other more general societal trends affect the answer to this question, two of which are discussed below. First, people are living longer, yet the U.K. state pension reflects only 19% of the average wage. Employees must therefore consider not only their own support after retirement but also that of their parents (who probably expected to live on the state pension to which they had contributed all their working lives). Can employees freely choose to leave a job unless they are moving to one that is equally secure and equally compensated? Second, the social contract of the citizen with the state has changed more generally. The emphasis on social well-being of the post-World War II years has given way to a self-help ethic that has resulted in a middle-class rush to ensure health, life, mortgages, and salaries. In the meantime, the poorest 10% of the U.K. population have become poorer in real terms, and the gap between the rich and the poor has grown wider. This, then, is the context within which we seek to determine the extent to which the psychological contract is an appropriate concept to describe the state of the employment relationship in the United Kingdom today.

IS THE CONTRACT METAPHOR APPROPRIATE IN THE UNITED KINGDOM?

The above account makes it clear that the psychological contract metaphor does not face too much competition from the metaphors cited earlier. The central feature of the family metaphor, care, has not characterized recent employment history. The "clubbiness" of professionals has been dented as they too have been subjected to managerial accountability, and the legal rights of democratic citizens within the workplace have taken a pounding. On the other hand, the economic metaphor of human resources is a powerful alternative, with its strong connotation that business owns its human capital and uses it in its own best interests. Another alternative is the notion of the employment relationship as a crusade, with everyone buying into a common vision, mission, and values (although this last metaphor is more aspirational rhetoric than general perception).

For the psychological contract to be considered a useful description, we have to demonstrate that the concept draws attention to important features of the employment relationship. The core elements of the concept are its mutuality and its individualized nature: Each employee and employer perceives the mutual obligations involved differently. If the employment relationship in the United Kingdom were universally characterized by the unilateral use of power in imposing the terms of the employment relationship or by a complete uniformity in those terms, the use of the concept of the psychological contract would be entirely inappropriate.

As we will demonstrate in the rest of this chapter, although U.K. employers have increased their power and control in a variety of ways, many still engage in two-way dealing with many of their employees. And as our review of the U.K. context demonstrates, there is a wider range of contracts today than ever before. However, there are organizations that impose the terms and conditions of employment, and their number may increase as the organizations exercise ever tighter control.

THE CONTRACT AS PROCESS: WITH WHOM IS THE DEAL?

The fundamentally two-way nature of the employer-employee exchange relationship is a critical consideration. As a mere snapshot of what the employment deal consists of, the *content* of the psychological contract pertains to something so uniquely personal, context bound, and fluid as to render it impossible to make generalized statements. Taking the contract as a *process,* however, raises questions about whom the deal is made with, how the deal is made, what constitutes a breach in the deal, and what the consequences of any such breach are.

It is commonly assumed within the psychological contract literature that the deal is made between employer and employee and that the identification of the two parties in the exchange is nonproblematic (Coyle-Shapiro & Kessler, 1998; Sparrow, 1998). But who is the employer? In a small organization, there is likely to be little doubt. In a large and highly complex multinational or transnational organization, however, the answer is less likely to be so straightforward. With the devolution of responsibility to divisions, departments, or even teams, employers may be more appropriately construed in local day-to-day terms (divisional manager, department manager, team leader).

In the contracted-out employment scenario that is increasingly common within the United Kingdom, the employer is legally the recruitment or contracts agency. However, at a more psychological level, the employer is likely to be more meaningfully located in the host organization or division in which an employee actually works. Many contractors are members of professional institutions to which they feel first and foremost obligated and in which they strongly invest their identity and self-esteem. Multiple exchange scenarios may be operating at any given moment (e.g., between the employee and the agency, the host organization, the profession, and the division, department, or team in which one also invests time and energy). There is indeed some evidence to show that "deals" can be forged at all these levels (Millward, Brewerton, & Hopkins, 1998; Millwood & Hopkins, 1998).

The complexity of the contemporary U.K. workplace in its devolved and deregulated state, coupled with an increasingly matrix-managed and "virtual" form, points toward the need for caution in assuming that the "employer" side of the exchange relationship can be lumped into one homogeneous category of employers. If we take the term *employer* to mean *organization,* thus denoting the need to adopt an "organizational" level of analysis, it becomes equally clear that what constitutes the organization is not obvious either. When employers are equated with organizations as a whole, the latter group is anthropomorphized in a way that may not be realistic. As Rousseau (1995) stipulated, organizations cannot enter into psychological contracts; rather, we need to think in terms of "organizational representatives" (p. 61).

Despite the heterogeneity of large and many medium-sized enterprises within the United Kingdom workplace, and despite the large number of potential "representatives" who might take on the persona of employer, researchers have seldom questioned who the other party is in the exchange relationship. Millward and Hopkins (1998) found that commitment to one's job was a far stronger predictor of the psychological contract than commitment to one's organization. They took this to suggest that contracting is more appropriately construed at a more concrete and day-to-day level of reality than that signaled by the abstract term *organization.* In many cases, *organization* is little more than an umbrella term denoting a bundle of activities that are pursued in the organization's name but have little substantive meaning beyond that of the activities themselves. Very little is known about who employees believe to be their ultimate employer or about the appropriate level of analysis needed to talk about the kinds of deals that are made.

THE ORGANIZATION AS A
FRAMEWORK FOR CONTRACTING

The above analysis may take a rather extreme view on the organization, construing it in terms of the "empty raincoat" image of Handy (1994). A distinction between "make" and "buy" organizations (Miles & Snow, 1984) may be useful at this stage. A "buy" organization is one that purchases labor on an as-needed basis and is therefore highly cost driven. Employee regulation strategies in such organizations are largely economic. A "make" organization, on the other hand, seeks to forge a lasting relationship with employees, provides them with an important source of social identification and self-esteem, and develops their skills and knowledge. In a "make" organization, employee regulation strategies are likely to focus on winning the hearts and minds of employees. These subjective regulation strategies strive to harness a deeper social and emotional level of investment in the organization and its interests than is possible within a purely economic exchange relationship. Handy, however, predicted an employment scenario whereby organizations would shift from "make" to "buy" strategies.

In recent years, the United Kingdom has witnessed a major expansion in the contracts industry. In mid-1996, demand for temporary staff in the United Kingdom had risen by 23% from the previous year and stood at its highest level since 1982. Workplace restructuring, driven by cost and economic concerns, has involved not only mass downsizing but also the introduction of contractualization as the primary means of enhancing numerical and financial flexibility (Tooher, 1996). Underpinning this movement is a change from traditional working patterns to a "core/complementary" employment structure— that is, organizations' employment of core workers whose tenure is long term and contract based along with complementary short-term, contract-based employees (Brown, 1997).

Because large organizations commonly outsource their peripheral activities to external agencies, many workers are employed on short-term or part-time contracts. The result is reduced job security and a continuously changing work environment. It is estimated that the average number of functions outsourced by organizations has risen 225% (from 1.2 to 3.9) in the last 5 years, and this growth area is expected to continue into the new millennium. At the same time, it is anticipated that core workplace activities will also be strategically put out to tender as a means of in-house value creation (Brown, 1997). Whereas employment relations at one time prevailed over labor contracting, the opposite is now increasingly true.

The move toward the "externalization" of employees reflects a shift away from a reliance on social exchanges to a reliance on economic exchange considerations. Employees are taken on as calculated risks (i.e., a "buy" employment model) rather than as people who have needs, concerns, and interests of their own. Though it is clear that economic concerns reign supreme and that cost cutting has often been pursued with little regard for its human costs, research suggests that many organizations are now urgently trying to remake themselves, along with the employees who survived the previous cuts.

Both "make" and "buy" strategies have always coexisted comfortably in certain U.K. organizations and still do coexist, even in organizations that have contracted out most of their peripheral functions to agency regulation and control (Williamson, 1991), a finding consistent with that obtained by Pearce

(1993) in the United States. There is also a major increase in human resource management interest in changes to organizational culture and the management of those changes, partly due to the fear of potential cultural dilution or confusion resulting from merger, acquisition, or major reorganization. All this suggests that organizations are still very much intent on making rather than simply buying at least some of their employees, while adopting a transactional approach with others (Hirsh & Jackson, 1996).

Yet we must question whether employees can be "remade" in the image of the new organization. This was more feasible in the days when organizations could guarantee their workers employment for life in exchange for employee loyalty and commitment. The flexible, amoebic organization of the cost-conscious 2000s no longer provides the security it once did for its employees. The security of tenure—with its concomitant predictability of payment for services rendered, life/workplace routine, and sense of belonging—has been largely replaced by insecurity over the prospects of employment and promotions and hesitation in taking on long-term financial burdens such as mortgages and loans. The substitution of fixed-term for permanent contracts even for "core" employees (i.e., those who take on primary organizational responsibilities), coupled with mass redundancy of friends and colleagues, has exacerbated the insecurity felt by otherwise secure employees in the contemporary marketplace.

This picture of widespread employee insecurity is the context in which U.K. organizations are attempting to reconstitute themselves and prepare for the future. It is commonly noted that although the old employment deal is clearly dead, new deals that harness the time, energy, and commitment of employees have yet to be formulated and articulated within organizational contexts. The "deal" that exists at the social level of analysis (i.e., the social contract) is primarily economic in character. This binds individuals to their organizations only loosely, a fact that does not bode well for organizations in the long run.

Herriot, Hirsh, and Reilly (1998) noted that many organizations seeking to reanchor and reintegrate employees on a more "make" than "buy" basis face the fundamental challenge of rebuilding lost trust. By breaching the old employment deal or social contract, these firms have undermined employee trust to the point where social capital within organizations is at an all-time low. Social capital, which denotes the willingness of people to trust in and collaborate with others, is further undermined by management rhetoric that, more often than not, does not tally with the realities of organizational life. The general absence of reserve social capital within the stock of U.K. society (due to the large-scale disintegration of institutions, such as the family and the education system) has made it less and less likely that trust can be effectively secured.

Thus, organizations face the immediate challenge of rebuilding social capital before they can forge more integrative deals with employees. This is the context within which new psychological contracts can emerge. It may therefore be appropriate to construe the organization as affording a normative framework in which psychological contracts can be made. Rousseau (1995) noted that contracts forged at the normative level denote shared psychological contracts. It is logical to contemplate a process of contracting at a normative level, which in turn provides the interpretative backdrop within which contracting can be pursued at the more psychological level.

Most organizations, it seems, have not yet reinvented themselves at the normative level, let alone at the more individual level of the psychological contract. Many employees have turned to their professions or occupations as suitable anchors for their identity and self-esteem (Tolbert & Stern, 1991). Many perceive organizations as mere employment zones rather than meaningful institutions where one can carve out a viable niche in society. Many organizations are still fumbling with "buy" and "make" considerations, without articulating any basis for employment relationships beyond the purely financial.

It is important when thinking about the normative context in which deals are forged not to suggest that any one new deal will provide the ultimate collaborative solution. As noted above, a deal is a two-way affair that must be negotiated. Although many different types of deal scenarios are in operation, many organizations have attempted to *impose* new deals on their employees (Noon & Blyton, 1997; Parsons & Strickland, 1996). In their efforts to change both structurally and culturally while also enhancing performance, organizations can encourage their employees to accept deals that ignore their long-term personal interests and needs. For the sake of stability and financial survival, many employees find it difficult to resist the offer of a deal that promises short-term security.

In the United Kingdom, it also appears that many employees (across a wide range of industries and service organizations in the public and private sectors) are heavily preoccupied with so-called "hygiene" factors such as pay and security (Herriot, Manning, & Kidd, 1997; Millward & Brewerton, 1998). This raises the question of exactly what constitutes a psychological contract. How can psychological contracts be described, and what is the underlying psychological dynamic?

TYPES OF DEALS

Psychological contracts can be described in terms of content (the perceived terms of the deal) and process (how the deal was arrived at). Here we take the view that content can only be examined at a single moment in time. Questions about content enable us to describe a current relationship between employer and employee and hence can point us to the product of the contractual process.

Psychological contract terms have been described by Rousseau and colleagues (Robinson & Rousseau, 1994; Rousseau, 1990; Rousseau & Parks, 1993) as either transactional or relational. Contracts composed of transactional terms are based largely on remuneration and other short-term benefits to the employee. Relational ones, however, are more akin to a partnership between the employer and employee (MacNeil, 1985). A relational contract can engender feelings of affective involvement or attachment in the employee and can commit the employer to providing more than just monetary support to the individual through investments in training, personal development, and career development. The two constructs (transactional and relational) can be equated to the notions of economic and social exchange, terms used earlier when describing the more economic than social character of the contemporary workplace climate in the United Kingdom.

Research in the United Kingdom has confirmed the distinction between transactional and relational contracts. Millward and Hopkins (1998) used findings from focus group discussions to formulate a scale that measured these two aspects of the employment relationship. Their work was informed by Rousseau's conceptualization (1995, pp. 91-98), which used the following several dimensions: emotional versus economic focus; inclusion, or the extent of individual integration within an organization; short-term versus long-term time frame; contract formality, as measured by the degree of performance specification; stability (static or dynamic); contract scope; and subjective versus objective tangibility. Millward and Hopkins conducted factor analysis on 32 items, yielding two factors that were used to produce subscales for the transactional and relational aspects. These subscales were subsequently tested for validity. The researchers found the relational subscale to be more strongly linked to permanent contracts, full-time work, and long-term employment relationships than to temporary contracts, part-time work, and short-term employment. Moreover, the relational subscale was positively correlated with job and organizational commitment as well as with an expressed willingness to work overtime without pay (i.e., to go the extra mile for the organization). In contrast, the transactional subscale was more strongly associated with a temporary workplace relationship and was negatively correlated with commitment and willingness to work overtime.

These findings validate the idea of relational contracts that are based on trust, high commitment, a high degree of integration and identification with the organization, expectations of stability and long-term commitment, and a reciprocal exchange with the employing organization. Likewise, the findings support the idea that transactional psychological contracts are characterized by a short time frame and an attitude of limited organizational contribution, low commitment, weak integration and identification, limited flexibility, and easy exit. The findings also suggest that the construct of the psychological contract can explain substantially more variance in organizational behavior than either organizational or job commitment, including extraordinary activities, intention to stay or leave, and absenteeism (Coyle-Shapiro & Kessler, 1998; Rousseau, 1990, 1995). The psychological contract is powerful as an explanatory tool because of its reciprocal nature.

Millward and Brewerton found that employees' perceptions of the opportunities to develop, belong, and obtain recognition within an organization are correlated with their scores on the relational and transactional subscales. The perceived absence of these opportunities predicts a heightened score on the transactional subscale, whereas the opposite is true for the relational subscale. We cannot assume a causal link between what the organization is perceived to offer and what the employee might then offer in return, but the research suggests that psychological contracts are inextricably tied to the employer-employee exchange. Coyle-Shapiro and Kessler (1998) reported similar findings and operationalized that exchange as the extent to which various relational and transactional obligations on the part of the organization of both a relational and transactional kind are deemed fulfilled. Their results, derived from public sector employees such as teachers and firefighters, demonstrated that exchange relationships are driven by the extent to which employees perceive themselves to be valued and supported.

BREACHED DEALS

U.K. commentators such as Charles Handy (1994) commonly argue that employees are experiencing a breach in the psychological contracts that they have formed with their employers. In particular, breaches occur in the relational aspects of the psychological contract, to the point where an exchange relationship based on mutual loyalty and commitment can no longer be guaranteed. Economic pressures have created a workplace characterized by transactional forms of dealing. Critics believe that this shift will fashion a calculating, self-interested, and opportunistic workforce that stays within the bounds of the contract and goes no further than is necessary to fulfill the agreed-on terms, in return for high compensation.

This analysis assumes a direct link between economics and psychology. It also assumes that transactional deals are intrinsically bad, yet there is little evidence to date that the United Kingdom is experiencing a greater prevalence of transactional than relational psychological contracts. Although some employees may feel that their psychological contracts have been breached, it is unknown whether this has led them to become more transactional in their exchange relationships (Millward & Hopkins, 1998; Sparrow, 1998). There is some suggestion that many employees have been forced into situations in which their short-term survival is of paramount importance, but this does not necessarily equate to transactional psychological contracts. Instead, the issue may be more complex—before relational considerations can come into play, employees must ensure that basic transactional requirements are met (Herriot et al., 1998, p. 161).

Herriot and Pemberton (1996) pointed out that transactional deals may be appropriate in some instances for both parties in the exchange. More crucially, it can be argued that although transactional deals need not preclude loyalty when psychological contracts are defined in terms of content, it might be difficult to reconcile transactional deals with relational-type content. In terms of process, however, transactional deals denote a strictly defined exchange of goods that indicates nothing about the actual content of the exchange. Instead, an employee operating primarily within a transactional deal is likely to value distributive equity (i.e., a fair exchange of goods). Likewise, what differentiates the relational contract is not its content (of long-term loyalty, commitment, identification, and so on) but reciprocity on a broader, longer-term scale. In this case, an employee is more likely to value procedural equity (i.e., fair decision-making procedures). An employee operating primarily within a relational deal is thus more likely to tolerate distributive inequity at one point in time because he or she expects justice to be served in the long term.

Thus, transactional and relational contracts are not necessarily at odds with one another, as research conventionally assumes. Rather, it seems that the exchange relationship can be characterized as a uniquely complex hybrid containing both relational and transactional aspects (Millward et al., 1998; Rousseau, 1995). Employees may put their efforts into building trust in a company with the expectation of a high return on that investment, while also retaining a practical, transactional attitude in case their contract is terminated. In this sense, loyalty and commitment may follow on the fulfillment of transactional needs and interests (Meyer, Allen, & Smith, 1993).

The term *social capital* can be best understood in the context of general, rather than job-specific, reciprocity. As trust grows and workers become more willing to collaborate over the long term, it is logical to believe that a breach of reciprocity could have serious costs in terms of organizational survival (Herriot et al., 1998). For example, when employees believe that an employer has not honored a commitment to provide for personal growth, increased pay, and/or autonomy, they may become angry, leave the company, or withdraw the organizational-level investment that they have made (Goffee & Scase, 1992; Robinson, Kraatz, & Rousseau, 1994). Many employees have construed employer actions such as compulsory relocation, demotion or job change, threats of layoffs, and intensified workloads to be fundamental violations of the long-term reciprocity deals characteristic of the relational psychological contract.

We must point out that not all U.K. researchers view the psychological contract with as much anxiety. Some in the human resource management field have wondered whether we have overstated the violation of relational contracts because there is only limited evidence of any overt employee reaction to contractual violation within the United Kingdom (Guest, 1998; Guest, Conway, Briner, & Dickman, 1996). Guest and Conway (1997) reported findings from a recent telephone survey of 1,000 employees indicating higher feelings of security and trust in the employer than had been forecast and employees' fairly optimistic view of their future. Trust, commitment, and satisfaction are reported to be slowly recovering, with 79% of employees saying they trust their managers a lot. Although 25% of the U.K. workforce have experienced redundancy, their expectations of future redundancy are low. Although 53% say they are working harder, nearly half of these say it is because they want to (42%). Moreover, those on temporary or fixed-term contracts are more satisfied on average than those with full-time contracts. Although media stories in the United Kingdom document mass insecurity and opinion polls demonstrate declines in job security, a more detailed investigation shows that deterioration in the psychological contract is restricted to around 20% of employees, most of whom are less well-educated employees in peripheral jobs. This may point toward a process of "self-correction" among those who have survived structural adjustment and job dislocation. It may also be the case that human resource management strategies designed to reengage employees and rebuild their commitment have paid off.

Many of the young employees entering the labor market today have tempered their expectations in light of the increasing individualization of the employment experience and their realization that there are no longer any guarantees of long-term, full-time employment. These changes to the workplace—viewed by older employees as a new set of employment rules—are the only reality that young workers have ever experienced. Because the psychological makeup of employees may be evolving, with workers placing a higher priority on their personal, rather than organizational, identities, human resource management strategies must also evolve. Moreover, it is likely that many older workers—for whom the "job-for-life" scenario was the reality during much of their careers—have been able to adapt to the new employment scene. They may have found satisfaction in the autonomy and flexibility that go along with explicit transactional deals, or perhaps they have figured out how to reinvest their time and effort in a new, more transactional way. Of course, some employees will not respond to conventional attempts to raise their levels of organizational trust and commitment to their previous levels and will find it difficult to adapt to the new contract terms (Guest & Conway, 1997). The violation of old relational contracts may have hit these employees the hardest, threatening or undermining their self-esteem. For these employees, the language of transactional contracts is not yet meaningful, and newly designed human resource strategies must also take their needs into account.

In sum, there is likely to be more than one broad psychological contract scenario within the U.K. workforce. We have not yet addressed whether employees and employers vary widely in the extent to which they seek, require, or negotiate relational and/or transactional contracts. The potentially wide variation in needs and interests can become clouded by the use of categorical terms to describe particular types of contracts. Moreover, a preoccupation with documenting content over process has meant that the dynamics of contracting within the U.K. workplace are poorly understood. In fact, we know very little about whether true contracting takes place.

THE DYNAMICS OF CONTRACTING

Herriot et al. (1998) described the dynamics of psychological contracting as an interplay of "wants" and "offers" on the part of employees and organizations. A psychological contract is formed when there is a match between what is wanted and what is being offered. Because it is unlikely that a perfect match will simply happen, the contracting process involves negotiation of wants and offers. Potentially, what employees want from their employment relationships varies much more than what an organization wants in return (Guest, 1998). In the contemporary economic climate, organizations are likely to desire employee investment in optimal performance, flexibility, and the ability to adapt to rapid change. However, without considering the employees' wants, organizations are effectively imposing a deal on their workers that does not, in the strictest sense, constitute a psychological contract.

Schein's (1993) model of work values is one extremely useful way to view differences in the things employees look for in their employment relationships. Schein listed eight categories of work value: security, autonomy/independence, technical/functional, managerial, entrepreneurship, service/dedication, challenge, and lifestyle integration. Note that many sectors of the U.K. workforce have such predominant financial security needs that anything beyond this basic transactional requirement is purely academic (Herriot et al., 1997). Some employees are "working to live" rather than living to work. Yet research to date has focused primarily on the latter group, studying employees who seek relational contracts with their employing organizations rather than transactional ones.

It is tempting to segment the workforce in terms of predominant work values. It may be likely, for example, that professionals seek autonomy and independence in their relationship with an employer and that female employees with families will be more interested in lifestyle integration. However, such simplistic divisions must be avoided because they are inconsistent with the process of contracting, which addresses individual needs and interests. Moreover, conventional divisions such as age, sex, and occupation are no longer viable ways of segmenting the U.K. workforce, which is diverse and may be infinitely variable (Sparrow, 1998).

Human resource management experts now agree that the diverse nature of the workforce, coupled with the demands placed on organizations to innovate and adapt in order to survive, requires highly individualized strategies of psychological contract management (Herriot et al., 1998; Parsons & Stickland, 1996; Sparrow, 1998). Organizations tend to underestimate the diversity of their employees' needs, assuming that their cultural values and therefore their personal values are the same. Thus, organizational norms can obscure individual needs and interests to the point of neglect. This is particularly true of employees lower in the organizational hierarchy or in peripheral roles.

Some role-model organizations have attempted to establish individualized deals with employees in all types of jobs and at all levels of status. Vauxhall Motors, for example, affords all employees the opportunity to identify and pursue their personal development needs, both within and outside the employing organization (Parsons & Stickland, 1996). Since this plan was introduced, more than 60% of workers have taken the opportunity for personal development, and employee turnover has dropped substantially. Other examples include First Direct and also Lloyds TSB, who give supervisors the ability to tailor work patterns to suit the lifestyle needs of their telemarketers (Herriot et al., 1998).

In summary, it seems from what limited evidence we have that true contracting is occurring in some leading-edge organizations, where organizational offers are reconciled with individual needs and wants. U.K. organizations do seem to be taking more seriously the need to adapt quickly to changing economic realities and to prepare their workforces for the future. In so doing, many have reconfigured themselves and their employees in terms of new employment deals that address a diverse set of employee needs and requirements. Other organizations, however, use the term *psychological contract* merely as rhetoric that hides the reality of imposed deals and ill-thought-out attempts to reenergize an insecure workforce. Some individuals have harnessed the new freedoms afforded by contemporary employment realities and pursued avenues that had been unavailable under the old deal. Unfortunately, others have suffered profoundly in terms of identity and self-esteem from the violations they have experienced.

The above analysis assumes that the zone of negotiability within which psychological contracts are formed is not limited by legislation and the relative bargaining power of each party in the equation. In practice, there are likely to be structural and cultural limits that constrain the range of terms available for consideration and also affect the extent to which individuals perceive negotiation to be viable.

ANSWERING THE QUESTION

We began with the question of whether the psychological contract metaphor is an appropriate way of describing the contemporary U.K. employment scene. One test of this, we argued, is the extent to which organizations engage in contracting in the strictest sense of a two-party exchange. Research on the process of contracting is scarce within the United Kingdom, and most has focused on contractual content from the employee point of view. We know very little about the extent to which true psychological contracts are formed. However, there are indications that some U.K.-based organizations are attempting to forge two-way contracts and that the language of contracts and contracting has taken a foothold in the thinking of many employees. However, there is also evidence of the arbitrary, wholesale imposition of new deals, as well as an assumption that social or normative contracts automatically generate the required psychological contracts. The metaphor of the psychological contract certainly exists in the United Kingdom, but its use is only partially justified.

REFERENCES

Brown, M. (1997, January). Outsourcery. *Management Today,* pp. 56-58.

Coyle-Shapiro, J., & Kessler, I. (1998). *Consequences of the psychological contract for the employment relationship: A large scale survey.* Paper presented at the British Academy of Management Conference.

Goffee, R., & Scase, R. (1992). Organizational change and the corporate career: The restructuring of managers' job aspirations. *Human Relations, 45,* 363-385.

Guest, D. (1998). The role of the psychological contract. In S. Perkins & St. John Sandringham (Eds.), *Trust, motivation, and commitment.* Strategic Remuneration Research Centre, Oxon. Farringdon, UK.

Guest, D. E., & Conway, N. (1997). *Employee motivation and the psychological contract* (Issues in People Management Rep. No. 21). Institute of Personnel Directors, London, UK.

Guest, D. E., Conway, R., Briner, R., & Dickman, M. (1996). *The state of the psychological contract in employment* (Issues in People Management Rep. No. 16). Institute of Personnel Directors, London, UK.

Handy, C. B. (1994). *The empty raincoat.* London: Hutchinson.

Herriot, P., Hirsh, W., & Reilly, P. (1998). *Trust and transition: Managing today's employment relationship.* Chichester, UK: John Wiley.

Herriot, P., Manning, W. E. G., & Kidd, J. M. (1997). The content of the psychological contract. *British Journal of Management, 8,* 151-162.

Herriot, P., & Pemberton, C. (1996). Contracting careers. *Human Relations, 49,* 757-790.

Hirsh, W., & Jackson, C. (1996). *Strategies for career development: Promise, practice, and pretence* (Rep. No. 280). Brighton, UK: Institute for Employment Studies.

Institute of Employment Studies. (1998). *Long Term Survey of Employment Trends.* Brighton, UK: Author.

MacNeil, I. R. (1985). Relational contract: What we do and do not know. *Wisconsin Law Review,* pp. 483-525.

Meyer, J. P., Allen, N., & Smith, C. A. (1993). Commitment to organizations and occupations: Extension and test of the three-component conceptualisation. *Journal of Applied Psychology, 78,* 538-551.

Miles, R. E., & Snow, C. C. (1980, Summer). Designing strategic human resource systems. *Organizational Dynamics,* pp. 36-52.

Millward, L. J., & Brewerton, P. (1998). *Validation of the Psychological Contract Scale in an organizational context.* Unpublished manuscript. University of Surrey, Guildford, UK.

Millward, L. J., & Brewerton, P. (1999). Contractors and their psychological contract. *British Journal of Management, 10,* 253-274.

Millward, L. J., & Hopkins, L. J. (1998). Psychological contracts, organizational and job commitment. *Journal of Applied Social Psychology, 28*(6), 16-31.

Noon, M., & Blyton, P. (1997). *The realities of work.* London: Macmillan Business.

Parsons, G., & Strickland, E. (1996). How Vauxhall Motors is getting its employees on the road to life-long learning. *European Journal of Work and Organizational Psychology, 5,* 597-608.

Pearce, J. L. (1993). Toward an organizational behavior of contract laborers: Their psychological involvement and effects on employee coworkers. *Academy of Management Journal, 36,* 1082-1096.

Robinson, S. L., Kraatz, M. S., & Rousseau, D. M. (1994). Changing obligations and the psychological contract: A longitudinal study. *Academy of Management Journal, 37,* 137-152.

Robinson, S. L., & Rousseau, D. M. (1994). Violating the psychological contract: Not the exception but the norm. *Journal of Organizational Behavior, 15,* 245-259.

Rousseau, D. M. (1990). New hire perceptions of their own and their employees obligations: A study of psychological contracts. *Journal of Organizational Behavior, 11,* 389-400.

Rousseau, D. M. (1995). *Psychological contracts in organizations: Understanding written and unwritten agreements.* Thousand Oaks, CA: Sage.

Rousseau, D. M., & Parks, J. M. (1993). The contracts of individuals and organizations. In L. L. Cummings & B. M. Staw (Eds.), *Research in organizational behavior.* Greenwich, CT: JAI.

Schein, E. H. (1993). *Career anchors: Discovering your real values* (Rev. ed.). London: Pfeiffer.

Sparrow, P. R. (1998). Can the psychological contract be managed? Implications for the field of rewards management. In S. Perkins & St. John Sandringham (Eds.), *Trust, commitment and motivation.* Strategic Remuneration Research Center, Oxon Farringdon, UK.

Tolbert, P., & Stern, R. (1991). Organizations and professions: Governance structures in large law firms. *Research in the Sociology of Organizations, 8,* 97-118.

Tooher, P. (1996, July 15). Temps take over the British workplace. *Independent.*

Williamson, O. E. (1991). Comparative economic organization. The analysis of discrete structural alternatives. *Administrative Science Quarterly, 36,* 269-296.

14

Psychological Contracts in the United States

Diversity, Individualism, and Associability in the Marketplace

Denise M. Rousseau

I took one draught of life,
I'll tell you what I paid,
Precisely an existence—
The market-price, they said.
—Emily Dickinson

The United States is a veritable laboratory for developing idiosyncratic and distinct employment relations. In contrast with other industrialized nations, the country has few laws guaranteeing employment conditions such as salary levels or job security; instead, negotiations between firms and workers form the basis for most employment arrangements. New businesses are founded every day, and old ones are frequently transformed; with each occurrence, new and revised employment arrangements emerge. The United States is also a big country with geographically diverse history, resources, culture, and law. What is true in Pittsburgh may not be in San Francisco or Fargo.[1] The country is

AUTHOR'S NOTE: Paul Goodman, René Schalk, Jianmin Sun, and Snehal Tijoriwala Shah provided very helpful comments on earlier drafts of this chapter.

socially complex, with a wide range of socioeconomic groups, ethnic differences, and a several-hundred-year history of immigration. It has a complex workforce structure: Each of the 50 states has unionized factory workers, professionals in entrepreneurial firms, and temporaries who line up each morning for unskilled industrial jobs. The employment arrangements and psychological contracts of these varied workers can be markedly different.[2]

This chapter first considers how social institutions, particularly culture and law, shape American employment relationships. Throughout society, three core themes—diversity or pluralism, individualism, and the formation of flexible communal relations (referred to here as *associability*)[3]—play out repeatedly.

Pluralism, defined as the coexistence of interdependent subcultures to which Americans belong, leads to a preference for transparent and explicit employment arrangements and results in psychological contracts that contain both idiosyncratic features for individual workers and terms that are common across coworkers. Diverse psychological contracts characterize the U.S. workforce and employers, supported by individualistic achievement and choice. Relationships are often built around tasks, based on an American capacity for associability that spurs various ways of organizing to get work done. As a result of these societal features, American psychological contracts tend to mix both relational and transactional elements.

The chapter next presents several labor market factors and human resource strategies that vary within the United States and have consequences for the diverse psychological contracts of American workers. The segmented U.S. labor market leads to different employment arrangements and psychological contracts for different types of workers, as do the various human resource strategies that firms adopt to meet their strategic demands and the preferences of their founders, shareholders, and managers.

Third, I describe general patterns in U.S. psychological contracts that result from the forces described above. In particular, this chapter notes that relational contract terms are widespread in the United States, along with a variety of other employment conditions. Finally, the generalizability of psychological contract theory to the American experience is discussed.

CULTURE

Any attempt to summarize the social institutions that shape psychological contracts in a nation as large and complex as the United States runs the risk of being superficial or imbalanced. But social institutions must be considered to understand the dynamics of American psychological contracts.[4] An array of cultural aspects affects employment, including government, education, religion, the media, and the marketplace (Rousseau & Tinsley, 1997). In the third century since the nation was founded, these institutions have become intertwined, and though they are sometimes in conflict, they also reinforce each other in many ways. From the perspective of employment relationships, and psychological contract issues in particular, three cultural features are key: diversity, individualism, and associability.

Diversity

All cultures have intrinsic sources of ambiguity and nonconformity. America's diversity has fueled this ambiguity and created a variety of behavioral norms and social obligations (Williams, 1960). The country's size, geographic variety, continuous immigration over several centuries, and decentralized, permissive power structure have led to a highly pluralistic society. Nationwide, pronounced subcultures have emerged based on ethnicity, religion, and an inherent variety of interests and values; sociologist Robin Williams (1961) suggested that the United States is a conspicuous case of "subcultural pluralism."[5] This means that U.S. subcultures place different emphases on particular cultural values. Though specific subcultural differences are beyond the scope of this chapter (Cox, Lobel, & McLeod, 1991), the interplay of differing subcultural perspectives regarding the individual and the group shape how two fundamental values, individualism and associability, shape the everyday lives of Americans.

Individualism

Both individualism and associability are influenced by the enduring diversity of American society. The first large wave of immigrants (Irish Catholic refugees) after the country's founding brought normative values distinct from those of the largely Protestant English founders. Subsequent immigration from eastern Europe reinforced a more community-oriented value system by adding Judaism and Asian collectivism to the cultural mix. Despite an acrimonious labor history in which immigrant laborers were frequently in conflict with native, white Protestant owners and managers, the social gaps were reduced over subsequent generations. Part of this reduction in differences is attributable to rising economic opportunities and wealth among laborers; another part was an increase in the expression of community values and recognition of shared interests between management and labor.[6]

Individualism respects people for their achievements rather than their status. This value derives from the broad Western cultural trends around which the United States was initially formed: impersonal justice, universalistic ethics, achievement, equality, and freedom (Williams, 1961). American individualism is strongly task oriented and success centered. The pressure for successful goal accomplishment fuels individual deviation in the pursuit of wealth and prestige (Williams, 1960, p. 378). In keeping with this emphasis on worldly success, individualism is associated with attempts to actively master one's environment rather than passive acceptance, an open (rather than closed) worldview emphasizing change and flux, and refusal to accept things because they have been done before.

Americans tend to view themselves as equals. American individualism is based on the assumption of a level playing field, particularly in the economic marketplace. Despite disparate incomes and labor market positions, equal opportunity (though not necessarily equal outcomes) is a related cultural assumption. The freedom to follow one's personal preferences and beliefs is rooted in the ideologies dominant at the time the United States was founded. The decade between 1770 and 1780 was the height of philosophical liberalism and classical contract theory among English-speaking intellectuals, articulating the rights of individuals to freely enter into obligations (Atiyah, 1989a). The founding ideology of colonial America regarded free choice as the ultimate good and left a very small role for community values.[7]

Associability

Associability is an American variation on collective or community-oriented values, based on the capacity to form associations for a common purpose. American associability is, like American individualism, strongly task centered: Sharing, mutual support, and concern for the broader community reflect the value of cooperating to achieve goals that individuals cannot readily accomplish on their own. As defined by Leana and Van Buren (1999), associability is the willingness and ability of participants in a collective to subordinate their individual goals to those of the collective. America's orientation toward collective action differs from the traditional notion of collectivism that social scientists use to describe societies such as Japan or China. Elsewhere, *collectivism* typically means the subordination of individual freedom to focus on group identity and relationships (Markus & Kitayama, 1991). In contrast, American associability emphasizes active participation, cooperation, attachment, and the creation of associations to address personal needs and shared social problems. The collective to which the individual is attached need not necessarily be stable or enduring, in contrast with the Asian view of collectives, although it can be. Some constructs of American associability overlap with collectivism, such as identification with a broader group, a sense of obligation, and a sense of belonging. Other aspects of collectivism, such as group control over individuals, may be less relevant. American associability involves creating and participating in multiple associations, from the nuclear family, to volunteer associations in church, charities, and civic organizations, to professional associations, to boosterism for children's education and sports.

Markus and Kitayama (1991) and Hofstede (1980) characterized a more traditional collectivism that is often higher among America's ethnic minorities, reflecting cultures of their countries of origin. This traditional collectivism has to some extent been transformed by America's open social stratification and decentralized economic structures, which have contributed to the development of private voluntary associations. Of necessity, these associations extended beyond blood relations as people formed kinlike ties with others, both inside and outside their ethnic groups (Fukuyama, 1995). American associability overlaps with collectivism but has a distinctive focus on collective interdependence and joint action. DeToqueville (1945) commented in the 19th century on the American gift for organizing volunteer associations to get work done. Even today, Americans participate in volunteer organizations in large numbers.[8] Moreover, the formation of voluntary associations is fostered by shared values of equality and individualism. Associability makes the formation of new alliances with diverse people possible by identifying common interests and a willingness to trust one another.

The Interaction of Individualism and Associability

Individualism and associability coexist in the United States, each playing an important role in the broader society.[9] However, the value of equal opportunity for individuals has become increasingly at odds with the desire for stable communal relations.[10] The core concepts of individualism are the achievement of work and wealth through individual efforts that reflect contributions of the self and relations with others that are based on competition for scarce resources. In contrast, the core concepts of associability are cooperation to achieve common goals and the presumption of enough resources for everyone to share. These two models also maintain opposing attitudes toward low performers and others in marginal positions. Whereas the individualistic view would help only those who appear worthy, the associability view would provide help to all who need it. Another striking difference is attitudes toward achievers: Whereas the individualistic view idealizes the successful, the associability view tends to be suspicious of achievers.

The two values also give rise to divergent attitudes toward fairness. Throughout U.S. history, there has been a tension between equal opportunity and equal outcomes, evident in the distinct ideologies of the two prevailing political parties and the ongoing public debate over preferential treatment for women and minorities.[11] Interestingly, research indicates that Americans often combine an individualistic orientation with the communal orientation of associability. Thus, although they may manifest a more communal orientation, individualism may still be present in their thinking and actions (Cox et al., 1991; Hegelson, 1994).

The influence of diversity on individualism and associability contributes to some distinctive characteristics of American psychological contracts. Three of these features are idiosyncratic employment arrangements, a preference for transparency in organizational roles and relations, and an expanding market mentality coupled with worker access to capital markets.

Idiosyncratic Employment Arrangements

American workers' diverse interests and individualistic orientations give rise to individually distinct agreements, even within the same firm. Because people can bargain for and choose to participate in a variety of employment relations, a workplace can have any number of different psychological contracts. Women in a largely male-oriented firm may negotiate more flexible work schedules than their male colleagues (Klein, Berman, & Dickson, 1998). Companies frequently use cafeteria-style benefit plans and reward systems to meet the needs of a differentiated workforce. In addition, the various ways in which individualism and associability's communal emphasis manifest can generate different psychological contracts through the ways rewards are allocated. Firms often overpay low performers and underpay high performers but give the latter public recognition and status in an effort to reward individual merit while sustaining a sense of shared organizational membership. The psychological contracts of American workers are also likely to combine individual- and community-oriented elements (e.g., rewards based on performance along with attachment to the larger organization) as well as unique features negotiated by the employer and the worker.

Preference for Transparency

Because of the diverse values and multicultural heritage of Americans, U.S. workers find it more difficult to interpret subtle cues regarding roles, responsibilities, and performance requirements because the person sending those signals often has a different background. Diversity results in a preference for simple social structure ("What you see is what you get") and direct and explicit communication leaving little room for ambiguity. Because reading subtle signals is difficult in a culturally heterogeneous society, direct and explicit communication becomes socially valued and culturally accepted.[12] Indeed, there is evidence that the firms with the most explicit performance expectations are the most successful in addressing diversity issues (Moskos & Butler, 1996; Rousseau, 1996).

This preference for transparency is linked to a widespread American belief that mutuality is possible in employment relations. Consensus-based solutions to problems at work are reflected in popular American self-help books that advocate the formation of mission statements, explicit goals, and direct communication (Covey, 1990). A basic faith in the potential for a voluntary consensus is perhaps a crucial element in the American "dream" of the country as an ethnic melting pot, with people from disparate backgrounds coming together as a cultural whole.

In the United States, direct communication of worker and firm interests is important to the creation of mutual psychological contracts between workers and employers. We would expect more explicit communication in U.S. organizations than in those in other countries. American workers can also have more or less heterogeneous values depending on their different genders, ethnicities, geographic regions, and previous work experiences. The psychological contracts of coworkers who have widely different backgrounds are expected to be based on more explicit performance requirements. In contrast, we would expect more implicit communication underlying psychological contracts in firms whose members have homogeneous backgrounds.

Transparency is also supported by the individualistic emphasis on achievement, which makes it acceptable to specify work requirements and performance measures. Individualism further reinforces the preference for transparency by idealizing those whose actions are governed by their own internal principles (Markus & Kitayama, 1991). Thus, the individualistic culture prizes those who maintain consistency between word and deed ("walking the talk") and behavioral consistency across situations (avoiding hypocrisy), as evident by American management books extolling the virtues of principle-centered leadership. Given the country's limited legal interventions in employment, it is not surprising that workers in firms operating within the United States tend to value procedural justice within firms, such as personnel procedures that are applied consistently and impartially while providing an opportunity for the affected parties to participate (Sitkin & Bies, 1994). Interestingly, Americans tend to respect the rules that do exist inside and outside firms (e.g., most Americans file their tax returns on time and honestly). Research conducted in the United States indicates that in firms as well as in government, procedural justice based on transparent practices reinforces the public's perception that loyalty to its institutions is appropriate and justified even in the face of negative outcomes (Tyler, 1992).[13]

This preference for transparency in social interactions was supported in the early years of the 20th century by the rise of scientific management, which criticized arbitrary or "unscientific" decisions on the part of employer (Guillen, 1994, pp. 41-58). More recently, the push for transparency has been supported by the scientific endeavors of American industrial-organizational psychologists. Since the Civil Rights Act of 1964 (described in further detail below), this field has developed a set of rational, scientific bases for hiring, firing, promoting, and motivating workers. Current trends in human resource practices toward explicit job performance criteria and two-way or even multiple performance appraisals (such as 360-degree feedback) are consistent with a continued movement toward transparency in employment (Lancaster, 1998).

Expanding Market Mentality and Worker Access to Capital

The increasing salience of financial markets in the minds of American workers, regardless of rank, is influenced by the dynamics of both individualism and associability. The rising market mentality accompanies an increasingly blurry boundary between workers and owners. As pension funds grow and the population ages, a growing number of Americans will track the value of their holdings, worry about the inflationary consequences of higher wages, and support the financial sector's drive for higher profit margins (Carnoy, Castells, & Benner, 1997). Ease of access to capital markets afforded by public stock trading and customer service-oriented investment houses help make stock market participation commonplace.

The individualistic emphasis on property and wealth accumulation and the social institutions that often accompany individualism are tied to the development of markets for capital and for labor. This value is also associated with use of market pricing to allocate societal resources and make decisions (Fiske, 1995). Perhaps it is not surprising, then, that American workers are increasingly aware of the effects of economic markets, both on the firm and on individuals.[14]

The conflicts of interest characterizing owners and labor from the industrial revolution to the mid-20th century have to some extent been transformed in many American firms, both union and nonunion, by a shift toward employment relations based on trust and partnership.[15] Partnership injects the value of associability into the worker-employer relationship. Using trust as a basis for cooperation, partnership often entails greater sharing of financial information with workers, which makes employees more cognizant of external market issues than was traditionally the case (Case, 1998). Partnership and shared information reinforce both the individualistic value that persons are equal and the community-oriented message that labor, management, and owners have common goals and interests. The distinction between labor and management has been reduced further by higher education among workers, the rise of white-collar professionals, the growing service economy, and demographic changes. Convergence in at least some psychological contract terms can be expected from such a commonality of interests, which has contributed to economic growth for both American firms and the U.S. economy as a whole. Greater risk sharing between workers and owners is evident in the shift from fixed pay (i.e., salaries) to variable pay (i.e., incentives) based on firm performance (Rynes & Gephart, 2000). As a result, those who enter the American labor market as workers or as managers are more likely to expect an equity stake in the firm or a profit-sharing program of some type. These forces—coupled with another feature of U.S. institutions, the relatively weak retirement support from the government-maintained social security system—increasingly lead workers to participate in the stock market and become familiar with financial issues.[16]

LAW

Four types of laws are particularly relevant to psychological contracts in the United States: employment, agency, contract, and tax. In the United States, laws affecting employment exist at the federal, state, and local levels. The general types of laws addressed below refer to the federal level.[17] These laws intertwine with the cultural factors described above to shape the patterns of psychological contracts that American workers and employers manifest.

U.S. *employment laws* reflect the cultural tradition of free choice coupled with concerns born from the diverse American workforce. In comparison to most developed countries, U.S. laws offer workers relatively little protection from termination, except for those who are covered by formal, written employment contracts or collective bargaining agreements. Commentators in the United States and elsewhere have remarked that America offers fewer job property rights and protections from dismissal than any other industrialized nation (Glendon, Gordon, & Osakwe, 1985).[18] However, America has enacted a number of laws governing worker health and safety, as well as various "fair employment" laws that are designed to protect historically disadvantaged groups, such as women, minority populations, older workers, and people with disabilities.

In the 19th century, the legal principle of mutuality was widespread, which meant that unless the parties agreed otherwise, employment could be freely terminable for any reason or no reason at all, subject to the giving of reasonable notice. Most industrialized nations (e.g., Germany, France, Sweden) eventually discarded the doctrine of mutuality in favor of worker security and protection from dismissal. In contrast, U.S. employment law maintains the principle of mutuality, giving rise to the common practice of "employment at will," which maintains that workers can be discharged for good reason, bad reason, or no reason whatsoever.[19]

The two implicit principles underlying job security are protection from arbitrary or unjust dismissal and the accrual of job property rights through the contributions that senior workers make to the firm. With regard to the first principle, U.S. law makes only a few exceptions to at-will employment. Some reasons for these exceptions are public policy (e.g., some whistle-blowers are protected when a public interest is identified), good faith and fair dealing (e.g., terminating someone to avoid paying a scheduled pension or bonus is generally prohibited), and violation of implied contract agreements (e.g., offering a person a transfer to another location and terminating him or her on arrival at the site). The second principle, job property rights, is typically associated with some degree of seniority-based pay, signaling that an individual who contributed to the firm in the past has a reasonable expectation of future raises. Although prohibitions against age discrimination for workers between 40 and 70 can make termination of senior workers difficult (or at least costly), job property rights prohibiting termination of people without cause are relatively rare. Exceptions include union contracts and academic tenure. However, cultural beliefs in fair treatment (coupled with the desire to avoid litigation, because even winning a long, drawn-out court battle can be costly) have led to the common practice of providing severance pay to individuals who are willing to leave the firm voluntarily.

To some extent, employer reputation acts as an alternative to stricter labor laws. Because U.S. workers are more mobile than workers in other industrialized nations, American employers have an incentive to maintain a reputation as "an employer of choice" to attract to competent workers. Thus, newspapers and magazines frequently headline the "Best Companies to Work For," and television news specials showcase firms that are "family friendly" or "great workplaces for women and minorities." Even workers who are not looking for jobs read help-wanted ads and business articles highlighting on practices used by other employers, in large measure to educate themselves on what to demand from their current as well as future employers (Rafaeli, 1998; Rafaeli & Oliver, in press). Creation of a marketplace for reputation among employers via word of mouth and the media gives rise to institutional supports that to some extent compensate for the absence of job property rights. One example is that of AT&T Corporation, which laid off massive numbers of employees despite a high stock price and generous CEO compensation. Newspaper and magazine headlines helped lead to a backlash, as customers shifted their phone service to AT&T competitors.

Cultural beliefs regarding the rights of employers and employees can differ from the letter of the law, which creates accountabilities that firms seeking a good reputation must recognize. For example, the American public generally believes that firms have an obligation to retain senior employees as long as their performance is satisfactory (Rousseau & Anton, 1988; 1991). The prevalence of this belief is evident in the seniority-based renumeration practices of downsizing firms, which frequently tie severance packages to years of service. Firms seeking to protect their reputations as good employers and avoid litigation provide terminated workers with benefits without being legally required to do so.

Moreover, the congested and costly U.S. legal system, coupled with media scrutiny of aversive employer behavior, creates incentives to settle disputes out of court through internal due-process mechanisms such as progressive discipline systems that promote a sense of fair treatment at work. Although companies are not required to provide due process when disciplining or terminating workers (except when union agreements or workers from protected groups are involved), many U.S. firms have created such mechanisms. Thus, I suggest that a certain degree of equifinality exists in employment relations: Though U.S. law does not explicitly provide workers with job property rights, institutions such as the media and prevailing cultural beliefs can give workers some protections by making unjustified dismissals socially costly for employers.

In contrast to its weak protections from dismissal, the United States has an array of "equal employment opportunity" laws enacted to offset historical discrimination and other factors that might disadvantage groups or individuals in the labor force. For decades, Americans have labored in a two-tiered workforce: temporary and low-paid jobs typically held by women, minorities, and young people and more stable, higher-paying jobs held by white men. Since the 1960s, however, women and members of minority groups have made tremendous inroads in employment—a trend fueled by new laws and the creation of new jobs. The Civil Rights Act of 1964, for example, specifically barred employers from discriminating against workers or applicants due to their race, ethnic origin, religion, or gender. Implementation of this and other equal opportunity laws required firms to demonstrate that employment decisions that had adverse effects on women and minorities were based on job-relevant factors. Fair employment laws and the human resource practices developed in response to them have extended the American cultural preference for transparent social relations into increasingly transparent employment relations.

One unintended consequence of the shift toward scientific management in personnel decisions may be a new focus on hiring persons on the basis of their ability to perform in specific jobs rather than on their suitability for the organization as a whole. As personnel researchers have noted, European and Japanese firms select workers on the basis of criteria of fit or value congruence, whereas Americans are more often selected for a specific job (Herriot, 1992). To some extent, America's sensitivity to discrimination and desire to appear objective in personnel decisions may have led to a downplaying of implicit, relational criteria in favor of explicit and concrete indicators of competence.

Laws of agency form the basis for U.S. employment, characterizing the responsibilities of firm owners and workers and addressing the relationship between principals (firm owners) and those they hire to do work (agents). Laws of agency largely focus on the responsibilities of agents whose actions put the principals' interests (and money) at risk, and they constitute a special form of contractual arrangement (see the discussion of contract law below).[20] An agent has the responsibility to act on behalf of the principal, and the principal has an obligation to compensate the agent in the agreed-on manner. Little is assumed or stipulated about the nature of the personal relationship between the parties.

Agency laws generally protect the interests of owners over those of workers. The rising involvement of workers in the stock market, as described above, is fueled at least in part by the fact that they have greater legal protections as owners of capital than as workers. However, a caveat is in order regarding the trend toward greater mutuality of interest among workers and owners (e.g., stockholders). Many workers have no ownership stake in their firm and cannot influence its strategic or business decisions. Even firms with reasonably effective labor management committees lay off workers, often with little notice. American financial markets tend to underemphasize the long-term economic value of labor and stable relations among workers, managers, and suppliers in favor of short-term gains (Leana & Rousseau, 2000). The legal claims of stockholders to the firm's wealth tend to dominate over those of employees (Ritter & Taylor, 2000; Schleifer & Summers, 1988). One result is that downsizing often leads to stockholders' reappropriating the wealth due to workers by firing senior workers before they access future wage gains. Pressure to reallocate risks and rewards among owners, managers, and workers is one likely consequence of the vulnerability felt by many workers in the face of innumerable restructurings and downsizings over the past decade. In effect, agency laws protecting the interests of owners, coupled with the absence of job protection laws, fuel worker interest in obtaining an equity stake in the firm as well as in being paid on the basis of their present value to the firm rather than waiting for seniority-based wages later.

U.S. *contract laws,* rooted in British common law, center on the concept of promise. They enforce promises made orally, implied, or made in writing to the extent that such a promise can be proven and evidence provided that one party relied on the promise of another to his or her detriment (Corbin, 1952). Enforcement can, however, take various forms and need not always result in judicial intervention. Most employment-related contract disputes, for example, are settled before legal action is taken, often prior to a formal hearing. Because there are far more lawyers than judges, most courts are backlogged with litigation. One result is that most cases get settled via out-of-court negotiations between lawyers regarding terms that need not reflect the specific details of any written contract or other legally enforceable agreement. Legal theorist Stewart Macaulay (1985) argued that American contract law guarantees little more than what parties can negotiate out of court. As Macaulay pointed out:

> [The] very limited practical role of what professors call contract law poses significant theoretical problems that we are only beginning to confront. . . . People and organizations bargain, they write documents, and they avoid, suppress, and resolve disputes little influenced by academic contract law. Some cases are taken to court and the formal process begun, although lawyers settle most of them. (p. 465)

A comparatively small segment of American workers have formal written contracts. Those with written contracts include workers covered by collective bargaining agreements and elite workers in high-demand professions ("superstars") who are able to demand formally binding arrangements (e.g., executives, professional athletes) (Frank & Cook, 1995). Most workers are party to implied contracts that are oral or otherwise informally expressed commitments between themselves and the firm. Note that these implied contracts need not pertain so much to job security as to promised inducements, such as bonus pay, that may have occurred during the course of employment. It appears that many aspects of these informal agreements are honored to the reasonable satisfaction of both parties (Robinson & Rousseau, 1994). Courts can and do adjudicate breaches of implied contract, as in the case where a company terminates a salesperson rather than pay that person a scheduled bonus.

Tax laws define which workers are true employees, for whom the firm must pay specified benefits, and which are contract laborers who do not access benefits. American tax laws create incentives for firms to avoid paying benefits by using contract labor on a contingent basis to limit the number of workers defined as "employees." Because tax laws affect the cost of labor, they are an important factor in promoting diversity in employment relations because firms can avoid paying the specified benefits associated with full-time employees through use of independent contractors and temporary and part-time workers.

The various types of U.S. laws raise several salient issues that make American employment practices distinctive in the formation, maintenance, and violation of psychological contracts in employment:

- The foundation of U.S. employment is a voluntary relationship that can be terminated by either party (with a few exceptions).
- To some extent, employers' concern for their reputations substitutes for worker protections from unjust dismissal. An employer's reputation shapes individual beliefs regarding employer promises and can thus shape psychological contracts between a firm and its workers. A firm seeking to protect its reputation as a good employer (particularly a high-profile employer such as a large corporation) and to avoid costly litigation will rely on internal procedural justice mechanisms to give employees the sense that they are being treated fairly. Keeping psychological contracts with workers is just one of these mechanisms.
- Laws of agency protect the rights of firm owners, and related laws dealing with financial investments protect the rights of stockholders. Thus, owners of capital tend to have greater legal protections than do workers, creating incentives for workers to seek equity stakes in firms.
- Equal employment opportunity laws have given rise to the use of scientific criteria emphasizing competence and performance in specific jobs as a basis for selection, promotion, and retention. Such employment arrangements are based on job-related criteria rather than on personal relationships or organizational fit. These practices also emphasize transparent employment relations that protect participants from the influence of non-job-related factors.
- Tax laws give firms an incentive to limit the number of workers defined as employees and to use contract and contingent labor to avoid paying benefits. These laws contribute to the formation of an array of alternative employment arrangements.

LABOR MARKET FACTORS AND
HUMAN RESOURCE STRATEGIES

Given the limited legal constraints on employment conditions in the United States relative to other countries, American individualism expressed as idiosyncratic individual choices, associability's varied forms of organizing, and the country's diverse subcultures, psychological contracts can vary widely across workers. Workers with high labor market power tend to have a greater capacity to tailor a bargain to their personal preferences, leading to widely divergent psychological contracts.

Labor Market Factors

Over the past 25 years, the U.S. labor market experienced massive growth. The majority of new jobs have gone to women, who first flooded the market in the 1970s, once largely in part-time work but now shifting to full time. The overall number of jobs for men has also increased substantially, especially compared with that of other industrialized economies.[21] The U.S. labor market offers different opportunities based on skill levels and education. Distinct work experiences, stable jobs, and promotion opportunities associated with a worker's market position can give rise to varied psychological contract patterns.

Labor Market Segments

Global competition and new technology have spurred significant changes in the labor market. A saying favored by supply-side politicians, "A rising tide raises all the boats," argues that a growing economy benefits everyone. Of course, these benefits are not necessarily evenly distributed. The uneven consequences of economic change raise the issue of labor market segmentation and the impact of different employment relations on worker well-being. In the decades following World War II, the labor market had two categories, "core" and "contingent" (Osterman, 1988) (see Figure 14.1). Core workers traditionally advanced within an organization's internal labor market because they provided skills deemed critical to organizational success. Such workers, typically adult men but increasingly adult women too, were unwilling to move from firm to firm because of their investments in career, family, and skills. Core workers had high job attachment, opportunities for training and promotion (rising age-income profiles), little direct supervision, and job stability (Doeringer & Piore, 1971). Contingent workers, comprising mostly youth and women, moved frequently among firms because of weak commitment to career, lower attachment to a particular firm, and little power to demand anything else. Their jobs were largely unstable, with high supervision, low wages, and little opportunity for promotion (resulting in flat age-income profiles).

Recent changes have further differentiated workers with greater labor market power from those with less. Core workers traditionally had both market power and long-lasting attachment to a single firm. Increasingly, however, workers with all the characteristics of traditional core workers are exhibiting a willingness to move frequently from firm to firm, particularly in high-demand markets such as information technology. This sharp increase in core-worker mobility corresponds to a newly recognized labor-market segment identi-

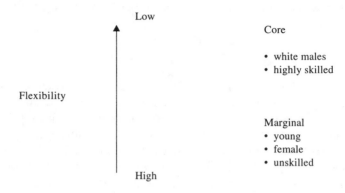

Figure 14.1. Post-World War II Labor Market Segments

fied as "boundaryless workers" or "careerists" (Arthur & Rousseau, 1996) (see Figure 14.2).

Labor market changes have made the differences in workers' market power even more salient. Many older workers have been displaced from the core labor market through the combined effects of downsizing and "upskilling" of jobs. Over the past 15 years, the advantage of earning a college degree versus a high school diploma has doubled in response to skill demands associated with new technologies and new forms of work organizations (Carnoy, Castells, & Benner, 1997). Less educated workers have seen their wages decline as the manufacturing base shrinks, leaving behind jobs that generally require a higher skill level, at the same time that unionization has also declined.[22]

Contingent work has also undergone striking changes. Firms seeking to hire workers on a contingent basis are facing ever tighter labor markets. Analyses indicate that forces affecting the demand for labor rather than the supply are responsible for the rise in temporary employment (Davis-Blake & Uzzi, 1993). High demand for female labor has led firms to adopt flexible scheduling policies, with firms that are more dependent on women typically being early adopters of such practices.[23] Thus, the market power of some traditionally marginal workers has increased, as has the quality of work life for part-timers and temporaries. Workers who indicate that they are temporary or part time by their own choice are most likely to be in this category; frequently they are women raising young children or "retired" workers (Bureau of Labor Statistics, 1995). In the United States, part-time workers make up the largest category of contingent labor—although many part-timers actually have long-term relationships with their employers.

The segmented U.S. labor market gives rise to a variety of psychological contracts between American workers and their employers. On the basis of psychological contract theory, we can predict the following patterns:

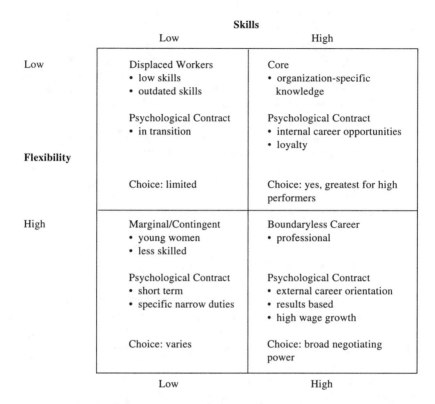

Figure 14.2. Contemporary Labor Market Segments

- Divergent forms of psychological contracts are expected across labor market segments. This is because the U.S. workforce varies in its job security, advancement and development opportunities, and access to benefits and pension funds.

- Workers with greater market power will have psychological contracts that reflect more idiosyncratic individual demands.

- Core workers by definition will display greater commitment to develop organization-specific skills and remain with a firm over time. The psychological contracts of such workers are expected to reflect greater convergence of interests among themselves, their managers, and the firm's owners. This convergence manifests itself in a broader array of socioemotional exchanges than would be observed in the contingent workforce.

- Employees who are in the contingent workforce by choice can enjoy greater market power in a growing economy and tight labor market. Increased market power among contingent workers generates new psychological contract terms, including wage growth over time, the capacity to demand flexible scheduling, and other benefits. Through this greater market power, some segment of the contingent workforce is shifted into the boundaryless career category.

- Labor shortages have created external market opportunities for those with boundaryless careers, and downsizing has made these opportunities more attractive for workers once considered part of the core workforce. Psychological contract terms promoting greater employability (e.g., opportunities to develop skills valued on the external labor market) are becoming increasingly valued by both workers and firms.

- Low-skilled workers are increasingly disadvantaged in the knowledge-based economy, a problem exacerbated by firms' relatively low investments in training. These workers have extremely limited employment choices. We expect that the disadvantaged segment of the labor force will participate in limited voluntary employment agreements, report fewer obligations to their employers, and expect fewer obligations from their employers in return.

Human Resource Strategies

At the same time, employers can more freely create employment arrangements based on their business needs, shaped by the human resource strategies that give them comparative advantages in the marketplace. These human resource strategies are themselves influenced by legal and cultural factors as well as business strategies.

Human resource management concerns how firms acquire, develop, maintain, and terminate workers. It is increasingly thought of as a strategic decision where particular combinations of human resource practices tend to position firms to implement specific business strategies—although widespread discussion of human resource practices and their connection with business strategy emerged only in the 1980s (Jackson, Schuler, & Rivero, 1989; MacDuffie, 1995; Miles & Snow, 1984; Rousseau & Wade-Benzoni, 1994). These practices affect employee contributions to the firm and ultimately firm performance (Rousseau & Wade-Benzoni, 1994). High-performance firms, which derive their competitive advantage from product innovation and customer service, are more likely to develop and maintain a highly skilled workforce that works interdependently and provides quality customer support. In contrast, a firm whose strategy is to provide a commodity at the lowest price may treat its workforce as a variable cost, hiring, outsourcing, and firing employees as needed to meet short-term market demands. Although innovative workplace practices originating in the 1980s are widely diffused in the United States (e.g., performance-based pay, total quality management), firms use various combinations of workplace practices. A major industrial firm and a privately held company can create comparable employment relations with their respective workforces—or not, depending on decisions each makes regarding its business and human resource strategies (Osterman, 1988). Viewing human resource practices as "strategic bundles" prompts firms to create the types of psychological contracts that are consistent with their business strategies.

Limited government restraints on U.S. employment make human resource practices even more subject to strategic choices, market pressures, and preferred management styles. However, firms not only choose the human resource practices that suit their business strategies but also choose their business strategies on the basis of their human resource capabilities. Despite the relative absence of governmental controls, it appears that even in the United States it is often easier to change business strategy than human resource strategy (Hannan, Burton, & Baron, 1996).

Human resource strategies and the psychological contracts resulting from them are often powerfully shaped by the choices and preferences exercised by the organization's founder(s)—a phenomenon referred to as "imprinting" (Stinchcombe, 1986). A founder's values and the conditions existing at the time of the firm's establishment have long-lasting effects on human resource practices, even when a new CEO is brought in from outside the firm (Baron, Burton, & Hannan, 1996). The effects that founders have on the nature of the human resource system are even stronger in a firm's first decade, and many U.S. firms are young. Employment arrangements that are more relational in nature (stressing loyalty, employment stability, and concern for worker needs) are more likely to exist when friends and family members of the founder were involved with the firm in its earliest stages and in cases where the firm remains privately held.[24] In contrast, firms with diffuse ownership are likely to have transactional employment arrangements. However, even in established firms, distinctive managerial ideologies can influence the kinds of employment arrangements and psychological contracts created with the workforce.

The diversity of human resource practices within the United States is also attributable to regional differences in worker skills and experience, laws, and economic conditions. Geographic variety means that location can be a strategic human resource choice. Software firms that compete heavily in the tight information technology labor market might locate in rural areas and subsidize home purchases to keep people attached to the firm and reduce poaching by competitors (see specific examples described in Cappelli, 1998.) Manufacturing firms seeking to operate leanly in a nonunion environment might build plants in states with weak labor laws and recruit workers with limited exposure to worker-management conflicts.

The implications for American employment relationships are:

- Human resource practices can differ substantially between firms and are shaped by the demands of business strategy as well as by the firm's history. The differences in such practices create different psychological contracts among workers in different firms.

- Choices made by firm founders have considerable impact on the human resource practices and resulting psychological contracts of the workforce, particularly in the early years after a firm's founding. Firms in which founders have hired family members are more likely to create employment arrangements that include relational contract terms than firms founded without family members or founded by a collection of investors rather than a single individual.

- A firm's location can also be a strategic choice. Various locations differ in their labor laws, worker values, and constraints on mobility, which contribute to the kinds of employment relationships firms create with their workers.

TRENDS IN PSYCHOLOGICAL CONTRACTING

The content of psychological contracts and the processes shaping their change and violation vary with a society's view regarding the meaning of promises. Legal scholar Patrick Atiyah (1981) has argued that the concept of promise is like the idea of a goal in hockey: It can only be defined against the background of the game's rules. Similarly, promises in American employment and the psychological contracts they give rise to must be interpreted against the conventions of U.S. society. This section describes how Americans tend to think about promises, their enforcement, and their impact on employment arrangements. It then addresses how features of psychological contracts interact with contemporary employment arrangements.

Promises

In American culture, commitments regarding a future course of action can be oral, written, or implied. Though society values consistency in word and deed, inconsistency occurs and is tolerated to some extent. Recall from the first chapter of this book the story of the Japanese student in America who braved a blizzard to keep an appointment with an American friend, only to have that person not show up. The American student's assumption that no reasonable person would expect him to go out in a blizzard suggests that the meaning of a promise depends on the controllability of the circumstances surrounding it as well as its likely impact on the parties involved.

Uncertainty also plays a role because unforeseen events can interfere with promise keeping. A hurricane knocking down a manufacturing facility in Florida is likely to be viewed as an acceptable reason to at least temporarily terminate employment. Despite this cultural acceptability, a national hero emerged in 1994 when the owner of a business continued to pay workers after the manufacturing facility was destroyed in a fire. Generally speaking, Americans accept and tolerate uncertainty, which means that the interpretation of a promise can vary with the situation, shifting the meaning of promise keeping from "to do" to "to try."

Organizations undergoing changes that create losses for their employees can reduce the likelihood of psychological contract violation by offsetting or reducing those losses through training, severance packages, advance notice, and worker participation in the introduction and management of the change (Rousseau, 1995). For example, an employee who has been promised a promotion may not receive it due to unforeseen circumstances such as an economic downturn or political difficulties within the firm. To mitigate the loss from this broken promise, that person could be assigned to a project that enhances his or her future advancement potential. In other cases, senior workers have frequently accepted early retirement packages with cash or years of service added to their pension; these payouts are intended to compensate for loss of future employment with the company. It is commonly observed that workers who report good relations with their employer also indicate that their employers have broken promises made to them at various points in time. These employees with otherwise satisfying employment relationships reported mitigating circumstances and the employer's willingness to honor its commitments to them in some other way. (See, e.g., Robinson & Rousseau, 1994; Rousseau, Kraatz, & Robinson, 1993.)

When an employee or employer fails to honor a commitment, the situation often ends in a negotiation. Research on employer violations of psychological contracts suggests that employees may come to believe that the employer is basically fulfilling its end of the deal if the employee voices concern over the violation and the employer offers some form of remedy in response (Rousseau, Robinson, & Kraatz, 1992). When violation is treated as a conflict to be managed, resolution is possible. Fulfillment in the midst of changes is likely to be greatest for those employees with high levels of trust in and commitment to the employer. Promises tend to be interpreted in the context of the overall quality of the employment relationship, which creates flexibility regarding the meaning of contract fulfillment. Because quitting one's job can be costly even in a relatively mobile society, an employee might adjust his or her perception of a given situation in order to remain in an otherwise acceptable employment arrangement. If an American worker feels that the spirit of the deal has been honored, the letter of the deal may be less important.

Emerging Patterns

The U.S. business world is transforming itself, moving in two fundamentally divergent directions. First, many businesses are shifting toward "contingent capitalism," which puts short-term market factors and the interests of owners ahead of workers; at the same time, a number of firms are embracing "cooperative capitalism," which builds a community of interests that blurs the boundaries between workers and owners (Carnoy et al., 1997, pp. 54-55). Lean production firms make up the former category, and team production systems the latter. However, this dichotomy is not always clear-cut in practice: Even high-performance firms that are committed to teamwork and humanized labor management relations (both union and nonunion) have been known to subcontract business services and downsize their core labor forces. And most lean production firms have fairly stable core labor forces that receive relatively high wages and benefits.

Psychological contracts are frequently characterized as "transactional" or "relational." Transactional terms include basic job specifications that detail the duties to be performed. Relational terms entail obligations between parties based on socioemotional considerations, including loyalty and concern for the welfare of the other party. In the United States, transactional and relational terms are mixed and matched in a variety of ways, from purely relational or transactional agreements to hybrids that combine elements of each. How individual American workers and their managers experience psychological contracts is shaped to a great extent by business strategies, human resource practices, and the labor market position of the individuals involved. Following are some general observations regarding contemporary American psychological contracts.

Relational Contracts:
More Widespread Than Americans
(and Their Lawyers) Often Believe

Relational contract terms have been found in virtually every study of psychological contracts conducted in the United States, in the form of promises regarding loyalty, commitment, and concern for worker security and well-being (Robinson, Kraatz, & Rousseau, 1994; Rousseau, 1990; Shore & Barksdale, 1998). Despite high turnover and unemployment, the U.S. labor market has provided stable, near-lifetime employment to nearly a third of the labor force (particularly for men and Caucasians). Increasingly, U.S. firms prefer the term *regular* rather than *permanent* to identify long-term employees. At the same time, strong shared beliefs persist regarding respect for seniority, particularly as an indicator of expertise and past contribution (though not necessarily as a basis for allocating rewards).[25]

There is evidence that the zone of negotiability is broadening to include employment conditions influencing the balance of work and nonwork life. It has long been true that higher performers were better able to negotiate unique deals, particularly with regard to flexibility in the time and place of work. Increasingly, this flexibility is being extended to a broader array of employees to help support family and lifestyle needs. Charles Perrow (1996, note 83) has pointed out that the rise of corporations in 20th-century America and the resulting mobility contributed to an erosion of "civil society," the local community of family and stable relations that once provided child care, entertainment, and support in times of need. Many American firms that had traditionally taken on the role of supportive protectors to keep a reliable committed workforce shed this role by the 1990s in order to reduce overhead costs. Nonetheless, a recent survey[26] indicates that commitment is highest to employers that recognize the importance of personal and family lives. Moreover, support for personal and family lives is more predictive of commitment than is the ability to buy stock, participate in profit sharing, or receive bonuses.

Contingent workers also manifest some aspects of relational agreements in their employment arrangements. Associating contingent work with relational agreements may seem odd, but U.S. employment statistics suggest some surprising trends. Though many equate contingency with instability, research suggests that more than half of all part-time workers 25 and older had 3.9 or more years' tenure with their current firm (described by Carnoy et al., 1997). Not all part-timers are contingent: Many are long-standing employees working reduced hours for some reason (e.g., phasing in retirement, rearing young children). However, temporary employment firms do a sizable business in supporting dedicated relationships between temporaries and those firms seeking skilled and highly motivated workers who will remain with the firm for several years. Many firms are finding it advantageous to create long-term, stable relations with the firms to which they outsource. In their research, Davis-Blake and Broschak (2000) indicated that hiring firms have diverse strategies in contracting with labor intermediaries, from short-term, hire/fire arrangements to long-term, ongoing contracts that reflect a preference for the greater familiarity and firm-specific knowledge that stability brings. In universities, adjunct faculty hired on a course-by-course basis have an average tenure of 6.5 years, and some remain 40 years or longer.

Carnoy et al. (1997) suggested that a worker's attachment to an employer should be judged by the length of time spent working with the firm, regardless of the legal status (i.e., a full-time vs. part-time contract) of the relationship. Many American firms swayed by legal counsel and the threat of litigation assert that there is no commitment or regular contract, even while they act as if there is—as in the case of moral tenure in universities for adjunct professors and non-tenure-track faculty members.[27]

One challenge for firms is to sustain relational agreements, which often emphasize equal treatment among employees, while hiring workers who have different, inherently unequal, employment agreements. The attachment that long-term employees feel toward their employer appears to be eroded when they work alongside contingent employees (Pearce, 1993). Firms that diversify their employment arrangements to promote flexibility signal their reliance on market pressures and their greater managerial control over workers (Carnoy et al., 1997, p. 57). The U.S. labor market has always been marked by highly stable employment for one segment of workers and high turnover and job changes for another, a pattern that has remained largely unchanged since the 1960s.[28] What has changed—literally—is the "face" of the individuals in these differential roles. Whereas white men once had stable, relational jobs and most women and minorities occupied more transient positions, today's workforce is more demographically diverse. With fewer obvious differences between individuals in stable jobs and those in more flexible ones, it is easier for people to compare themselves with each other and identify inequities.

Independent Contractors: The Expansion of Self-Employment

Historically, self-employment and employment of limited duration were common, especially prior to the founding of large corporations. Today, these practices are clearly returning in large measure for workers in sales, professional, and technical areas who contract their services to interested firms (Bradach, 1997).

Individualistic U.S. values place self-employment in a positive light. Such workers have no full-time contract, pay their own benefits, and earn less on average than those who are not self-employed. The work can be insecure, unstable, and marked by a relentless pursuit of billable hours (Bradach, 1997). When self-employment is voluntary, nonpecuniary rewards may offset the insecurity. Although the proportion of self-employed workers has remained below 10% for the past two decades, some of the growth of self-employment may actually be among organizational employees who operate businesses on the side ("Don't quit your day job").

A variant of the independent contract model is exemplified by workers in geographically diffuse "networked" firms, such as information technology consultants and sales representatives. Some of these workers move back and forth in status from "employee" to "contractor." It is important to note that independent contractors can have a variety of relationships with the firms with which they do business and that these relationships shape the formation of their psychological contracts. Major differentiating factors include the extent to which contractors do repeated business for the same firm(s) and their previous status with that firm. Some contractors are retired workers or former employees who opt to stay with their former employer while cutting back on paid employment to raise children, to pursue more education, or for other reasons. Thus, the psychological contracts that individual independent contractors form differ greatly.

The Toll of Transition: The Rat Race and Displacement

Increased global competitiveness has escalated the performance demands that firms place on workers. Two consequences of escalating performance pressures are higher workloads and a greater sense of vulnerability. There is a "rat race" quality to work in many American firms that makes the once standard 8-hour day a thing of the past. Competitive pressures and downsizing have led to flatter firms, with fewer employees doing the work once done by many more.

From a psychological contract perspective, there is a general lack of choice for many workers regarding these new employment conditions. Pressure from the transition to higher performance standards is expected to be high, but there is an added vulnerability regarding the need to demonstrate continually one's value to the employer. It is unclear whether these pressures and vulnerability are a sign of transition from an old employment arrangement to a new one or a new, enduring way of life for many. The popular press highlights workers' reluctance to take vacations lest they look dispensable. In the words of one human resource manager trying to reconcile the vacation benefits of his U.S. workers (who typically receive 2 to 3 weeks' vacation but take less than half of it) and his expatriated German workers (who typically receive at least 5 weeks of vacation and tend to take much of it all at once), "If you can be gone a month, you can be gone forever." The German-style vacation system is not likely to be adopted widely in the United States anytime soon.

The escalating pressure for high performance is institutionalized in so-called "up or out" professional firms such as accounting, consulting, and law. Rebitzer and Taylor identified a phenomenon that they labeled the "rat race redux": Workers rewarded for putting in long hours consistently indicate that they would be willing to accept lower pay to work fewer hours. However, when an individual worker is offered the chance to work less for lower pay, few actually elect to take the reduction. But if their coworkers also agree to work fewer hours for less pay, workers are more likely to be willing to take the cut themselves. This is because people fear that if only they elect to work fewer hours, they will be less competitive than their colleagues for any future rewards. The rat-race phenomenon suggests that people will continue to work long hours when they would prefer not to in order to avoid losing their standing among their peers.

Global competitiveness has led to workforce displacement in many countries, including the United States. Displacement is the loss of and failure to replace a valued employment relationship. Older male workers have experienced greater declines in real income in comparison with prime-age workers (35 to 44 years of age). Older workers and those with more education tend to have more influence on the public mood, so that layoffs of white-collar workers send shock waves through American society (Cappelli, 1998; Farber, 1995). Despite popular management books claiming that continuous change is the wave of the future, the U.S. experience suggests that even people who are relatively tolerant of uncertainty and flexible in ways of organizing work, as Americans tend to be, may not cope well with rampant change and unpredictability.[29]

GENERALIZABILITY OF
PSYCHOLOGICAL CONTRACT THEORY

Given its foundation at the height of liberal thinking regarding free choice, the United States is a likely locale for the concept of a psychological contract to emerge. Many core assumptions of psychological contract theory are at home in American culture and law:

- Individuals are autonomous entities who exercise free choice.
- Only a willing individual can enter into a binding agreement.
- Mutuality in understanding is possible between parties in an exchange agreement.
- Promise keeping can take a variety of forms, which depend on situational factors such as controllability.
- Parties to a contract are relatively equal, making possible the negotiation of terms in each's own interest.

However, some distinctively American characteristics should also be considered before generalizing research conducted in an American context to another society. Americans tend to tolerate uncertainty and appear willing to accept promise keeping that is often less than the specific terms agreed to, as long as a good-faith effort was made and a good relationship exists between the parties. The principle of mutuality can be problematic in other cultures, where the idea of two parties' mutually agreeing to transparent contract terms may seem "too pure and too simple." Americans have numerous opportunities to create new and varied forms of associations. In this context, obligations tend to be viewed positively, advantaging both parties who voluntarily enter an agreement. Individuals also tend to have the capacity to fulfill the promise to which they commit. American society lacks social stratification and power differences that would make such obligations more complex and burdensome.

CONCLUSION

In the United States, *freedom* means the right to have a voice in critical factors affecting one's life, well-being, and property. One product of a free system is the principle of contracts, which in the context of employment includes the freedom to hire, fire, join, or quit. As Atiyah (1989b) argued, freedom of contract is always a matter of degree in any society, although to date it has appeared as a "seemingly irreversible trend" (p. 31). From an American perspective, freedom of contract is similar to romantic love—once experienced, it is difficult to relinquish. America may place less emphasis on security than other societies, instead expressing security through associability, the formation of relationships that fulfill needs through collective rather than individual action.

In the United States, the parties to employment contracts potentially have a broad ability to negotiate the contract terms. The pendulum swings between equal opportunity and equal outcomes, with an ongoing tension between individual rights and collective well-being. This tension gives rise to flexible, innovative ways of organizing and a wide variety of psychological contracts.

NOTES

1. The effects of place on people and firms, particularly in the United States, are described by Blau (2000).

2. Psychological contracts are defined here as individual beliefs regarding an exchange relationship with an employer, based on promises conveyed both explicitly and implicitly (Rousseau, 1989).

3. *Associability,* the willingness and ability to organize collectively by subordinating individual goals to collective goals and action, for the purpose of accomplishing some common purpose, is used here as defined by Leana and Van Buren (1999).

4. In-depth treatment of the history of law and employment relations is found in several books and articles that have informed the writing of this chapter: Atiyah (1981) on contracting, Miles and Creed (1995) on employment relations, and Bendix (1974) and Guillen (1994) on firm-worker relations.

5. Williams (1961, p. 375) contrasted a Mexican American village in Arizona with a backcountry town in New Hampshire. Despite a common allegiance to the same federal government, shared voting rights, and obligations to pay taxes, these communities represent subcultures differing in religion (Catholic vs. Protestant) and social life (centrality of family vs. the individual).

6. Miles and Creed (1995) provided evidence over 150 years of increasing trust and concomitant reduction in social differences between workers and managers. However, Barley and Kunda (1992) suggest that the rhetoric of community was commonly manifested by management during times of economic expansion.

7. One prominent exception then and since has been in the role of women in sustaining a community orientation (typically through traditional family roles or unpaid volunteer activities), which remained relatively unchanged in domestic life until the late 1960s. The legal system that this liberal tradition produced has emphasized the rights of the individual (despite the striking anomalies of slavery, which defined the majority of African-Americans as property until 1864, and the disenfranchisement of women until 1920), gradually extending who was defined as a person from white males with property to all men and women regardless of rank or origin.

8. This communalism, often referred to as participation in the civil society, has been described by some scholars, notably Putnam (2000) and Perrow (1996), as breaking down in the face of the power of modern business corporations and erosion of nonwork life by work. In particular, Putnam (2000) labeled the phenomenon as "bowling alone," noting that bowling leagues have declined in many parts of the United States since the 1950s. An opposing view, offered by Nicholas Lemann (1996) argues that American civil society is alive and well. Rather, bowling leagues have declined for demographic reasons, with civil activities shifting to focus on more child- and family-centered activities, such as the rise of soccer leagues for children that are coached by parents.

9. Other value differences also exist, including some that are regional, such as distinctions between work orientations of urban and rural workers, northern industrial laborers (union) and southern industrial laborers (nonunion), and workers on the West Coast and in other regions (with West Coast workers being more entrepreneurial and technology oriented).

10. The debate surrounding equal opportunity versus equality of outcomes reflects several related ideological dichotomies: Max Weber's (2000) *gesellschaft* and *gemeinschaft;* the Protestant versus the Catholic ethic in sociology and social commentary as described by Tropman (1995); and agency (self) versus communion (collective) orientations in psychology (Hegelson, 1994).

11. In recent U.S. history, the most contentious legal issue addressing community versus agency concerns has been equal employment laws, sometimes referred to as "affirmative action." Crosby (1994) has argued that affirmative action "poses a threat" (p. 34) to the ideal of individualism. Persons with community-oriented or egalitarian values are more positively disposed toward affirmative action than those with individualistic values (Fried, Levi, Billing, & Browne, in press). Gaining support for affirmative action among Americans, particularly among those who do not benefit from it, tends to be linked to framing such programs in terms of individualistic goals such as business necessity (Levi & Fried, in press).

12. Edward Hall (1976) described U.S. culture as low context, where individual behaviors tend to be relatively interpretable by others without many contextual cues. In contrast, Hall characterized Japan as a high-context society.

13. The link between transparency and procedural justice is also underscored by recent analysis of postcommunist reorganization of firms in eastern Europe, where, in effect, there is insufficient bureaucracy and consistency in practices to create a sense of fairness and organizational rationality. See Pearce, Bigley, and Branyiczki (1997).

14. The increased salience of the market in everyday lives of Americans is not without its detractors (see Cox, 1999). Moreover, despite the expanded role of markets, Americans do not always know the implications of their financial decisions.

15. For the most part, employee-owned firms have not been economically more successful than those where owners and labor are distinct, a result attributable at least in part to the fact that most employee-owned firms became so by buying out the owners of less profitable firms. However, law partnerships and medical practices traditionally are owned by at least some of their members.

16. Worker consciousness of economic markets has increased markedly in the past decade. Declining voter perceptions since the 1980s regarding the government's power to influence markets in an increasingly global economy (Castells, 1997), coupled with a shift away from the New Deal policies formulated under President Franklin Roosevelt and toward private markets during the Reagan era, have altered wage profiles and made the market a more salient force in wage determination than collectively negotiated contracts or wage norms. Stock ownership by employees is another relevant trend (see Parus, 1998).

17. Laws can vary at the state and municipal levels. For example, Casimir Pulaski, a Polish general who fought in the Revolutionary War, enjoys his own holiday in the state of Illinois, which has a strong Polish-American community. Aside from federal laws, state laws affecting unionization activities are perhaps the most relevant to employment. Several states are referred to as "right-to-work" states where workers in firms with col-

lective bargaining agreements need not join the union, though they may still benefit from union negotiations. In contrast, some states give unions greater power, permitting "closed shops" that require all workers covered by a collective bargaining agreement to join the union.

18. Note that as Glendon et al. (1985) pointed out, in the United States, as in most countries, labor laws are not true codes but rather collections of diverse statutes at the federal and state levels pertaining to employment. American labor laws do vary somewhat from state to state, particularly with regard to laws governing union activity. It should be noted, however, that fair employment laws are highly developed in the United States, prohibiting discrimination in employment based on gender, race, ethnicity, religion, national origin, age (i.e., over 40), and disabilities.

19. In its "at-will" practice, the United States is at odds with standards established by the International Labor Organization in 1963 concerning termination of employment on the initiative of the employer (Glendon et al., 1985, p. 1038).

20. See Stinchcombe (1986) for a discussion of the implications of agency laws for workers. One alternative to laws of agency as a basis for employment would be those dealing with rentals, which can cover services as well as property. Such was the case in Roman law, which formed the basis of employment laws in much of Europe through the 19th century; see Prichard (1967).

21. This rapid growth of employment suggests that investment in new technology is not an overall employment inhibitor (Carnoy, Cassels, & Benner, 1997).

22. There is some debate whether these new jobs are higher paying (professional and managerial). At this writing, the wage curve appear to be relatively flat. It does seem, according to Carnoy et al., that the middle has declined: Higher-paying jobs are expanding and, to a lesser extent, lower-paying jobs, but middle levels have been reduced, a trend not accounted for by traditional notions that technology deskills people. It is evident too that the high-end jobs have gone to white men and women and the low-end jobs to blacks and Latinos disproportionately.

23. Later-adopting firms tend to do so to protect their image as a "good employer" (Ingram & Simon, 1995).

24. See, for example, firms such as Fel-Pro, the Skokie Illinois manufacturer of gaskets, recognized as one of the top family-friendly firms in the United States until a recent takeover (Knapp, 2000).

25. For the value placed on seniority, see Rousseau and Anton (1991) and Rusbult, Insko, and Lin (1995). For the sense of unfairness generated by using seniority as a basis for allocating rewards, see Ganesan and Weitz (1996).

26. America at Work Consulting Survey, conducted by Aon Consulting, Chicago. See also Friedman et al. (1998).

27. Adjunct faculty tend to have relatively stable and enduring arrangements with the universities that employ them. Levesque and Rousseau (1999) reported high commitment among adjunct faculty, particularly those who have regular contact with full-time members and those included in social activities.

28. See Carnoy et al. (1997) for a review.

29. Early evidence from workers in firms undergoing massive changes suggests that an individual's capacity to revise his or her own psychological contract lags behind the recognition that a fundamental change has occurred (Rousseau, 2000).

REFERENCES

Arthur, M. B., & Rousseau, D. M. (1996). *The boundaryless career: A new employment principle for a new organizational era.* New York: Oxford University Press.

Atiyah, P. S. (1981). *Promises, morals, and law.* Oxford, UK: Clarendon.

Atiyah, P. S. (1989a). The binding nature of contractual obligations: The move from agreement to reliance in English law and the exclusion of liability relating to defective goods. In D. Harris & D. Tallon (Eds.), *Contract law today: Anglo-French comparisons.* Oxford, UK: Clarendon.

Atiyah, P. S. (1989b). *An introduction to the law of contract* (4th ed.). Oxford, UK: Clarendon.

Barley, S., & Kunda, G. (1992). Design and devotion: Surges of rational and normative ideologies of control in managerial discourse. *Administrative Science Quarterly, 37,* 363-399.

Baron, J. N., Burton, M. D., & Hannan, M. T. (1996). The road taken: Origins and evolution of employment systems in emerging companies. *Industrial and Corporate Change, 5,* 239-275.

Bendix, R. (1974). *Work and authority in industry: Ideologies of management in the course of industrialization.* Berkeley: University of California Press.

Black, S. E., & Lynch, L. M. (1996). Human-capital investments and productivity. *American Economic Review, 86,* 263-267.

Blau, J. (2000). Spatial capital. In C. Leana & D. M. Rousseau (Eds.), *Relational wealth.* New York: Oxford University Press.

Bradach, J. L. (1997, May). *Flexibility: The new social contract between individuals and firms.* Working paper. Harvard Business School.

Brown, C., & Medoff, J. (1978). Trade unions in the production process. *Journal of Political Economy, 86,* 335-378.

Bureau of Labor Statistics. (1995, August). *Contingent and alternative employment arrangements* (Rep. No. 900). Washington, DC: U.S. Department of Labor.

Cappelli, P. (1998). *The new deal at work* [Monograph]. Philadelphia: University of Pennsylvania, Wharton School.

Carnoy, M., Castells, M., & Benner, C. (1992). *What is happening in the U.S. labor market? Part 1: Review of the evidence.* Unpublished manuscript, Stanford University.

Case, J. (1998). *The open-book experience: Lessons from over 100 companies who successfully transformed themselves.* Reading, MA: Perseus.

Corbin, A. L. (1982). *Corbin on contracts.* St. Paul, MN: West Publishing.

Covey, S. (1990). *Seven habits of highly effective people.* New York: Fireside.

Cox, H. (1999, March). The market as God. *Atlantic Monthly,* pp. 18, 20-23.

Cox, T. H., Lobel, S., & McLeod, P. (1991). Effects of ethnic group cultural differences on cooperative versus competitive behavior in a group task. *Academy of Management Journal, 34,* 827-847.

Crosby, F. (1994). Understanding affirmative action. *Basic and Applied Social Psychology, 15,* 13-41.

Davis-Blake, A., & Uzzi, B. (1993). Determinants of employment externalization: A study of temporary workers and independent contractors. *Administrative Science Quarterly, 38,* 195-223.

Davis-Blake, A., & Broschak, J. (2000). In C. Leana & D. M. Rousseau (Eds.), *Relational wealth*. New York: Oxford University Press.

DeTocqeville, A. (1945). *Democracy in America*. New York.

Doeringer, P. B., & Piore, M. J. (1971). *Internal labor markets and manpower analysis*. Armonk, NY: M. E. Sharpe.

Farber, H. S. (1995). *Are lifetime jobs disappearing?* (Working Paper No. 5014). Cambridge, MA: National Bureau of Economic Research.

Fiske, A. (1995). *Structures of social life*. New York: Free Press.

Frank, R., & Cook, P. (1995). *The winner-take-all society*. New York: Free Press.

Fried, Y., Levi, A. S., Billing, S. W., & Browne, K. R. (in press). The relation between political ideology and attitudes toward affirmative action among African-Americans: The moderating effect of racial discrimination in the workplace. *Human Relations*.

Friedman, S. D., Christensen, P., & DeGroot, J. (1998, November-December). Work and life: The end of the zero sum game. *Harvard Business Review*, 119-129.

Fukuyama, F. (1995). *Trust: The social virtues and the creation of prosperity*. New York: Free Press.

Ganesan, S., & Weitz, B. A. (1996). The impact of stafing policies on retail buyer job attitudes and behavior. *Journal of Retailing, 72*, 31-56.

Glendon, M. A., Gordon, M. W., & Osakwe, C. (1985). *Comparative legal traditions*. St. Paul, MN: West.

Guillen, M. F. (1994). *Models of management: Work, authority, and organization in a comparative perspective*. Chicago: University of Chicago Press.

Hall, E. T. (1976). *Beyond culture*. Garden City, NY: Doubleday.

Hannan, M. T., Burton, M. D., & Baron, J. N. (1996). Inertia and change in early years: Employment relations in young, high technology firms. *Industrial and Corporate Change, 5*, 503-536.

Hegelson, V. S. (1994). Relation of agency and community to well-being: Evidence and potential explanations. *Psychological Bulletin, 116*, 412-428.

Herriot, P. (1992). Selection: Two subcultures. *European Work and Organizational Psychologist, 2*, 129-140.

Hofstede, G. (1980). *Culture's consequences: International differences in work-related values*. Beverly Hills, CA: Sage.

Ingram, P., & Simon, T. (1995). Disentangling resource dependence and institutional explanations of organizational practice: The case of organization's adoption of flextime and work at home. *Academy of Management Journal, 38*, 1466-1482.

Jackson, S. L., Schuler, R. S., & Rivero, J. C. (1989). Organizational characteristics as predictors of personnel practices. *Personnel Psychology, 42*, 727-786.

Klein, K. J., Berman, L. M., & Dickson, M. W. (1998). *When employees seek to change their employment contracts: The influence of dependency and institutional pressures on employer responses*. Unpublished manuscript, University of Maryland, College Park.

Knapp, K. (2000). Fel-Pro family ways fade after takeover. *Crain's Chicago Business, 23*(5), 3.

Lancaster, H. (1998, December 1). Performance reviews: Some bosses try a fresh approach. *Wall Street Journal,,* p. B1.

Leana, C., & Rousseau, D. M. (2000). *Relational wealth.* New York: Oxford University Press.

Leana, C. R., & Van Buren, H. J., III. (1999). Organizational social capital and employment practices. *Academy of Management Review, 24,* 538-555.

Lemann, N. (1996). Kicking in groups. *Atlantic Monthly, 277,* 22-26.

Levesque, L. L., & Rousseau, D. M. (1999). *Socialization of adjunct faculty.* Technical Report, Carnegie Mellon University, Heinz School of Public Policy, Pittsburgh, PA.

Levi, A. S., & Fried, Y. (in press). The effects of organizational framing of affirmative action on program acceptance among white males: A contingency model. *Personnel Psychology.*

Macaulay, S. (1985). An empirical view of contract. *Wisconsin Law Review,* pp. 465-482.

MacDuffie, J. P. (1995). Human resource bundles and manufacturing performance: Organizational logic and flexible production systems in the world auto industry. *Industrial and Labor Relations Review, 48,* 197-221.

Markus, H. R., & Kitayama, S. (1991). Culture and self: Implications for cognition, emotion, and motivation. *Psychological Review, 98,* 224-253.

Miles, R. E., & Creed, W. E. D. (1995). Organizational forms and managerial philosophies. In L. L. Cummings & B. M. Staw (Eds.), *Research on organizational behavior.* Greenwich, CT: JAI.

Miles, R. E., & Snow, C. C. (1984, Summer). Designing strategic human resource systems. *Organizational Dynamics,* pp. 36-52.

Moskos, C. C., & Butler, J. S. (1996). *All that we can be: Black leadership and racial integration the Army way.* New York: Basic Books.

Osterman, P. (1988). *Employment futures: Reorganization, dislocation, and public policy.* New York: Oxford University Press.

Parus, B. (1998, September). Stock become prevalent as a compensation tool. *American Compensation Association News,* pp. 12-15.

Pearce, J. L. (1993). Toward an organizational behavior of contract laborers: Their psychological involvement and effects on co-workers. *Academy of Management Journal, 36,* 1082-1096.

Pearce, J. L., Bigley, G. A., & Branyiczki, I. (1990). Procedural justice as modernism: Placing industrial/organizational psychology in context. *Applied Psychology: An International Review, 47,* 371-396.

Perrow, C. (1996). The bounded career and the demise of civil society. In M. B. Arthur & D. M. Rousseau (Eds.), *The boundaryless career: A new employment principle for a new organizational era* (pp. 297-313). New York: Oxford University Press.

Prichard, A. M. (1967). *Leage's Roman Private Law: Founded on the Institutes of Gaius and Justinian* (3rd ed.). New York: St. Martin's.

Putnam, R. D. (2000). *Bowling alone: The collapse and revival of American community.* New York: Simon Schuster.

Rafaeli, A. (1998). Motivation at point of entry: The implicit employment contract in employment advertising. In M. Erez, H. Thierry, & U. Kleinbeck (Eds.), *A multilevel approach to employee motivation.* New York: Lawrence Erlbaum.

Rafaeli, A., & Oliver, A. (in press). Employment ads: A configurational research agenda. *Journal of Management Inquiry.*

Ritter, J. A., & Taylor, L. J. (2000). Are employees stakeholders? Corporate finance meets the agency problem. In C. Leana & D. M. Rousseau (Eds.), *Relational wealth.* New York: Oxford University Press.

Robinson, S. L., Kraatz, M. S., & Rousseau, D. M. (1994). Changing obligations and the psychological contract: A longitudinal study. *Academy of Management Journal, 37,* 137-152.

Rousseau, D. M. (1989). Psychological and implied contracts in organizations. *Employee Rights and Responsibilities, 2,* 121-139.

Rousseau, D. M. (1990). New hire perceptions of their and their employer's obligations: A study of psychological contracts. *Journal of Organizational Behavior, 11,* 389-400.

Rousseau, D. M., & Anton, R. J. (1991). Fairness and obligations in termination decisions: The role of contributions, promises and performance. *Journal of Organizational Behavior, 12,* 287-299.

Rousseau, D. M. (1995). *Psychological contracts in organizations.* Newbury Park, CA: Sage.

Rousseau, D. M. (1996). *Managing diversity for high performance.* New York: Business Week Executive Briefings.

Rousseau, D. M. (2000). *Psychological Contract Inventory. Technical Report, #3.* Carnegie Mellon University, Heinz School of Public Policy,

Rousseau, D. M., & Anton, R. J. (1988). Fairness and implied contract obligations in terminations: A policy capturing study. *Human Performance, 1,* 273-289.

Rousseau, D. M., & Anton, R. J. (1991). Fairness and implied contract allegations in job terminations: The role of contributions, promises, and performance. *Journal of Organizational Behavior, 12,* 287-291.

Rousseau, D. M., Robinson, S. L. & Kraatz, M. S. (1992). *Renegotiating the psychological contract.* Paper presented at the annual meeting of the Society for Industrial and Organizational Psychology, Montreal.

Rousseau, D. M., & Tinsley, C. (1997). Human resource are local: Society and social contracts. In N. Anderson & P. Herriot (Eds.), *Handbook of recruitment and performance appraisal* (pp. 35-62). New York: John Wiley.

Rousseau, D. M., & Wade-Benzoni, K. A. (1994). Linking strategy and human resource practices: How employee and customer contracts are created. *Human Resource Management, 33,* 463-489.

Rusbult, C. Z., Insko, C. A., & Lin, Y. W. (1995). Seniority-based reward allocation in the United States and Taiwan. *Social Psychology Quarterly, 58,* 13-30.

Rynes, S., & Gephart, B. (1999). *Compensation.* San Francisco: Jossey-Bass.

Schleifer, A., & Summers, L. H. (1988). Breach of trust in hostile takeovers. In A. Auerbach (Ed.), *Corporate takeovers: Causes and consequences.* Chicago: University of Chicago Press.

Shore, L. M., & Barksdale, K. (1998). Examining degree of balance and level of obligation in the employment relationship: A social exchange approach. *Journal of Organizational Behavior, 19,* 731-744.

Sitkin, S. B., & Bies, R. J. (1994). *The legalistic organization.* Newbury Park, CA: Sage.

Stinchcombe, A. (1986). Contracts as hierarchical documents. In A. Stinchcombe & C. Heimer (Eds.), *Organizational theory and project management* (pp. 121-171). Oslo: Norwegian University Press.

Tropman, J. E. (1995). *The Catholic ethic in American society.* San Francisco: Jossey-Bass.

Tyler, T. (1992). *Why people obey the law.* New Haven, CT: Yale University Press.

Weber, M. (2000). *The Protestant ethic and the spirit of capitalism.* Los Angeles: Roxbury Publishing Co.

Williams, R. M. (1961). *American society: A sociological interpretation* (2nd ed.). New York: Knopf.

15

Learning From Cross-National Perspectives on Psychological Contracts

Denise M. Rousseau
René Schalk

This book is evidence why multinational research teams are needed to uncover both generalizable and society-specific phenomena. Appreciation of the complex layers of institutions, cultural beliefs, and group dynamics that constitute the context of employment relations necessitates comparable complexity on the part of researchers, which only a diverse team can provide. This final chapter, therefore, would have been impossible to write without the collective insights of our international team of scholars. Our purpose throughout the book has been to examine the broader society's influence on the formation and maintenance of psychological contracts of employment, as well as changes that occur in those contracts over time. Across the countries represented, societal effects are evident in the diversity of worker-employer obligations and employment practices. In an effort to better understand these effects, this concluding chapter addresses core concepts that have come out of our authors' description and interpretation of their societies' employment relationships and resulting psychological contracts. We address the theoretical features of psychological contracts, highlighting similarities and differences across

AUTHORS' NOTE: We thank Loïc Cadin, Anton Dorst, Paul Goodman, and Jianmin Sun for helpful input during this chapter's preparation. Cathy Senderling did her usual fine job editing this manuscript. Parts of this chapter are based upon a presentation by the first author at the European Association of Work and Organizational Psychology, Helsinki, May, 1999. The first author wishes to acknowledge the H. J. Heinz II endowment for support provided during the writing of this chapter.

societies, and then present some caveats regarding our analysis along with implications for future research.

A CROSS-NATIONAL LOOK AT THE BASIC COMPONENTS OF PSYCHOLOGICAL CONTRACTS

Similarities and differences across societies are apparent in the basic building blocks of psychological contract theory. A psychological contract is an *individual's interpretation* of (a) an exchange of promises that is (b) mutually agreed on and voluntarily made (c) between two or more parties. Each of these components can vary in response to the social context in which employment is embedded. In all cases, the essential building block of a psychological contract is what one party believes to be the *intent* of the other in making a commitment. Our authors provide evidence of both societal similarities and differences in the workings of these components of the psychological contract.

An Exchange of Promises

At the core of psychological contract theory are issues regarding the willingness of workers and employers to rely on each other's promises, what it means to keep a promise, and the array of promises potentially exchangeable within a given employment relationship, also known as the zone of negotiability.

Credible Promises

From a psychological contract perspective, the key components of promise making are the words, deeds, or other indicators that are construed as promises, the credible signals of future intent. Credible signals are a function of the trustworthiness of the signal and its sender in the particular setting in which promises are conveyed. *Within* a society, features specific to a given employment relationship will shape how the parties interpret commitments made by one another. Employees will read the promises of an employer who has laid off people during economic downturns differently from those from an employer who has sustained its workforce despite downturns. Similarly, workers who negotiate to work at home can be viewed differently from those whose requests for such arrangements are turned down because high performers are more likely to get this opportunity than others who are deemed less hard working (and thus less trustworthy).

However, differences *between* societies exist in the extent to which promises are enforced, which in turn affects what promises can be credibly made by either workers or employers. All of the societies surveyed here have sanctions in place for violating certain preset conditions of employment (e.g., cutting wages is illegal in Mexico under most conditions, and employee termination is legally constrained in France, Belgium, and Japan). Specific commitments arising within the relationship (e.g., promotion opportunities promised by firms, or levels of contributions promised by workers), in particular those that are implied rather than stated explicitly, are more difficult to enforce. It is not surprising to find a good deal of workplace innovation and experimentation in New Zealand and the United States, where employers are more able to terminate workers who appear to breach their commitments to work effectively at home or on a part-time schedule, and where a firm's reputation as an innovative employer is attractive to many workers participating in the external labor market. In contrast, for countries that make termination of unsatisfactory employment relationships difficult for firms through legal restrictions and for employees by the absence of labor market opportunities, greater standardization of employment conditions is expected. This is the case in France and Belgium.

The Meaning of Promise Keeping

The degree of tolerance for less than full performance of contract terms varies considerably across societies. Whether individuals are obligated "to do" or "to try" (to honor the strict letter of an agreement or simply to make an effort to keep the agreement) is related to the degree to which societies factor uncertainty into the definition of what it means to keep a promise. Japan's high value on mutual consensus and predictability generates considerable effort to remove uncertainty from social relations in the pursuit of greater harmony. Promise keeping is held to a rigorous standard. In contrast, the inconsistent rules and regulations that are a way of life in France provide a socially acceptable explanation for failure to keep commitments. Dutch and American societies offer a middle ground, where a variety of social accounts can be accepted as honoring the spirit of the promise if not the letter. Where some degree of uncertainty is expected, the quality of a relationship between employer and worker is especially influential in shaping how the parties react to discrepancies between promises and results. Several countries are undergoing major upheavals in their employment relations (Australia and the United Kingdom in particular), suggesting that workers will rely increasingly on an employer's reputation as a basis for gauging whether it is credible. Discrepancies between promises and results are expected in transitions along with greater monitoring and suspicion.

Other things being equal, the explanations, excuses, and justifications that people accept in interpreting promise fulfillment are far broader than those recognized by any society's laws of contract. Rather than holding people rigorously accountable for commitments made and promises understood, parties often suppress, ignore, or compromise on potential disputes in the service of "keeping the relationship alive" (Macaulay, 1985, pp. 467-468). Enforcing any specific promise is weighed against that promise's significance in the broader context of the relationship. What constitutes a credible reason for failing to keep a promise or motivating a change in a psychological contract is likely to differ significantly across particular worker-employer relationships. Societal factors come into play when one considers the possible adverse consequences that the parties incur from a broken promise. The basic norm of reciprocity appears to operate universally; one feature of that norm is the obligation to avoid harming the party who has trusted (Gouldner, 1960). How society defines promises and promise keeping is related to how harm resulting from promise breaking is construed. In Japan, where pension benefits come from employers rather than the state and labor markets tend to operate at the entry level, employer reputation suffers tremendously if a layoff occurs, commensurate with its adverse consequences for worker well-being. Japanese workers who leave an employer who has invested heavily in their skill development can experience similar social sanctions. By contrast, workers and employers in Singapore and New Zealand, where labor markets are relatively open and laborers' skill levels tend to be general rather than company specific, typically are subject to far fewer aversive consequences in the event of job terminations.

The Zone of Negotiability

Which employment conditions are on the bargaining table varies both within and between countries. The *zone of negotiability* refers to the negotiable, or variable, conditions of employment available for negotiation. Every society examined in this book sets a zone of negotiability through its own set of constraints and guarantees, which establish certain conditions of employment (e.g., wage rates, retirement benefits, termination practices) or custom (e.g., separation of work and nonwork). In effect, much of what employment "promises" to workers derives from societal stipulations regarding employment per se, not from a relationship with a particular employer.

A variety of factors shape variations in the zone of negotiability. Within societies, the personal power of individuals in constructing an idiosyncratic arrangement with the employer and the employer's willingness to demand or offer unique or varied employment conditions to individual workers affect the zone of negotiability. Between societies, the zone of negotiability is shaped by societal tolerance for unequal outcomes and, relatedly, by societal regulation of employment. Our focus here is on the factors shaping differences between countries.

Societal Tolerance for Unequal Outcomes

The social implications of unequal outcomes shape the variability among individual workers' psychological contracts. Particular employees may have a broader zone of negotiability if they have the advantage of a special relationship with a supervisor, are recognized as high performers, or have alternative employment options. However, differentiated and unequal employment conditions must be socially acceptable for an individual to readily exercise that leverage. One Japanese saying, "The nail that sticks up gets hit," essentially is an injunction to adhere to group norms and avoid behaving in ways that would create differences between oneself and one's peers. Even when a society might tolerate a certain degree of individual variability, in the form of freedom to be a character or act out, notions of distributive justice can still limit that society's tolerance for unequal outcomes. Thus, some deviant behavior may be tolerated in Australia, but the "tall poppy" who is paid considerably more than others is not. Similarly, Dutch society values "being normal," meaning that a high performer works hard without demanding particular attention or compensation. In contrast, in the United States, it is culturally acceptable to seek more lucrative employment arrangements than one's peers have and for employers to reward workers differentially. These cultural differences can be reinforced by law: legal mechanisms such as Australia's industrial relations laws and the general absence of comparable mechanisms for standardizing wages in the United States.

The clash of varying societal tolerance for outcome inequality is illustrated by the merger of the American Chrysler Company with Daimler-Benz of Germany, creating Daimler Chrysler. Notable differences in how American and German top executives were compensated required some degree of integration between the compensation systems of the two firms, including what to do about the American executives' multimillion-dollar compensation packages. Jurgen Hubbert, head of the Mercedes luxury car unit of Daimler Chrysler, stated that he wouldn't want to be paid as highly as an American manager in Detroit because of the social consequences of large reward differentials in Germany: "In the small town where I live, if I went to the market after someone had said I made $20 million . . . they'd destroy my house" (quoted in Jenkins, 1999, p. A23). Variations within a society regarding individual-level zones of negotiability are directly tied to its tolerance for unequal distribution of wealth and benefits. Assuming that an employer or worker is motivated to cut a deal that would give the worker a distinctly different arrangement from peers, societal norms can constrain whether this can readily occur or what forms those differences take. The addition of perks (such as cars or houses) to the compensation and benefit packages of senior workers in many societies such as Germany or Japan is a means of rewarding high contributors without greatly widening the pay gap. It is noteworthy that even in the more meritocratic United States, high performers tend to be underpaid relative to their contributions in comparison with average or low performers, though the pay gaps are typically greater than in other industrial societies (Bloom & Milkovich, 1996). High performers receive titles, recognition, and greater flexibility in work styles—compensation that does not widen the more socially sensitive pay gap.

One result of intolerance for unequal outcomes is greater homogeneity among the psychological contracts of workers within a firm. In some societies, psychological contracts may be subordinate to normative contracts, which are shared understandings regarding terms of employment within a particular work unit (local or firmwide) or occupational grouping (e.g., steel workers). These can be a more accurate representation of the reality of employment arrangements in some occupations, industries, or societies than the notion of idiosyncratic individual contracts. Normative contracts are likely to be prevalent where individual workers have limited zones of negotiability (e.g., Australia, Belgium, and France). In contrast, the zone of negotiability will be greater and psychological contracts more idiosyncratic when individuals and employers can demand or negotiate distinct terms, as appears to be the case in New Zealand and the United States. Laws reinforce a society's tolerance or intolerance for unequal distribution of wealth and benefits by whether they support or eschew standardization of compensation.

Societal Regulation

State intervention and central collective bargaining agreements have the most salient cross-national effect on the range and boundaries of what is negotiable between employers and workers. Governmental regulations stipulate diverse conditions of employment, including minimum wages, standard pay systems, holidays, health and safety protections, and job security. For example, in Mexico and New Zealand, the wage rate set at the time of hire cannot be reduced later; no such enforcement exists in the United States.[1] Central agreements, negotiated collectively, limit individual variability in psychological contract terms. Both appear to be more prevalent in societies that are relatively intolerant of outcome inequality or in which there are institutional concerns regarding disparities in power between labor on the one hand and management and owners on the other. All societies use regulations and/or collective agreements to put boundaries on what is negotiable. The difference is one of degree.

Societies also vary in whether their legal protections are accessed by all classes of workers or focus on particular segments (white- vs. blue-collar workers, government employed vs. private employed, contingent vs. non-contingent). Protections that are widely shared by French and Australian workers across a variety of occupations are less broadly applied in Belgium and Mexico, and even less so in India, New Zealand, the United Kingdom, and the United States. Such protections are more likely to exist where historical concerns regarding the relative differences in power between employers and workers are part of the institutional framework of employment (as discussed in detail in chapters on Australia, Belgium, France, and Mexico).

It would be inaccurate to infer that government can constrain the zone of negotiability only in firm-employee negotiations. The rule of law promotes enforcement of both implicit and explicit employment agreements, a condition critical for meaningful employment negotiations. Such enforcement naturally enhances the credibility of promises.[2] Thus, government can expand the zone of negotiability by making credible commitments possible between workers and employers through the enforcement of both formal and informally made commitments.

Nonlegal factors can also constrain the zone of negotiability. Cultural norms in particular can effectively remove certain employment terms from the bargaining table. Belgian culture, for example, inhibits employers from negotiating overtime work on weekends, given cultural distinctions between work and nonwork life and the high value placed on the quality of one's personal life. (On the basis of the contrasting societal norms of the Netherlands and the United States, perhaps the reader can guess which of the editors works in a university where the heat is turned off over the Christmas holiday and employees are locked out of the building. The other editor has keys to get into the building and would encounter more than a few colleagues working in their heated offices even on Christmas Day.) From the worker's perspective, such practices also can be interpreted as a source of freedom and flexibility, not necessarily constraint, because there is no need to negotiate respect of one's personal time.

In societies with strong state influence or central agreements, the focus of negotiation and flexibility shifts to what is possible within the rules or how those rules can be bent. There tends to be relatively clear demarcation of which issues are on the negotiation table and which ones are off. Yet even when the wage system has been standardized, with strict rules for salary ranges for a certain job, there is often room at the level of the individual worker to negotiate a salary within the given range or the title of a particular job.

Terms set by statute or regulation are not optional and therefore become part of the context of employment for broad classes of employers and workers. Although these aspects certainly affect subjective understandings of the employment relationship, we know relatively little about how such conditions shape the interpretation of other terms of the psychological contract. We suspect that the presence of preset guarantees provides a context for interpreting the employment relationship's more idiosyncratic terms. Thus, for example, where job security is mandated by law, a company's signals to workers about its financial viability and long-term health are likely to mean far less than in a society with fewer job protections. In the latter, firms are more likely to justify changes and solicit worker contributions using the advantages of financial stability as an incentive. In such a situation, workers can exchange higher performance for the promise of stable employment.

Implications

The interplay of fixed conditions of employment with idiosyncratic and variable ones raises interesting questions. How do the proportions of fixed relative to variable terms influence the ways in which individual workers and employers interpret the psychological contract? How do differences in levels of security (pension or employment guarantees, for instance) affect the ways in which variable terms are experienced and implemented? Though as yet unanswered, these questions are important to understanding how the zone of negotiability functions in creating psychological contracts to the advantage of both workers and employers.

Mutuality and Voluntariness

A psychological contract derives from one party's perception of a mutual agreement between him- or herself and another. A meeting of the minds is implied in the term *mutuality,* but whether there is actually a moment when the parties share a crystal-clear understanding regarding the terms of their exchange is irrelevant. A psychological contract is based on the *perception* of agreement and not necessarily agreement in fact, an important distinction. The principle of *perceived mutuality* underlying the psychological contract makes it distinct from the broader class of employment-related beliefs, including expectations, norms, and preferences. However, perceived mutuality can be difficult to achieve where conflicts are institutionalized within a society, where large social differences exist between the workforce and owners, and where parties have limited opportunity or rights to influence the terms of employment.

Institutionalized Conflict as an Organizing Principle

When parties have deep-rooted suspicions regarding the intentions of others, reinforced by culture and social institutions, an employment model based on the perception of agreement breaks down. Loïc Cadin (Chapter 4) challenges the broad applicability of agreement-based models of employment, noting that the French accept conflict as an inherent feature of society. Cadan suggests that aligned interests rather than agreement may be more a common basis for pacts between labor and firms in some societies. No common set of interests might appear to exist between the firm and the worker, yet their separate concerns might be met through a combination of dispute, negotiation, and intervention. Overall, we need to better understand the different meanings that *agreement* can take. One possibility is that aligned interests can give rise to a generally agreed-on course of action in which disputes are seen as inevitable events to be handled as they arise, as in the case of many collective bargaining agreements worldwide.

Large Social Differences Between the Parties

Large social differences between the parties can reduce shared understanding due to limited opportunities for interaction and the absence of common frames of reference. We suspect that in cultures of high power distance, it may be difficult to freely enter into mutual agreements. Power differences between the parties can affect the ability of those who are weaker to directly communicate their interests. Highly autocratic leaders can constrain the amount of information shared. Directly asking an employer for something may be considered a sign of disloyalty or selfishness. Social psychologist Jianmin Sun comments that in many Chinese firms, workers are expected to "inspire their supervisor" to know their needs, because asking directly is seen as disrespectful. Mutuality, in contrast, is fostered when each party has the power or the right to ask for terms deemed in his or her own interest because more direct communication is possible.

Research into the dynamics underlying perceived agreement is critical. In contemporary employment, workers and managers can have different cultural backgrounds or social status. Societies where social hierarchies are relatively closed may inhibit negotiated agreements between parties of different backgrounds and instead rely on collective agreements or regulations. When members of different social groups negotiate (in contrast to members of the same group negotiating among themselves), there is typically more mistrust, more common negative stereotyping regarding intentions, and greater use of threats (Insko, Scholper, Hoyle, Dardis, & Graetz, 1990).

Voluntariness

Whether parties have the right to ask for, consent to, or reject the terms of employment affects the extent to which they perceive such an agreement to be mutual. Voluntariness—the exercise of free choice in entering into an employment arrangement—is always a matter of degree, in part stipulated by laws and in part based on the power and influence of the parties involved. It is made possible when individuals have the right to control their own time and the use of their skills and when employers are able to adapt their practices to suit their organizational and business goals. We note that the difference in formal and informal power and the legal rights of the different participants make it questionable whether the promises exchanged between parties can always be described as voluntary. Social factors, employer beliefs, organizational culture, and the skills and resources that workers possess all shape the level of voluntariness in the employment relationship. For example, employers who believe that their workers have few alternative employment opportunities may offer fewer benefits in exchange for employee contributions.[3] In addition, the notion of an autonomous individual, capable of making and receiving commitments, is not the cultural ideal in every country (Markus & Kitayama, 1991). However, we note that the chapters on Hong Kong and Japan (Chapters 5 and 8) discuss psychological contracting in more collectivistic societies and suggest that many similar dynamics exist across collectivistic and individualistic societies.

When workers identify with their employer, the differences between employees and the firm become less evident (Buroway, 1979). In firms where worker identification arises in the context of long-term relationships, the interests of the two parties are more likely to converge, particularly where relational agreements are made and kept. Despite this, it can be difficult to make and keep relational commitments in more competitive marketplaces because competition increases the need for parties to share in the risks and to be ready to pursue alternative courses of action. Any arrangement of long duration will need to weather unanticipated events, but the interests of workers and employers must be made more transparent if real choices are to exist among available alternatives. Because not every contingency can be addressed in advance, employment arrangements contain more implied terms, particularly when the relationship is expected to last over time. Contemporary employment, particularly in firms that compete globally, is replete with implied terms of employment—signaling that workers will be required to adapt to new methods and techniques as needed (Hough & Stewart-Taylor, 1999).

Obligations need not be viewed as positive. Although the idea of voluntariness is rooted in the notion that individuals will access benefits by choosing to obligate themselves to others, people can be burdened by their obligations or find themselves agreeing to something that conflicts with their obligation to another party. Although individuals are assumed to be able to fulfill their commitments (or else they would not have made them), webs of obligations sometimes entail little if any sense of choice and a real risk that some of the commitments may not be met. The situation is particularly evident in collectivistic cultures, where social and work roles are created through complex networks of exchange. In general, a complex social structure and high power distance between workers and employers can undermine the sense of voluntariness. The latter is particularly likely where there is little societal infrastructure to protect parties from the abuse of power. Limited economic opportunities, as experienced by displaced, unemployed, and underemployed workers around the world, also constrain voluntariness. Authors report that in India, the United Kingdom, and to some extent, Australia, current economic conditions have created a sense of limited personal choice.

Governments often intervene in the labor market to mitigate the effects of power difference between workers and firms. Yet the presence of government regulations also raises issues regarding the degree of voluntariness in employment relations. Power differences are directly addressed in the French,

Belgian, and Australian employment systems and are downplayed in the United Kingdom and United States. Whether and how governments address power differences has implications for the terms, conditions, and degree of choice present in exchanges between workers and employers.[4] How society interprets the power differences between labor and management is directly tied to the definition of who the parties are in the employment relationship, as discussed in the following section.

Agreement Between Two or More Parties

Who the parties are to the employment agreement varies considerably across countries, as does the level at which the exchange agreement was created (individual, work group, industrial sector).

Who the Parties Are

Each society's law and culture directly influence whom participants view the other parties to their psychological contract to be. Typical parties to an individual's psychological contract are the individual worker and the firm and its representatives. Other parties might also include, as in Australia, one's co-workers ("mates"); the union or professional association; the state, which has brokered the agreement and is looked to for settling disputes, as in France; and even God among Israelis and Muslims (Rayner, 1991). Many Americans are loath to think of the government as being part of their employment arrangement, whereas French workers believe that the government helps to protect them against the interests of a more powerful employer. The status of and esteem for government differ considerably across countries, affecting how workers and employers view it in relation to psychological contracts of employment.

Societal constructs regarding capital and labor influence how differently the two basic parties to the psychological contract (workers and employers) are viewed. The distinction between owners and workers is not just a feature of economic theory. Societies differentiate between the parties through laws that protect the interests of each, to varying degrees. Laws can protect investors' rights over workers, protect worker's rights over owners, or seek to balance these interests. The relative status of each group is evident through such indicators as how worker claims against firm assets are handled in bankruptcies and whether workers may hold an equity stake in firms (Ritter & Taylor, 2000). Where social hierarchies are relatively closed, the distinction between owners and workers will loom large. European countries traditionally view owners and workers as culturally distinct, and equity stakes that would move workers closer to owners are not widely accepted. In contrast, Americans typically

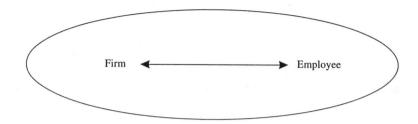

Figure 15.1. Direct Firm-Employee Exchange

have greater access to capital markets, and the boundary between owners and workers is blurring in many firms.

Levels of Agreements

Because the parties to employment agreements can include a wide range of societal actors, employment agreements can arise at several levels: between the individual worker and the firm, between groups of workers and the firm, between groups of workers and groups of firms, and through central agreements that involve groups of workers, employers, and the state (Dunlop, 1993). Among the 13 countries on which this book is based, direct exchanges between firm and employee predominate (see Figure 15.1). Direct firm-employee exchanges are more prevalent in countries such as Israel, New Zealand, Singapore, and the United States (except in the case of unionized firms). Second most prevalent are central collective bargaining agreements between employer and unions (or comparable parties) (see Figure 15.2). Central agreements play an important role in Australia, Belgium, India, Mexico, and the Netherlands. Last are the employment relationships anchored in society—that is, the state and institutions—where regulations and statutes predominate in the construction of the employee-employer exchange (see Figure 15.3). Regulations along with central agreements play a significant role in France and Japan.

An industrial relations system involves three sets of actors: employers, workers, and the government. Workers are typically in groups, either within or between firms, and the government can include direct negotiation involving government officials, mediation of employee-employer agreements, or the creation of laws specifying employment conditions (Dunlop, 1993). Individual parties to any of these forms of agreement can have their own subjective understandings of the exchange. However, individual psychological contract terms are likely to be less variable where individuals are party to collective bargaining agreements or have employment conditions largely set by government statute.

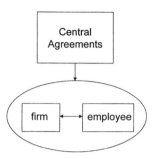

Figure 15.2. Central Collective Bargaining

For the vast majority of employers and workers, psychological contracts in employment are a response to phenomena occurring across several levels (individuals, groups, firms, etc.) (Rousseau & House, 1994). In effect, higher-level processes shape individual-level psychological contracts, and individual psychological contracts add up or interact to create higher-level patterns and practices.

Looking at psychological contracts from a cross-level view suggests that normative contracts—that is, those higher-level patterns of employment relations—can occur through a variety of mechanisms (Chan, 1998). First, direct consensus occurs where members of a social unit (work group, union) share the same higher-level normative contract. Where there is individual agreement regarding the terms and conditions of employment, this local consensus arises because of higher-level forces shaping and constraining variability in individual employment relations. Normative contracts of this form can occur where higher-level factors give rise to a critical mass of common perception. Belgium and France would exemplify the conditions under which such effects exist. Higher-level patterns of agreement can also result from the summation of lower-level perceptions. Such additive arrangements are based on self-organizing processes, more common in New Zealand and the United States.

A less convergent higher-level perspective regarding the conditions of employment is evident in the dispersion model developed by Chan (1998). Under conditions of dispersion within a collective, the meaning of a higher-level normative contract is captured in the variance among lower levels (how mutual agreements vary and overlap across social strata, company levels, and industry segments). Australia and the United Kingdom, both undergoing societal transitions in employment relations, may exemplify this pattern. Collective or normative perspectives are likely to be more important when negotiations regarding employment conditions occur at higher levels of analysis as opposed to individual levels of negotiation. Societies vary considerably in their poten-

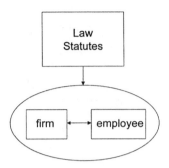

Figure 15.3. Law/Status Model

tial to create higher-level normative contracts as opposed to individual psycho-logical contracts. Choosing the appropriate level of analysis for studying exchange agreements is critical to understanding their dynamics.

CAVEATS AND QUALIFIERS

Our Sample

The countries in this sample provide a basis for comparative analysis of psy-chological contracting across societies with different employment-related institutions. It is important to acknowledge that all of the societies share sev-eral features: a developed market economy, democratic political processes, and the rule of law.[5] This commonality is far from accidental. Democratic soci-eties where mechanisms for freedom of choice in employment exist are those in which psychological contracts are most likely to function. Our treatment of psychological contracts internationally omits the developing economies of eastern Europe and most of the Third World. Nonetheless, we hope that by exploring the formation of psychological contracts where individuals play an active role in shaping at least some conditions of employment, we can contrib-ute to the understanding of how effective psychological contracts in employ-ment can emerge in developing nations. Comparisons among the democratic societies represented here provide a sort of laboratory for examining the conse-quences of differing societal effects on how workers and employers under-stand the employment relationship. As market economies and democratic institutions develop, the expansion of psychological contract research into eastern Europe and the Third World offers exciting possibilities for observing the formation of employment relations.

Exaggerating Differences and Similarities?

By focusing on a country-by-country basis, it is possible to exaggerate apparent differences between societies and miss their similarities. Within most countries represented here, substantial variation exists among terms of employment relations and resulting psychological contracts. Though all countries demonstrate differences across segments of their labor forces (e.g., lifetime employment in Japan is available only for male workers; government employees in India have high levels of job security, but other white-collar Indian workers do not necessarily share that benefit), differences are increasingly observable at the firm level. In part, firms implement strategic changes through human resource strategies that obtain new and different contributions from their workforce. As global competition increases, it is plausible that strategic issues at the level of the firm will offer increasingly more powerful explanations of psychological contracts with the workforce than societal institutions.

Psychological Contracts Versus Legal Contracts

In considering the creation, change, violation, and fulfillment of psychological contracts, questions arise regarding the role that contract law plays. The societies represented here possess legal systems ranging from those founded on English common law (Australia, Hong Kong, New Zealand, the United Kingdom, and the United States), to those founded on Germanist and Romanist codes (Belgium, France, and the Netherlands), to those founded on the more diversified legal codes of Israel, Mexico, and Japan. Nonetheless, the shared features of psychological contracts across different legal traditions underscore the importance of not equating psychological contracts with legal ones. Though law influences some employment conditions and shapes the nature of enforcement mechanisms, legal mechanisms do not fully mirror psychological ones. In particular, contract law as discussed by scholars is often more of a rhetorical ploy in a much larger struggle involving perception, power, and social norms. Lawyers, employers, and workers can use legal vocabulary in the process of dealing with a dispute, but they typically settle out of court via various forms of "bargaining in the shadow of the law" (Mnookin & Kornhauser, 1979, cited in Macaulay, 1985, p. 477). It is noteworthy, however, that the Romanist legal codes view employment as renting services or selling one's time. In contrast, English common law and that of countries derived from it, particularly the United Kingdom and United States, tend to view employees as agents risking someone else's money. The impact of legal underpinnings on assumptions regarding employment and the dynamics of psychological contracts is an important issue for further research.

Relational Versus Transactional Contracts

Throughout this book, the authors note a trend toward a more transactional employment arrangement and away from a relational one. The use of *transactional* and *relational* as descriptors necessitates some discussion, and this apparent trend needs some interpretation. There has been confusion in scholarly writings pertaining to psychological contracts regarding the meaning and usage of the terms *relational* and *transactional*. Transactional employment in its theoretically pure form entails a short-term exchange of labor for compensation, with limited involvement between employee and employer. Relational employment in its ideal form is an open-ended, potentially long-term agreement with economic as well as socioemotional involvement between worker and employer. The confusion in using these concepts arises from the unannounced shifting of conceptual levels back and forth from discrete *terms* in the psychological contract to the *global qualities* of the overall composite psychological contract.

A temporary accountant helping a small business with its records might be participating in short-term work, doing a specific job with clear standards and a narrow scope, with no attachment between the accountant and the employer. A clerk working with that same company's records over a longer period of time might have just returned from a training program where she learned strict quality standards for which she will be held accountable as part of the company's push to meet ISO 9000 standards. Both workers have explicit job requirements and are held accountable for their performance, but neither explicitness nor accountability constitutes a purely transactional psychological contract. The first worker is likely to perceive a transactional contract based on the congruence among a set of well-specified and limited employment conditions. The second worker may have a largely relational psychological contract, but in the context of incentives supporting increasingly higher levels of performance and escalating specificity in job requirements. Explicitness and accountability may be necessary conditions for an observed exchange to fit the criteria of a "transactional" arrangement (Macneil, 1985; Rousseau, 1995). In and of themselves, however, they are not sufficient to turn a relational agreement into a transactional one.

The terms *relational* and *transactional* appear in virtually all the chapters in this book. Although they may at first glance have consistent meanings across societies, we suspect there might be salient differences in how each society constructs these concepts. Indeed, chapter authors indicate a variety of differing assumptions. For instance, Cadin (Chapter 4) observes that the focus on explicit performance terms (often characteristic of transactional work arrangements, as noted above) can indicate a project-oriented focus within the context of a broader employment relationship. Moreover, when explicit obligations are framed in terms of projects, their specification by management comes to be more culturally acceptable in the context of a relational contract. In another vein, because expressing dissatisfaction with the terms of one's employment is not culturally acceptable in Singapore, workers in that country's dynamic labor market are more likely to quit and go elsewhere when dissatisfied, even though there is a strongly relational quality of socioemotional concern and worker commitment to Singaporean employment arrangements.

Across chapters, many authors make the general observation that "transactional" employment is expanding. Let us examine the factors behind that apparent shift. Capital markets are becoming increasingly important in the day-to-day lives of managers and workers. Firms in many countries now compete on a global scale. Workers are held accountable for new, higher, and changing standards of performance. In understanding the implications of these trends for employment, we must differentiate two conceptually distinct conditions of employment: (a) the anticipated duration of employment and (b) whether rewards are accessed by fulfilling specific performance requirements. Across the countries examined in this book, the global changes above translate first into more explicit performance requirements and more frequently changing job requirements. The secondary impact of these changes has been to increase job insecurity and worker mobility in some nations. The first trend is perhaps more powerful than the second, and it may signal less about the transactionalization of the employment contract and more about accountability for high performance. Singapore offers an example of how conditions of employment combine various economic and relational features. Employment relations, as Soon Ang and her colleagues describe in their chapter (Chapter 12), blend external mobility, high pay, and rapid advancement based on short-term contributions to the firm (a high drive to show results and cost consciousness) but also include provisions for generalized training and a very broad and flexible role orientation. Such a pattern cannot easily be labeled transactional, because of the flexibility, supportiveness, and training, but it cannot easily be labeled relational either, because of the acceptance (if not virtual inevitability) of mobility.

There are nonetheless differences between countries in the explicitness about both the worker and the employer's obligations. In Japan, key characteristics of traditional (post–World War II) employment include the pervasive relational quality of the psychological contracts between male workers and their employers, evaluations based on capabilities, and development of the potential to make some form of unspecified contributions over a career with the firm. In contrast, psychological contracts in New Zealand are characterized by highly specific performance demands accepted by workers as a means of contributing to the firm's competitiveness, along with employers' obligations to provide good workplace relationships. Explicitness in performance demands and in the broader terms of employment generally appears increasingly characteristic of the United States, where a preference for transparency and an expanding market mentality is evident for both workers and employers. We suspect that as explicitness in conditions of employment becomes more salient, we may learn more about the underlying dynamics of both short-term transactions and longer-term relationships.

Focusing on Different Employment Sectors

Our authors have attempted to provide a balanced view of the psychological contracts arising across different labor markets and sectors within their respective countries. Nonetheless, more research is often available for some types of workers and industries than for others.

It is apparent that different employment sectors can be characterized by different psychological contracts even within the same society. First, government jobs have much in common across many countries. Not surprisingly, workers employed by governmental organizations worldwide appear to have more relational contracts, long term and without explicit links between performance and rewards. This is true in countries as diverse as Belgium, India, and Japan (and perhaps in all countries represented in this book). Government employment is likely to differ from the private sector because of the relatively small influence of market factors on public employment.

The extent to which firms have globalized also gives rise to variations in psychological contracts within a society due to different business and human resource strategies. Several authors, including those from Australia, Japan, and the United States, make a point of addressing how changing business dynamics have given rise to diverse employment practices and psychological contracts. For example, high-involvement firms valuing in-house innovation and learning place different demands on their workforce than firms whose strategies are more short term or limit worker involvement. It is likely that the globalization of competition will lead to greater firm-level variability in employment relations within countries as some firms seek to compete internationally and others remain domestic or regional in focus. Thus, differences in employment arrangements and resulting psychological contracts can be greater within a society than between societies.

Psychological Contracts Between
Members of Different Societies

With the rise of multinational firms, it is common for managers from one country to supervise workers from another. We know little about how cross-cultural differences influence each party's interpretation of the psychological contract and how each assesses the degree to which contract terms are fulfilled or breached. In this book, our focus has been primarily on employment relations between members of the same society. However, evidence from relationships between in-group members, in contrast with those between members of different groups, indicates different bases of interpersonal trust and differing reactions to discrepancies between promises and behavior. Not surprisingly, outsiders are more likely to be viewed as breaking their promises. Part of the explanation for this has been the greater emphasis on reliability as a basis for interpersonal trust between members of different groups. In effect, consistent behavior is more important for trustworthiness when people are from different groups than when they are from the same group (Insko et al., 1990). Further exploration of the bases of trust, performance, and fulfillment is needed in psychological contracts where the parties are from different cultural groups.

CONCLUSION

The results of our cross-national analysis indicate that the psychological contract as a promise-based exchange is widely generalizable to a variety of societies. It is true that variations and difference are endemic to human experience and social organization. Yet distinctiveness, as Philip Selznick (1996) has cautioned, should not be taken too literally. Even differences can be patterned, and apparent differences can reflect the formation of certain *kinds* of psychological contracts and employment exchanges, which psychological contract theory can help us understand. Theory building and research into psychological contracting in employment must take to heart both factors promoting similarity and those that create differences.

Although a general trend toward more flexible employment relationships (in terms of performance requirements, incentives, and work conditions) can be found all over the world, it is too simple to conclude that the "transactional" psychological contract is the contract of the future. Local values give different meanings to seemingly similar practices, such as increasingly explicit performance demands. This is also true of a movement seen in some countries away from centrally negotiated agreements and toward direct negotiation between firm and employee. Social preferences to view exchanges as personal relationships or as market transactions may endure to some extent, although manifest in new and varied forms. It is likely that Asian preferences for first establishing a relationship and then carrying out transactions and the Western style of creating a relationship through transactions will remain relevant in some form to psychological contracting.

The expanded market mentality, which increasingly frames both business and personal decisions in terms of the dynamics of economic markets, affects societal institutions as well as the culture-based responses of workers, managers, and owners. The effects of this mentality include new conceptions of the roles played by labor and capital and reallocation of business risks between owners/investors and workers. Creating an equity stake for a broader proportion of the workforce is one means of establishing a collective interest in the firm's market performance. However, the legitimacy of this practice can vary considerably as a function of the cultural views of owners and labor; the role of third parties such as workers' councils, unions, employers' associations, and government; and the extent to which social hierarchies are open or closed.

We have also seen that societies vary in their tolerance of risk and uncertainty. Mexicans and Americans are relatively accepting of uncertainty; the Belgians and the French are less so. We previously postulated that greater tolerance for uncertainty could make the breach of contract terms more acceptable to employees or employers. However, cultures vary in their reactions to uncertainty, which is likely to influence the mechanisms whereby psychological contracts are changed or revised. This means that societal preferences are likely to influence the degree to which future psychological contracts entail greater risks for workers. The changing allocation of business risks is reflected in the use of pay contingent on performance, equity stakes for workers, and contingent employment in which core workers are differentiated from more peripheral ones. Risk tolerance can yield different reactions to adjustments in risk allocation, from the vantage point of individuals as well as that of broader societies. Mechanisms available within societies for risk absorption (e.g., pension funds and social security) can shape reactions to changes in risk allocation between workers and owners.

Creating and sustaining psychological contracts enables arrangements made in the present to influence worker actions and organizational outcomes in the future. Social rules and moral values regarding honesty, reciprocity, and keeping commitments are not simply arbitrary constraints on individual choice but a precondition for any kind of cooperative enterprise (Fukuyama, 1999). Workers and employers amplify their own power and abilities by following cooperative rules that constrain their freedom of choice because these allow them to communicate with others and coordinate their actions. The psychological contracts that parties commit to have a tangible economic value and help foster collective goals. Understanding the dynamics of psychological contracting across societies sheds light on one of the basic mechanisms of effective organizing.

NOTES

1. Note that there is protection of wages already earned, under the principle of "good faith and fair dealing." But no guaranteed wage rates exist in the United States, unless a legal contract so stipulates.

2. Note that a variety of other institutional mechanisms affect the credibility of the employer and constrain the zone of negotiability for those with poor reputations. Where direct negotiation between employer and employee predominates, nongovernmental institutional mechanisms typically promote promise keeping (e.g., customs, media). When employers behaving in bad faith are sanctioned by the media (as in the case of AT&T's conducting massive layoffs while making substantial profits), employers with better reputations have the advantage of attracting workers through their ability to make credible promises.

3. A pattern referred to as "rational selective exploitation"; see Rusbult, Lowery, Hubbard, Maravankin, and Nieses (1988). Evidence of the cross-cultural generalizability of this pattern is provided in Lin, Insko, and Rusbult (1991).

4. Issues relevant to understanding the distribution of power in employment include the extent to which workers have access to resources external to the employment relationship (e.g., access to savings or capital markets, self-employment, alternative employment opportunities, government subsidies), how work-related training is accessed (controlled by broader society, employers, or workers), and how easy it is for each party to exit the employment relationship.

5. We note that as of this writing the takeover of Hong Kong by Communist China has begun to alter the legal and political systems in Hong Kong.

REFERENCES

Bloom, M. C., & Milkovich, G. T. (1996). Issues in managerial compensation. In C. L. Cooper & D. M. Rousseau (Eds.), *Trends in organizational behavior* (Vol. 3, pp. 23-47). Chichester, UK: John Wiley.

Buroway, M. (1979). *Manufacturing consent: Changes in the labor process under capitalism.* Chicago: University of Chicago Press.

Chan, D. (1998). Functional relations among constructs in the same content domain at different levels of analysis. *Journal of Applied Psychology, 83,* 234-246.

Dunlop, J. T. (1993). *Industrial relations systems* (Rev. ed.). Boston: Harvard Business School Press.

Fukuyama, F. (1999). *The great disruption: Human nature and the reconstitution of social order.* New York: Free Press.

Gouldner, A. W. (1960). The norm of reciprocity: A preliminary statement. *American Sociological Review, 25,* 161-179.

Hough, B., & Stewart-Taylor, A. (1999). A common law agenda for labor law. *Web Journal of Current Issues,* http://webjcli.ncl.ac.uk/1999/issue2/hough2.html

Insko, C. A., Scholper, J., Hoyle, R. H., Dardis, G. J., & Graetz, J. A. (1990). Individual-group discontinuity as a function of fear and greed. *Journal of Personality and Social Psychology, 58,* 68-79.

Jenkins, H. W. (1999, May 26). Just another German car company. *Wall Street Journal,* p. A23.

Lin, Y. W., Insko, C. A., & Rusbult, C. L. (1991). Rational selective exploitation among Americans and Chinese: General similarity, with one surprise. *Journal of Applied Social Psychology, 21,* 1169-1206.

Macaulay, S. (1985). An empirical view of contract. *Wisconsin Law Review,* pp. 465-482.

MacNeil, I. R. (1985). Relational contract: What we do and do not know. *Wisconsin Law Review,* pp. 483-525

Markus, H. R., & Kitayama, S. (1991). Culture and the self: Implications for cognition, emotion, and motivation. *Psychological Review, 98,* 224-253.

Rayner, S. E. (1991). *The theory of contracts in Islamic law: A comparative analysis with particular reference to the modern legislation in Kuwait, Bahrain, and the United Arab Emirates.* London: Graham & Trotman.

Ritter, J., & Taylor, L. J. (2000). Are employees stakeholders: Corporate finance meets the agency problem. In C. Leana & D. M. Rousseau (Eds.), *Relational wealth.* New York: Oxford University Press.

Rousseau, D. M. (1995). *Psychological contracts in organizations: Understanding written and unwritten agreement.* Newbury Park, CA: Sage.

Rousseau, D. M., & House, R. (1994). Meso organizational behavior: Avoiding three fundamental biases. In C. L. Cooper & D. M. Rousseau (Eds.), *Trends in organizational behavior* (Vol. 1, pp. 13-30). Chichester, UK: John Wiley.

Rusbult, C. L., Lowery, D., Hubbard, M. L., Maravankin, O. J., & Nieses, M. (1988). Impact of employee mobility and employee performance on the allocation of rewards under conditions of constraint. *Journal of Personality and Social Psychology, 54,* 605-615.

Selznick, P. (1996). Institutionalism "old" and "new." *Administrative Science Quarterly, 41,* 270-277.

Index

About the Contributors

Soon Ang heads the Division of Strategy, Management and Organization at the Nanyang Business School in Singapore. She is Director of the Singapore-Human Resource RoundTable (HARRT-Singapore), an institutional affiliate with HARRT-UCLA, and is Deputy Director of the Information Management Research Center (IMARC). She received her PhD from the University of Minnesota in management information systems with concentrations in management and industrial/organizational psychology. She specializes in cross-cultural OB, managing high-technology professionals, and outsourcing. Her papers have appeared in the *Academy of Management Journal, Organization Science, Social Forces, Information Systems Research, MIS Quarterly,* and other journals. She has won Best Paper Awards at the Academy of Management Meetings and the Hawaiian International Conference in Systems Sciences (HICSS) for research in compensation and outsourcing of information technology professionals. She is an associate editor for *Information Systems Research* and *MIS Quarterly* and serves on the editorial boards of *Group and Organizational Management* and *Journal of Organizational Behavior.*

Loïc Cadin (ESSEC, Doctorat de gestion) is Associate Professor at ESCP-EAP (Paris, Oxford, Berlin, Madrid), Graduate School of Management. Before becoming a full time professor he had different positions in the Human Resource Management function in several companies. His current research deals with careers and international comparisons of Human Research Management practices. He has also published about organizations and competencies development. He contributed recently to a book edited by M. Peiperl, M. Arthur, R. Goffee, T. Morris, *Career Frontiers: New Conceptions of Working Lives.*

George Zhen Xiong Chen received his PhD from the Hong Kong University of Science and Technology and is currently Assistant Professor at Hong Kong

Baptist University. He specializes in organizational commitment, loyalty to supervisor, and Chinese management. His current research focuses on cross-cultural management, leader-member exchange, organizational justice, and psychological contracts in Chinese context.

Hector R. Diaz-Saenz is working on his PhD in organizational communication in the Department of Communication Studies at the University of Texas at Austin. Formerly, he was Director of Executive Education at the Graduate School of Business and Leadership of ITESM, Monterrey Campus (Monterrey Institute of Technology). His areas of interest are organizational culture and leadership, with a focus on change and the usage of internal communication practices in organizations established in Mexico. He has published articles in *COMARI,* the Mexican Confederation of Industrial Relations magazine, and coauthored a recent article in *Management Communication Quarterly.* He is a member of the Monterrey (Mexico) chapter of Executives of Industrial Relations Association.

Charissa Freese received her master's degree in work and organizational psychology from Tilburg University in the Netherlands, where she is working on a dissertation on the dynamics of psychological contracts during organizational transformation. The English-language journals in which she has published are *Leadership and Organization Development Journal* and *European Journal of Work and Organizational Psychology.*

Peter Herriot is consultant with CSA Management Consultants, UK. He is Visiting Professor at the City University Business School and at the University of Surrey. He has consulted and written widely on career management and the nature and conduct of the employment relationship. His most recent book is *Trust and Transition: Managing Today's Employment Relationship* (with Wendy Hirsh and Peter Reilly, 1998). He is about to retire as editor of the *European Journal of Work and Organisational Psychology* (1995-2000). He is a convinced Europhile and is concerned about relating more closely the practitioner and academic perspectives on work and organizations.

Kerr Inkson is Professor of Management at the Auckland campus of Massey University, New Zealand. He has held positions at the University of Aston (UK) and the Universities of Otago and Auckland in New Zealand. His research areas have included organization structure, orientations to work, and, more recently, career theory and development. He has published eight books and many refereed papers. In 1997 he was awarded Best International Paper at the Academy of Management. His most recent book (with Michael B. Arthur and Judith K. Pringle) is *The New Careers: Individual Action and Economic Change* (1999).

Maddy Janssens joined the faculty of the Applied Economics Department of Catholic University of Leuven in Belgium after receiving her PhD in Psychology in 1992. She studied at Northwestern University, where she received a Master of Science degree in Organization Behavior. She held a faculty appointment at INSEAD in France during 1996 and was a visiting faculty at the Stern School of Business, New York University, during 1999. Her research is oriented toward Intercultural Management and Human Resource Management. She has published international articles in the areas of expatriate management, cross-cultural methodology, transnational teams, and international HRM. As guest editor, she just finished a special issue about new theoretical developments within Human Resource Management. Her current research interests focus on diversity in HRM, intercultural processes in transnational teams, and multiparty collaboration in the context of minority children's integration in the school system.

Nerina L. Jimmieson received her PhD in 1998 from the University of Queensland, where she examined a range of different organizational characteristics as moderating variables in the stress-strain relationship. She is currently a full-time Lecturer in the School of Management at the Queensland University of Technology, where she teaches research methodology and topics related to human resource management. Employing both laboratory and field methodologies, her research is concerned with the identification of organizational characteristics that may assist employees to use work control opportunities more effectively under conditions of work stress. Recent publications have appeared in the *International Review of Industrial and Organizational Psychology, Journal of Organizational Behavior, Journal of Occupational and Organizational Psychology, Applied Psychology: An International Review,* and *Journal of Occupational Health Psychology.*

Boris Kabanoff received his PhD in 1979 from the Flinders University of South Australia, where he examined the effects of task type and group structure on group performance. He is currently Head of School in the School of Management at the Queensland University of Technology. He has published more than 40 book chapters and journal papers, including papers in such leading international journals as *Psychological Bulletin, Academy of Management Review, Academy of Management Journal,* and *Journal of Applied Psychology.* For the past 8 years, his main research concentration has been on the application of computer-aided text analysis (CATA) methodology to the study of a number of issues in industrial and organizational psychology. His leadership role in this emerging methodology has been recognized in the form of his editorship of a special issue for the *Journal of Organizational Behavior* in 1997 and the publication of some 10 papers and chapters employing this methodology.

Moshe Krausz is on the faculty of Bar Ilan University's Psychology Department in Ramat Gan, Israel. He received his doctorate from the University of California at Berkeley. His research focuses upon absenteeism and turnover and the effects of shiftwork and employment status on job attitudes.

Cynthia Lee received her PhD from University of Maryland and is currently Associate Professor at Northeastern University. She specializes in managing change, performance management, and work motivation. Her current research focuses on cross-cultural management including interaction and effectiveness in teams, understanding the changing nature of psychological contracts, and justice perceptions in Chinese contexts.

Malcolm J. Lewis has a Diploma of Business, a Bachelor of Business (public administration), and a Master of Business Administration. He is currently a full-time Lecturer in the School of Management at the Queensland University of Technology. He has an extensive background in human resource management and management consulting in both the public and private sectors. His particular interests are in the human resource aspects of work and performance, training and development, and organizational consulting. He consults to a wide range of organizations related to his research and teaching interests.

Lynne Millward (BA Hons, PhD. CPsychol, AFBPSs) is Course Director of the Master of Science course in Occupational & Organizational Psychology at the University of Surrey, Lecturer in Organizational Psychology and part of the Centre for Defence Psychology. Her research interests include issues pertaining to the Psychological Contract, and also Team and Group Processes. Before arriving at Surrey in 1994, she was a Consultant Business Psychologist at Walpole Ltd. in Farringdon, London where she specialized in the design and implementation of training and development solutions to organizational problems.

Motohiro Morishima (PhD, University of Illinois, 1986) does research on the strategic aspects of Japanese corporations' human resource management and industrial relations and has published widely in both U.S. and Japanese journals. He is currently Professor of Human Resource Management at the Graduate School of Business Administration at Keio University and also Special Visiting Researcher at the Japan Institute of Labour. Previously, he taught in the Faculty of Policy Management at Keio University; served as Visiting Associate Professor in the Institute of Labor and Industrial Relations at the University of Illinois and as Visiting Professor at the Institute of Economic Research at Hitotsubashi University; and was Senior Research Fellow at the Wharton School at the University of Pennsylvania. He also consults with major firms in Japan and conducts management development seminars for them. Recent publications include "Strategic Diversification of Japanese HRM" in *Research in Personnel and Human Resource Management,* edited by P. Wright, L. Dyer, J. Boudreau, and G. Mikovich.

Human Resource Management, edited by P. Wright, L. Dyer, J. Boudreau, and G. Mikovich.

Kok Yee Ng is a doctoral student in organizational behavior at Michigan State University and a Senior Tutor with the Nanyang Business School in Singapore. She received a first-class honors bachelor's degree in accounting from the Nanyang Business School and was awarded the prestigious Senior Tutorship overseas scholarship to pursue her doctoral studies at Michigan State. To date, she has published and presented her research at the Academy of Management meetings and has won the 1998 best paper award from the Human Resources Division. She has also presented research at the European Minority Influence Conference. Her primary research interests include cultural influences on psychological contracts, devil's advocacy, and extrarole behaviors. Her recent research examines the role of individual differences in motivation in dual-task environments.

Bert Overlaet received his PhD in psychology in 1985 with a study on small group communication. He worked for 14 years at the Department of Work and Organizational Psychology at the Catholic University of Leuven, Belgium. His research and teaching focused on group dynamics, communication, and distributive justice. For 3 years he was management trainer in industry and works since 1988 as a freelance management consultant. Projects focus on management development, teambuilding, improvement of work systems, and crisis management. Since 1993, he is a full-time faculty member of the OB-group of the Department of Applied Economic Sciences. He teaches the Organization Theory and Organization Behavior classes in the MBA program and Philosophy of Science in the doctoral program. Present research interests include organizational knowledge and learning, membership processes, culture studies, and unconscious processes in organizations.

Simon Peel is a Lecturer in Management and International Business at Massey University, Albany Campus, in Auckland, New Zealand. He has also taught at the University of Auckland and Auckland University of Technology. His teaching has been in the areas of management and organization, human resource management, and organizational behavior. He is currently on the editorial board of the *Journal of Organizational Behavior.* His primary and present research is into issues surrounding the management of contractors. Other research interests include psychological contracts, performance appraisal, and organizational justice.

Denise M. Rousseau is H. J. Heinz II Professor of Organizational Behavior and Public Policy at Carnegie Mellon University, jointly in the Heinz School of Public Policy and Management and in the Graduate School of Industrial Administration. A graduate of the University of California at Berkeley, she has been a faculty member at Northwestern University, the University of Michigan, and the Naval Postgraduate School (Monterey) and visiting faculty at Renmin University (Beijing), Chulalongkorn University (Bangkok), and Nanyang Technological University (Singapore). Her research, which addresses the changing psychological contract at work, has appeared in academic journals such as the *Journal of Applied Psychology, Academy of Management Review, Academy of Management Journal, Journal of Organizational Behavior,* and *Administrative Science Quarterly.* Her books include *Psychological Contracts in Organizations: Understanding Written and Unwritten Agreements,* which won the Academy of Management's best book award in 1996; the Trends in Organizational Behavior Series with Cary Cooper; *Developing an Interdisciplinary Science of Organizations* with Karlene Roberts and Charles Hulin; *The Boundaryless Career* with Michael Arthur; and *Relational Wealth* with Carrie Leana. She is a Fellow in the American Psychological Association, the Society for Industrial/Organizational Psychology, and the Academy of Management and is editor-in-chief of *Journal of Organizational Behavior.*

René Schalk is currently Assistant Professor of Work and Organizational Psychology at Tilburg University in the Netherlands. He has also worked at Utrecht Business School, Tilburg Institute for Academic Studies, and Nijmegen University, from which he earned his PhD in social and organizational psychology. His research focuses on the issues of organizational psychology, personnel assessment and selection, quality of work, stress and health, motivation and commitment, and employee-organization linkages, with a special focus on the psychological contract, international differences, and (virtual) teamwork. He is a consulting editor for *Journal of Organizational Behavior,* and his books (in Dutch) include *Determinants of Frequent Short-Term Absenteeism* and *Older Employees in a Changing World.* Among the English-language journals in which he has published articles are *Journal of Organizational Behavior, International Journal of Selection and Assessment, Leadership and Organization Development Journal, Journal of Social Behavior and Personality,* and *European Journal of Work and Organizational Psychology.*

Luc Sels is Associate Professor of Human Resource Management at the Department of Applied Economics of the Katholieke Universiteit Leuven in Belgium. After receiving his PhD in the Social Sciences in 1995, he served as Project Manager at the Higher Institute of Labor Studies, an institute specialized in research-based consultancy and contract research. He joined the Applied Economics Department of the University of Leuven in 1996. His primary substantive research interests center around developments in human resource management and the analysis of organizational transformation. He has published international articles on the diffusion of innovative organizational practices, trends regarding the nature of the employment relationship in European countries, and social systems theory. His current research deals with the salary policy of Belgian companies, new tendencies in numerical and temporal flexibility, emic features of Belgian psychological contracts, human resource management in small and medium-sized companies, and training investment policy.

Snehal Shah is a PhD student at Carnegie Mellon University. Her research has primarily focused on different aspects of understanding organizational change. Specifically, she has looked at the impact of managerial factors on employees' reactions to organizational changes such as empowerment. Her PhD thesis, which is a combination of field and experimental research, attempts to study the role of attributions and social accounts in the context of organizational change in general and managerial directives in particular. Her research also includes published work in the area of psychological contracts. Her articles coauthored with Professor Denise Rousseau have appeared in *Journal of Applied Psychology* and *Journal of Organizational Behavior,* among others.

Mei Ling Tan is a doctoral student in the Division of Strategy, Management and Organization at the Nanyang Business School in Singapore. She holds a first-class honors bachelor's degree in accounting, and a Master of Business (with a special concentration in organizational behavior). Her current research interests include the management of technicians and paraprofessionals, psychological contracting, and workforce diversity. Her papers on psychological contracting in Singapore and the mediating effects of trust on *guanxi* in Chinese business ventures have been presented at the Academy of Management meetings and the American Sociological Association conference. Her most current research examines the psychological contracts of information technology professionals and the effects of status inconsistencies on workplace attitudes and performance of foreign paraprofessionals.

Catherine H. Tinsley received her PhD from Northwestern University and is currently Assistant Professor at Georgetown University. She specializes in the comparative analysis of conflict resolution across cultures. Her current research focuses on understanding conflict in the Chinese culture, new approaches to the study of culture in organizational psychology, and comparative models of conflict resolution in Japan, Germany, and the United States.

Inge Van den Brande studied at the Catholic University of Leuven, where she received her licenciate in Applied Economics. In 1995, she joined the Applied Economics Department of the Catholic University of Leuven, Belgium, as research and teaching assistant in the OB-group. Her doctoral research is about psychological contracts in Flanders, Belgium. In particular, she works on the operationalization of different types of psychological contracts in Flanders and on the role of formal contracts and HR policies in understanding these different types of psychological contracts.

Patricia D. Witherspoon is Chair of the Department of Communication Studies at the University of Texas at Austin. She teaches and conducts research in the areas of organizational leadership, organizational change, and the improvement of internal communication in large organizations. She has been Visiting Professor in the Graduate School of Business and Leadership at ITESM, Monterrey Campus (Monterrey Institute of Technology). Her most recent book is titled *Communicating Leadership: An Organizational Perspective* (1997).